Nathaniel Hawthorne

and the

Romance of the

Orient

LUTHER S. LUEDTKE

Nathaniel Hawthorne

and the

Romance of the

Orient

Indiana University Press

BLOOMINGTON AND INDIANAPOLIS

© 1989 by Luther S. Luedtke

MANUFACTURED IN THE UNITED STATES OF AMERICA

Library of Congress Cataloging-in-Publication Data
Luedtke, Luther S.
   Nathaniel Hawthorne and the romance of the Orient / Luther S.
Luedtke.
     p. cm.
   Includes index.
   1. Hawthorne, Nathaniel, 1804–1864—Knowledge—Orient.
2. Literature, Comparative—American and Oriental. 3. Literature,
Comparative—Oriental and American. 4. Romanticism—United States.
5. Exoticism in literature. 6. Orient in literature.   I. Title.
PS1892.O73L84   1989
813'.3—dc19   88-46018
ISBN 0-253-33613-9   CIP

1 2 3 4 5 93 92 91 90 89

For Carol, Pehr, and Pia
My faithful fellow-travelers

———————

CONTENTS

PREFACE AND ACKNOWLEDGMENTS

This journey along Nathaniel Hawthorne's road to Xanadu began in November 1965 on a New England railroad with a foreign traveler's account of America. En route back to Providence from New Haven, I wondered about a paper topic for Hyatt Waggoner's *The Blithedale Romance* seminar at Brown University while also reading Harriet Martineau's *Society in America* (1837) for William McLoughlin's course in United States Social and Intellectual History. One passage in the English visitor's chapter on "Utterance" particularly caught my attention. After giving qualified praise to Irving, Cooper, and Bryant, Miss Martineau came to a voice she thought truly worthy of the new national literature:

> I met with one gem in American literature, where I should have least expected it:—in the Knickerbocker; a New York Monthly Magazine. Last spring, a set of papers began to appear, called "Letters from Palmyra." ... These letters remain in my mind, after repeated readings, as a fragment of lofty and tender beauty. Zenobia, Longinus, and a long perspective of characters, live and move in natural majesty; and the beauties of description and sentiment appear to me as remarkable as the stong conception of character, and of the age. If this anonymous fragment be not the work of a true artist,—if the work, when entire, do not prove to be of a far higher order than anything which has issued from the American press,—its early admirers will feel yet more surprise than regret.

A literary precursor to Zenobia—the dark heroine of Hawthorne's *The Blithedale Romance*—based on a historical original somewhere in the East? The possible connections intrigued me more than another biographical comparison of Hawthorne's regal figure with Margaret Fuller or Freudian thrust into Priscilla's purse.

A couple hours' searching the next day validated Miss Martineau's prophecies. Published in book form in 1837 as *Letters of Lucius M. Piso from Palmyra, to His Friend Marcus Curtius, at Rome*, and again the next year as *Zenobia: or, The Fall of Palmyra*, the Rev. William Ware's historical romance had reached its eighth American edition when Hawthorne's novel appeared in 1852. What happened to the kingdom of Palmyra? Why did its fate appeal so strongly to the tastes of young America? Did Hawthorne knowingly ally his work with the third-century Syrian empire and its rebellious queen? This was my introduction to the Orientalism of the American Renaissance as well as the inspiration for a seminar paper on representations of Zenobia by Edward Gibbon, William Ware, and Nathaniel Hawthorne.

What I began as a first year graduate student in American Civilization I returned to a decade later as a member of the English and American Studies faculty at the University of Southern California and a reader at the Huntington Library. Guided particularly by Marion L. Kesselring's directory *Hawthorne's Reading 1828–1850*, I started to reconstruct and duplicate the author's unexpectedly extensive readings of voyages, travels, histories, and imaginative literature of the East. The influence of Hawthorne's Eastern interests on individual tales, as well as on his understanding of the Romance, became the topic for a first rough draft of this study. Encouraged initially by Hyatt Waggoner, at the Huntington Library my speculations passed through the hands of Claude Simpson and Arlin Turner, to whose personal generosity and scrupulous scholarship on Hawthorne I also can finally express my thanks.

For several years the course of life again led me down paths unconnected with Hawthorne. When appointed Director of the American Studies Research Centre in Hyderabad, India, in 1984, however, the time came to repack my notes and ideas. Thoughts of the Hawthornes followed me throughout India: to the Coromandel Coast at Madras, where Captain Nathaniel Silsbee and Mate Nathaniel Hathorne (the author's father) arrived from Boston on June 25, 1800; to the docks of the Hooghly River at Calcutta, where they traded the *Herald*'s cargo before re-embarking for America; to the U.S. Information Service offices in Bombay, where Manning Hawthorne, the author's great-grandson, spent part of his diplomatic career and is still remembered by the Indian academic community. At Hyderabad, Hawthorne's attraction to "all the gorgeous East" was in my mind repeatedly, whether climbing the steps of Golconda, listening to trouvère and troubadour music at the tombs of the sixteenth-century Qutb Shahi kings, or hearing the muezzin's call to evening prayers resounding from the Charminar and Mecca Masjid of the Old City. I am grateful to all those persons in India who in one year provided hospitality and stories for a lifetime, but especially to the officers and staff of the American Studies Research Centre, the USIS, and the U.S. Educational Foundation in India—and, in an exceptional way, to Chandrikant and Lalita Gir and to H.E.H. Mukarram Jah, the last Nizam of Hyderabad.

Inasmuch as this study relies heavily upon Hawthorne's readings in the years between his graduation from Bowdoin College in 1825 and the publication of *Twice-told Tales* in 1837, it is indebted to Kesselring's invaluable bibliography and to the libraries that have enabled me to retrace the events and fancies with which he filled his mind and imagination. The Huntington Library yielded more than half of the classical and contemporary works charged to Hawthorne's membership at the Salem Athenaeum on which this study is largely grounded and most of the additional Eastern works he mined for the *American Magazine of Useful and Entertaining Knowledge* or is otherwise known to have read. For the remainder I have depended upon the Salem Athenaeum itself, the Houghton Library of Harvard University, the New York Public Library, the William Andrews Clark Memorial Library, and the inter-library loan facilities of the Doheny Memorial Library at the University of Southern California. I am grateful to each of these institutions, especially to the Readers' Service staff of the Huntington Library and to Cynthia Wiggin, Librarian of the Salem Athenaeum.

My final trip to Salem was supported by a Travel to Collections grant from the National Endowment for the Humanities, whose support I am also pleased to acknowledge. The grant provided an opportunity to browse again through the material artifacts of Salem's maritime history, including the collections of The Salem East India Marine Society, so beautifully displayed at the Peabody Museum, and to select illustrations for the book. In Salem the staff of the Essex Institute library, especially Prudence Backman and Eugenia Fountain, gave immediate access to the Hawthorne–Manning collections and, importantly, to logbooks kept by Captain Nathaniel Hathorne on his voyages to the East Indies. The title of this book was suggested by the Essex Institute's exhibit in 1987 "The Romance of the Orient."

Recent scholarship has made it possible to trace patterns of association, thought, and language through Hawthorne's life and writings with a wholeness and subtlety impossible a decade ago. While my obligations mainly have been relegated to footnotes, I do want to mention here my appreciation for the biographies of Arlin Turner and James R. Mellow; the critical studies of Neal Frank Doubleday, Alfred Weber, Nina Baym, and Michael Colacurcio; C. E. Frazer Clark, Jr.'s descriptive bibliography of Hawthorne's writing; Lea Bertani Vozar Newman's guide to criticism on the short stories; the latest volumes of The Centenary Edition of the Works of Nathaniel Hawthorne, especially the author's letters; and John R. Byers, Jr., and James J. Owen's concordances to the novels and tales.

Finally, I am most indebted to Terence Martin and Thomas Woodson, whose careful, generous readings of the text have improved it in countless ways. My research and writing have been supported by a sabbatical leave from the Division of Humanities of the University of Southern California.

REFERENCES TO
HAWTHORNE'S WORKS

Unless indicated otherwise, quotations from Hawthorne's works are taken from the nineteen volumes of the Centenary Edition published to date (Columbus: Ohio State University Press, 1962–   ). They are identified in the text and notes through volume and page numbers only. Quotations from Hawthorne's *Letters* are footnoted to include date and recipient. Titles alone are used in the notes for the following:

Hawthorne's Lost Notebook 1835–1841, transcript and pref. Barbara S. Mouffe; intro. Hyatt H. Waggoner (University Park: The Pennsylvania State University Press, 1978).

The English Notebooks, ed. Randall Stewart (New York: Modern Language Association of America, 1941).

INTRODUCTION

"all the gorgeous East"

Nathaniel Hawthorne is usually read against the background of two cultures. His seminal role in our national literature has led scholars painstakingly to map the historical and moral landscape of Hawthorne's America from the founding of the Massachusetts Bay Colony to the social movements of the nineteenth century. Students of his style and literary heritage inevitably extend the framework of analysis to include the land of Edmund Spenser and Sir Walter Scott, which Hawthorne memorialized with *Our Old Home* and the "bloody footstep" of his late unfinished romances. To most readers trained in departments of English and American literature these frames of reference have seemed natural and sufficient.

Occasionally, though with less certainty, the radius of Hawthorne's consciousness has been projected beyond the Anglo-American spheres into Western and Southern Europe, where he expatriated for a time in the late 1850s and wrote his longest romance, *The Marble Faun*. The journals he kept at each stage—first *The American Notebooks*, then *The English Notebooks*, and finally *The French and Italian Notebooks*—are an indispensable guide to what he knew and thought of the world. All are safely bounded, however, within Western Civilization. Rarely have readers of Hawthorne shown any cognizance of the fourth zone of culture—the cradle of civilization and home for most of mankind—in the *East*.*

The maps that shape the worldview of twentieth-century Americans, centered somewhere below the Great Lakes, have kept Europe intact but divide and scatter Asia to both east and west. The maps of Hawthorne's time, based on the world of Mercator and centered on Greenwich, presented the East as one vast whole—and North America as still largely a vacancy, what F. Scott Fitzgerald called a century later the "ragged edge of the universe." Reading their atlases and navigational charts from right to left (from East to West), Hawthorne's contemporaries traced not only the course of empire but also the history of civilization. Reading from left to right (from America to Asia), they charted new paths of commercial exploration and cultural rediscovery. Between lay England and Europe, Rome and Greece, the Renaissance and the Middle Ages.

During an age that thought in terms of universal history it would have been surprising to discover an educated citizen of Massachusetts whose cul-

---

* Throughout this study *East* and *Orient* are used interchangeably, as in Hawthorne's time, to designate lands and cultures that were generally equivalent to the Ottoman Empire [Turkey, Syria, Palestine, Egypt, Mesopotamia, Arabia, the Barbary states], Persia, Afghanistan, India, and the other East Indies. At its outermost edge the East included China and Japan, but not until the late nineteenth century did America begin to think of the Far East as the principal Orient.

tural horizons stopped short of the Orient. A note Hawthorne recorded at Arezzo, Italy, in June 1858 captured the wholeness of his historical vision, encompassing the ancient East, the Mediterranean Renaissance, "Our Old Home," and the new civilization in America. Musing over Petrarch's birthplace and a water well mentioned in Boccaccio's stories, Hawthorne marveled that once he had taken hold of the handle of the Salem Town-Pump "a rill gushed forth that meandered as far as England, as far as India, besides tasting pleasantly in every town and village of our own country" (XIV, 270).

Anyone reading Hawthorne's major romances of the 1850s soon encounters his dark Oriental heroines. Hester Prynne's "rich, voluptuous Oriental characteristic—a taste for the gorgeously beautiful"—bewilders and invigorates the Puritan Rev. Arthur Dimmesdale in *The Scarlet Letter*. Zenobia in *The Blithedale Romance* bears the name and tragic majesty of an "Oriental princess," specifically of the proud Syrian queen whom Aurelian vanquished at Palmyra in A.D. 272. Like her dark sisters, Miriam in *The Marble Faun* displays "a certain rich Oriental character in her face."

Until now only D. H. Lawrence and John Updike seem to have tapped the root of this "voluptuous, Oriental characteristic" or realized its significance for the "blue-eyed darling" Hawthorne.[1] Usually the Eastern figures in Hawthorne's works, when recognized at all, have been taken simply as lineal descendants of the dark women of romantic fiction, "from the Rebecca of Scott's *Ivanhoe* to the Zahara of Prescott's *History of the Reign of Ferdinand and Isabella*."[2] Neither critical nor biographical importance has been attributed to Hawthorne's use of the East. Nor have efforts been made to chart his readings and exact knowledge of the Eastern half of the world that was yielding its mysteries to the West in his time.

The Orient, I will demonstrate, played a significant role both in Hawthorne's choice of life and in the development of his tales and romances. Speaking through a persona in "Fragments from the Journal of a Solitary Man" (1837), Hawthorne remarked: "The time has been when I meant to visit every region of the earth, except the Poles and Central Africa. I had a strange longing to see the Pyramids. To Persia and Arabia, and all the gorgeous East, I owed a pilgrimage for the sake of their magic tales. And England, the land of my ancestors!" (XI, 315). He achieved his secondary ambition in 1853, when he was appointed U.S. Consul to Liverpool. His primary wish, to follow the course of his father and townsmen to "all the gorgeous East," he realized vicariously through his readings and maritime occupations ashore. Hawthorne's imaginative pilgrimages to the East show a habit of mind that persisted throughout his life and helped shape the form, characters, and themes of his writing.

Critics have been uncomfortable with the intention Hawthorne declared in the opening lines of "The Threefold Destiny" (1838) to present "an allegory, such as the writers of the last century would have expressed in the shape of an eastern tale, but to which I have endeavored to give a more lifelike warmth than could be infused into those fanciful productions" (IX, 472). Belittling the importance, formal or thematic, of the story cycles and apologues of the East, they have hurried to situate Hawthorne in the tradition of the great English allegorists. "Placed beside a Spenserian allegory like 'Rappaccini's Daughter' (1844)," Buford Jones wrote, "The Threefold Destiny" is "positively embarrassing. The pat conclusion reminds us of an undistinguished eighteenth-century moral tale."[3] Neal Frank Doubleday attributed the apparent feebleness of this and other apologues in Hawthorne's earlier period to "the weaknesses of their models." They pose no real problems in interpreting Hawthorne's use of allegory, he suggested, if one only assigns them to a conventional genre and thus isolates them from his pieces of serious intent.[4] In general, critics of the mid-twentieth century immediately have assumed: "When he writes, for instance, that the world requires 'a deeper moral, and a closer and homelier truth' than is supplied by Scott and Dickens, he has obviously in mind the rich spiritual significance of his favorites, Spenser, Milton, and Bunyan."[5]

Aside from inflicting modern tastes and critical standards on works written for audiences in the middle third of the nineteenth century, such approaches categorize rather too quickly the fluent body of Hawthorne's writing while simplifying the cosmopolitan origins of his presumed models. "Rappaccini's Daughter" differs from "The Threefold Destiny" less in kind than degree and derives as much from the "poison-damsel" tales of the *Secretum Secretorum* and Indian mythology as from *The Faerie Queene*. As Hawthorne and his contemporaries knew, the masters of European and British literature from Boccaccio and Chaucer to Bunyan and Coleridge themselves built upon stories of more ancient Eastern origins. Hawthorne's obvious affection for British literature has led us to limit the catholicity of his taste and to neglect evidence for other sources and models. While he was influenced throughout his life by Spenser, Shakespeare, Milton, and Bunyan, it is prudent to remember Nina Baym's admonition that "he was so to a much smaller degree than by his own time and the literary era immediately preceding his own. That is, he is a product of the late eighteenth and early nineteenth centuries, and not of some magical literary kingdom peopled only by the Great English Writers."[6]

It is well known that Washington Irving, James Kirke Paulding, Edgar Allan Poe, and other early nineteenth-century American storytellers experimented with Oriental narratives. Attracted by the East in his formative years, Hawthorne, too, explored this realm of the world and imagination through every means at his disposal: through authentic Arabian, Persian, and Indian literature, the Oriental tales of eighteenth-century England and France, and the verse narratives of Byron, Southey, and Moore; but before all, through the abundant literature of discovery that poured forth from the time of the Renaissance travelers down to his own day, including, most significantly, logbooks kept on his father's East India voyages.

Areas of darkness still spotted the maps of Hawthorne's time, but the age possessed an exploring spirit, a sense of possibility and discovery, adventure and the unknown that have been mostly forgotten. As he wrote in "The Custom-House," two decades before Hawthorne's birth "India was a new region, and only Salem knew the way thither" (I, 29). Throughout the nineteenth century merchants, missionaries, scholars, naturalists, and professional travelers pushed back the borders of the known world in search of the antiquities and myths—of the "connection"—that would complete what Walt Whitman and E. M. Forster called the "Passage to India."

William Goetzmann has characterized the late eighteenth and the nineteenth centuries as a "Second Great Age of Discovery in the midst of which America as a nation was born, and into which Americans eagerly entered on a global scale."[7] Henry the Navigator inaugurated the First Great Age when he established his maritime observatory on the southern tip of the Iberian peninsula in 1419. By the end of the century Bartolomeu Dias had reached the Cape of Good Hope (1487–1488), Vasco da Gama had opened the sea road to India (1497–1498), and Christopher Columbus had found a land mass impeding his westerly route to the East. Eventually North America became a separate jewel in the crown of British empire. The passage to the Indies, however, remained a principal object of European and American rivalries. By the end of the eighteenth century Massachusetts and New York merchants were actively engaged in exploring the commercial and cultural possibilities of the Orient, usually in the path of Da Gama. Associations like the Salem East India Marine Society organized the gathering of maritime charts and sealogs by East India captains and collections of artifacts from the farthest lands of exploration. In 1802, two years before Nathaniel Hawthorne's birth, Salem's famous mathematician and astronomer Nathaniel Bowditch, following several voyages to the East Indies, published the *New American Practical Navigator*.

While the Lewis and Clark Expedition of 1803–1806 inaugurated a century of explorations in the interior of the continent, Americans also followed their European peers in charting the rest of the globe. European Catholics pursued their historic missions in India, China, and the Philippines. A question that intrigued the Western world for two millennia was answered when the Scottish explorer James Bruce established the source of the Blue Nile in 1770 and John Speke and J. A. Grant, for the Royal Geographical Society, identified the source of the White Nile in 1861–1862. Before completion of the Suez Canal in 1869, the concern for commercial, postal, and strategic links with India led the British East India Company to seek alternatives to the standard Overland Route from Cairo to Suez; beginning in 1829, Francis Chesney and Henry Lynch explored the Euphrates and Tigris rivers for that purpose. The scientifically most important of the American contributions was Captain Charles Wilkes's famous Exploring Expedition of 1838–1842, which proved the Antarctic to be a continent, mapped the South Sea islands, and sought the possible outlet of a Northwest Passage on the coasts of Oregon. Hawthorne tried to obtain the post of historian on the voyage and in *The Blithedale Romance* attributed the same wish to Miles Coverdale. In 1852–1854 Commodore Matthew G. Perry's expedition to the China Sea and Japan put American commercial and military interests in the farthest East on a permanent footing. Born in the international seaport of Salem, Massachusetts, the son of an East India captain in a century of expanding cultural horizons, no wonder

Hawthorne wished himself to explore "every region of the earth"—especially all the gorgeous East.

Each Great Age of Discovery had its renaissance in scholarship and the arts. The Greek manuscripts and Byzantine commentators that reached the West after the fall of Constantinople to the Ottoman Turks in 1453 inspired a classical Renaissance in the Mediterranean. Likewise, the explorations of the eighteenth and nineteenth centuries inaugurated a new age of literature and ideas in Germany, France, England, and the United States. Some 175 archaeologists, artists, scholars, and engineers accompanied Napoleon on his Egyptian campaign in 1798, just six years before Hawthorne's birth. The removal of Egyptian inscriptions and antiquities to England after the defeat of the French in the Near East in 1802, and Jean-François Champollion's deciphering of Egyptian hieroglyphic writing in 1821–1822 with the aid of the Rosetta stone, heralded an Egypt-mania that swept both Europe and the United States in the early nineteenth century.

While Western scholars gradually revised their notions of the "barbaric" Near East, philologists and explorers also were unlocking the secrets of the ultimate East: of India. In 1783 the immensely talented jurist and linguist Sir William Jones realized his yearning to travel to India when he obtained a judgeship on the Supreme Court in Calcutta. The Asiatic Society of Bengal, which he founded in January 1784, almost immediately began to publish translations from Sanskrit texts. Before his death ten years later, Jones had postulated the common ancestry of Sanskrit and Greek and had translated Kalidasa's treasure of Hindu theater, *Shakuntala; or, The Fatal Ring*, as well as the great legal codes of the Orient, the *Muhammedan Law of Inheritance* and the *Institutes of Hindu Law, or the Ordinances of Menu*. Each volume of *Asiatic Researches* published by the Society in Calcutta further disclosed the recency and tentativeness of what until then had seemed an autonomous Occidental universe. As his translations became known in the United States, Jones was elected a corresponding member of the Massachusetts Historical Society.

Since the last century the French have called this period, especially the years 1770 to 1850, *La Renaissance orientale*: a time when the language, literature, and imagination of Europe were reborn through Indic rather than Hellenistic inspiration. Raymond Schwab brilliantly interpreted the excitement and effect of the cultural exploration of the East in *The Oriental Renaissance: Europe's Rediscovery of India and the East, 1680–1880*. The Oriental Renaissance was inaugurated by two events: Antoine Galland's translation from the Arabic of the *Mille et une Nuits* (1704–1708) and Abraham Hyacinthe Anquetil-Duperron's translation of the Zoroastrian *Zend–Avesta* (1771). The former inspired the exoticism and proto-romanticism in European literature, associated with the Orient, that displaced the century of Louis XIV; the latter revolutionized linguistic and historical studies. Within a few years, Schwab wrote:

A whole world that had been entirely lost became . . . completely known. For the first time the image of India regally entered the configuration of the universe.

Except perhaps in those times drowned in legend, when more rumor than information would have reached him, a "cultivated" man would not necessarily have included India in his considerations of the cosmos. Judea would have been included because of biblical tradition; Persia because of wars and its traditions of magic; Arabia because of its conquests and physicians, the Crusades and the schoolmen; and, for the last two hundred years, China, seemingly because of its missions. The Indic world alone remained behind its wall. And then, in a single wave, it poured forth.[8]

The newly revealed texts incited a debate in the West, lasting throughout Hawthorne's lifetime, about primitivism, genius, and the origins of civilization. The opening of the East both multiplied the world and made it a whole, replacing the unitary Greco-Latin culture of the classical Renaissance with an expanded universe of comparativism, relativism, and historicism. Even while the West sought to integrate the East in its understanding of mankind, "The prestige that India, of all the orients, enjoyed among the Romantics arose from the fact that it posed, in its totality, the great question of the *Different*."[9]

In his study *Orientalism*—an analysis of the West's "coming to terms with" *and invention of* the Orient—Edward Said has gone beyond Schwab's thesis of multiplicity and difference to argue that the interaction of artists and politics in the British, French, and American empires led to an epistemological antithesis between East and West and the emergence of the Orient as one of the Occident's "deepest and most recurrent images of the *Other*."[10] By the late eighteenth century Europe had begun to draw strength and identity from the very unlikeness of the Orient, simplifying the East in such terms of mystery and inferiority as would maintain the dominance of the Occident. Orientalism, according to Said, was an exercise in hegemony, a Western "cultural enterprise . . . whose dimensions take in such disparate realms as the imagination itself, the whole of India and the Levant, the Biblical texts and the Biblical lands, the spice trade . . . a complex array of 'Oriental' ideas (Oriental despotism, Oriental splendor, cruelty, sensuality), many Eastern sects, philosophies, and wisdoms domesticated for local European use."[11]

European, British, and American Romanticism particularly welcomed the influx of the Orient. The coincidence of the Oriental Renaissance with the Romantic movement in the West gave the latter "its complex dimensions and led it to the reformulation of human limits—indeed, to that frontier where the unconscious and even the monstrous can claim the title of natural."[12] Like the manuscripts carried from Constantinople to Venice in the fifteenth century, the texts and tales brought home by Massachusetts merchant-voyagers in the early nineteenth century were midwife to a renaissance in art and philosophy.

A crude measure of the contours that the world assumed through the Second Great Age of Discovery and the Oriental Renaissance can be taken from *Peter Parley's Universal History, on the Basis of Geography*, a schooltext that Hawthorne and his sister Elizabeth wrote in 1836. The Hawthornes informed their young readers that the population of Asia, about four hundred millions, exceeded that of the two Americas tenfold. "Asia . . . contained the first human inhabitants, and from this quarter, all the rest of the globe has been peopled. Here, too, the most remarkable events took place that belong to the history of man. Here the most wonderful personages were born that have ever trod this earth; and here, too, the mighty miracles of Jehovah were wrought." When they first introduced the inhabitants of the several continents, the authors devoted sixteen lines to Asia but only three lines to Africa, four lines each to Europe and America, and seven to Oceania. They were writing to a formula, to be sure, but there is no reason to think they disbelieved the prefatory remark that "it is very desirable that every person should, at an early period of life, have imprinted on his mind, in bright and unfading colors, a clear outline of the story of mankind, from its beginning in the plains of Shinar, down to the present hour."[13] Whatever pride Nathaniel Hawthorne and his contemporaries felt for their new nation, they regarded it as one chapter in the long cultural evolution of mankind that had begun in the East. When young America chose symbols for its *novus ordo seclorum*, it turned its eye not only to the fasces of Rome but, beyond, to the pyramids of Egypt.

The discovery and celebration of Eastern Otherness at the same time that the new American nation was struggling to establish a cultural identity of its own, independent of European parentage, predisposed American artists and scholars to look Eastward across their maps, to incorporate the Oriental birthplace in the American Renaissance. It is not at all eccentric that *Father Bombo's Pilgrimage to Mecca* (1770), by Hugh Henry Brackenridge and Philip Freneau, was "the first American novel"; or that *The Arabian Nights' Entertainment* was one of four "best sellers" published in the United States in 1794 (the others: Benjamin Franklin's *Autobiography*, Thomas Paine's *The Age of Reason*, Susanna Rowson's *Charlotte Temple*); or that Thomas Moore's elaborately annotated *Lalla Rookh: An Eastern Romance* (1817) was the best-selling title in America between Walter Scott's *Waverley* (1815) and *Rob Roy* (1818).[14]

We have significant studies of the Transcendentalists' reading of Indian mythology and Persian poetry, the symbolism of the hieroglyphs in American literature, the Oriental tales of Irving, Paulding, and Poe, and American literary travelers in the Holy Land. The "orienda" of Herman Melville, the writer most often associated with Hawthorne, also has been well mapped.[15] There is no comprehensive interpretation, however, of the Orientalism pervading the literature of the United States, especially during the development of nineteenth-century Romanticism. And no serious recognition has been given to the Orientalism of Nathaniel Hawthorne. The present study, while primarily an exploration of Hawthorne's life, imagination, and work, will also deepen and enrich our understanding of the culture of the American Renaissance.

Hawthorne was never so overwhelmed by the East as to have given himself up to raptures like Emerson's, at Concord, where "the very cattle that lie on the ground seem to have great thoughts & Egypt & India look from their eyes."[16] If the current of Hawthorne's life had carried him to the Holy Land, like his friends Herman Melville and George William Curtis, or around the Cape of Good Hope to the East Indies, in the path of his father, he would have left a set of fascinating Asian notebooks and perhaps produced works of such emphatic Orientalism as *Clarel* or *Nile Notes of a Howadji*. He did not.

The following study, nevertheless, reveals a stratum of Hawthorne that we have not known—or have forgotten to remember, anyhow, in this century—and brings out Oriental patterns tightly woven into the fabric of his tales and romances. The source for themes, symbols, settings, character types, and storytelling techniques in Hawthorne's writings, the Eastern connection turns back one more corner of the veil that concealed what he called the "Inmost Me." It illuminates the tension of the foreign and the domestic, of wandering and homecoming, of "fantastic dreams" and "actual circumstances" that, together with excursions into the historical past, underlay his particular contribution to an American *romance*. Hawthorne's response to the real and the legendary East, what is more, can help us better appreciate what M. de l'Aubépine in the preface to "Rappaccini's Daughter" called his "unfortunate position between the Transcendentalists . . . and the great body of pen-and-ink men who address the intellect and sympathies of the multitude" (X, 91).

Hawthorne's encounters with the Orient were both recurrent and enduring—sometimes overt and self-conscious, at other times latent and subliminal, episodic but cumulatively providing a significant subtext, as well as context, for his life and writing. The world beyond the civilizations of America, England, and Europe had both personal and literary meaning for him. The East weighed in the young man's uncertain choice of a career; the traveler's search for his *destiny* figures prominently in the major romances as well as the early tales.

The first two chapters of this book are principally biographical and historical. Chapter 1 recreates a personal legacy that, contrary to much literary lore, was affected less by the dusky and distant Puritans of the seventeenth century than by the century of Salem sea captains in the immediate, still vivid background. The logbooks of Captain Nathaniel Hathorne's East India voyages in 1795–1804 particularly stirred the imagination of his son, as boy and man. While one modern critic has dismissed the writer's later positions at the Boston and Salem Custom Houses as providing only for "his physical existence, his merely animal nature," the life at sea, and intercourse with the farthest ports of the rich East, remained for some time a possible and attractive destiny for the young Salemite.[17] He needed to look no farther, however, than the nearest wharf in Salem for real-life travelers and storytellers like those who populate his fictions. The chapter concludes with a brief overview of Oriental manifestations in the culture of Salem and America in the early nineteenth century.

Chapter 2 considers the library of travels, voyages, histories, and literary and religious works concerning the East that Hawthorne explored. The two most detailed records of his reading interests are Marion Kesselring's inventory of his borrowings from the Salem Athenaeum, chiefly in 1826–1838, and Arlin Turner's identification of references in the six issues of the *American Magazine of Useful and Entertaining Knowledge* that he prepared in 1836. Eastern materials from these two sources, along with 69 items on the East that Hawthorne wrote or selected for the *American Magazine*, are fully indexed in Appendixes A and B. They are discussed in Chapter 2 together with other Eastern voyages and tales, authentic and imitative, that he knew. Hawthorne's readings reveal both periods of concerted study and a manifold knowledge of the cultures, histories, customs, and products of the East. There he found a "fairy land," storytellers, images of woman, and a gorgeous antithesis to the unromantic West that influenced his subsequent work.

Chapters 3 and 4 reconstruct creative interests and designs during Hawthorne's first decade as a writer, between his graduation from Bowdoin College (1825) and his emergence as author of *Twice-told Tales* (1837). The three works discussed in Chapter 3—*Fanshawe*, "The Wives of the Dead," and "The Gentle Boy"—all written before 1830, dramatize precepts of destiny, resignation, and hospitality that eighteenth-century moral philosophers and religious scholars associated particularly with the devoutness of Islam. The Happy Valley of Samuel Johnson's *Rasselas* and the theodicy of Voltaire's *Zadig* are especially important to establishing the form and meaning of the first two works. Previous commentary on Hawthorne's "The Gentle Boy" has been defined mainly by the intellectual and theological controversies of seventeenth-century Massachusetts. In his celebrated tale, however, the nineteenth-century man of letters drew on original histories of the Ottoman Empire to project the religious factionalism of Puritan New England against the natural religion and charitable creeds of the Muslims and to reveal, beyond the heterodoxies of Islam, Christianity, and Judaism, the common progenitor Abraham.

Chapter 4 considers the Eastern inspiration for *The Story Teller*, the two-volume book of sketches and tales, narrated by a traveling storyteller, that Hawthorne sought unsuccessfully to publish in 1834 and issued piecemeal thereafter in periodicals and annuals. While the works discussed in the previous chapter were notably affected by eighteenth-century British and French adaptations, in *The Story Teller* Hawthorne drew on authentic Oriental models as he knew them from *The Arabian Nights* and the testimony of European and American travelers in the East. In the original design, Hawthorne's Story Teller joined American pilgrims on their *hadj* from New England to Niagara Falls, the tourists' Mecca of the 1830s: an application of Eastern models to native materials one encounters frequently in his romances. The sketches, apologues, and essays written for *The Story Teller*—from "Little Annie's Ramble" to "Young Goodman Brown"—are best understood when restored to their original generic and narrative context. Other sketches and tales collected in *Twice-told Tales*, *Mosses from an Old Manse*, and *The Snow-Image*—from "The Threefold Destiny" to "Ethan Brand"—sustain motifs established there.

Against this background Chapter 5 assesses the place of the Orient in Hawthorne's own concept of the Romance. The East offered a ready-made "neutral territory," such as he sought, "somewhere between the real world and fairy-land, where the Actual and the Imaginary may meet, and each imbue itself with the nature of the other" (I, 36). Although scholarship on the romance tradition in America is usually silent on the matter, authors and literary historians in Hawthorne's time—including Walter Scott, the German and English Romantics, and Hawthorne's Bowdoin contemporary Henry Wadsworth Longfellow—weighed the claims advanced by Thomas Warton in his *History of English Poetry* (1774–1781) and by other comparativist critics for the Arabian and Indian origins of the Romance. The architecture of Hawthorne's "cloud castles" is Eastern in origin, and several of his recurrent symbols (the cavern, the carbuncle, the talisman) came to him from original Oriental sources or by way of Gothic-Orientalism.

Chapters 6 and 7 address the Oriental beauties of Hawthorne's major works in the 1840s and 1850s: Beatrice Rappaccini, Hester Prynne, Zenobia, and Miriam Schaefer. The intrigues between Hawthorne's bonded, passionate women and the male travelers who approach them with desire and fear, while Byronic in nature, were grounded in the many first-hand accounts Hawthorne had read of purdah, seraglios, and their captives in the East. The *visakanya* (poison-damsel) Beatrice Rappaccini, and each of the successive dark houris, exercises a nearly fatal charm on her male admirer, an ambiguous potion of naivete and sensuality that Europeans and Americans imagined of the East. Yet no significant attention has been paid to the manifestly Eastern origin of the "poison damsel" legend at the heart of "Rappaccini's Daughter," and no serious effort has been made to read the tale in a context more ancient and universal than that of sixteenth-century Padua. Explicitly in *The Scarlet Letter*—implicitly in "Rappaccini's Daughter," *The Blithedale Romance*, and *The Marble Faun*—Hawthorne considers the question "Doth the universe lie within the compass of yonder town?" and answers in the negative. The Eastern antithesis is particularly critical in his probings of the male-female relationship. Beginning in the eighteenth-century mode of moral and philosophical tales, then adopting the guise of an Oriental Story Teller, Hawthorne came in his major romances to a more psychological apprehension of the Eastern "Other." By *The Marble Faun* it had become difficult for him to subordinate his Eastern fancies to American actualities.

With only slight exaggeration, Harry Levin wrote of "the cult of the antithesis, which [Hawthorne] so assiduously practiced."[18] To the oppositions customarily used for interpreting his works—head and heart, light and dark, town and forest, fact and fancy, present and past, withdrawal and return—must now be added the dialectic of East and West. Hawthorne turned to the Orient not for ultimate spiritual unification, in the fashion of Emerson and Thoreau, but for cultural differentiation, and for a drama that carried forward from his life into his art. His world, in fact and imagination, was larger, richer, and more chromatic than we have known.

Nathaniel Hawthorne

and the

Romance of the

Orient

A HAWTHORNE
AND A SALEMITE

"To the Farthest Port of the Rich East"
(motto of Salem, Massachusetts)

Voyage of the Herald

THE SHIP *Herald* began its homeward voyage from Calcutta to America at the end of October 1800, slipping past the difficult shoals and Sand Heads of the Hooghly River into the Bay of Bengal and discharging its pilot on November 1 "At 4 P M ... in 6 Fathoms Water." According to the logbook kept by Nathaniel Hathorne,* first mate on the *Herald* and later father of the famous writer, the outbound journey to the Indies had been uneventful, blessed for the most part by "moderate breezes & smooth Sea."[1]

Departing Boston nine months earlier on January 29, 1800, the *Herald* had reached Madeira in just twenty days. Before weighing anchor a month later, on March 16, Captain Nathaniel Silsbee had disposed of his cargo of nankeen from China, rum, French brandy, butter, beef, tobacco, and codfish and had taken on in their place 260 pipes of Madeira wine for the "India market" and a score of "choice old London particular" for return to Boston.[2]

---

* The author Nathaniel Hawthorne, the subject of this book, began spelling the family name with a *w* around 1830, a usage then adopted by the household. To distinguish the generations, the names of Captain Nathaniel and his individual forebears are presented here as *Hathorne*; the names of the author, his mother, sisters, descendants, and the family at large, of all generations, as *Hawthorne*.

Hathorne's log recorded that the *Herald* passed the Cape of Good Hope and sighted Cape False on May 10 but proceeded on its way without touching shore. On June 8 the ship was "Keeping a good look out for the Island *Abu, Canda* and *Diego Garcia,*" and on June 12 "for the Southern *Maldivas* Island." On June 17 she was off "Cape Comorin" at the southern tip of India and shortly thereafter in sight of "Colombo Cove" on the coast of Ceylon. Avoiding the Gulf of Minnar between India and Ceylon, Captain Silsbee took the *Herald* southward round the island and on June 21 "At 10 P M came to Anchor in Back Bay of Trincomala" on the northeast coast of Ceylon, the *Herald's* first landfall since leaving Madeira. After a two-day layover she embarked for Madras "in Company with his Majesties Ship Sybel" taking in sail in order not to outrun the slower "Man of War." The 100-day passage from Madeira to India concluded "At ½ Past 8 A M" on June 25, when the *Herald* "came to in Madrass roads in 9 Fathoms water with the small Bower."

Hathorne's log does not tell how the ship's company was occupied over the following four months. His next entry, dated November 1, begins the return passage "From Calcutta to America Ship" *Herald.* In using this voyage to illustrate the importance of Madeira in the East Indies trade, Samuel Eliot Morison reported commercial activities on both coasts of the sub-continent:

> [The *Herald's*] genial cargo was carried around the Cape of Good Hope to Madras, where the India market wine was sold, and pepper, blue cloth, "camboys" and "Pulicate" handkerchiefs taken aboard. At Bombay and Calcutta, the bills and specie [silver dollars and bills of exchange carried by Silsbee] purchased pepper, sugar, ginger, and a bewildering array of India cottons, for which the fashions of that day, and the absence of domestic competition, afforded an excellent market in the United States. The *Herald's* invoice shows "Callipatti Baftas," "Beerboom Gurrahs," "Allabad Emerties," and a score of different weaves. Madras chintzes and seersuckers are the only names recognizable today.[3]

While goods might have been traded through factors in Bombay, it is doubtful that the ship visited the west coast of the Indian peninsula. In his own account of the voyage Captain Silsbee recalled: "After stopping at Madeira and Madras, we reached Calcutta the latter part of July and remained there until the last of October, procuring a return cargo."[4]

During the *Herald's* extended call at Calcutta Hathorne no doubt executed a small commercial "adventure" of his own. He became well acquainted with the fascinating capital of Britain's Indian empire, then in the middle of its most regal development. The new Fort William with its spectacular Maidan, twice the size of Hyde Park, had been completed in 1781 at a cost of £2 million. Hathorne might have visited the Royal Asiatic Society of Bengal, founded in 1784 by Sir William Jones, or worshipped at the imposing St. John's Church, which was finished about the same time. He could have strolled through Calcutta's new Botanical Gardens, where teas were cultivated for the plantations in Assam and Darjeeling, or stopped to watch the construction of the British Government House, modeled after Kedleston Hall in

Derbyshire, which the Marquess Wellesley had undertaken in 1799. Although a creation of the British East India Company, Calcutta was also a gateway to the real India. Behind the Western mask stared the dark face of Kali, the Hindu goddess of destruction and blood sacrifices from whom the original village had taken its name. The capture of the original Fort William by a native nawab and the infamous Black Hole of 1756 were still fresh in the minds of Western merchants at the turn of the century. After four months in the Orient Hathorne no doubt looked forward to home.

The *Herald's* return voyage was marked almost immediately, however, by one of the hazards of the East Indies trade that was to give this trip some celebrity in the annals of Massachusetts maritime history. The *Herald* entered the Bay of Bengal in company with four other American vessels—the *Perseverance*, *Cleopatra*, and *Grace* of Philadelphia, and the *Sphinx* of Baltimore— and with the *Cornwallis* of the British East India Company. The captains and supercargoes of the American ships, Silsbee later recorded, had:

> entered into an engagement, before leaving Calcutta, to keep company with each other until we passed the latitude of the southern part of the Island of Ceylon, with a hope that our united force (each ship having from eight to twelve guns) might enable us to defend our property against the attack of a single French privateer, several of which were known to be cruising in Bengal Bay. Of this squadron of American Indiamen, I was designated as the Commodore.[5]

The largest of the vessels, at 328 tons, and the best armed, the *Herald* took her place at the center of the convoy.

When day broke on November 3, the *Cornwallis* was found to have been set upon by a heavily armed privateer. Hathorne entered in his log this account of the ensuing battle:

> At 1/2 Past 5 A M saw two Sail to Eastward[.] [S]uppose one of them to be the Cornwallis. [A]t 10 A M saw the other Sail in chase of the Cornwallis. [I]t Proved to be a french Privateer, the Cornwallis steering right down for us with every sail sett[.] Tack Ship towards her, the Cornwallis and french Privateer firing continually at each other[.] [G]et all ready for action to receive the frenchman[.] The French Privateer prooved to be a Ship that M[r] Lynch an American sold in the Isle of France mounting 18 guns 12 & 9 Pounders[.] [S]he still keeps in chase of the Cornwallis[.] [T]he wind being very light both ships have there sweps out[.] At 2 P M the french ship being within reach of our shot, gave them a Gun, which was immediately followed by every american Ship in the fleet.   —The Privateer thinking (I suppose) if she came any nearer she would meet with too warm a reception to get off from us again immediately hauled by the wind[.] [W]e being apprehensive that she would bear down on us in the night keep all hands to 4[ers] ready to receive her[.] [T]he Cornwallis came along side of us and Capt Silsbee went onbord of her[,] was received with the greatest politeness and received the sincere thanks of the Capt[n] for resquing one of the Hon[ble] company, ship from a French rover[.]
> [T]he Cornwallis had no men kill'd[.] [T]he Batswain was slightly wounded[.] [H]er sails where very much torn by the frenchmans shot[.] [I]t was there

opinion if we had not assisted them that the would have been a prize to the frenchman[.][6]

Notwithstanding its proud name and crew of four hundred men, *La Glorie* abandoned its pursuit of the British East India ship.

The *Cornwallis* parted company with her redoubtable American protectors on November 5. The swifter *Herald* and the *Sphinx* separated from the other American vessels three days after, "there being so much odds in our sailing," Hathorne wrote, and they went on together until November 17, when "Capt[n] Lewis Brantz of Baltimore parted company with us." Captain Brantz later preserved this naval drama in a watercolor of the American, British, and French ships.[7]

The *Herald* touched land only once during the 118–day return voyage recorded by Hathorne, a stop at St. Helena January 15–16, 1801, for "16 Casks of Water" and "several necessary jobs." The *Herald* also "received a Sailor onboard as passenger" before leaving behind in port four "English Indiamen," three "south Sea Whalemen," and two other ships engaged in trade with Bombay and Calcutta. Two weeks later Hathorne recorded a "nearer view of the Island (or rather Rocks) of St. Paules," colored white "by the Birds dung upon them." Long Island and Block Island came into view on February 24, and the following day Hathorne made his final entry in the *Herald* log: "At 3 P M took a Pilot.... At 9 P M came too at Old town harbour in Four Fathoms Water, the weather not looking prudent to run over the Shoals to Night we are determin'd to wait for good weather and fair wind." According to "Nautical Intelligence" printed in the *Salem Gazette* a few days later, after its stop at New York, the *Herald* reached the port of Boston on February 27, 1801.[8]

Hathorne's quarto-size logbook—bound in marbled boards, each page meticulously lined for two days' record and inscribed in a firm, graceful hand—served both public and personal ends. In charting the course of the *Herald* he added to the growing body of exact knowledge about the water routes to the East that Salem, Massachusetts, merchants had accumulated since December 1785, when Elias Hasket Derby sent the *Grand Turk* around the Cape of Good Hope and on to Canton.[9] The chief business of Hathorne's log was to record, hour by hour, the distance traveled, bearings, winds, currents, sea conditions, setting of sails, and taking of latitude and longitude. But while carefully mapping a path thirteen thousand miles from Massachusetts to India, he also chronicled an experience by which a reader, even today, can relive the destiny and romance of the young men of Salem.

Hathorne's notes were concerned for the most part with weather conditions and routine duties on board. Days "Squally with heavy Rain" alternated with others on which he wrote, "Latter part moderate breezes & pleasant smooth Sea people Employ'd at Ships duty." As one of a thirty-man crew, mate Hathorne lent a hand in "hoging the Bottom," "Scraping the Quarter deck," and "other necessary Jobs." He showed a particularly lively interest, however, in the "Bobbies, Gannetts & Man of War hauches round the Ship" and liked to record his sightings of "Great numbers Albatross, Cape Pidgeons and Silver Birds," "Flying Fish," and "Plenty of Porpoises, Blackfish and Bonetoes." He wrote with the voice of a veteran mariner as he noted once, "I never saw so few Birds before in this Track," and again, "I never experienced so moderate weather here before but on the contrary a fine breeze." The fern fronds and other shoots and leaves still pressed between the pages of the *Herald* logbook are mute witnesses, two centuries later, to his naturalist bent and his exotic ports of call.

Occasionally notes of mortality interrupted Hathorne's ocean pastoral. Entries like "Struck 2 Porpoises and lost 2 Harpoons" appear with some frequency. "Shot one Albatross," he wrote on May 13, 1800, just east of the Cape of Good Hope, apparently undisturbed by the publication of Coleridge's "Rime of the Ancient Mariner" a year and half earlier. By the time the *Herald* reached St. Helena, "Three men onbord were sick with the Scurvy." A fourth fell ill days later. But the *Herald* seems to have lost only one man in its thirteen-month voyage. Two days after the engagement with the French privateer, on November 6, Hathorne's log read: "A 1/2 past 11 P M departed this life Michael Philby, Carpenter." Whether sailor Philby died as a result of the battle, or accident, or the contagions of Calcutta, and how his body was committed to the sea, were matters too commonplace to elaborate.

However Hathorne might have reflected on the dangers of the Indies trade, the conditions and place of his own death—by yellow fever in Dutch Guiana, March 1808—were over a farther horizon. In the winter of 1800–1801 he was homeward bound to Elizabeth Clarke Manning. They would marry the coming August and have the first of their three children, a daughter Elizabeth, the following March. When a son, also named Nathaniel, was born July 4, 1804, the elder Hathorne was again on a return voyage from the East Indies, this time as captain of the *Mary and Eliza*.

A Son's Legacy

Following the birth of his son in 1804 and the death of his only brother, Daniel, at sea later the same year, Nathaniel Hathorne gave up the East Indies trade for shorter voyages to Europe and the West Indies. In all, however, Captain Hathorne spent less than a year at home in Salem from 1804 until his death in 1808 at age thirty-three.[10] Three-year-old "Natty" had just begun to know his father when the boy was called into his mother's bedroom and told, simply, that his father was dead.[11] The modest estate left to Captain Hathorne's widow and children included a set of monogrammed chinaware from Canton, "an India box and an India punch-bowl and pitcher" from Calcutta[12]—and his logbooks.

While other items in the library of Nathaniel Hawthorne were lost or dispersed during the author's frequent changes of residence, the *Herald* log stayed in the family for at least 108 years. On March 3, 1908, the novelist's own son, Julian Hawthorne, wrote inside the front cover:

> This Log-book was written by Capt. Nathaniel Hawthorne, father of Nathaniel
> Hawthorne, the novelist, during one of his voyages to and from the West and
> East Indies, in the year 1800. . . . This log was in possession of his widow, and
> became the companion of his son's childhood and boyhood; he was in the
> habit of poring over it, and made up many imaginative stories for himself about
> the events of the voyage. In particular he was interested in the fight with the
> French privateer, recorded on Nov. 3 & 4th 1800, when Hathorne's ship, "The
> Herald", beat her off when she was attacking the ship Cornwallis of the British
> East India Co. America was between two wars with England at the time, but
> at odds with France.—The signatures at the end of the book were written by
> Nath. Hawthorne the novelist, while at Bowdoin College in 1825: the writing
> on the preceding page was done, probably, about ten years later. . . . [13]

The frequency and nature of Hawthorne's annotations show an abiding
interest in his father's travels. While musing over the journals young Hawthorne frequently copied the original phraseology, sometimes imitating his
father's ornate script but usually standardizing the irregular spelling, capitalization, and punctuation. Some entries in the *Herald* log are duplicated whole.
At other points Hawthorne copied only a few words—e.g., "At day light saw
the other Ship" (November 8, 1800)—before letting his mind roam silently
with an idea. The signatures on the back page of the *Herald* log, both spelled
"Nathaniel Hathorne," are dated "Bowdoin College" and "Salem, 1825." The
writing that Julian Hawthorne believed was added around 1835—simultaneous
with the elusive travel work *The Story Teller*—follows the final entry on the
Herald's return to America:

> Wednesday 25th,
> 1801
> Old town Harbour.
> Old town Harbour.
>
> the weather not looking prudent
> to run over the shoals to night
> we are determined to wait for
> good weather and fair wind.

Other additions could have been made at either the earlier or later dates.
The marginalia are consistent with the author's handwriting during these
years.[14]

It is hardly surprising to find a boy so curious about his dead father—
imagining himself in the mariner's place, reliving his long voyages and months
ashore in the East Indies. It is more thought-provoking to see the young man
at twenty or thirty years of age still retracing his father's routes. Hawthorne's
enduring interest in his parent's life at sea was well known in the family,
however, as was his penchant for inscribing his name in the favorite books
of his youth. Elizabeth Hawthorne remembered in 1871: "When my brother
was young he covered the margins and the fly leaves of every book in the
house with lines of poetry and other quotations, and with his own name,
and other names. Nothing brings him back to me so vividly as looking at
those old books."[15]

Four of Captain Hathorne's logbooks have survived. His son perused them
all not only in childhood but at crucial stages of his passage from adolescence

into adulthood. Significantly, each of the dates recorded in his father's logs by Nathaniel Hawthorne or offered by Julian coincides with an important transition in Hawthorne's life as first (1820) the sixteen-year-old youth prepared himself for college, then (1825) the Bowdoin College senior struggled to find his course in life, and finally (c. 1835) the author looked back on ten years of anonymous and largely unfulfilled literary work before the appearance of *Twice-told Tales* and his courtship of Sophia Peabody. In the early 1850s Hawthorne reflected on this period in his life as he wrote to Richard Henry Stoddard, "and so, on leaving college, in 1825, instead of immediately studying a profession, I sat myself down to consider what pursuit in life I was best fit for. . . . And year after year I kept on considering what I was fit for, and time and my destiny decided that I was to be the writer that I am."[16]

Occasionally Hawthorne might have turned to the logbooks and imitated his father's hand in order to stir ideas for his writing. But their importance to him evidently ran much deeper. The continuing recourse to the journals manifests a need to establish his life purpose in relation, generally, to the expectations of the community and, specifically, to the path his father had taken. If Hawthorne was "in the habit of poring over" the logs during his "childhood and boyhood," as Julian later claimed, "and made up many imaginative stories for himself," he did not put signatures and dates on the logs until he was at an age to be concerned about his own occupation and destiny. The father's career and his journals held an authoritative place in Hawthorne's inner library.

Other Voyages to the East

Although Captain Hathorne presumably also kept logs on his North Atlantic and Caribbean voyages, the four preserved by the family all recorded voyages to the East Indies. He is thought to have traveled to the Orient five, and perhaps six, times in all. In "The Custom-House," the prefatory sketch to *The Scarlet Letter*, Hawthorne implies that his father went before the mast when a lad of fourteen as was typical for the town and the family. The earliest extant record of his maritime career, however, is the "Journal of a Passage from Bengall to AMERICA in the Ship America of SALEM, 1796," which Hathorne kept when he was twenty years old.[17] The *America* had been purchased for Elias Hasket Derby at the Isle of France (Mauritius) during the summer of 1795 by Jacob Crowninshield.[18] Hathorne was on the ship when it sailed from Calcutta on December 3, 1795, with Crowninshield as master, and until it reached Salem following a stop at New York in April 1796.[19]

On December 7, 1796, Hathorne embarked for the East Indies again on the *Perseverance*, owned by his brother-in-law Simon Forrester, who was rapidly becoming one of the wealthiest merchants in America. The *Perseverance*'s voyage to the Dutch East Indies, the Philippines, and China was the farthest journey of his career. Following a week at Batavia in May 1797, Captain Richard Wheatland took the ship on to Manila, which had opened to American trade only the previous year.[20] After eighteen days in Manila, the *Perseverance* made an extended call of three and a half months in Canton and Whampoa, and returned to Salem via New York on April 28, 1798, with a cargo of 158,000 pounds of tea. Hathorne's logs for the *America* and the *Perseverance* are bound together between leather, canvas-wrapped covers. Although they do not identify his role on the ships, he obviously was an officer rather than a common seaman.[21] The third known logbook records the *Herald's* voyage to Calcutta and back to America from January 1800 to February 1801.

Hathorne kept the fourth log on the *Mary and Eliza*, which left Salem in mid-December 1803, and after two months of trading in the Dutch East Indies, returned to Salem under his command on October 16, 1804, with a substantial cargo of coffee, sugar, sweetmeats, nutmegs, mace, chinaware, and camphor, including Hathorne's own adventure in the amount of five hundred dollars. The duties paid on the *Mary and Eliza's* manifests totaled $17,053.98.[22] Back in Salem after the quick ten-month run to Batavia, Captain Hathorne learned of the birth of his son and namesake on Independence Day, 1804, and of the departure of his brother, Daniel, for Malaga and the Azores the latter part of August as master of the brig *Morning Star*.[23]

Having commanded a vessel around the Cape, Captain Hathorne became eligible for membership in The Salem East India Marine Society and, on November 7, 1804, was inducted along with four other captains in ceremonies that included a procession through the streets of Salem and a dinner attended by members and local dignitaries.[24] Among the founding members of the East India Marine Society five years earlier, in October 1799, were Nathaniel Silsbee, whom Hathorne served on the *Herald* in 1800–1801, and his own elder brother Daniel, who apparently had helped open Salem's trade routes to the East but was lost at sea in 1804 with the *Morning Star*. Membership in the elite East India Society was restricted to shipmasters, factors, and supercargoes who had navigated around the Cape of Good Hope or Cape Horn and in the East Indies. Its founders had declared their threefold purpose: to "assist the widows and children of deceased members"; to "collect such facts and observations as may tend to the improvement and security of navigation" (especially shiplogs and "all approved Books of History of Voyages and Travels and of Navigation"); and to "form a Museum of natural and artificial curiosities, particularly such as are to be found beyond the Cape of Good Hope and Cape Horn."[25]

Captain Hathorne's journals do not record his activities in the Eastern ports, nor do they list the cargoes carried by the respective vessels. Such information was readily available to his son in later years, however, not only from family memories but from his first-hand observation of the Salem and Boston harbors and from the newspaper files he was fond of studying. The *Salem Gazette's* "Ship News" for October 23, 1804, for instance, reported of the *Mary and Eliza*:

COMMERCIAL. Capt. Hathorne, who had left Batavia about the 15th June last, reports, that all the crop of Coffee was exhausted, and no more was to be had for the season. 6 or 7 American ships had been obliged to leave the port for Bengal and other places, without procuring any. No less than 45 neutral ships, principally American, had loaded there from September to June.

There is some evidence that after the return of the *Herald* and his marriage to Elizabeth Manning in 1801, Captain Hathorne had reembarked in December of that year for Sumatra and Java on Elias Hasket Derby's *Astrea*, returning to Salem in the spring of 1803 with a cargo of sugar, pepper, and coffee.[26] It is also possible that in the summer of 1805 he transferred from the ship *Neptune*, in France, to another vessel bound for Batavia.[27] Whatever knowledge of additional trips to the Orient existed in the family, no journals are known today. From the birth of his second child and only son in 1804 until his death in Surinam four years later, Captain Hathorne concentrated on less exotic trading with Europe and the West Indies.

The contents of the *America, Perseverance,* and *Mary and Eliza* logs are much like the report of the *Herald*'s trip to Madras and Calcutta. As Captain Hathorne's responsibilities on the East Indiamen grew, his accounts became increasingly businesslike. The *America* and *Perseverance* logs are the most narrative and expressive; the *Mary and Eliza* log, entirely matter-of-fact. Since these other three logs have been described elsewhere in some detail,[28] it is only necessary here to suggest a few episodes that later exercised his son's imagination.

After at least five weeks at Calcutta late in 1795, where the *America* took on its cargo of rice, coffee, and bales of textiles, Nathaniel Hathorne evidently was homesick for Salem.[29] Written across the title page of his logbook, perhaps on setting sail from Bengal on December 3, is the sententious remark: "Let this Auspicious day be ever sacred." On March 10, 1796, after stops at St. Helena and Ascension islands, Hathorne again showed a yearning for home: "this Night we saw the North Star which I think is a great Pleasure to a homeward Bound Mariner after a Long Voige to India." Throughout the voyage he displayed his usual interest in the bird and fish life surrounding the ship. But without question the most notable animal on this trip was the young female elephant Captain Crowninshield had purchased for forty-five pounds in Bengal. Hathorne recorded the provisioning of "Greens for the Elaphant" at St. Helena, February 17, 1796. Two months later the New York *Minerva* (April 18) announced:

> The America, Capt. Jacob Crowninshield, of Salem, Mass. commander and owner, has brought home an ELEPHANT, from Bengal, in perfect health. It is the first ever seen in America, and a very great curiosity. It is a female, two years old, and of a species that grows to an enormous size. This animal is sold for Ten Thousand Dollars, being supposed to be the greatest price ever given for an animal in Europe or America.[30]

Between his return to Salem in the spring of 1796 and the departure of the *Perseverance* in December Hathorne had the opportunity of seeing the pachyderm on display in his own town.

The notes in Hathorne's *Perseverance* logbook reveal a pensive if sometimes pious and platitudinous nature. He remarked on February 21, 1797, for instance—"This day by my account I am in East Longitude. God send us into West Long. again after a prosperous Voyage"—and on February 22—"This is the Anniversary of the Illustrious Washingtons Birth Day, may every succeeding year heap New honours upon Him." Hathorne had reason to be reflective, for the *Perseverance* was frequently in peril during its seventeen month journey. At least two sailors died of disease, and a third was almost lost in an antic Hathorne recorded on January 24, 1797: "at Meredian a Very Large Fish came along Side, hove the Harpoon into it. but the Carpenter being in the Coil of the line the Fish hauled him over the Stern so that we were obliged to let the Fish go harpoon line and all to get the Carpenter onboard again[.]"

Other adventures on the *Perseverance* would remind the modern reader of Joseph Conrad's Lord Jim. Having cleared the Straits of Sunda and rounded Java Head at the beginning of May, the *Perseverance* was approached by an unidentified shore boat, which she warned off by firing a blunderbuss. All American vessels were not so fortunate. On May 10, when leaving Batavia harbor, the *Perseverance* received a party from the ship *Eliza* of Providence who informed her that they had lost their captain, "by the name of Page," and two men "in an Engagement with a Mallay Prow." For safety in the pirate-infested China Sea the two ships agreed to sail on to Manila together. This rescue might have been known to Edward Everett when he wrote his tale "The Modern Job; or, The Philosopher's Stone" for *The Token* (1834) and credited a "Captain Hathorne" from Salem with picking up the survivors of a Massachusetts pepper ship pillaged by Sumatran pirates.[31]

Hathorne was obviously relieved to reach Manila without further accident and composed there one of the few pieces of verse found in his logbooks:

> Place me where never Summer breeze
> Unbinds the Glebe or warms the Trees
> Where ever Lowering Clouds appear
> And angry Jove deforms the inclement Year

On a loose sheet in the same part of the Journal he devoted another set of couplets to the girl he had left behind in Salem:

> In Storms when clouds obscure the Sky
> And Thunders rool and lightning fly
> In the Midst of all these dire allarms
> Ill think dear Betsey on thy Charms

Perhaps it was during the *Perseverance's* three months in Canton and with his "dear Betsey" Manning in mind that Hathorne ordered the set of china, monogrammed with "N. H.," that passed down through the Hawthorne household.

As in the case of the *Herald* log, young Nathaniel Hawthorne sometimes merely duplicated his father's notes on sea and weather conditions when reading the logbooks for the *America* and *Perseverance* voyages. But he also copied each of the quatrains above—normalizing the spelling and capitalization—and, perhaps, added the assessments "Romantic"[32] and "Beautiful" that appear respectively under the two verses. When twice copying his father's paean "Let this Auspicious day be ever sacred" on the title page of the *America* log, he added a like-spirited query—"For what?"—whether in impatience or puzzlement is not clear. Finding one's destiny, and one's Faith, at home after a world-wearying search later would become a major theme in Hawthorne's fiction as the "The Threefold Destiny," "The Great Carbuncle," "Young Goodman Brown," and other tales manifest.

Hawthorne might have had his father's sentiments still in mind when he published Lydia H. Sigourney's poem "The Mariner to the First-Seen Mountain, on Approaching His Native Coast" in the March 1836 issue of the *American Magazine of Useful and Entertaining Knowledge*. Although he otherwise had little regard for this "Infernal woman!"[33]—the final stanza of her poem expressed feelings well known to his father and the community:

> I've roam'd where Himmaleh aspires
> With snowy breast o'er Indian vales,
> And where, perfumed from spicy groves,
> The freighted vessel spreads its sails,—
> But most my heart doth joy to climb,
> Thy breeze-swept hills, dear native clime![34]

In his father's journals young Hawthorne found not only a personal affection for travel but the professional discipline and routines of life on the trade routes to the East. Log-keeping by common sailors and lesser officers was both an avocation and practice for the day when they, too, expected to become chief mates or shipmasters. Captain Hathorne's first logs probably served such an apprenticeship, and at least once the son made his own imaginative start in that direction. Finding the back page of the *Perseverance* logbook blank, the future novelist organized it in the fashion of his father and then set down "Remarks Tuesday Aug. 15, 1820," beginning "This 24 hours begins with gentle breezes and passing clouds," and closing "Latter Part cloudy with some drops of rain."

Hawthorne's appropriation of his father's experience is most boldly illustrated on the title page of the first log, for the *America*. There, in block letters framed by intricate designs spanning the middle of the sheet, the future romanticist asserted: "NATHANIEL HATHORNE'S BOOK, 1820, SALEM." On the facing page, surrounding an original inscription reading—

> Nathaniel Hathorne's Book
> Presented By his Esteamed Friend
> Mr. Robert Robinnet October 25ᵗʰ 1795
> CALCUTTA

he stamped his own name nine times. The father's and son's signatures were made a generation apart but at similar points in both lives.[35]

While most adolescents practice their names as a matter of self-definition and personal style, Hawthorne's signatures and inscriptions witness an exceptional desire to connect with the experience of his seafaring father. Biographers who have worked closely with the Hawthorne family papers are inclined to find "that the life of the father and its attending circumstances deeply impressed and largely tended to shape the writer of fiction."[36]

The Sea of Literature

In his essay "Captain Nathaniel Hathorne" Hubert Hoeltje remarked, "The fact of this possession and perusal [of the shiplogs] is of importance, certainly, in any attempt to evaluate the influence of father upon son."[37] There can be no doubt that young Hawthorne turned to his father's East India logs at times when most people are setting the compass for their careers. That he sought a response from them about his own choice of life seems probable.

Beyond their importance as a record of his heritage, his father's journals also provided Hawthorne a bridge between the factualities of life in early nineteenth-century America and the realm of imagination. Since the age of Ulysses and Sindbad, mariners' accounts have been the keel of myth and story. Americans of Hawthorne's time were quick to recognize the romantic resources of travel. Among the contemporary novelists who exploited real or imaginary sea voyages were not only Herman Melville but also Timothy Flint in *Life and Adventures of Arthur Clenning* (1828), Edgar Allan Poe in *The Narrative of Arthur Gordon Pym* (1838), James Fenimore Cooper in *Afloat and Ashore* (1844) and *The Crater* (1847), and a host of other penmen who appealed to the popular rage for travel narratives. In *Astoria* (1836) Washington Irving described the displeasure of an "honest captain" that "Some of the young clerks, who were making their first voyage, and to whom everything was new and strange, were, very rationally, in the habit of taking notes and keeping journals. . . . 'The collecting of materials for long histories of their voyages and travels,' said he, . . . 'appears to engross most of their attention.' "[38]

As a mature writer Hawthorne knew the popular taste as well as the techniques for transmuting travel notes into literature. When his college classmate and lifelong friend Horatio Bridge was appointed purser of the USS *Saratoga* on its cruise along the west coast of Africa in 1843, Hawthorne encouraged him to keep a detailed journal for the purpose of producing magazine articles and later helped Bridge edit his notes into a book to which Hawthorne gave his own name. He wrote to Bridge:

Allow your fancy pretty free license. . . . This is the secret of all entertaining travellers. . . . Begin to write always before the impression of novelty has worn off from your mind; else you will begin to think that the peculiarities, which at first attracted you, are not worth recording. . . . After you have had due time for observation, you may then give grave reflections on national character,

customs, morals, religions, the influence of peculiar modes of government &c. . . .
I shall merely arrange them [the sketches], correct the style, and perform other
little offices as to which only a practiced scribbler is *au fait.*[39]

"I should like well," Hawthorne had told Bridge in a previous letter, "to
launch you fairly on *the sea of literature.*"[40]

In noting the place of the father's logbooks in Hawthorne's library, B.
Bernard Cohen emphasized their proto-literary quality. "Hawthorne's youth-
ful imagination was stirred by memories of stories about his seafaring father,"
Cohen wrote. "Here may have been the beginning of his interest in the art
of fiction—the altering of reality by the moonlight and firelight which in the
Custom House essay symbolizes the creative imagination." Cohen also thought,
"This early interest in his father's world-wide trips probably accounts for the
heavy proportion of travel books which Hawthorne drew from the Salem
Athenaeum years later. His was a mind enchanted by travel and by the ro-
mance of adventure."[41]

Hawthorne would not make an ocean passage until the Cunard steamer
Niagara carried his family to Liverpool in July 1853, but the experience of
travel and homecoming was indigenous to his life in Salem. Despite the boy's
extreme youth and his father's long absences, there is a core of fact in Julian
Hawthorne's reminiscence a century later:

> When his tall, grave father came home, he would take little Nathaniel between
> his knees, and tell him tales of the sea and of foreign countries; how, once, he
> helped an English merchant captain fight off a French sloop of war . . .; how,
> in the remoter Indies, were strange temples and dark-skinned, turbaned myriads
> of people speaking outlandish tongues. From these places he sometimes brought
> home wonderful objects of carved ivory and sandalwood; baskets of grass cur-
> iously woven, and rainbow shells and coral beads from the islands of the Pacific;
> and once, a superb set of the finest porcelain from China, with his own initials
> painted on each piece in a gold monogram.

"Some of these ancient pieces," Julian said, "still survive unscathed." According to his son, the future novelist "pored over the carvings and the
pictured porcelain; but he lacked the clue to them. Sometimes his amiable
uncle Robert or his queer uncle Ebenezer would take him down to Salem
wharves, and he would gaze at the ships and at the sea, and feel a deep longing
to sail far away and see for himself the wonders of the unknown world."[42]

Like Father Like Son

The early family biographers are agreed both about the character of Captain
Nathaniel Hathorne and resemblances in the son. Captain Hathorne was
remembered to be a reserved man, slender and athletic, inclined to melancholy
but kindly and fond of children.[43] "The chief testimony one gets of Captain
Nathaniel Hathorne" from the early accounts, Manning Hawthorne noticed,
"is that of silence."[44] He did not share the reputation for bluster and severity

of his own father, "Bold Daniel" Hathorne, but maintained the stern composure of the family line. According to the author's sister-in-law Elizabeth Peabody, Nathaniel Hawthorne "used to say that he inherited the granite that was in him [from the Hawthorne line], in such strong contrast to the Manning sensibility";[45] and he acknowledged himself in later years, "I had always a natural tendency (it appears to have been on the paternal side) towards seclusion."[46] Hawthorne noticed in 1851 the "singular resemblance" in expression between an engraving made from his own portrait and a miniature of his father.[47]

The temperamental affinities were even stronger than the physical. Like his son, Captain Hathorne was said to have been "a great reader, employing all his leisure time at sea over books."[48] The occasional verse, the ornamental script, and the appreciations of nature in Captain Hathorne's logbooks were enough to have caused Arlin Turner to consider: "If a choice had been open to his father, might not he too have passed over the professions and trades and business, and the possibilities of wealth, and chosen instead the realms of thought, dreams, speculation, and creative imagination?"[49]

Such faculties might have been even more responsible than poor business acumen or mere bad luck for the senior Hathorne's failure to rise as rapidly and far through the ranks of Salem's maritime aristocracy as other men of his age and breeding, including his brother-in-law Simon Forrester and his relatives in the Archer, Peabody, and Crowninshield families. Jacob Crowninshield was only twenty-four years old when he commanded the *America* on its celebrated voyage in 1795. Nathaniel Silsbee—just twenty-seven when leading the defense of the *Cornwallis* in the Bay of Bengal in 1800—thought one more voyage like that of the *Herald* would enable him to retire from the sea. By contrast, when he died in Dutch Guiana at age thirty-three in 1808, Captain Hathorne left virtually no estate. His father's worldly misfortune surely vexed young Nathaniel Hawthorne as he mused over the logbooks before, during, and after Bowdoin College in 1821–1825. He wrote out of family pique when he chided Salem's new and short-lived aristocracy in "The Custom-House":

> Here, no doubt, statistics of the former commerce of Salem might be discovered, and memorials of her princely merchants,—old King Derby,—old Billy Gray,— old Simon Forrester,—and many another magnate in his day; whose powdered head, however, was scarcely in the tomb, before his mountain-pile of wealth began to dwindle. The founders of the greater part of the families which now compose the aristocracy of Salem might here be traced, from the petty and obscure beginnings of their traffic, at periods generally much posterior to the Revolution, upward to what their children look upon as long-established rank. (I, 28–29)

Too much critical capital already has been made of Hawthorne's "Oedipal conflict" with his missing father.[50] Recent efforts to establish the importance of Hawthorne's mother, and of the maternal relatives whose house, support, and affection the widow Hawthorne and her three children shared, have helped balance the young author's life. It is unnecessarily reductive, however, to claim as one Hawthorne scholar has: "Given the limited biological understanding of the child, young Hawthorne probably never missed his dead father consciously, and since there were male heads of the Manning household in abundance he probably never grasped, at any level, the fact that he was lacking a father until be was beyond childhood."[51] Gloria Erlich's connections of the oppressive father figures in Hawthorne's fiction with the Manning uncles, especially the benevolent and authoritarian Robert Manning, give even more reason to suspect that, as he moved into adulthood, Hawthorne invoked the romantic image of his father as a standard for defining himself.[52]

If Hawthorne had only a hazy personal memory of his father, for that very reason, Manning Hawthorne suggested, "the consequences of the Captain's death would . . . be the more powerful and mysterious." "Raised by the Mannings, educated by the Mannings, in their society constantly, for even in Raymond [Maine] there was a Manning uncle, Hawthorne in spite of it all, remained fundamentally a Hawthorne."[53] He was pleased when an old sailor stopped him on the steps of the Salem Custom House one day in the late 1840s to ask "if he had not once a relative . . . who died in Surinam." The sailor had recognized his father's likeness in him.[54] The substantial, hardworking traders and businessmen on the mother's side, while successful in the field of money-making, were unlikely to attract the imagination of the young writer. The uncles' coach lines gave him transportation within New England. His father's logbooks carried him to the farthest ports of the rich East.

A Sailor or an Author?

The few characterizations of Hawthorne's earliest childhood that have been passed down through the family agree on his dream of going to sea and his imaginative accounts of the journeys he would make. His older sister Elizabeth told James T. Fields in 1870, six years after Hawthorne's death: "He used to invent long stories, wild and fanciful, and to tell us where he was going when he grew up, and of wonderful adventures he was to meet with, always ending with 'and I'm never coming back again.' "[55] Hawthorne's son-in-law, George Lathrop, associated the pretend journeys definitely with the sea in his Study of Hawthorne in 1876, writing:

> . . . he would break out from the midst of childish broodings, and exclaim, "There, Mother! I is going away to sea, some time"; then, with an ominous shaking of the head, "and I'll never come back again!" The same refrain lurked in his mind when, a little older, he would tell his sisters fantastic tales, and give them imaginary accounts of long journeys, which he should take in future, in the course of which he flew at will through the air; on these occasions he always ended with the same hopeless prophecy of his failing to return.[56]

In view of the number of Hawthornes who had disappeared at sea over three generations, and the widows at home, the boy's threat was not a negligible one.[57]

Hawthorne's passion for the sea did not leave him as he grew. A merchant-father and other East Indies sailors figure prominently in the novel *Fanshawe* (1828), which he began at college, and his first book of stories, to be called *Seven Tales from My Native Land*, although abandoned and mostly destroyed before publication, reportedly contained tales both of witchcraft and of pirates and privateers.[58] In "The Custom-House" Hawthorne acknowledged Salem's grip on his adult affections, and after finishing *The House of the Seven Gables* in the Berkshires of Western Massachusetts, he longed to be near the sea once more.[59] In 1859 Hawthorne took his family and the draft of *The Marble Faun* from Italy back to England, where he had first gone as United States Consul in 1853, and chose a house in Redcar, overlooking the North Sea, as a quiet and consanguineous site for finishing his book. Fields, who traveled with Hawthorne by ship back to America in 1860, later wrote:

> Hawthorne's love for the sea amounted to a passionate worship; and while I (the worst sailor probably on this planet) was longing, spite of the good company on board, to reach land as soon as possible, Hawthorne was constantly saying in his quiet, earnest way, "I should like to sail on and on forever, and never touch the shore again." He liked to stand alone in the bows of the ship and see the sun go down, and he was never tired of walking the deck at midnight. I used to watch his dark, solitary figure under the stars, pacing up and down some unfrequented part of the vessel, musing and half melancholy.[60]

According to Hawthorne's family, "he used to declare that, had he not been sent to college, he should have become a mariner, like his predecessors"; and "if he had not been an author he should have been a sailor."[61] Perhaps his Bowdoin classmates knew of these inclinations and of the family shiplogs in his room when they elected him Commander of the Navy Club in 1825, a "rear-guard" of those fourteen graduates who had no role in the class commencement exercises.[62]

Although Hawthorne never went to sea professionally, his work life shifted several times from writing to maritime employment. Except for the utopian experiment at Brook Farm, his non-literary occupations were all related to shipping and trade, first as weigher and gauger of salt and coal at the Boston Custom House in 1839–1841, then as "Surveyor for the District of Salem and Beverly and Inspector of the Revenue for the Port of Salem" in 1846–1849, and finally as U.S. Consul to Liverpool and Manchester in 1853–1857. He avidly pursued the support that secured each of these political appointments.

Hawthorne wrote to Henry Wadsworth Longfellow in anticipation of his first post in Boston—"I shall be a sort of Port-Admiral, and take command of vessels after they enter the harbor, and have control of their cargoes"—and imagined drolly the sketches he could write with his leisure time and new experiences: " 'Passages in the life of a Custom-House Officer'—'Scenes in Dock'—'Voyages at Anchor'—'Nibblings of a Wharf-Rat'—'Trials of a Tide-Waiter'—'Romance of the Revenue Service.' "[63] He expected "not utterly [to] lay by the story-telling trade" while at the Boston Custom House.[64] Although he ultimately tired of his customs and consular roles, his letters and other testimony show him to have worked capably and with some satisfaction at his duties ashore. "After all," he wrote to Sophia Peabody in 1840, "a human spirit may find no insufficiency of food fit for it, even in the Custom-House. And with such materials as these, I do think, and feel, and learn things that are worth knowing, and which I should not know unless I had learned them there." He preferred, however, "ten million times," being out of the office and on the ships themselves, "for there the sky is above me, and the fresh breeze around me, and my thoughts, having hardly anything to do with my occupation, are as free as air."[65]

The decade Hawthorne spent among the ships and cargo, the masters and seamen of Boston, Salem, and Liverpool were fallow interludes preceding major bursts of creativity. His career as a whole shows a diastolic-systolic rhythm of matter-of-fact engagements alternating with acts of imagination for which his seaside life ideally prepared him. Burns and Chaucer had been custom house officers in their days, Hawthorne noted, and he tweaked himself for not "writing out the narratives of a veteran shipmaster" at the Salem Custom House who stirred him "to laughter and admiration by his marvellous gifts as a story-teller. Could I have preserved the picturesque force of his style," Hawthorne thought, "and the humorous coloring which nature taught him how to throw over his descriptions, the result, I honestly believe, would have been something new in literature" (I, 26, 37).

Before his appointment to the Boston Custom House, Hawthorne had sought through the support of Franklin Pierce and other political friends to secure the office of historian on the Great Exploring Expedition that mapped the shores of Antarctica, the Pacific Ocean islands, and the northwest coast of American from August 1838 until July 1842. Called "the largest and most elaborate exploring squadron that any nation had yet sent to sea at one time," the Expedition under Lieutenant Charles Wilkes returned with 160,000 scientific specimens that provoked the construction of a national museum at the Smithsonian Institution.[66] Hawthorne's sister Elizabeth later believed that although "on some accounts it would have been a good thing for him . . . , he never would have written The Scarlet Letter, if he had succeeded in getting that appointment." The experience would have "hardened his heart."[67] Horatio Bridge held a similar opinion: "Had his aspirations in that direction been successful the current of his life would have been strangely disturbed, and his later writing would, I think, have taken on an entirely different coloring—whether for the better, who shall say?"[68] The paranoia of Lieutenant Wilkes, a vainglorious martinet who wanted to write his own narrative of the Expedition, would have frustrated Hawthorne intolerably, and by the time the Expedition sailed, Twice-told Tales (1837) had launched him fairly on his own sea of literature. But Hawthorne was still writing to Longfellow as late as June 1837: "If such a post were attainable, I should certainly accept it; for, though fixed so long to one spot, I have always had a desire to run round the world."[69]

Hawthorne was attracted above all to that romantic zone extending from Asia Minor eastward to the "Celestial Empire" which was opening to American economic and political interests in the course of the century. In 1854, when Commodore Matthew Perry approached him at the consulate in Liverpool with the notion of preparing an account of Perry's historic cruise in the China Sea and of the famous treaty of commerce that opened Japan to the West, Hawthorne wrote in his journal: "It would be a very desirable labor for a young literary man, or, for that matter, an old one; for the world can scarcely have in reserve a less hackneyed theme than Japan."[70]

Hawthorne's penchant for travel and his actual tours across young America are a matter of record. "Once in a while, every summer if he could, he went out of town for four or five weeks." According to his sister, "he went to Niagara, to Nantucket, and Martha's Vineyard and other places"—as far as Detroit.[71] Hawthorne claimed that in his annual excursions, he "enjoyed as much of life as other people do in the whole year's round."[72] He must have agreed with the editor and translator of Carsten Niebuhr's *Travels through Arabia and Other Countries in the East*, when he read the Danish explorer's account in the mid-1830s:

> He who spends his life without wandering ever more than a few miles from the spot of his nativity, or without mingling with any other but the first circle, whether of courtiers, of cit[izen]s, or of rustics, into whose society he has been introduced, can know little of the dignity, of the meanness, of the capacities of his nature,—and but little of the beauties and the wonders of this great theatre of human exertions.
>   . . . To enlarge, in any considerable degree, the extent of our knowledge, we must change the scene. . . . [73]

Why Hawthorne did not go to sea when other future Massachusetts literati like Charles Eliot Norton were still shipping as supercargoes to India in the 1840s is a matter of speculation. There is some truth, no doubt, in Julian Hawthorne's suggestion that this only son conceded to the wishes of the family, which generation after generation had sent its young men to sea "never to return." Following "an ancestral bias toward the sea," Julian pointed out, "would have left his family unprotected."[74] Inertia, lack of encouragement from the landsmen in the Manning household, and doubts about his temperamental suitability for the aggressive commercialism of the Indies trade also might have held Hawthorne back.

He was well aware, too, that by the 1830s the golden age of Salem was receding into the past as changing demography, commodities, and transportation systems rerouted trade from Salem in the direction of Boston, New York, Baltimore, and other ports to the south and as industry inexorably replaced commerce as the business of Salem. In his reproachful "Custom-House" essay Hawthorne noticed how rarely in the 1840s a florescence of affairs in the port of Salem "might remind the elderly citizen of that period, before the last war with England, when Salem was a port by itself; not scorned, as she is now, by her own merchants and ship-owners, who permit her wharves to crumble to ruin, while their ventures go to swell, needlessly and imperceptibly, the mighty flood of commerce at New York or Boston" (I, 6).

He had watched his father's once-proud ship *America* decaying at Downer's Wharf, and in 1846, the year he assumed his Surveyorship, the final pepper ship from Sumatra entered at the port of Salem.[75]

Puritans or Seafarers?

The imaginative power of *The Scarlet Letter* and Hawthorne's unforgettable images of black-browed Puritans in "sad-colored garments and gray, steeple-crowned hats" (I, 47) have fixed the impression that his ancestry consisted principally of severe Puritan magistrates. Although the earliest American progenitors came to Hawthorne's aid in works like "The Gentle Boy," "Young Goodman Brown," and *The Scarlet Letter*, they were neither the most accessible nor necessarily the most representative of the Hawthorne line. Only after he graduated from college and began searching the early history of Massachusetts for literary materials did Hawthorne become particularly aware of the lineage before his father and grandfather, or of the role the Hawthornes had played in the history of seventeenth-century Salem.[76] While he later researched the life of the Massachusetts settlements with the interests of a romanticist and a family historian, the experiences of Hawthorne's youth were those suitable to a world seaport in the first quarter of the nineteenth century.

The history of the Hawthornes in America from the arrival of William Hathorne at the Massachusetts Bay Colony, possibly with Governor John Winthrop on the *Arbella* in 1630, to the sixth generation of Nathaniel and his sisters Elizabeth and Louisa, born in the first decade of the nineteenth century, divides into two stages. Major William Hathorne (1607–1681), persecutor of Quaker heretics, and Colonel John Hathorne (1641–1717), judge at the Salem witchcraft trials in 1692, developed their considerable estate through farming, real estate, and maritime adventures that included a wharf, warehouses, and vessels for trade with Newfoundland, England, and the West Indies. Except for John Hathorne's occasional voyage as supercargo, however, the first two generations of Hawthornes apparently remained close to home.[77]

The second stage of the Hawthorne family's history in America began with the third generation. All five of John Hathorne's sons, including the novelist's great-grandfather Joseph (1692–1762), turned to lives at sea. Following the death of his daring younger brother, Captain Benjamin Hathorne, in a storm in April 1732, Joseph retired to a quiet life of farming—but only after two decades of voyages along the Atlantic Coast and to the West Indies and Europe. He demonstrated his skill as a captain in 1724, as well as considerable heroism, by rescuing the crew of a foundering craft bound for the Azores and bringing his own disabled vessel safely back to Salem.[78]

The most celebrated of the fourth generation of Hawthornes was Joseph's sixth son, Daniel (1731–1796), who came under the spell of the sea at an early age. "No childhood experience could have pleased [young Daniel] more," Vernon Loggins thought, "than hearing his father tell the story of the rescue of Captain Willard and his men in the storm. The boy's first hero was perhaps his drowned uncle, Captain Benjamin Hathorne." Daniel Hathorne grew into a blustering, fearless shipmaster—according to one witness, "the sternest man that ever walked a deck!"[79] His career reached its apogee in the latter half of 1776 when he captained the privateer *True American* on a triumphal cruise against British shipping during which he took several prizes and, while losing three men and himself suffering a musket wound, overpowered a British ship bound for America with troops for General Howe. The naval battle was memorialized by the ship's surgeon in a ballad called "Bold Hathorne" that became popular among Yankee sailors and was referred to by his grandson in the early 1850s.[80] The second and last stanzas are typical of the thirteen-part panegyric:

> Bold Hathorne was commander,
>   A man of real worth,
> Old England's cruel tyranny
>   Induced him to go forth;
> She, with relentless fury,
>   Was plundering all our coast,
> And thought, because her strength was great,
>   Our glorious cause was lost.
>
>   . . . .
>
> Ten other men were wounded
>   Among our warlike crew,
> With them our noble captain,
>   To whom all praise is due;
> To him and all our officers,
>   Let's give a hearty cheer:
> "Success to fair America,
>   And our good privateer!"[81]

Captain Daniel Hawthorne saw his daughters married to Simon Forrester, John Crowninshield, and George Archer and his two sons, Daniel and Nathaniel, launched at sea. Unlike both his sons, however, "Bold Hathorne" died at home, in 1796.

While one of the biographers most attentive to the author's maritime heritage, oddly, has remarked that "in his own immediate family, there was no such long sequence of sea-faring ancestors" as Hawthorne's description in "The Custom-House" would indicate,[82] the family had turned decisively to the sea beginning at the third generation, early in the eighteenth century, with the author's great-grandfather Joseph and his brothers. The sharp distinction Hawthorne made in "The Custom-House" between the first two generations of Puritan magistrates and the century of seafarers that followed is based precisely on family genealogy:

From father to son, for above a hundred years, they followed the sea; a gray-headed shipmaster, in each generation, retiring from the quarterdeck to the homestead, while a boy of fourteen took the hereditary place before the mast,

confronting the salt spray and the gale, which had blustered against his sire
and grandsire. The boy, also, in due time, passed from the forecastle to the
cabin, spent a tempestuous manhood, and returned from his world-wanderings,
to grow old, and die, and mingle his dust with the natal earth. (I, 11)

To be sure, "The Custom-House" represents the Puritan forebears as
being the primary family influence on the novelist. "The figure of that first
ancestor, invested by family tradition with a dim and dusky grandeur, was
present to my boyish imagination, as far back as I can remember," Hawthorne
wrote. "It still haunts me, and induces a sort of home-feeling with the past,
which I scarcely claim in reference to the present phase of the town" (I, 9).
This post facto account, however, is at least semi-fictional and, like Surveyor
Pue's manuscripts and the embroidered letter A, constructed more from later
readings in local history than from experience. Once Hawthorne had introduced "the old trunk of the family tree"—with himself "its topmost bough"—
the logic of the metaphor obliged him to expose "the deep and aged roots
which my family has struck into the soil" (I, 8, 10).

Led by the examples of Walter Scott and Washington Irving, in the introduction to *The Scarlet Letter* Hawthorne moved his scene backwards
through successive shades of time until he arrived at the heroic age of his
culture. The same romantic distancing that Scott achieved through the folklore of the Scottish borderlands and Irving through the old wives tales recorded by Diedrich Knickerbocker, Hawthorne sought to attain through the
antiquarian papers of Surveyor Pue. He did not entirely foresake the Salem
Custom House but, archaeologically, peeled away layers of history until he
arrived at the ideal types of an earlier age, imaginatively recreating his Puritan
ancestry in the process.

If it suited the conceptual purposes of "The Custom-House" to discover
a "dim and dusky" ancestor in Hawthorne's "boyish imagination," biographical evidence points to a more typical acquaintance with his immediate ancestors. In describing his origins for Richard Henry Stoddard shortly after writing
The Scarlet Letter and *The House of the Seven Gables*, Hawthorne began: "I
was born in the town of Salem, Massachusetts, in a house built by my grandfather, who was a maritime personage." He went on to explain the situation
of the house and gardens planted by "this old man of the sea" but made no
mention, at least in the text that has come down to us, of the Puritan forebears.[83]

With a particularly well-chosen metaphor Hawthorne referred in "The
Custom-House" to the "oyster-like tenacity with which an old settler, over
whom his third century is creeping, clings to the spot where his successive
generations have been imbedded." By contrast, "The new inhabitant—who
came himself from a foreign land, or whose father or grandfather came—has
little claim to be called a Salemite" (I, 11). While acknowledging that he felt
Salem "almost as a destiny," Hawthorne resolved to sever the family connection. "My children have had other birthplaces," he wrote, "and, so far as
their fortunes may be within my control, shall strike their roots into unaccustomed earth" (I, 12).

The family's romance with the East, however, continued into subsequent generations. In 1897 *Cosmopolitan* magazine appointed his son Julian its "Special Commissioner" to report on the plague and famine that were devastating India. Counting the tour of Bombay and stations to the north "among the keenest experiences" of his life, Julian returned to write a five-part series that began with "The Horrors of the Plaque in India" and concluded with "Beauty and Charm in India."[84] After the lapse of another generation Julian's grandson, Manning Hawthorne, at mid-life became a South Asia specialist in the United States Information Service and served successively in New Delhi, Tokyo, Bombay, and Penang.[85] Salt water and spice were the Hawthorne heritage.

Salem and the Orient

Contrary to general impressions, far from spending his youth and young manhood physically removed from the world, Nathaniel Hawthorne grew up in the heart of Salem's maritime activity, like his father, "literally on the waterfront, among ships and sailors and tales of the sea."[86] Both father and son were born in the house chosen by "Bold Daniel" at 27 Union Street, "near the wharves, and convenient to his business," where the boy "rolled on a grass-plot under an apple-tree, and picked abundant currants."[87] The Manning household on Herbert Street, to which Captain Hathorne's widow moved her three children in 1808, and which adjoined the back of the Hawthornes' Union Street property, was equally proximitous to the central wharves and warehouses of Salem's South River. A few rods to the south, the block bordered by Union and Herbert Streets looked across Derby Street immediately onto Union Wharf (earlier called Long Wharf). A short distance to the north, Union and Herbert Streets terminated at Main Street (now Essex), where merchant grandees built their square white mansions with profits from the East Indies trade, conveniently close to their ships and counting houses.

Less than a block away, the Salem wharves were close enough for Hawthorne to hear "the dark and weather-beaten ships . . . creaking and murmuring with the movement of the water and the wind" and to smell "the briny tonic in the air, bracing and yet melancholy at the same time."[88] "Even when he was a little lad," his great-grandson wrote, "Hawthorne was attracted to the wharves. He used to see the schooners come around Naugus Head, their white sails flashing and dipping in the sunshine, their sharp prows cutting the water and sending up a spray of foam on either side. Or he would walk down the length of the Long Wharf, under the bowsprits of the vessels, staring at their figureheads, which gazed back at him blankly with their unseeing eyes. The small boy followed them, no doubt, in his imagination."[89]

On shore, between the wharves and the Yankee skippers' mansions, were a small shipyard, a distillery, and the inevitable taverns. Vernon Loggins has reasoned that, "Often, when their elders were not looking, the children darted from their front door down to Derby Street, ran past the wicked tavern as they had been told to do, and . . . found a place to stand and watch ships going out to sea and ships coming in. Ebe, envied because of her recollection of their father, was able sometimes to identify a vessel he had sailed."[90] As he grew older, both before and after college, Nathaniel Hawthorne's life fell into a pattern; he "sat at home, and read, and walked to the seashore."[91]

During the first half of the nineteenth century Salem was a major international port for products both from the East Indies and China and from the Eastern Mediterranean, the Red Sea, and the Persian Gulf. Besides silk, tea, and chinaware, following the inaugural voyage of the *Grand Turk* in 1785, Salem's East Indiamen accounted for a massive trade in Eastern textiles and indigo. The cargo of Jacob Crowninshield's *America*, in addition to its famous elephant, might have been represented in the *Salem Gazette* ads on May 3, 1796, for "a few bales of INDIA GOODS, Consisting of Madras and Bengal Plain Musslin; Madras and Bengal Handkerchiefs"; "Gurrahs, wide and narrow Sannas, Black and colour'd Persians of a very superior Quality"; "Sistusoy Handkerchiefs."

The fortunes of the Peeles, Crowninshields, Silsbees, Popeses, and other Salem merchants rested heavily on the pepper trade. Between 1799 and 1846, 179 pepper ships entered at Salem. The pepper trade not only contributed a large part of the five percent of its total revenue that the United States government derived from the port of Salem, but as the city became the world emporium for pepper, it also furnished the basis of Salem's trade with the Baltic and the Mediterranean. Without an accessible hinterland Salem depended for its livelihood on the transshipment of goods between major world sources and markets—like Venice, Lisbon, and Antwerp in other ages. The last vessel of Sumatra pepper to reach America, which entered New York in 1867, like the first sailed under a Salem captain and first mate.[92]

"No young man" of Hawthorne's time, a Salem pastor wrote, "considered his education finished before he had visited India, China or the Malay Archipelago."[93] By 1799 forty-one Salem vessels had called at Calcutta, Madras, and Bombay; twenty-two at Batavia, Sumatra, and the Dutch East Indies; and five at Canton.[94] "Boston was the Spain, Salem the Portugal, in the race for Oriental opulence," Samuel Eliot Morison noted. "Boston followed Magellan . . . westward, around the Horn; Salem sent her vessels eastward . . . , around Africa, along the path blazed by Vasco da Gama." Morison imagined a typical scene at the Salem wharves: "The crowd parts deferentially as master and supercargo stalk ashore, gapes at a turbaned Oriental who shipped as cabin boy."[95] Little wonder that a Rome bookseller, who offered George Bancroft a book on Hindostan in 1821, mistook India for the city of Boston.[96]

Salem's commerce with the Middle East was of little less importance than the China and East Indies trade. Massachusetts was engaged in trade with the Mediterranean as early as 1614, when Captain John Smith began exporting dried codfish to Spain and Portugal. By the late 1790s Massachusetts merchants were reconveying Canton tea to Southern Europe and the Levant, along with their consignments of domestic wheat, codfish, lumber, tobacco, cotton goods, and rum. The return cargoes, arranged by American factors in Turkey and unloaded on the wharves of Salem and Boston, made an exotic cornucopia of oranges and lemons, wine and currants, nuts and raisins, figs, sponges, wool, damask silks, olive oil, perfumes, corkwood, carpets, and drugs like myrrh and scamony, which ante-bellum physicians prescribed in profusion. In 1830 twenty of the thirty American vessels calling at Smyrna—the "Pearl of the Orient" and the principal mart of Asia Minor—were from Massachusetts. Late in the 1820s hustling Yankee merchants took almost the entire crop of Turkish opium for domestic consumption and shipment to China and the Indies, completing a three-cornered trade with the Near and Far East that had begun early in the century.[97]

Enterprising merchantmen from Salem regularly passed through the Arabian Sea at the turn of the century. When Elias Hasket Derby, Jr., hauled a cargo of Mocha coffee thirteen thousand miles around the Cape and back to Smyrna in 1788, he inaugurated a lucrative carrying trade between the Red and Mediterranean Seas that often yielded as much as three hundred percent profit. In 1805 Salem alone imported two million pounds of Arabian coffee.[98] In 1825 the brig *Laurel* out of Salem opened the Islamic sultanate of Zanzibar to American commerce, and in the years 1832–1834 nearly half of all foreign vessels (twenty of forty-one ships) entering Zanzibar hailed from Salem. Traffic further increased with the ratification of a bi-national diplomatic treaty in 1835 and the installation of Richard P. Waters of Salem as a consul at Zanzibar. So energetic and intrepid were the Massachusetts merchants in exploiting every prospect for a cargo of copal gum and ivory or a sale that a British officer of the East India Company remarked in admiration:

> Go where you will, on the wildest shores of Africa, from Madagascar to the Persian Gulf, there is hardly a petty harbor or sheltered bay large enough to admit a square-rigged craft, but you will find a Yankee boiling his oil, repairing his vessel, or in a tent planted on shore, driving a hard bargain with the natives.[99]

In the Eastern Mediterranean and the Arabian Sea trade steadily expanded in volume and importance from the 1820s to the 1850s until the Boston and Salem harbors babbled with foreign tongues. Although Salem was but half the size of Boston, in the commercial ports of foreign lands it was perhaps the best known of all American cities and as late as 1860 accounted for more ships trading with East African ports than any two other American towns. "In the Dutch East Indies, Manila, Mauritius, both coasts of Africa, and the smaller islands of the Pacific," Morison observed, "SALEM had the same connotation as BOSTON on the Northwest Coast; it stood for the whole United States."[100]

The prominence of Salem as a general seaport was in decline by 1846, the year Hawthorne became Surveyor of the Customs; yet then, as before, "pepper-bags, and baskets of anatto, and cigar-boxes, and bales of all kinds of dutiable merchandise" passed under the Custom House marker, which bore Hawthorne's insignia (I, 27). The palm tree, Parsee, and ship emblazoned on the city seal—and its motto *Divitis indiae usque ad ultimum sinum* ("To the Farthest Port of the Rich East")—continued to identify the worldly foundations of Salem's culture, while the port of Boston, where Hawthorne had worked as measurer of salt and coal in 1839–1841, remained the chief North American bazaar for East Indian and Mediterranean products until the Civil War.[101] The names bestowed on the ships of Salem—from the *Arab, Bengal,* and *Borneo* to the *Ganges, Grand Turk,* and *Hindoo;* from the *Malabar, Malay,* and *Manchu* to the *Tigris, Yumchi,* and *Zenobia*—foretold their destinations into the 1860s.[102]

For generations the Orient signified wealth and adventure to all levels of Salem society. The sight of the recently arrived sailor, Hawthorne wrote— "pale and feeble, seeking a passport to the hospital"—did not deter "the smart young clerk, who gets the taste of traffic as a wolf-cub does of blood" (I, 6). The estates of the merchant grandees, for their part, disclosed "a style of luxury and magnificence, which we do not usually associate with our ideas of the time," Hawthorne wrote in "Old News" (1835): "silk beds and hangings, damask table-cloths, Turkey carpets, pictures, pier-glasses, massive plate, and all the things proper for a noble mansion" (XI, 150). "The china, ... the ivory figurines and fans, the enigmatic Chinese idols, the silks and shawls" from the East, Manning Hawthorne noted a century later, served to "soften the Puritan harshness of the household furnishings."[103] After his removal from the Salem Custom House the author typified their proprietors less charitably in "The Great Stone Face" (1850): "All the countries of the globe appeared to join hands for the mere purpose of adding heap after heap to the mountainous accumulation" of Gathergold's wealth:

> ... hot Africa sifted for him the golden sands of her rivers, and gathered up the ivory tusks of her great elephants out of the forests; the East came bringing him the rich shawls, and spices, and teas, and the effulgence of diamonds, and the gleaming purity of large pearls. (XI, 29–30)

By 1817 George Crowninshield, Jr., was cruising the Mediterranean in his magnificent yacht *Cleopatra's Barge.*

It was not only mariners and their immediate families who shared the Eastern adventures. "There was a constant influx of new ideas," a Salem clergyman later reported, "foreign fashions, curios from every land, young men with traveller's stories to tell, adventurers who had made fabulous fortunes in amazing countries."[104] As early as the 1730s Boston was visited by a "Schick Sidi" from Syria, and periodically over the next century travelers from the East, from cabin boys to potentates, appeared in the coastal towns. The Rev. William Bentley, pastor of some thirty sea captains at the liberal East Church of Salem, "Had the pleasure of seeing for the first time a native of the Indies from Madras" sometime in 1790–1792, and by 1805 he possessed sufficient classical Arabic to exchange letters with an Arabian Chief, Said Aimed.[105] In the 1830s merchants' representatives from Smyrna took up residence in Boston.

Particularly sensational was the arrival of *Al-Sultanah* in New York in April 1840. The first Arabian vessel to visit American shores, the *Sultanah* carried a special emissary from Sayyid Said bin Sultan, "Ruler of Muscat,

Zanzibar, and their dependencies," who was bent on extending good will and commercial ties with the United States. Sayyid Said's representative on board the *Sultanah* was the corpulent and elegant Ahmad bin Na'aman. For five months before their vessel sailed again for the Arabian Sea, Ahmad and his exotic crew entertained the journalists, socialites, and commoners of New York by their ornate dress, dark complexions, courtly manners, incredulity about American women, and Oriental tales. "Graphically, were harrowing, personal adventures on storm-tossed seas related to ever credulous listeners. Time and again, too, did the well-worn tales of Sindbad and other legendary Eastern merchant-mariners lend vicarious pleasure to rapt listeners."[106] During his stay at the Navy yard in New York, Ahmad sat for a three-quarter length painting by the eminent New York portraitist Edward Mooney. A replica of the painting, likewise done by Mooney, now hangs in the Peabody Museum, where it is accompanied by the description: "Ahmad bin Na'aman, Emissary from Muscat to the United States, Friend of Salem Merchants." Also on display at the Museum, which has incorporated the collections of the Salem East India Marine Society, is the only known portrait of Sayyid Said, painted by Lieutenant Henry B. Lynch, RN.

A half century before the Smithsonian's Gothic "castle on the Mall" was built in Washington, D.C., to house the artifacts of the Wilkes' Exploring Expedition, the Salem East India Marine Society was developing a *Wunderkammer* of instructive and entertaining materials from the Orient. What Hawthorne's father and uncle might have contributed from their voyages is unknown, but he visited the Society's exhibition hall periodically and, it has been suggested, based his sketch "A Virtuoso's Collection" (1842) on its contents.[107] There he saw such "natural and artificial curiosities" as hooks for impaling the human body in Kali ceremonies, a stone hand from the cave temples at Elephanta, a hookah and hubble-bubble, a tamboor and turban, and figures of Krishna, Rama, Sita, and Lakshmi. A diorama depicting the unloading of a China and East Indies brig at a Salem wharf in 1820 anticipated his pictorial machines in tales like "Ethan Brand." In the center of the Society's hall he faced life-size portrait mannequins or dressed clay figures of Eastern merchants well known to the Salem captains: of Yamqua, a Hong merchant of Canton, carved by Samuel McIntire and dressed in "Yamqua's own costume brought from China by Captain Benjamin Hodges in 1801";[108] of the Bombay Parsee Nusserwanjee Manackhaee Wadia, in a suit of clothes he gave to the museum in 1803; and later of Calcutta banians like Ragindar Dutt and Door Gapersand Ghose.[109]

The Society's exotica could also be seen out of doors in Salem as "its hundreds of members paraded the streets before their annual dinner, dressed as Chinese Mandarins, Indian Rajah, or Arabian Sultans, carrying their palaquins and other Far Eastern curios."[110] The appearance of the palanquin given to the Society by Moses Townsend and four others in 1802 and still on display was described in the *Salem Register* in 1823: "a boy apparelled in the most gorgeous habitments, borne by Black fellows, sweating under the unaccustomed burthen, in the East Indian dress attended with fan and hookah bearers and every other accompaniement of an East India equipage."[111]

The Oriental figures that appeared in Hawthorne's milieu, like the Oriental carpets and draperies of the wealthier houses, softened the commercialism of everyday life and suggested realms of idleness, imagination, and sensuality quite contrary to Puritan Massachusetts. "A lithograph of a Turk and of a Turkish lady" overlooked the eating and drinking that Hawthorne enjoyed at Parker's saloon in Boston (VIII, 495). He represented his countrymen in "My Kinsman, Major Molineux" as using their inn "somewhat after the fashion of a Turkish Caravansary" (XI, 213). In "Little Annie's Ramble" "a turbaned Turk, threatening . . . with his sabre, like an ugly heathen as he is," glared out from a toy-shop window upon the narrator and his little mistress (IX, 124).

By the 1870s and 1880s odalisques, cloisonne, sandalwood, and other Oriental bric-a-brac had become part of the general atmosphere of the "twilit world of the later New England."[112] But for Hawthorne, living on Union and Herbert Streets, walking along the wharves of Salem or looking down from his "dismal chamber" Paul Pry-like on the cosmopolitan traffic below, the Orient was a present reality. It was not unnatural for Elizabeth Peabody to refer to the widow Hawthorne's "all but Hindoo self-devotion to the manes of her husband," and for Julian Hawthorne to mention the "almost Hindoo-like construction of the law of seclusion which the public taste of that day imposed upon widows."[113] Salem sailors came home with stories of suttee in India as well as seraglios in Turkey.

American Orientalism

Although Salem enjoyed a special relationship with the East, all of America shared a mania for Oriental objects and sensations during the first decades of the nineteenth century. Before all else the East was a literary force, and fashion, in Hawthorne's time—a matter that will be explored in the next chapter. But the East also manifested itself in many other social and cultural forms.

Archaeological treasures and exotic beasts materialized throughout Massachusetts and the Atlantic states. Egyptian sarcophagi and mummies that later came into the hands of P. T. Barnum appeared in Boston in 1823 and at Peale's Museum and Gallery of Fine Arts in New York in 1826.[114] On his daily foray into Boston the gentleman might wonder at: "The camel, that strange beast from Africa, with two great humps, to be seen near the Common." It caused the narrator of "Old News" to speculate, "Methinks I would fain go thither, and see how the old patriarchs were wont to ride" (XI, 140). Children flocked to see lions and lionesses, Bengal tigers, and Egyptian hyenas. Even at the inland town of North Adams in 1838 Hawthorne encountered a caravan of rough circus people, who took lodging in the house while their elephant occupied the barn (VIII, 140–142).

The popular fascination with the East was heightened by an element of violence, for as Salem and Boston knew well, the costs of doing business in the Indian Ocean and Arabian Sea ran high. The plundering of the *Essex* in the Red Sea off the coast of Mocha in 1806, and the murder and mutilation of the crew under Captain Joseph Orne, horrified Salem for years.[115] At the beginning of the nineteenth century the Eastern Mediterranean was in continual ferment. Joel Barlow, while serving as consul at Algiers, had scarcely secured the release of the "Algerine Captives," memorialized in Royall Tyler's play of that name (1797), before Barbary piracy sent American warships back to the Mediterranean for the Tripolitan Wars of 1801–1805 and the war with Algiers in 1815.

The United States' political and moral concern with the Near East intensified during the Greek War of Independence (1821–1829). Among the liberal democrats of New England and the Middle Atlantic states feelings ran strongly against the Ottoman Empire for its enslavement of the Greeks. Bitter Turkophobic sentiments were expressed in poems by Bryant, in plays like John Howard Payne's *Ali Pacha* (1823) and Mordecai Noah's *Grecian Captive* (1822)—performed by a cast that included "a live elephant and a camel, a philhellene American officer, and a Turk named 'Nadir' "[116]—and later in Hiram Powers's arousing work of classical nudity, *The Greek Slave* (1843). At Bowdoin College at the height of the Greek fever in the spring of 1823, Hawthorne and his schoolmates, inspired by the example of Lord Byron, organized the Bowdoin cadets and played at sacrificing themselves in the noble struggle.[117]

The image of Byron dying for the cause of freedom, the moral armament of Christians against the "infidel" Turks, and the prodigious relief work of Dr. Samuel Gridley Howe excited the growing taste in the United States for information and lore about the East. When Turkey sought to improve its diplomatic relations with the United States in the 1830s, a reviewer for the *Knickerbocker* magazine expressed the opinion: "It is time that our knowledge of a nation, with which, as a commercial country, we have so much to do, should be enlarged and purified. The Turks are infinitely better than we have been accustomed to think them."[118] As a gesture of good will Commodore David Porter in Constantinople ordered Boston rocking horses for the children of the Sultan's harem.[119] Because of the new cultural detente the traffic of persons between America and the East became steadily heavier and, with the introduction of steam navigation, more convenient.

In step with America's expanding commercial and political interests in the East came a heightened desire for knowledge about the origins of civilization and the capacity to satisfy this desire through exploration and exact scholarship. Although an American Oriental Society was not constituted until 1842, the writings and translations of Sir William Jones circulated widely in the United States before the turn of the century. The Bible lands of Syria, Egypt, Arabia, and Palestine became a special destination of American as well as British and European explorers. The new interest in comparative religions, the emergence of Higher Criticism of the Bible, and the study of "sacred geography" fostered a wave of archaeological discoveries in the Middle East in the first half of the nineteenth century. The excitement of Napoleon's Egyptian campaign and the finding of the Rosetta Stone in 1798–1799 helped launch the Swiss Johann L. Burckhardt's journeys through Palestine, Arabia and Egypt, and his discovery of Petra (1812–1817); the Italian Giovanni Belzoni's spectacular excavations of temples, tombs, and pyramids in Egypt and Nubia, and his location of the ancient city of Berenice (1817–1819); and the French Jean-François Champollion's decipherment of the hieroglyphs, which provided the key to Egypt's past.

American scholars and explorers added substantially to Eastern studies. The publication of the Rev. Edward Robinson's *Biblical Researches in Palestine, Mount Sinai and Arabia* in 1841 revolutionized the study of Palestinian archaeology;[120] and six years later a crew of United States navymen, commanded by Lieutenant William F. Lynch, carried out the first scientific survey of the Dead Sea, which was reported in Lynch's fast-selling *Narrative of the United States Expedition to the River Jordan and the Dead Sea* (1849). At the same time Sir Austen Henry Layard, with whom Hawthorne dined in April 1855, was at work excavating Nineveh.[121] His account *Nineveh and Its Ruins* (1849), like each of the earlier discoveries, was reviewed enthusiastically in American newspapers and journals.[122]

The new knowledge of Eastern antiquities and customs, combined with a general Romantic tendency to identify the beautiful with the remote, soon began to alter the art forms and physical features of this country, notably its monumental and domestic architecture. Reservoirs, prisons, cemetery gates, and tombs copied the massive pylonic form of Egyptian temples; Cairo and Memphis reappeared as small towns along the Mississippi River (called the "Nile of America"); and in 1828 Frances Trollope opened her famous Oriental bazaar in Cincinnati. The Egyptian Revival has been called "the most important moderating influence on the Greek revival in American architecture."[123] It set its mark alike on the New York Halls of Justice (1836–1838)— the "Tombs" prison where Melville's Bartleby gave up his life—and on the towering obelisk of the Washington Monument.

By the 1840s "Moorish," "Turkish," and "Oriental" houses faced Grecian and Federal styles in builders' manuals of design inspiring a particularly keen interest in garden structures and Turkish baths. Orientalisms entered the nation's architectural vocabulary with such now familiar terms as *verandah* (Sanskrit), *alcove* (Arabic), *bungalow* (Hindi), *pagoda* (Tamil or Cantonese), and *kiosk* (Turkish). Fanciful styles were imported from Persia and Arabia. In 1848 P. T. Barnum raised his elegant fairy palace *Iranistan* in Bridgeport, overlooking Long Island Sound.[124] Nor was New England immune. In 1853 George W. Curtis likened the terraces, arbors, and pavilions Bronson Alcott had erected on the "homely steppes of Concord," behind Hawthorne's Wayside home, to the delightful gardens of Babylon. He promised his readers: "The hanging gardens of Semiramis were not more fragant than Hawthorne's hill-side during the June blossoming of the locusts."[125]

The germ of an unwritten tale recorded in Hawthorne's journal in 1836–1837—"A missionary to the heathen in a great city. To describe his labors, in the manner of a foreign mission"—suggests that the author was well aware not only of the travels and letters of the Jesuits in Asia but, too, of the New England evangelists who set out in search of the Coptic and Nestorian Christians.[126] The American Board of Foreign Missions was formed in 1810; two years later the first five young men, ordained at Salem, set sail for Calcutta.[127] Simultaneous with Hawthorne's journal entry the *American Magazine of Useful and Entertaining Knowledge* concluded an essay on "Bowdoin College" by noting the conspicuous success of "this Seminary" in "the promotion of vital, expansive, and comprehensive piety. The waste places of India have witnessed the adventurous and glowing devotion of those sons of Bowdoin, who have joined in carrying the cross back to the original, extremest east."[128]

The Eastern Mediterranean soon took a precedence among the foreign mission fields that lasted until the end of the century. The missionaries' narratives of glorious tribulations in the service of the Lord—alternately picturesque, chilling, and maudlin—summoned from the towns of New England a class of recruits who might have scorned the worldly adventures of a life at sea. "The first half of the nineteenth century," David Finnie has pointed out, "saw a constant procession of essentially nonpolitical Americans to the Middle East: missionaries, of course, but also merchants, engineers, inventors, promoters, and artisans; scientists, scholars, and literary figures; philanthropists, adventurers, tourists, and eccentrics; naval officers and sailors; and even a farmer or two."[129]

East Is East

Fred Lewis Pattee's remark in 1923 that Hawthorne "knew only New England, and he cared to enter no wider field," was at best unhistorical.[130] Yet as concerns the molding of his imagination, past scholarship has taught that when Hawthorne traveled away from New England, in imagination as well as fact, the road from Salem led either across the Atlantic to the "old home" in England, and eventually on to Rome in *The Marble Faun*, or westward into the American forests. Edwin Fussell expressed the latter disposition:

> Like Cooper, Hawthorne was at heart a Western writer; and even more persistently than Cooper, he was determined to see himself in a Western light. . . . The gist of the matter is that Hawthorne, like many another writer confined to the Atlantic seaboard, made what he could of what he was born with and what he was able to lay hands on. By a judicious use of the Romantic imagination, and sustained by precious little actual experience, he transformed New England into an available prototype of the West.[131]

The intent of this introductory chapter has been to show that what Hawthorne was born with and was able to lay his hands on in Salem was nothing so raw as the American West. When the literary impulse throbbed "one idle and rainy day" in the late 1840s, and sent him burrowing into the moldy, antiquarian records of the Salem Custom House for a scarlet letter, he exerted his fancy "to raise up from these dry bones an image of the old town's brighter aspect, when India was a new region, and only Salem knew the way thither" (I, 29). A decade later, at Arezzo, Italy, he marveled that the rills from his Town-Pump had "meandered as far as England, as far as India." Hawthorne would have been gratified to know that his schoolbook *Peter Parley's Universal History* was the basis of the Western civilization curriculum at Keio University, Japan, in 1870.[132] England and Europe were not the outermost reach of his fancy. Before and beyond lay another dimension of history and story—the *East*.

It should not surprise us that the male protagonists of Hawthorne's tales and novels are predominantly travelers, pilgrims, wayfarers, and sightseers. While he returned to live several times in his home port of Salem and did his most inspired work there, he was, as he confessed in "The Old Manse," characteristically "as uncertain as the wandering Arabs where our tent might next be pitched" (X, 33). When not actually tumbled in the stream of affairs, he was living and observing by the "wayside"—a name he naturally chose for his last home in Concord, Massachusetts.

One of Hawthorne's more revealing short works is "The Toll-Gatherer's Day: A Sketch of Transitory Life" (1837). It opens with the notion: "ME-THINKS, for a person whose instinct bids him rather to pore over the current of life, than to plunge into its tumultuous waves, no undesirable retreat were a toll-house beside some thronged thoroughfare of the land." The narrator imagines "how pleasant a miracle" it would be for "natures too indolent, or too sensitive, to endure the dust, the sunshine, or the rain, the turmoil of moral and physical elements, to which all the wayfarers of the world expose themselves" if the great globe would "perform its revolutions and shift its thousand scenes before his eyes without whirling him onward in its course" (IX, 205).

The distant roll of wheels at the start of day, "creaking more and more harshly," gradually replaces the toll-gatherer's "dream ... with realities" of commerce and society passing both over and beneath the drawbridge he oversees (IX, 206). As day begins, "the old man looks eastward, and (for he is a moralizer) frames a simile of the stage-coach and the sun" (IX, 207). The sun moves westward during the course of the day. But as the day ends, the old toll-gatherer again "looks seaward, and discerns the light-house kindling on a far island, and the stars, too, kindling in the sky." And once more "all the dusty pilgrimage which he has witnessed, seems like a flitting show of phantoms for his thoughtful soul to muse upon" (IX, 211–212). While the course of empire led Westward, the reflective, moralizing observer continued to look across the sea, Eastward, for the stuff of dreams and story.

HAWTHORNE'S
READING

"all most all the Books which have been published for the
last hundred Years"

AFTER WRITING *Nathaniel Hawthorne in His Times* (1980), James Mellow
offered a piece of advice for all biographers: "*Pay attention to dreams and the
weather.*" By weather, Mellow meant the personal and social circumstances,
"those *necessary* details which place the subject inescapably in his time—not
our time, which would be an anachronism"; by dreams, the inward fantasies
and associations and desires, "that mysterious realm of the mind and the
imagination from which his or her art proceeds."[1] The previous chapter has
charted a pattern of circumstances—in the Hawthorne family, the city of
Salem, and American culture of the earlier nineteenth century—that colored
Nathaniel Hawthorne's eventual choice of vocation and his literary materials.
Looking out from his room on Herbert Street towards the wharfs and traffic
below, Hawthorne watched the weather and dreamt of sailing away to the
farthest East. Inside his room, meanwhile, he was exploring an even richer
province of dreams.

The traffic of images in the author's mind throughout many "a rainy
winter's day, within doors" at home, is vividly depicted in the long and
contemplative introduction to "Night Sketches Beneath an Umbrella" (1838):

> The best study for such a day, or the best amusement,—call it which you will,—
> is a book of travels, describing scenes the most unlike that sombre one, which
> is mistily presented through the windows. I have experienced, that fancy is
> then most successful in imparting distinct shapes and vivid colors to the objects

which the author has spread upon his page, and that his words become magic spells to summon up a thousand varied pictures. Strange landscapes glimmer through the familiar walls of the room, and outlandish figures thrust themselves almost within the sacred precincts of the hearth. Small as my chamber is, it has space enough to contain the ocean-like circumference of an Arabian desert, its parched sands tracked by the long line of a caravan, with the camels patiently journeying through the heavy sunshine. Though my ceiling be not lofty, yet I can pile up the mountains of Central Asia beneath it, till their summits shine far above the clouds of the middle atmosphere. And, with my humble means, a wealth that is not taxable, I can transport hither the magnificent merchandise of an Oriental bazaar, and call a crowd of purchasers from distant countries, to pay a fair profit for the precious articles which are displayed on all sides. True it is, however, that, amid the bustle of traffic, or whatever else may seem to be going on around me, the rain-drops will occasionally be heard to patter against my window-panes, which look forth upon one of the quietest streets in a New England town. After a time, too, the visions vanish, and will not appear again at my bidding. Then, it being nightfall, a gloomy sense of unreality depresses my spirits, and impels me to venture out, before the clock shall strike bedtime, to satisfy myself that the world is not entirely made up of such shadowy materials, as have busied me throughout the day. A dreamer may dwell so long among fantasies, that the things without him will seem as unreal as those within. (IX, 426–427)

Reading, especially in fancy-stirring books of travel, played an exceptional role in shaping Hawthorne's mind and imagination. The cosmopolitan life that his townsmen and schoolmates pursued in commerce, politics, the mission fields, and the merchant marine he lived for many years chiefly through the printed word. Hawthorne's withdrawal into the vicarious world of literature was partly accidental. His introspection and habit of constant reading emerged during a period of lameness, at age nine, that kept him home from school for two years and intensified when, in June 1816, his mother took her three children from Salem to live on the large tract of land that the Mannings were developing at the new frontier town of Raymond, Maine. There, in the forests around Lake Sebago, the imaginative faculty "waxed and grew rich ... which was thereafter to delight his countrymen and the world."[2] The boy's correspondence with his mother and sisters in Raymond in 1819–1820, after he had returned to Salem to prepare for college, indicates a well-established taste for the remote and the fanciful. By September 1819 he had read *Waverly* and the first volume of *The Arabian Nights*, and by the following fall, all of Scott's novels except *The Abbot*. "I have read," he wrote around this time, "all most all the Books which have been published for the last hundred years."[3] The practical bookkeeping tasks he performed at the office of the Manning stage lines on Union Street in Salem apparently did not keep him from long hours and nights in the world of books and newspapers.

There is some evidence that when he again returned to Salem in 1825, after four years at Bowdoin College, Hawthorne already was determined to carve out a new family career in letters. But his self-effacing remark in 1853 also seems essentially accurate: "And year after year I kept on considering what I was fit for, and time and my destiny decided that I was to be the writer that I am."[4] The dozen years between his graduation from college and his appearance before the world as author of *Twice-told Tales* in 1837 have had a special fascination for students of his life and work. Depending on mood and circumstance, Hawthorne gave varying accounts of this seminal period. In the exchange of letters that followed publication of *Twice-told Tales* he answered his Bowdoin classmate Henry Wadsworth Longfellow's query about his *environments* by claiming that he had been "carried apart from the main current of life" and for the last ten years had "not lived, but only dreamed about living."[5] Returning temporarily to his room on Herbert Street in October 1840, after two years at the Boston Custom House, he wrote to his "Dove" Sophia Peabody in a similar vein: "This deserves to be called a haunted chamber; for thousands upon thousands of visions have appeared to me in it; and some few of them have become visible to the world. . . . [S]o much of my lonely youth was wasted here; and here my mind and character were formed."[6] Both laments, which were written in the first flush of his new publicity as an author and his late-developing courtship, no doubt embellished the hardships of the seclusion from which he was then emerging. A more balanced depiction of his life from 1825 to 1837 probably was that which he gave years later as an established citizen, husband, father, and author of *The Scarlet Letter, The House of the Seven Gables,* and several volumes of tales: "Meanwhile, strange as it may seem, I had lived a very tolerable life, always seemed cheerful, and enjoyed the very best bodily health. I had read endlessly all sorts of good and good-for-nothing books, and, in the dearth of other employment, had early begun to scribble sketches and stories, most of which I burned."[7]

Before undertaking his life study of Hawthorne, Arlin Turner identified "his reading and his response to what he read" as the most promising area for new understanding of the man and the novelist.[8] Subsequent years have not lessened appreciably the need to appraise Hawthorne's reading habits, especially during his residence in Salem in the later 1820s and the 1830s. The decade Hawthorne spent at home following his four years at Bowdoin was both his post-graduate education and his apprenticeship. Notwithstanding his deferential remark to Longfellow that he had "turned over a good many books, but in so desultory a way that it cannot be called study," Hawthorne's readings after 1825 manifest an organized and thorough-going investigation of several fields of interest that exposed him to a good deal of the world and provided the equivalent of what a novelist, historian, or scholar would call research.[9]

The Salem Athenaeum

According to his sister Elizabeth, after college Hawthorne "depended for books principally upon the Salem Athenaeum and a Circulating Library, the latter of which supplied him with most of the novels then published."[10] While his personal library and the circulating library he patronized in Salem are known only circumstantially today, his borrowings from the Salem Athenaeum have been carefully established by Marion L. Kesselring in *Hawthorne's Reading 1828–1850* (1949).[11] First under the name of his aunt Mary Manning, and then in his own right, Hawthorne held a share in the Athenaeum from 1826 to 1839 and again on his return to Salem in the late 1840s. During the former period he relied on his sister Elizabeth to withdraw materials which he then read at home. As a result, the Athenaeum's chargebooks provide a detailed chronicle of Hawthorne's developing interests and knowledge through the formative years of his career. Between memberships he also kept the privilege of reading at the Athenaeum although not the borrowing of books. "I went to the Athenaeum this forenoon," he wrote to Sophia Peabody in September 1841, "and turned over a good many dusty books." Three years later he again wrote to Sophia, who was in Boston: "I spend almost all my afternoons at the Athenaeum."[12] Although her list does not include Hawthorne's readings at the Athenaeum itself, or materials used between memberships, Kesselring's bibliography is the single most comprehensive index to his taste and world of reference.

The Salem Athenaeum, incorporated in 1810 through the merger of an earlier Social Library and the Philosophical Library, offered one of the young nation's finest collections of materials in history, natural science, philosophy, and literature. Before and after their educations at Harvard and Bowdoin, the citizens of Salem depended on the Athenaeum for classical treatises as well as contemporary British, European, and American periodicals. Here Salem's Nathaniel Bowditch educated himself in mathematics, astronomy, and general science; and here Joseph Story, later Supreme Court justice and the nation's foremost legal writer, pursued much of his exhausting study. As one would expect from the times and from the commercial and cultural interests of Salem, the Athenaeum offered a particularly extensive collection of voyages and travels (ten pages in the printed catalog of 1842) and other significant materials on the Orient in its history, religion, biography, and literature collections. Between the Museum of the East India Marine Society, the holdings of the Salem Athenaeum, and the wharves on the South River, Hawthorne had abundant opportunity to make his "Voyages at Anchor."

In all, Hawthorne borrowed 487 titles from the Athenaeum (counting each multi-volume work or serial as a single title). Thirty-six of these were exclusively or substantially concerned with the East. A complete list of titles and dates of use appears in Appendix A, along with comments on Elizabeth Hawthorne's role in their selection. The borrowings include such authentically Eastern tales as *Antar, A Bedoueen Romance* and *The Adventures of Hajji Baba of Ispahan*, Camoes's epic of Portuguese exploration *The Lusiad: or, The Discovery of India*, and religious works like the Koran and Picart's *Religious Ceremonies and Customs*. Above all, however, Hawthorne turned to the Athenaeum collection for histories, voyages, and travels into the East.

Hawthorne's borrowings began on October 24, 1826, during an important transitional period. Between his ill-fated *Seven Tales of My Native Land* and the publication of *Fanshawe* in 1828, Hawthorne wondered how to reconcile, personally and professionally, the simultaneous callings of literature and the sea. It is particularly remarkable that he withdrew, in sequence throughout 1827, the Athenaeum's copies of John Lockman's *Travels of the Jesuits into Various Parts of the World* (1743), Ogier Ghislain de Busbecq's *Travels into Turkey* (1744), *The Famous Voyages & Travailes of Vincent Le Blanc* (1660), Adam Olearius's *The Voyages and Travels of the Ambassadors Sent by Fredrick, Duke of Holstein, to the Great Duke of Muscovy and the King of Persia . . . whereto are added The Travels of John Albert de Mandelslo, from Persia, into the East-Indies* (1662), *Memoires of the Baron de Tott, on the Turks and the Tartars* (1785), George Sandys's *A Relation of a Journey Begun An:Dom:1610. Foure Bookes. Containing a Description of the Turkish Empire, of Egypt, of the Holy Land* (1627), and Thomas Coryate's *Crudities* (1776). This same year, if indeed not earlier, he also took up George Sale's translation of the Koran (1734), prefaced by Sale's brilliant "Preliminary Discourse" on the Mohammedan religion.

In 1828 Hawthorne read either Richard Chandler's *Travels in Asia Minor* (1776) or his *Travels in Greece* (1776); in 1829, Sir Paul Rycaut's *The History of the Turkish Empire from the Year 1623 to the Year 1677* (1679–1680); and in 1830, Joseph Pitton de Tournefort's *A Voyage into the Levant* (1741) and John Harris's *Navigantium atque Itinerantium Bibliotheca. Or, A Complete Collection of Voyages and Travels*, which he borrowed again in 1831.

After the more sporadic readings of 1828–1830, Hawthorne resumed his Eastern studies forcefully in 1831 with a syllabus of narratives and histories as extensive as the course he had followed in 1827. His renewed readings reflected his literary plans at the time as well as his general interest, for by then he had begun to formulate the cycle of tales, narrated by a traveling storyteller, that produced first "The Seven Vagabonds" (1832) and then the manuscript for the two-volume work called *The Story Teller* that he sought to publish in 1834. He had the following seven works in his hands during 1831, the last six in close succession from October through December: Henry Maundrell's *A Journey from Aleppo to Jerusalem at Easter, A.D. 1697* (1810), a volume of *Asiatic Researches* (published by the Asiatic Society of Bengal), John Cochrane's *Narrative of a Pedestrian Journey through Russia and Siberian Tartary* (1824), *The Travels of Sir John Chardin into Persia, and the East Indies* (1686), Alexander Russell's *The Natural History of Aleppo* (1794), Jonas Hanway's *An Historical Account of the British Trade over the Caspian Sea: with the Author's Journal of Travels from England through Russia into Persia* (1754), and Richard Pococke's *A Description of the East, and Some Other Countries* (1743–1745).

From 1832 to 1834, Hawthorne withdrew from the Athenaeum Edmund Chishull's *Travels in Turkey and Back to England* (1747), James Bruce's *Travels to Discover the Source of the Nile* (1790), Reginald Heber's *Narrative of a Journey through the Upper Provinces of India, from Calcutta to Bombay, 1824–1825* (1828), and Richard Madden's *Travels in Turkey, Egypt, Nubia and Palestine* (1829). In 1836, while Nathaniel and Elizabeth Hawthorne were editing the *American Magazine of Useful and Entertaining Knowledge* and compiling *Peter Parley's Universal History*, they checked out George Bush's *The Life of Mohammed* (1830), David Porter's *Constantinople and Its Environs* (1835), Jeremiah Reynolds's *Voyage of the United States Frigate Potomac . . . During the Circumnavigation of the Globe* (1835), and Hiob Ludolf's *A New History of Ethiopia* (1682).

The periods and order of Hawthorne's readings reflect a desire to sharpen his familiarity with the still evolving genre of travel writing as well as to enlarge his knowledge about the lands and peoples of the East. The titles themselves show a thorough acquaintance with the classical as well as the contemporary literature of Eastern exploration. From *The Naturall Historie of C. Plinius Secundus* in the first century A.D. to *The Travels of Sir John Mandeville* in the fourteenth century and David Porter's *Constantinople and Its Environs* in the 1830s, a massive library of travel literature had developed, interconnected and continually self-correcting, that pushed back the borders of the marvelous with ever more empirical if no less romantic accounts of the East. Annotations and remarks in the accounts he read referred Hawthorne constantly on to earlier commentaries. He had already read Busbecq's letters and Maundrell's *Journey*, however, when he took up Edmund Chishull's *Travels into Turkey* and saw a dedicatory compliment there to these earlier "ingenious and learned" travelers, who "are repeatedly read, and always with new pleasure."[13] Carsten Niebuhr's *Travels through Arabia, and Other Countries in the East* (1792), which provided information on the Parsees of Bombay for Hawthorne's essay "Fire Worshippers" in the August 1836 *American Magazine of Useful and Entertaining Knowledge*, acknowledged the same commentaries by James Bruce, Jonas Hanway, Hiob Ludolf, and Pliny the Elder that Hawthorne was using at the time or had read earlier. If not so exhaustive as the scholarly citations of Thomas Moore's *Lalla Rookh* or Robert Southey's *Thalaba the Destroyer* and *The Curse of Kehama*, the record of Hawthorne's reading nonetheless demonstrates a broad engagement with the romantic explorations of the East.

In preparing her directory of Hawthorne's borrowings from the Salem Athenaeum, Marion Kesselring noted the prominence of foreign travels. "Books of travel to exotic lands were favorites with him," she wrote. "Even when he was busy in the workaday world upon his return to Salem, travel books did not lose their fascination for him." However, while indeed, "There seemed no limit to the horizons he reached through his reading," Kesselring's own data belie her further observation that there was no "favorite spot that lured him back."[14] Had she concentrated on the travels as a genre, and gone beyond short titles into the contents of the works themselves, she would have found that Hawthorne's vicarious travels turned repetitively Eastward.

Inattention to the Orientalism pervading Salem and American culture early in the nineteenth century apparently caused Alfred Weber, too, to overlook the locale and destination of Hawthorne's readings in his important reconstruction of Hawthorne's early "framed tales." Referring to Kesselring's bibliography for evidence that Hawthorne participated in the tradition of travel literature, Weber listed the identification numbers of forty titles drawn from the Salem Athenaeum between 1827 and 1834, when *The Story Teller* was completed. If he had given the titles behind the numbers, however, or considered the contents behind the titles, Weber would have noticed the marked and continuing interest in the East. Twenty-two of the forty works he indicated are exclusively or predominantly set in the Orient. Great Britain and all of Europe account for just eight titles; North America, including Canada and Mexico, for only seven. The East was represented by eight of the nine items Weber identified for 1827, and in each year thereafter.[15]

The thirty-six titles listed in Appendix A do not exhaust the observations and explorations of the East that Hawthorne drew from the Salem Athenaeum. No attempt has been made, for example, to inventory Oriental materials dispersed in the twenty-eight different magazines that he used or in the voluminous writing of Voltaire that he studied in 1829–1831. True to the multifaceted Orientalism of their times and the interests of their subscribers, magazines like the Philadelphia *Museum of Foreign Literature, Science, and Art*, the London *Monthly Magazine*, and the *Gentleman's Magazine* disseminated a wealth of useful and entertaining travel sketches, review essays, and disquisitions on the natural history, customs, religions, mythologies, languages and literatures, commerce, technology, and sexual practices of the East.

The American Magazine of Useful and Entertaining Knowledge

After the charge records of the Salem Athenaeum, the most extensive index to Hawthorne's reading in this period is a result of his own experience as a magazine editor. In 1836, following the appearance of some thirty of his tales anonymously over the previous five years, Hawthorne edited six issues of *The American Magazine of Useful and Entertaining Knowledge*. The position required that he move to Boston, and it opened an intercourse with the world that was enhanced, the next year, by publication of *Twice-told Tales* and, later, by his appointment to the Boston Custom House. From January to August 1836, Hawthorne mixed daily with a larger circle of writers, printers, and publishers in the metropolis. The rigorous demands of preparing a monthly magazine for an expectant audience also imposed the discipline and responsibilities he associated with the professional man of letters. His correspondence with Longfellow a year later indicates that, after failing to secure a berth with the Great Exploring Expedition, Hawthorne continued to think of making his way through the combination of editing, reviewing, and creative work that characterized the careers of other literary men of the time.

The usual dismissals of Hawthorne's "drudgery" and "hack" work for the *American Magazine* have underestimated its importance both as a product of authorship and editing and as a reflection and summation of what he was learning and thinking in the decade following his return to Salem in 1825. The contents of Hawthorne's issues, Arlin Turner has pointed out, are a valuable indication of "what he was reading, what in his reading attracted him most, and his own estimates of what he read."[16]

To be sure, Hawthorne's correspondence gives much evidence of dissatisfaction with his publishers, the Boston Bewick Company, and the conditions under which he was forced to work. He railed against their general penury, their failure to pay his salary, and their cheapness in not buying a membership at the Boston Athenaeum that would enable the editor to withdraw materials. In a farewell message to readers in his last issue, he complained particularly about the need to suit his literary copy to the crude engravings that were a principal object of the publishers.[17]

Hawthorne's complaints were largely related to the impending bankruptcy of the Bewick Company, however, rather than intrinsic to the task of writing and editing materials for a popular audience. Indeed, he showed considerable pride in his ability to produce the 256 double-column pages he put into print from March to August of 1836. "I make nothing of writing a history or biography before dinner," he wrote to his sister Elizabeth on January 25. He stayed home on Sunday, March 13, to compose a dissertation on the Tower of Babel and observed with some satisfaction that he had written all but about half a page of the first two issues, except for the extracts from other sources provided by his collaborator Elizabeth.[18]

The distinctiveness and quality of Hawthorne's editorship is especially conspicuous when one compares his work with the issues that Alden Bradford edited both before and after his tenure. In the six issues prepared by Hawthorne readers were temporarily relieved of Bradford's temperance crusading, abolitionism, and general pedanticism. Hawthorne obviously drew from a much wider range of knowledge and tolerances and rendered his material with a cosmopolitanism and color, so different from Bradford's wooden copy and narrow ideals, that still make entertaining reading today. His sister's appraisal years later was just and accurate: "[I]ndeed all that he wrote for the Magazine did him great credit, evincing not only much miscellaneous information, but a power of adapting himself to the minds of others whose culture and pursuits were unlike his own."[19]

The American Magazine introduced Hawthorne to the daily life of the pen-and-ink men of America and led to the series of books for adolescent readers—beginning with Peter Parley's Universal History (1837), Grandfather's Chair (1841), and Biographical Stories for Children (1842)—that he thought for a time might become his particular literary realm. Despite his suspicion that Samuel Goodrich had misappropriated his salary from the magazine, he did not hesitate at the opportunity Goodrich gave for writing the Peter Parley's history the same year. The challenge to produce both "useful" and "entertaining" knowledge was quite congenial to this self-proclaimed "idler" who still felt the need for solid and substantial work. Hawthorne's issues of the American Magazine merit further study both as a source of ideas developed in his subsequent fiction and as a reflection of literary taste and culture in the 1830s. As Arlin Turner observed in his study Hawthorne as Editor, it is not difficult to find in the American Magazine "gleams of the mind" that produced "The Birthmark" and "Rappaccini's Daughter" and forestudies of his later writings.[20]

Most important at the moment, however, is the guide the magazine provides to Hawthorne's readings and his interests in the preceding years. His need to produce voluminous copy, often on a day or two's notice, left him little time to explore new territory. The pace of the work required that he pull together topics and information already stored in his memory, or return to familiar genres of material through the Boston and Salem Athenaeums or other sources.

It is highly significant, therefore, to find so many essays, sketches, extracts, and notes on the Orient during Hawthorne's term with the *American Magazine*. His six issues contain, in all, sixty-nine items dealing chiefly with Eastern matters, not including items on sub-Saharan Africa or Oceania or general pieces in which the East makes only a minor appearance. Hawthorne prepared the majority of these from his own general knowledge and without indicating sources. His references in the *American Magazine*, however, include at least twenty travel commentaries, histories, and fictions that were wholly or largely concerned with the cultures extending eastward from the Barbary States to China. Complete lists of the Eastern materials and source references in the *American Magazine* from March to August 1836, with remarks on the role of Elizabeth Hawthorne, are found in Appendix B. Comparison of the references and readings listed in Appendixes A and B illustrate that, for the most part, Hawthorne was mining contemporary accounts of the East for the *American Magazine* while his borrowings from the Salem Athenaeum in the preceding decade had emphasized more classical histories, travel narratives, and literature.

To some extent Hawthorne's devotion to travel books simply reflected the conventions of the time. "The present age seems to be peculiarly distinguished, as favourable to great travellers," the *Portico* noticed in 1816. The *American Quarterly Review* was more emphatic about the popularity of travel books in 1829: "Authorship and travelling are all the fashion. Sailors wash the tar from their hands and write verses in their logbooks; midshipmen indite their own adventures; and naval commanders, not content with discovering countries and winning battles, steer boldly into the ocean of literature."[21] As the "original, extremest" East, India was a particularly beloved destination. In its review of Emma Roberts's *Scenes and Characteristics of Hindostan*, from which Hawthorne drew three lengthy extracts in May and June 1836, the London *Monthly Review* remarked:

> Many parts of India seem to be almost as familiar to us, from the numerous works recently published, descriptive of them, as were certain parts of Britain to our fathers half a century ago. This is the age of travellers and authors. War, science, and religion, have each their intelligent and enterprising servants. The curious, the idle, and the wealthy, are upon the wing, over every accessible region of the earth.[22]

If travel writing, and especially observations of the Levant and the East Indies, were a literary fashion in the 1830s, Hawthorne not only acknowledged but embraced and encouraged the convention. The Eastern contents of the issues he prepared significantly exceeded the Oriental materials in the *American Magazine* both before and after his editorship. Where Hawthorne provided sixty-nine such items, the six issues before he took office contained only thirty-nine comparable pieces, and the six issues following (stimulated perhaps by his model) supplied fifty-two.

So far as he was able, Hawthorne stretched the editorial limits of the *American Magazine* to accommodate his own interests and knowledge. He inherited an editorial policy that declared: "The work is designed to be *American*, and to give articles relating to the natural history, geology, and geography of this continent; to the political history, the means of education, the literature, the institutions, the discoveries in useful arts, in the United States, with whatever may occur important and useful, on a perusal of respectable European publications of the day."[23] While his predecessor did include instructive foreign examples, the magazine had been resolutely nativist as well as moralistic. Hawthorne found his own first number in March, which contains only three pieces on the East, "very dull and respectable—almost worthy of Mr. Bradford himself."[24] In his effort to broaden and enliven his materials, he extended his Eastern coverage in the April, May, and June issues to eight, fourteen, and nineteen items respectively. Bradford had introduced Eastern customs mainly to assault infidels and exalt American civilization; Hawthorne combined exoticism, utility, and genuine comparativism in the choice and presentation of his Eastern materials.

The breadth of the varied and gorgeous East that he offered to his readers is represented by two adjacent articles in the May issue: "The Valley of the Sweet Waters," extracted from Commodore Porter's *Constantinople and Its Environs*, and "An Annual Fair, in India," from Miss Roberts's *Scenes and Characteristics of Hindostan*. Porter had been privileged to observe a holiday at the Valley of the Sweet Waters, on the Asiatic side of the Bosphorus, where Turkish wives and children spent each Friday in fine weather amusing themselves with minstrels, love stories, fortune tellers, coffee, sherbets, and ice cream—away from their husbands and fathers. Porter, a celebrated veteran of America's wars with the Barbary pirates and chargé d'affaires to Turkey at the time, was charmed by the "oriental splendour" of the ornamented carriages, the carpets, and the marble Persian fountains, but most of all by the extreme loveliness of the young women, with "their brilliant black eyes, their beautiful arched eyebrows, and their long and glossy black hair almost reaching the ground." His perspective on the natural, unrestrained pleasures of these Eastern beauties foreshadowed Coverdale's voyeurism a decade and a half later in *The Blithedale Romance*. "I had seen the Turkish character in a new point of view," Porter wrote; "the film had dropped from my eyes." "The Turks are a noble race of men, and the women being generally of Circassian origin, it is natural that the daughters of the Turks should be beautiful" (AM, 361–362).

Immediately following the four-column selection from Porter's *Constantinople*, a two-page extract from Miss Roberts's *Hindostan* provided the description of another fair, this time in Hurdwar, where "Arabs, Cingalese,

Persians, Tartars, Malays, Sikhs, people from Gutch, Gudjarat, Nepal, and all other provinces of India" gathered in one vast camp to trade precious jewels, elephants, camels, books, watches, medicine, and other exotic commodities (AM, 363–364). Subscribers to the American Magazine in 1836 learned a good deal about the geography, ethnicity, manners, and popular culture of the Orient.

As the realm of humanity most remote in space and time, the East offered a romantic antithesis to the bromidic sameness of the Jacksonian age and an ancient standard against which contemporary American life and character could be measured. Although Hawthorne presented much of his Eastern material for its sheer exoticism and entertainment value, he used other articles to satirize Western manners and morals or to offer practical lessons for American horticulture and technology. Mentioning a few further items from the American Magazine will accentuate Hawthorne's personal attraction to the Orient while also foreshadowing motifs, counterpoints, and morals that can be traced through his tales and romances in subsequent chapters.

Hawthorne's first article on the East appeared on the fourth page of the March issue. Beginning "Jerusalem was first called Salem," it insinuated comparisons between the holy city and his home town that certainly did not escape the author and which he, indeed, had anticipated in his juxtaposition of seventeenth-century Turks and Massachusetts Puritans five years earlier in "The Gentle Boy." The two-page essay "Jerusalem" is notable for the ease with which Hawthorne described the tempestuous history of the city ("a dismal history of siege, storm, intestine commotion, captivity, famine, pestilence, and every sort of ruin"), the Crusades and the respective dominions of the Saracens and Turks, the settlement of Christians in Jerusalem, and the Church of the Holy Sepulchre. After mentioning the ugly contention between the monks of the Greek Orthodox Church and the Church of Rome over the privilege of celebrating mass at the Holy Sepulchre, Hawthorne concluded: "It is a curious and rather melancholy fact, that these Christians have shed blood in such a quarrel, in that place of awful sanctity—and the unbelieving Turks have interfered to keep the peace!" (AM, 269–270).

Hawthorne further contrasted the Oriental and the Western by placing the essay on "Jerusalem" immediately next to his piece "An Ontario Steamboat," which was based on a trip he had made himself in the early 1830s. The former traces Christian pilgrimages Eastward, back to the polyglot Holy City. The latter offers a pilgrim's account of travel Westward, amidst a tourist and immigrant cargo ("the pauper dregs which England flings out upon America") crossing the Great Lakes towards Niagara Falls and on into the wilds of America. "An Ontario Steamboat," which probably had been written several years earlier for The Story Teller, served Hawthorne both as instant copy for his magazine and a native companion piece to "Jerusalem." The celebrated hospitality of the Eastern nations was also the first topic addressed in a long extract on "The Turcomans" from Arthur Connolly's Journey to the North of India that Hawthorne published in the June American Magazine. The selection is particularly interesting for Connolly's account of living prototypes for the romance among the pastoral, nomadic peoples of Asia:

> To a European, the description of many simple Oriental customs appears a romance; and, connected as they are with so much miraculous anecdote, it is gratifying to be assured that those who describe the lives and actions of people of antiquity, did it not in any sense of exaggeration, and that relations, which appear to us highly coloured, are told in the simple and natural idiom of the countries and days the writers lived in. (AM, 427)

In the *American Magazine* Hawthorne typically represented the flora and fauna of the East as a different order in greatness from Western products. He noted in the April issue: "In India, the system of Nature is on a grand scale. The bamboo, which answers to the reed of other countries, grows to the height of fifty feet, and is eight feet in circumference. Other productions are of proportionate magnitude" (AM, 335). He might have remembered accounts in his father's logbooks of the taking of turtles and turtle eggs on homeward voyages from the East Indies when, in the May issue, he described the six and eight hundred pound turtles of Ascension Island and reported the trading of turtle shells between the Persian Gulf and China. Prepared in a simple sailor's style, he wrote, "turtle is a more delicious food than the most elaborate art of cookery can render it in Europe, where the animals arrive in a sickly and dying condition, having lost much of their original richness of flavour" (AM, 369). The extensive descriptions of Asia in *Peter Parley's Universal History*, too, abound in superlatives of "most remarkable," "most wonderful," and "mighty miracles," whether in reference to natural phenomena or to storytelling, poetry, and human virtues.

Now and then Hawthorne simply communicated a useful model from the East. In the June *American Magazine*, for instance, he mentioned the practice in parts of India of marking the progress of time by placing a perforated metal cup in a vessel of water—a practice he thought would be a "valuable acquisition" for families in the American back country "who have no better method of noting the lapse of time, than by the height of the sun" (AM, 424).

Other comparisons took a jocular turn, like two items in the magazine for May. In a note called "Female Protection" the cry *fy ard el harym*, by which a fleeing criminal at Cairo could claim the asylum of a harem, reminded Hawthorne that, "Recently, in our own country, a body-guard of petticoats has been found a surer protection than the civil authority" (AM, 389). In a longer piece titled "Moorish Peculiarities, Taken at Random," the white shroud-like *hayk* of the Moorish women, which concealed their face and form but disclosed their bare legs, was contrasted with the European fashion of concealing legs but showing the face. Although he also extracted an article "Dress of the Turkish Ladies" from Commodore Porter's *Constantinople* (AM, 467), there is no indication that Hawthorne lifted his "Moorish Peculiarities" from another source. His ironic voice is conspicuous in remarks like, "Beauty among the Moors consists in corpulency. . . . A lady who weighs a ton, and whose girth is equal to that of a hogshead, may aspire to be a

Sultana." Taking Tangier as "a good specimen of a Moorish city," he held up a kaleidoscope of wandering Bedouins, jugglers, storytellers, wells and granaries, diseases like elephantiasis, bastinados, beheadings, and other forms of punishment (AM, 368–369).

Manning Hawthorne found the July and August issues of the *American Magazine* "almost barren of interest," and Arlin Turner noted, too, that as the months passed, extracts generally took the place of Hawthorne's earlier original work.[25] His selection and use of Eastern material, however, remained fresh and pertinent to the end. Three items from the final, August issue will illustrate this fact: the first, a long extract from Jeremiah Reynolds's *Voyage of the United States Frigate Potomac*; the other two, essays of his own composition.

The eleven paragraphs that Hawthorne reprinted from Reynolds's work, concerning "Transplantation of Foreign Goods," compared the climate and environment of the United States with China and recommended "the benefits which might result to agriculture, and particularly to horticulture, from an expedition to the coast of China." The antiquity of Chinese civilization and its long history of cultivators, Reynolds believed, would give America "the advantage of a thousand or more years of acclimation" if the new land only turned to Asia, rather than to England and France, for produce. He cited the wealth and epicurean pleasure already derived from the import of the Chinese hog, wondered what American gardeners would think "of the immense piles of headed lettuce, described by travellers in China as heaped up at the gates of the cities," and noticed the superior quality of Formosan Iron. Reynolds commended these and other commodities as matters of importance to all classes of society in the new republic (AM, 486).[26]

Although Hawthorne did not rework Reynolds's material, the selection itself is interesting. His uncle Robert Manning was the foremost pomologist in the United States and the author of a book on fruits of New England. Hawthorne's long essay "The Culture of Rice" in the April *American Magazine* had demonstrated his own synthesizing knowledge of the horticulture of China, India, and Egypt, as well as Sumatra and Java, and his curiosity about the effects of cross-breeding the domestic and the foreign reappeared years later in "Rappaccini's Daughter," *The Scarlet Letter*, and *The House of the Seven Gables*.

The second item from the August magazine, titled "Fire Worshippers," is only some 250 words in length but entirely Hawthorne's writing and noteworthy both as a forestudy for his sketch "Fire Worship" (1843) and as an avenue into the Zoroastrianism that waits beneath the surface of such other tales as "Ethan Brand" (1850). "Fire Worshippers" begins and ends:

> There is a sect in Hindostan, who call themselves descendants of the ancient Persians, and, like their ancestors, pay adoration to the sun, the moon, and stars, but especially to fire, esteeming all these objects as visible emblems of the invisible Deity. . . . Niebuhr affirms, that he saw, in one of the temples of these people, at Bombay, some fires which had been kept perpetually burn-

ing for two hundred years. . . . It has been remarked, that if there could possibly exist an idolatry founded on reason, and which did not degrade the Divine Majesty by the symbols of its worship, it would be that of the adorers of fire, and of the eternal lustres of the firmament. There is, in truth, nothing that can be seen or felt, which combines so many symbolic attributes of splendor, terror, and beneficence, as fire. (AM, 494)

Hawthorne's perfunctory contrast between the "senseless" idols of the Hindus and the Christian's "surer trust" in his March sketch "Death of Hindoos on the Ganges" (AM, 297) was all the comment the engraving imposed on him there deserved. His "Fire Worshippers," on the other hand, discloses a broader religious and imaginative tolerance and seems to have lingered in the family's mind. A painted fire screen by Sophia Hawthorne, addressed to "fire worshippers," still stands before the hearth in the Wayside at Concord.

Hawthorne wrote the last essay to be mentioned here, "Natural History among the Ancients," with the end of his authorial and editorial labors in sight. Reflecting back over a half year with the *American Magazine*, he was reminded of "the most laughable absurdities" in Pliny the Elder's *Historie of the World*. "In a comparison between ancient and modern times," Hawthorne wrote, "nothing is more remarkable than the ignorance and misconceptions of the learned men of old, in regard to natural science. Their strictly intellectual cultivation was the most perfect of which human powers are susceptible; but they were mere children in all matters that are to be learned by physical experiments, the observation of facts, and scientific analysis." Among the "fabulous varieties of the human race" that have disappeared "in the progress of modern intelligence," he cited Pliny's legendary accounts of the peoples of India: "In India, there are men seven and a half feet high, and of such excellent constitutions, that they are never troubled with head-ache, tooth-ache, or sore eyes, and very seldom with diseases of any kind. Among the hills of that region, dwell people with heads like dogs, and whose conversation is carried on by barking." The same country was inhabited by pygmies a foot and a half in height, a one-legged race called Monoscelli, another people who lived two hundred years, at the headwaters of the Ganges "a nation that have no mouths, and do not subsist by eating and drinking, but by inhaling sweet perfumes through their nostrils," and many other most remarkable species of humanity. Hawthorne thought their memory worth preserving as "a sample of what would have been the contents of a Magazine of Useful Knowledge, about eighteen hundred years ago," but also as a reminder, lest the elder times be regarded too scornfully, that "future investigations will convict the present age of absurdities as . . . ridiculous, as any in Pliny's Natural History" (AM, 489–490).

The space between fable and empirical analysis, the unknown and the known, as Hawthorne understood, is the realm of the imagination and romance. In his remarkable *The Road to Xanadu*, John Livingston Lowes represented voyages and travels as part of a continuous, "almost cosmic process":

Not only on the fascinating fringes of early maps, but universally, the advancing territory of the known is rimmed and bounded by a dubious borderland in which the unfamiliar and strange hold momentary sway. And that zone of the marvellous . . . draws like a loadstone the incorporating energy of the imagination, which penetrates to the core of the familiar behind the outward semblance of the strange, and completes the conquest which discovery began.[27]

The Eastern travels and voyages Hawthorne read reduced the more laughable absurdities of the ancient historians, but they also gave credibility to remarkable productions and customs just beyond the edge of the known, Western world and established an intermediate zone in which the dialectical and assimilating romantic imagination was free to work.

When he added the *American Magazine of Useful and Entertaining Knowledge* to the canon, Arlin Turner saw, "In truth, on page after page Hawthorne's peculiar characteristics come to light: his interest in early American history, his predilection for moralizing, his comparisons of America with Europe. . . ."[28] Fully as characteristic, as a result of his heritage and a factor in the development of his romance, are his comparisons *and his counterpoints* of America with the East.

Destinations: From Constantinople to Canton

The purpose of describing the milieu and contents of Hawthorne's readings at some length in this chapter is to dispel two equally false impressions. The first, suggested by the few scholars who have mentioned an Oriental element in passing, is the notion that Hawthorne derived his idea of Eastern storytelling incidentally from the moral and philosophical tales of eighteenth-century Europe and England without further thought. The other, held by persons interested in his themes of travel, is the assumption that the East was but one of many regions that Hawthorne visited indiscriminately in his fireside voyages. When John Christie undertook to trace the global readings of another Massachusetts writer known for "celebrating the regional and insular in a period of unprecedented expansion and universality," he was able to draft a simple map of "Thoreau's Literary Travels in Asia" based on six works read by this citizen of Concord.[29] A similar cartographic feat incorporating the voyages of Captain Nathaniel Hathorne and the fifty-plus Eastern travels and histories included in his son's borrowings from the Salem Athenaeum and issues of the *American Magazine of Useful and Entertaining Knowledge* would be so intricately laced and criss-crossed as to leave few areas of darkness from Constantinople and Cairo to Calcutta and Canton. Hawthorne's readings should put us on guard against the idea once expressed by Norman Holmes Pearson: "His writings never mention a wishing-ring of travel. History interested him, but principally that of England and America. . . . He was satisfied with the White Mountains, with Niagara, and with New Haven."[30]

The true compass of Hawthorne's historical interests and satisfactions is suggested by his passing reference in the July 1836 *American Magazine* to "Purchas's Pilgrimage" (AM, 476), a work of religious geography that drew heavily upon Giovanni Ramusio, Richard Hakluyt, and earlier historians and political geographers.[31] *Purchas His Pilgrimage, or Relations of the World and the Religions* (1613) is not to be mistaken for the more famous *Purchas His Pilgrimes* (1625), which continued and enlarged Hakluyt's *Principall Navigations, Voyages, Traffiques and Discoveries of the English Nation* (1589–1600). While there is no direct evidence yet, Hawthorne may well have read both Hakluyt's *Navigations* ("the prose epic of the modern English nation") and *Purchas His Pilgrimes*, which incorporated many additional voyages of Dutch, Spanish, and Portuguese explorers. The great collections and translations of Hakluyt and Purchas, reaching back to the first known English voyage to the Levant in 1458, did much to stimulate seventeenth-century travel for both adventure and trade.

Even if Hawthorne did not go back to Hakluyt, he twice spent a week with the first volume of John Harris's two-volume *A Complete Collection of Voyages and Travels, Consisting of Above Six Hundred of the Most Authentic Writers* (1744–1748), which began with "The History of the circum-navigators" and continued "Comprehending the Discovery, Settlement, and Commerce of the East-Indies." Harris's large-quarto volume of 984 double-column pages drew heavily from Hakluyt, Purchas, Ramusio, and earlier compilers for historical accounts of Egypt, Arabia, Persia, India, and China, the voyages of Columbus and Drake, the travels of Marco Polo, John Albert de Mandelslo, and John Baptist Tavernier, and explorations of the British, French, Dutch, Danish, Swedish, and Imperial East India companies. Harris lavishly illustrated his *Collection* with maps and engravings of harbor scenes, animal and plant life, and such human exotica as a Chinese prostitute on sale.

Hawthorne surely was acquainted also with the marvelous *Voyages and Travels of Sir John Mandeville* (c. 1356). Accepted for three centuries as an authentic record of travels undertaken by an English knight from 1322 to 1355, the immensely popular and picturesque travel book was fabricated from contemporaneous encyclopedias and various genuine accounts of travel to Turkey, Palestine, Egypt, Persia, Tartary, India and beyond to China and Southeast Asia. A citizen of Liège named Jean d'Outremeuse pressed his own claim for authorship of this travel romance, which fired the imagination of medieval Europe. Throughout the Renaissance and later Pliny the Elder and Mandeville continued to create European expectations about the mysterious East and, at "the outer edge of the literature of real travels," to inspire other fireside writers who, supplied only with "a good library and an imagination," produced accounts that anticipated the genre of the novel.[32]

Surprisingly, Mandeville's *Voyages and Travels* is not recorded in the Salem Athenaeum's 1842 catalog, and there is no immediate proof that Hawthorne studied it. Among his contemporaries, however, the young Longfellow was particularly stirred by Mandeville's prodigious adventures in strange places. Inspired by Mandeville as well as by Irving's *Sketch Book*, Longfellow called his first book—a travel work published in 1833–1834 while he was a professor at Bowdoin—*Outre-Mer: A Pilgrimage Beyond the Sea*, and he derived his first headnote from the fourteenth century progenitor. *Outre-Mer* both began and ended by associating itself with a fictionalized journey to the East. Byron's *Childe Harold's Pilgrimage* provided the epigraph to Longfellow's last chapter:

> Ye who have traced the Pilgrim to the scene
> Which is his last, if in your memories dwell
> A thought which once was his, if on ye swell
> A single recollection, not in vain
> He wore his sandal-shoon and scallop-shell.

When Hawthorne sent a copy of his *Twice-told Tales* to Longfellow in March 1837, he hoped it would repay him for "some part of the pleasure" he had derived from *Outre-Mer*. In his notable letter of June 4, 1837, which lamented his long disengagement from the "real world," Hawthorne continued: "You, who have the dust of distant countries on your 'sandal-shoon,' cannot imagine how much enjoyment I shall have" in a summer's tour somewhere in New England.[33] This succession from Mandeville to Byron and Longfellow was still in Hawthorne's mind fifteen years later when, in *The Blithedale Romance*, Coverdale considers an excursion away from Blithedale, after which, he says, "I might fling aside my pilgrim-staff and dusty shoon, and rest as peacefully here as elsewhere" (III, 140). Interestingly, in both his letter of June 1837 and his novel in 1852 Hawthorne introduced the pilgrim's dusty shoes only after mentioning a desire to join the Great Exploring Expedition and run round the world.[34]

The voyages and travels into the East that Hawthorne read began at the borders of Asia Minor with Richard Chandler's account of his journeys in 1764–1766. The English classicist was sent by the Society of Dilettanti in London to record inscriptions, ruins, and antiquities in Greece and Turkey. Among travelers who had prepared the way for Chandler was the Rev. Edmund Chishull, a fellow of Corpus Christi College, Oxford, who was chaplain to the Turkey Company at Smyrna in 1698–1702 and left a journal in the hands of his son that was first published in 1747. Chishull pursued his own antiquarian interests on several expeditions throughout Greece and Turkey, copying inscriptions and rendering a historical account that was of considerable value to his successors. The British Turkey Company, which Queen Elizabeth had established in 1581, was well grounded by the times of Chishull and Chandler.

At least a dozen of the accounts Hawthorne perused were set in Turkey and the Holy Land. Most vivid and memorable perhaps are those from the eighteenth century; however, Hawthorne's readings included richly informative and impressionistic works dating from the sixteenth century to his own time. Earliest in origin were the *Turkish Letters* of Ogier Ghislain de Busbecq, written when Busbecq was sent as ambassador from the Holy Roman Empire to Constantinople in 1554–1562 to negotiate the Turkish threat to Hungary. "Diplomatist, traveller, linguist, scholar, antiquarian, zoologist, and botanist, Busbecq was one of those many-sided men who seem to touch no department of human knowledge without making valuable contributions to it." His *Letters* were republished several times from the later sixteenth to the early eighteenth centuries and have been described by a modern translator as containing "the best extant description of the Ottoman Empire at the height of its glory [under Soleiman the Magnificent], when it was not merely a preoccupation but an actual menace to Europe. The letters are also full of the quaintest lore and the most delightful stories, several of which are quoted in Burton's *Anatomy of Melancholy*." Among Busbecq's other claims to fame is that he introduced the lilac and the tulip into Western Europe.[35]

The subtitle of Heinrich Bünting's *Itinerarium totius Sacrae Scripturae* (first published in German in 1585) explains its coverage: "The Travels of the Holy Patriarchs, Prophets, Judges, Kings, our Saviour Christ, and His Apostles, as they are related in the Old and New Testaments." Far more engaging than Bünting's scriptural geography, which Hawthorne had for five days in 1828, was Sir Paul Rycaut's *The History of the Turkish Empire from the Year 1623 to the Year 1677*, which he had for six days in 1829. One of the best religious and military accounts of Turkey, Rycaut's history was based largely on his own residence first as secretary to the British embassy at the Porte and then consul for the Levant Company at Smyrna from 1661 to 1679. Rycaut's work updated and was later published together with Richard Knolles' *The Generall Historie of the Turkes* (1603), which Samuel Johnson praised in his *Rambler* No. 122. Knolles greatly influenced young Byron's desire to visit the Levant, and Byron acknowledged that it "gave perhaps the oriental colouring which is observed in my poetry."[36]

One of the most successful accounts of a pilgrimage to the Holy Land, held by Hawthorne for nine days in 1831, was Henry Maundrell's description of *A Journey from Aleppo to Jerusalem at Easter*, A.D. *1697* (1703), undertaken while he was chaplain to the English factory at Aleppo. Fourteen Englishmen set out in February 1697 to observe the ceremonies of Easter. Approaching the Holy Land with attitudes of curiosity tinctured by skepticism, the English pilgrims were moved, nonetheless, by the devotion surrounding the sacred places. On his way back from Jerusalem, Maundrell made one of the first English accounts of the magnificent ruins of Baalbek.[37]

Joseph Pitton de Tournefort's *A Voyage into the Levant* recorded the natural history, geography, commerce, religion, and manners of the people he encountered on a scientific expedition from Asia Minor to the borders of Persia commissioned in 1699 by the king of France. Tournefort was accompanied by a physician and a painter and enriched the collections of the king and the Royal Academy on his return to Paris. Alexander Russell's *The Natural History of Aleppo*, despite its rather restricted title, became known as "one of the most complete pictures of Eastern manners extant" and recently has been called "a delightful and exhaustive survey of the society . . . of a major Ottoman city."[38] Russell had special privileges of access as physician to the Levant Company and St. Thomas's Hospital from 1745 until 1753, when he was succeeded by his brother Patrick, who edited the second edition of *The Natural History* (1794).

Perhaps the most celebrated Eastern correspondence in a century known for its excellent letter writers was the *Letters of the Right Honourable Lady*

M[ar]y W[ortle]y M[ontagu]e ... Which Contain, Among Other Curious Relations, Accounts of the Policy and Manners of the Turks, published in 1763 but written in 1716–1718 on Lady Montagu's travels from London to Vienna and thence to Adrianople and Constantinople as wife of the British ambassador. One of the first English women residents in the East, she gave spectacular accounts of the gardens, kiosks, and fountains of the Great Seraglio of Constantinople and the luxurious life of Turkish women. Dismissing the "absurdities" and fictions of earlier travelers to the Levant, Lady Montagu reported that, contrary to much European opinion, Turkish women enjoyed an enviable life.[39] The irrepressible traveler entered Hagia Sophia, a rare opportunity even for male diplomats, and overcame prejudice at home when she introduced to England the Turkish practice of inoculation against smallpox. Lady Montagu's letters appear neither in Kesselring's list of Hawthorne's readings nor in his issues of the American Magazine. However, in Our Old Home he remembered her familiarly as "a literary acquaintance of my boyhood" and "a friend" (V, 127). Her depiction of the daily romance of Eastern life, the smooth and polished bodies seen in the women's bagnio, and the Eastern instinct for storytelling complement if, indeed, they did not prompt Hawthorne's own representations.[40]

In his turn Baron François de Tott, the last of the eighteenth-century commentators included here, debunked the beauty and graciousness Lady Montagu had attributed to the life of Turkish women. His Memoires ... with Numerous Anecdotes, Facts, and Observations, of the Manners and Customs of the Turks and Tartars portrayed, instead, a female life of ignorance, pride, blind passion, and slavery. The son of a Hungarian refugee, but French in education and spirit, De Tott introduced Western military techniques to the army of Selim III at the time of the Turkish-Russian wars. Two contemporary accounts of Turkey and the Holy Land provided further material for Hawthorne's American Magazine: David Porter's Constantinople and Its Environs (1835) and an anonymous English account, Three Weeks in Palestine and Lebanon (1833), which was republished in New York and Boston by American Sunday school and missionary societies.

Beyond Turkey and the Holy Land, Hawthorne's literary travels took him both eastward into Persia and southward to Arabia, Egypt, and Muslim Africa. Adam Olearius, John Albert de Mandelslo, John Chardin, and Jonas Hanway all portrayed Persia and the overland route to the East Indies. Olearius was secretary in a German embassy to the Duke of Muscovy in 1633–1635 and the King of Persia in 1635–1639. His The Voyages and Travels of the Ambassadors Sent by Fredrick, Duke of Holstein (1622) had special cartographic importance and was later praised by Goethe. Mandelslo accompanied Olearius as far as Ispahan but then proceeded independently to India, China, and Japan. His Travels and Olearius's accounts were published together in 1662.

John Chardin, a Huguenot who emigrated to England, first visited the East in 1665, at age twenty-two, both for the love of travel and in pursuit of his career as a jewel merchant. The Travels of Sir John Chardin into Persia and the East Indies (1686) includes important voyages in the 1670s via the

Black Sea and intermediate countries as far as India. Chardin, who was fluent in Persian and described as having the "eyes of a philosopher," found the Persians the "most civilized people of the East," and he left a specially interesting account of the Persian court and his transactions with the Shah. Sir William Jones regarded his narrative as "the best yet published on the Mohammedan nations."[41]

A well-known merchant and philanthropist, Jonas Hanway was sent by the Muscovy Company in 1743–1745 to determine whether British trade with Persia over the northern route remained as impractical as in the previous century. His perilous journey, beset by robbers, confiscation of his goods, and near enslavement, convinced him this was still the case. He testily refused the attempt of the Shah's officials to compensate him for his lost properties in the form of concubines. Piqued by Hanway's attacks on tea-drinking, Samuel Johnson later said "that he acquired a reputation travelling abroad, but lost it all by travelling at home."[42]

The most entertaining depiction of Persian life and manners in the early nineteenth century was James Morier's The Adventures of Hajji Baba of Ispahan (1824), which Hawthorne read in July 1827. Morier was born in Smyrna, a son of the consul general of the Levant Company at Constantinople. After serving as secretary to Lord Elgin in the Egyptian campaign, young Morier became secretary to the British legation at the court of Persia in 1807 and secretary to the embassy of Sir Gore Ouseley at Teheran in 1810–1816. Accompanying the Persian ambassador Mirza Abul Hassan back to London became the occasion for Morier's sequel, The Adventures of Hajji Baba of Ispahan in England (1828), an amusing eighteenth-century-style satire on Western civilization. The tales and romance of Hajji Baba—robber, water-bearer, smoke-seller, pharmacist, lover, sub-lieutenant to the chief executioner, mullah, scribe, merchant, aga, impostor, and picaresque hero—were applauded both as superior imaginative literature and as an authoritative insight into Oriental fatalism, intrigue, changefulness, and destiny. Walter Scott called Morier "the best novelist of the day," and the Dictionary of National Biography said of him: "So accurate was his delineation of Persian life and character that the Persian minister at St. James's is said to have remonstrated on behalf of his government with the plain-speaking and satire of 'Hajji Baba.' "[43]

If the life of Persia was popularly known in Hawthorne's time through Morier's evocations, Arabia was imagined largely through The Arabian Nights' Entertainment and Antar, A Bedoueen Romance. The Arabian Nights was on every literate tongue in England and the United States early in the nineteenth century. Byron had read the tales by age ten, Hawthorne by age fifteen, and Cardinal John Henry Newman later wrote, "I used to wish the Arabian Tales were true."[44] The Thousand and One Nights were a general product of the East, not particular to Arabia in either origin or setting. Many of the tales are located in India and Central Asia. Persian, Iraqi, Egyptian, and Turkish elements all come together within the frame story of Scheherazade and the Sultan of Baghdad. The title by which they became popularly known, however, implied a special association with the Arab world, and it was accepted that some of the circumstances of the voyages of Sindbad "were founded on supposed fact; and that many descriptions were, in all probability, collected from real narratives of Arabian seamen who had navigated the Indian ocean."[45] Allusions to the *Arabian Nights* weave in and out of Hawthorne's stories, and it held a place in his small library until the end of his life.[46]

Antar was welcomed in the nineteenth century for its distinctive depiction of the pre-Islamic Arabian people, whose pride, boldness, desert chivalry and nobility of character it epitomized. The historical Antara Ibn Shaddad was a sixth-century Arabian prince and one of seven poets whose verses were hung at the door of the Kaaba. The heroic romance *Antar* was believed to have been written early in the ninth century by Admai, a renowned grammarian and theologian of the court of Haroun al Raschid. It found its way via Sir William Jones and other European commentators into the abbreviated translation by Terrence Hamilton (1819–1820), which Shelley responded to in "From the Arabic, an Imitation" (1821), and which Elizabeth and Nathaniel Hawthorne borrowed from the Salem Athenaeum in 1836. The *Encyclopedia Americana* said of *Antar* in 1829:

> This romance gives the most complete idea of the manners and life, of the way of thinking, of the opinions and superstitions, of the early Arabians before the time of the prophet, and the fidelity of the picture is even now to be recognized in many features of the modern Bedouins. It is written in the purest Arabic, and ranked among the classics of Arabian literature. It is so attracting that critics prefer it to the Arabian Nights.[47]

Antar provided a counterweight to the greater dream world of *The Arabian Nights* tales.

Hawthorne also knew the several quarters of Arabia (Arabia Felix, Arabia Petraea, Arabia Deserta) as well as Egypt, Nubia, and the Barbary States through several centuries of travel commentary. In *A Relation of a Journey Begun An:Dom:1610* George Sandys narrated his travels beyond Constantinople— where the lofty cypress trees and resplendent marble mosques filled his eyes as he first sailed up the Bosphorus—and on to Cairo. The son of a bishop and a staunch defender of Christianity against Islam, he crossed the "forsaken" Sinai Desert by camel and described the Turks' mania for coffee, which they had learned in the fifteenth century from Arab pilgrims to Mecca and which shortly would be introduced to Venice and London. Sandys subsequently became a treasurer of the Virginia Company in America.

The Famous Voyages & Travailes of Vincent Le Blanc ... through Most Parts of the World (first published in French in 1648) chronicled the observations of an inveterate wanderer who, from age fourteen to seventy-eight, included Persia, Morocco, Ethiopia, Egypt, and the East Indies in his personal survey of the world. Hiob Ludolf's *A New History of Ethiopia* portrayed the origins, natural history, politics, literature, and religious and social affairs of the Abyssinians in great detail. Richard Pococke's *A Description of the East, and some other Countries* (1743–1745), which Gibbon praised for its "superior learning and dignity," attained its celebrity partly because of 178 large engravings of city plans, flora and fauna, statues, tombs, temples, hieroglyphics, dress, and social life. The engravings of Baalbek are especially numerous and impressive. A well-to-do clergyman who explored Asia Minor, Palestine, Syria, Mesopotamia, and Egypt in 1737–1740, Pococke was one of the few travelers of his time to ascend the Nile beyond Cairo.

As intrepid an explorer as Hawthorne met anywhere in his readings, Carsten Niebuhr took part as astronomer and naturalist in the first scientific expedition to Arabia, dispatched by the King of Denmark in 1763. Niebuhr's *Travels through Arabia, and Other Countries in the East* chronicled his observations not only of Arabia but of the Nile, Mount Sinai, Suez, his overland journey to Mocha, and a fourteen-month sojourn in India. Niebuhr was the sole survivor of the five-man Danish expedition. He made his way back to Copenhagen in 1767 via Muscat, Persia, Mesopotamia, Cyprus, and Asia Minor, and delivered accounts of the lands he had explored that were among the best and most authentic of the day.

Hawthorne's interest in Abyssinia and the still mysterious origins of the Nile is particularly conspicuous in his reading of James Bruce's monumental and lavishly illustrated *Travels to Discover the Source of the Nile* (1790). He borrowed four of the five volumes of Bruce's epic of African adventure in order from February to April 1833. Bruce, who had served as British consul to Algiers and covered most of North Africa and Arabia in his travels, reached the headwaters of the Blue Nile in November 1770 after two years in Abyssinia. The extravagance of the explorer and his claims made him a convenient object of parody in the travels of the fictive Baron Münchhausen. As in the case of the Turkish empire, Hawthorne also drew on contemporaneous accounts of North Africa and Egypt for the *American Magazine*, including: the *Narrative of the Operations and Recent Discoveries within the Pyramids, Temples, Tombs, and Excavations in Egypt and Nubia* (1820) of the fearless Giovanni Belzoni, who excavated Karnak, penetrated the second pyramid of Giza, identified the ruins of Berenice, and shipped cargos of colossal antiquities to the British Museum; and Perceval Barton Lord's *Algiers, with Notices of the Neighbouring States of Barbary* (1835).

When Hawthorne renewed his borrowings from the Salem Athenaeum in 1848, he took Sir John Gardner Wilkinson's *Modern Egypt and Thebes* (1843) for five weeks. Wilkinson's tourist's guide, gratefully acknowleged by Harriet Martineau in her *Eastern Life, Present and Past* (1848) as "a daily benefactor to us in Egypt," covered in all practical detail travel schedules, connections, documents required, lodgings, meals, use of porters, and sites of interest from Europe to Bombay.[48] Hawthorne might have been thinking at the time of getting out from behind his desk at the Salem Custom House and acting on his chronic instinct for travel, or perhaps of seeking a foreign appointment. It is worth noticing that on the same day he returned Wilkinson's travel guide to the Athenaeum (November 14, 1848), he also gave up *The Journals of Major Samuel Shaw, the First American Consul at Canton* (1847), which he had had for seven weeks. Shaw was supercargo of the *Empress of China* on the first American voyage to Canton in 1784–1785 and made several prosperous trips in the years following. He was appointed consul in 1786, even before the ratification of the United States Constitution, but died in 1793 of a liver disease contracted at Bombay.

Of the works that extended Hawthorne's explorations, respectively, into India and China, the former derived for the most part from the Salem Athenaeum and the latter, as one would expect from the current opening up of the farther East, from presentations in the *American Magazine*. In 1830 Hawthorne had the Athenaeum's copy of Luiz de Camoes's *The Lusiad: or, The Discovery of India*, the epic of Portugal, which was patterned after the *Aeneid* and celebrated Vasco da Gama's discovery of the searoute to the East. Camoes was in Goa and Macao from 1563 to 1570. His great work must have attracted Hawthorne not only as a foreshadowing of his own family history and a drama of confrontation between Eastern and Western cultures but for its celebrated marriage of imagination with "the truth of history." In his introduction to the English translation, William Julius Mickle characterized *The Lusiad* as "the Epic Poem of whatever country has the controul and possession of the commerce of India."[49] To no small degree, by the early nineteenth century Salem, Massachusetts, had begun to play just such a role.

Through *Coryat's Crudities* Hawthorne followed the pilgrim's staff and dusty shoes of the "gentle traveller" Tom Coryat through the Levant and Persia, and farther east to Agra and the court of the great Mogul, in the years 1612 to 1617. The life of this witty buffoon, who entertained his contemporaries with letters and verses on his travels and embarrassed English officials in India by his unconventional behavior, ended at Surat in the latter year.

If the volume of *Asiatic Researches* Hawthorne looked at in 1831 was the first of the series, as Kesselring surmised, he probably was less taken by the scholarly material he saw there on orthography, inscriptions, language, deities, and Hindu literature than by Sir William Jones' inaugural discourse to the Asiatic Society at Bengal, which introduced the publication. Jones began by recalling the evening en route to India when he found:

> on inspecting the observations of the day, that *India* lay before us, and *Persia* on our left, whilst a breeze from *Arabia* blew nearly on our stern. A situation so pleasing in itself, and to me so new, could not fail to awaken a train of reflections in a mind which had early been accustomed to contemplate with delight the eventful histories and agreeable fictions of this eastern world. It gave me inexpressible pleasure to find myself in the midst of so noble an amphitheatre, almost encircled by the vast regions of *Asia*, which has ever been esteemed the nurse of sciences, the inventress of delightful and useful arts, the scene of glorious actions fertile in the productions of human genius, abounding in natural wonders, and infinitely diversified in the forms of religion and government, in the laws, manners, customs, and languages, as well as in the features and complexions of men.[50]

Hawthorne found further personal and pictorial tributes to the glories of India in the Rev. Reginald Heber's *Narrative of a Journey through the Upper Provinces of India, from Calcutta to Bombay, 1824–1825* (published posthumously in 1828), Arthur Conolly's *Journey to the North of India Overland from England, through Russia, Persia, and Afghaunistaun* (1830), Emma Roberts's *Scenes and Characteristics of Hindostan* (1835), and *The Oriental Annual; or, Scenes in India* (1834-1840). As Lord Bishop of Calcutta, Heber traveled tirelessly throughout his huge diocese from Bombay to Ceylon. Robert Southey and other contemporaries celebrated Heber's character, piety, and literary works with elegaic verse after his sudden death in April 1826, and Hawthorne mentioned the Bishop of Calcutta in "P.'s Correspondence" as late as 1845.

Aside from his father's log for the ship *Perseverance* in 1796-1797, Hawthorne visited China through John Lockman's *Travels of the Jesuits into Various Parts of the World* (1743), Earl Macartney's *An Historical Account of the Embassy to the Emperor of China* (1797), John White's *History of a Voyage to the China Sea* (1823), John Cochrane's *Narrative of a Pedestrian Journey through Russia and Siberian Tartary, from the Frontiers of China to the Frozen Sea and Kamchatka* (1824), Egor Timkovskii's *Travels of the Russian Mission through Mongolia to China* (1827), and Charles Gützlaff's *A Sketch of Chinese History* or his *Journal of Three Voyages along the Coast of China* (1834). He visited the Dutch East Indies both through Jeremiah Reynolds's *Voyage of the United States Frigate Potomac* (1835) and Edward Trelawny's *Adventures of a Younger Son* (1831), a work of Byronic imagination and autobiography celebrated for its brilliant local coloring, its strong narrative, and its violence. Trelawny had shipped to the East Indies with the Royal Navy, but depicted himself as deserting at Bombay and taking over a French privateer, and around the years 1811-1813 had various adventures off the coast of Java and in the Eastern archipelago.[51]

In addition to the foregoing voyages and travels Hawthorne also read a number of religious texts that characterized the East in general. Among these were the Koran and Bernard Picart's voluminous *Religious Ceremonies and Customs*, which he had respectively in 1827 and 1829. "From the Atlantic to the Ganges," Edward Gibbon wrote, "the Koran is acknowledged as the fundamental code, not only of theology, but of civil and criminal jurisprudence."[52] Picart's richly illustrated *Ceremonies and Customs* inspired Robert Southey's lifelong fascination with religious mythology and his poetic dramas of Hinduism and Islam.[53]

The Christians' Hebrew and Greek testaments are often excluded from discussions of the Orient. However, it is noteworthy that Hawthorne's favorite biblical text, the Book of Job, is an Arabian tale in both origin and form. Under the influence of Eastern archaeology and comparative textual studies, scholars in Hawthorne's time had begun to trace the story of Job— a rich, upright Arab sheik and "greatest of all the men of the east" (Job 1:3)— through the folklore of the ancient East and to explore its roots in Egyptian pessimism, Babylonian skepticism, and Akkadian theodicy. The story of the man of Uz derived most immediately from the Edomites, a seminomadic people who lived to the southeast of the Dead Sea and were renowned for their wisdom. In its essay "Arabian Literature and Language" the *Encyclopedia Americana* speculated in the 1820s: "If it were beyond doubt, that the poem of Job was of Arabian origin, this would show, not only that Arabia Petraea had its poets, but also the character of their productions. . . . The antiquity of philosophy among the Arabians might also be shown from Job."[54]

Hawthorne most likely turned to the Book of Job both for its pure religion—a submission to the will of God that one finds at the center of Islam and in such tales as Hawthorne's "The Wives of the Dead"—and for the intricacies and beauty of its language. Like other great works of Oriental literature the Book of Job is a framed narrative. It consists of a prose prologue and epilogue and a complex sequence of poems, soliloquies, and discourses concerning the meaning of life and religion. When Hawthorne conceived his *Story Teller* in the early 1830s, he showed a kindred spirit to the Jobian narrator, who was versed in the oral folk tales of the East and "heir to centuries of storytelling at night before the campfire."[55]

Literary Intermediaries

With the rise of Sanskrit studies in the nineteenth century, the conviction grew that India was the original source of Europe's stories and folktales, which, after passing through Arabic, Syrian, and Persian translations, had spread westward during the Crusades. An impressive scholarship has devoted itself to tracing the influence and development of Eastern prototypes, from the Christianized legend of *Barlaam and Josaphat* and medieval adaptations of *Kalilah and Dimnah* and *The Seven Wise Masters*, down to the nineteenth century. The Oriental frame structure, plots, and motifs of the *Decameron*, Chaucer's "Squire's Tale" (an "Arabian Nights" tale probably brought to Europe by Italian merchants), and the Eastern stories in the *Gesta Romanorum*—all of which Hawthorne is thought to have read[56]—popularized Eastern storytelling in Europe during the fourteenth century. Europe's indebtedness to Arabic poetry and prose literature during the Middle Ages is unquestioned.[57]

Although the classical discipline of the Renaissance restrained the Oriental influence, the East continued to provide characters, themes, and scenes of action in the following centuries. By one count, forty-seven plays dealing with Oriental matters appeared on the English stage between 1579 and 1642, inspired largely by the rivalry of the Ottoman Empire, whose territories then extended from the Persian Gulf to the borders of Vienna. In the age of Shakespeare the average citizen had at least "as wide and as accurate a knowledge of the Orient" as the average American of the twentieth century.[58] In the sixteenth and seventeenth centuries the works of Spenser, Milton, Bunyan, and Dryden variously reflected the influence both of travelers' histories of the East and the literary figures and motifs that had become naturalized in English literature. Dryden's heroic play *Aureng-Zebe* (1675) was contemporary with the reign of the austere and imperious Mogul emperor. One could troll endlessly through the ocean of story that stretched between the Eastern *Ursprung* of myth and imagination and nineteenth century America.

We can afford to suggest here only the most immediate channels that brought the Eastern stories to Hawthorne.

The tide of Oriental influences that swept Europe in the Middle Ages returned in the Romantic movement, beginning with the publication of Galland's translation of *The Arabian Nights* in 1704. The success of *The Arabian Nights*, which went through at least thirty editions in French and English during the next century, was both "immediate and complete." As it fired the imagination of the reading public, publishers brought out further editions of *Persian Tales* ("The Thousand and One Days") and *Turkish Tales*, and when genuine Oriental materials ran short, French and English writers created their own "Oriental" tales to satisfy the demand.[59]

In her study *The Oriental Tale in England in the Eighteenth Century*—describing "an episode in the development of English Romanticism"—Martha Conant identified four forms that the Eastern tale took. The "imaginative" tale, represented by the exotic settings and adventures of *The Arabian Nights* and subsequent imitations, was the earliest, but "moralistic," "philosophic," and "satiric" genres all waxed in prominence throughout the eighteenth century. The moral and philosophic tales were particularly prominent in the periodical literature from Joseph Addison's *Spectator* to Samuel Johnson's *Rambler* and *Idler*. Half or more of the Oriental tales in Addison's periodicals express a moral lesson.[60] Johnson followed his example with a series of tales in the *Rambler* in 1750–1752 (the stories of "Hamet and Raschid," "Obidah, the son of Abensina," "Nouradin the Merchant," "Morad the son of Hanuth," and "Seged, lord of Ethiopia," a precursor to *Rasselas*) and in the *Idler* in 1759–1760 ("Gelaleddin," "Ortugrul of Basra," and "Omar, the son of Hussan"). When Johnson first arrived in London, his calling card was a verse tragedy entitled *Irène* that told "the story of the love of the Sultan Mahomet for a beautiful Christian taken at the capture of Constantinople."[61]

The philosophical tale, superior in interest though inferior in number to the moral tale, reached its apogee in three English works: in Addison's "The Vision of Mirza" (*Spectator*, 1711), which particularly sparked the imagination of Robert Burns; in Johnson's *Rasselas* (1759), which was the most important of the serious English Oriental tales; and in Oliver Goldsmith's "Asem" (1759), also entitled "The Proceedings of Providence Vindicated, an Eastern Work." In France the Oriental tale reverted to its original apologue form in Voltaire's *Zadig* (1747)—a philosophic tale of a young man's encounter with chance and destiny—and in his other works of political and social satire.

The fourth form of Oriental tale described by Conant, the satire, developed out of Giovanni Paolo Morana's *L'espion Turc* (1684ff.), Montesquieu's *Lettres Persanes* (1721), and George Lyttelton's *Letters from a Persian in England to His Friend at Ispahan* (1735). These collections of letters by supposed Eastern visitors, ingenuously exposing the peculiar customs of Western society, culminated in English in Goldsmith's *Citizen of the World* (1762).

The effects of Hawthorne's readings in Johnson and Voltaire will be discussed in the next chapter. The extent and depth of his engagement with the eighteenth-century essayists, however, is immediately apparent. He wrote an adolescent newspaper, also called the *Spectator*, in imitation of Addison. According to his son its original held a place in the bookcase at the Wayside as late as the 1860s. The *Idler* and *Adventurer* also were part of Hawthorne's library. Julian Hawthorne reported that both his parents read "a good deal of French literature" at the Old Manse and that his father had "a nearly complete edition of Voltaire in duodecimo."[62] The degree of attachment Hawthorne felt for Goldsmith is suggested by his widow's gift of a volume of the English satirist's works, inscribed with Hawthorne's name, to Longfellow in 1864.[63]

The two single most impressive facts about Hawthorne's use of the Salem Athenaeum are his 130 withdrawals of the *Gentleman's Magazine* and the 49 volumes of Voltaire he borrowed (some twice) in 1829–1831. (His next most frequent reading, the *Collections of the Massachusetts Historical Society*, accounted for 39 loans.) On May 30, 1829, Hawthorne sat down with the first volume of the *Gentleman's Magazine* (for 1731), and by July 5, 1831, he had gone through nearly every issue up to 1821. Then in 1836–1838 he returned to peruse the issues for 1830–1837. When Hawthorne staged his "Earth's Holocaust" in 1844, "The small, richly-gilt, French tomes, of the last age, with the hundred volumes of Voltaire among them, went off in a brilliant shower of sparkles, and little jets of flame" (X, 395).

No other feature of Hawthorne's pastime at the start of his career so distinctly bears the marks of organized study as does his immersion in the *Gentleman's Magazine* and its compendium of eighteenth-century society, politics, and taste. Among other materials he found there a substantial literature on the East that mirrored the discoveries and changing interests of the period. Persian spy stories and pseudo-letters to Ispahan from London and Holland predominated in the 1730s and 1740s. In the 1750s the *Magazine* printed imitation Oriental fables like "Asem and Salned: An Eastern Tale," "Amurath, Sultan of the East," and "The Letter of Cosrou the Iman." Essays on travel, history, and diplomacy kept readers abreast of latest developments in the East. "Carazan's Dream" was followed immediately in the 1754 *Magazine*, for example, by a book review of *Ruins of Palmyra or Tedmor, in the Desert*. Persian songs and tales appeared into the 1780s. The 1790s saw a correspondence of considerable size and warmth concerning the authenticity of *The Arabian Nights* and the authority of competing manuscripts and translations. Learned speculation about the symbolism and interpretation of the hieroglyphs was another regular feature that continued into the 1830s. At the turn of the century the accounts of Eastern travels took a new archaeological turn, as readers vicariously explored the vast ruins of Jerrasch, Karnak, and Luxor, held their breath before the grandeur of Baalbek and Palmyra, probed subterranean caves for sarcophagi and scrolls, and suffered with Belzoni in the desert. In Hawthorne's period the *Gentleman's Magazine* regularly published "intelligence" from Persia, Arabia, Egypt, and Turkey, often concerning revolutions within the Ottoman Empire.

At the end of the eighteenth century the imaginative tale returned with a dark florescence on both sides of the English Channel in *The History of the*

Caliph Vathek (presented as "an Arabian Tale, from an Unpublished Manuscript"), which appeared in English and French in 1786. William Beckford's fusion of the Gothic romance with Oriental subjects and imagery anticipated and strongly affected the imaginative literature of the next half century predisposing "public taste for the reversion to the non-classical and medieval which goes by the name of the Romantic movement."[64] Beckford's story of the proud, sensual Caliph who sold himself to the powers of evil made a particular bridge between the eighteenth century Oriental tale and the verse dramas of Lord Byron, Robert Southey, and Thomas Moore. Beckford had steeped himself in the Orientalia of the period, briefly studied Arabic and Persian, and erected a great Egyptian Hall in his home at Fonthill. He dressed his romance in all the paraphernalia of Arabian Nights storytelling: genii, houris, a Prince of Demons, the beautiful princess Nouronihar, whom Vathek seduces, his evil mother Carathis, Gulchenrouz the lovelorn poet.[65] Notwithstanding, or perhaps because of these "sublime" effects, Byron said of *Vathek* in a note to *The Giaour*: "For correctness of costume, beauty of description, and power of imagination, it far surpasses all European imitations; and bears such marks of originality, that those who have visited the East will find some difficulty in believing it to be more than a translation. As an Eastern tale, even *Rasselas* must bow before it; his 'Happy Valley' will not bear a comparison with the 'Hall of Eblis.' "[66] Symbols and characterizations from *Vathek*, which reignited *The Arabian Nights*' gloomy and surreal magnificence for the first decades of the nineteenth century, have been traced in Hawthorne's *The Scarlet Letter* as well as *Fanshawe*.[67]

The incipient romantic spirit of the eighteenth century poured forth in a succession of major Oriental dramas in the first two decades of the new century that were inspired both by the demands of the reading public and by political events of the time, from the French retreat from Egypt to rebellions within the Ottoman Empire. Hawthorne knew the Oriental passages in Wordsworth's works and surely read the greatest romantic poem on the Orient, Coleridge's "Kubla Khan," which was published at the behest of Byron and inspired not only by a mild narcotic but by *Purchase his Pilgrimage*, the same work to which Hawthorne alluded in the *American Magazine* in 1836. Far more significant here, however, was the appeal of Byron and two contemporaries nearly forgotten today, however dominant their contemporary appeal: Robert Southey and Thomas Moore.[68]

Hawthorne tended to think of Byron, Southey, and Moore as a set, regardless of Southey's attacks on the "Satanic School" of poetry and Byron's lampoon of "Bob Southey" in the dedication to *Don Juan*. In "P.s Correspondence" the narrator's friend, "a great traveller" in the realm of fantasy and disordered reason, wrote that on making acquaintance with several distinguished characters he first availed himself to his letter of introduction to Lord Byron: "Southey and he are on the most intimate terms. You are aware that some little time before the death of Moore, Byron caused that brilliant but reprehensible man to be ejected from his house" (X, 365). When disposing of the Romantics in "Earth's Holocaust," Hawthorne contrasted Shelley's "purer light . . . with the fitful and lurid gleams, and gushes of black vapor, that flashed and eddied from the volumes of Lord Byron. As for Tom Moore, some of his songs diffused an odor like a burning pastille" (X, 397).

How little the late twentieth century appreciates the taste of the first decade of the nineteenth is obvious from the virtual disappearance of Robert Southey from our literary anthologies. Hawthorne's thorough acquaintance with and indebtedness to Byron have been well demonstrated, but Southey was also a main feature in his reading.[69] If Hawthorne did not quite feel the rapture of young Shelley, who embraced *The Curse of Kehama* as "my most favorite poem," the poet laureate's works nonetheless occupied a prominent place in his library.[70] Shortly before their marriage, when the Hawthornes were setting up a household at the Old Manse, Nathaniel suggested that a gift volume of Southey's poems be exchanged for some other book because his own copy of Southey already had gone to Concord with his furniture. He was still reading "a good deal of Southey" to his family in the winter of 1850–1851.[71] References to Ladurlad in his notebooks in 1838 (VIII, 176) and "Monsieur du Miroir" in 1837 (X, 164) suggest that he found *The Curse of Kehama* especially impressive.

Fascinated as a schoolboy by the sympathetic histories and famous engravings of Picart's *Religious Ceremonies and Customs*, Southey conceived the notion of dramatizing the world's principal mythologies in long narrative poems. He began in *Thalaba the Destroyer* (1800) with "the Mahommedan religion, as being that with which I was then best acquainted myself, and of which everyone who has read the Arabian Nights' Entertainments possessed all the knowledge necessary for readily understanding and entering into the intent and spirit of the poem." Southey committed himself to putting the most favorable light upon the morality of the Koran and upon "that system of belief and worship which had been developed under the Covenant with Ishmael," eschewing the profligacy commonly attributed to the Prophet, the "abominations" engrafted upon Mohammedanism, and the despotism that accompanied its political conquests. He called the unusual rhythms employed in *Thalaba* "the *Arabesque* ornament of an Arabian tale."[72]

In *The Curse of Kehama*, which followed ten years later (1810), Southey took up "that mythology which Sir William Jones had been the first to introduce into English poetry"—the still new and unfamiliar religion of the Hindus—and again strove for the "moral sublimity" he had achieved in the earlier work.[73] Both *Thalaba* and *The Curse of Kehama* were clearly influenced by Beckford's work of Gothic Orientalism. In the former work young Thalaba descends to Domdaniel ("a seminary for evil magicians, under the roots of the sea") to slay the powers of evil.[74] About the latter work, which was considered Southey's masterpiece, a late nineteenth century commentator first appreciated "the gorgeous shows of Indian courts and Indian nature admirably reproduced in intricate and sonorous rhymed stanzas," and then noted, "The striking catastrophe [in the Hall of Death] owes much to 'Vathek.' "[75] Southey's verse dramas had a pervasive influence on presentations of the marvelous in the early nineteenth century, and his annotations became a "mythic mine" for his contemporaries. Romantic mythmaking, according to Stuart Curran, "owes its most immediate debt to Southey's quest romances, both for its enlargement of the horizons open to narrative poets and for his almost abstract focus on the individual's quest against and for evil powers."[76]

The wide readership that was transported to the realms of Islam and the Hindus by Southey's romances in the first decade of the nineteenth century multiplied in the second decade as Byron's Oriental tales took England and Europe by storm. Byron's imagination was drawn Eastward first by his childhood readings in Richard Knolles' and Paul Rycaut's accounts of the Ottoman Empire, as well as by *The Arabian Nights* and *Vathek*. Unlike Southey his interest in the East became more than imaginary when he traveled to Greece and Asia Minor in 1809–1811. Because of his first-hand experiences Byron confined his Oriental locales to Greece and the Aegean while the armchair travelers Southey and Moore had the entire Eastern hemisphere at their disposal. Like Southey and Moore, however, Byron responded to the expectations of his audience by substantiating his wild adventures through learned annotations and references. The first cantos of *Childe Harold's Pilgrimage* (1812), a work which seems particularly to have captured Hawthorne's imagination, show the most immediate effects of his travels in Greece and Turkey.[77]

The first of Byron's complete Oriental works was *The Giaour, a Fragment of a Turkish Tale* (1813), which introduced the great theme of connection between a renegade Western male (a Christian "unbeliever," or *giaour*) and an Eastern maid locked in the grip of Islamic despotism. Byron claimed to have based his fragment on a story heard in the coffeehouses of the Levant about "the adventures of a female slave, who was thrown, in the Mussulman manner, into the sea for infidelity, and avenged by a young Venetian, her lover."[78] *The Giaour* marked a dark contrast to Mozart's depiction only three decades earlier of good-humored and magnanimous Turks in *The Abduction from the Seraglio* (1782). Rewarded by popular acclaim, Byron quickly added *The Bride of Abydos, a Turkish Tale* (1813), *The Corsair, a Tale* (1814), *Lara, a Tale* (1814), *The Siege of Corinth* (1816), and *Sardanapalus* (a drama, 1821), as well as Eastern stanzas in *Beppo* (1817) and *Don Juan* (1819–1824).

Thomas Moore's *Lalla Rookh*, which was published in 1817 on the crest of interest for Southey's and Byron's Oriental works, excelled its predecessors in popularity not only in England, where five editions appeared within the first twelve months, but in the United States, where it sold more copies than any other book in its year of publication.[79] Southern writer William Russell Smith said of it: " 'The Light of the Harem' glowed in every cottage, and flashed on every centertable. The book was the pocket companion of the boys and the bosom darling of the girls."[80] Moore had begun work on *Lalla Rookh* before the appearance of *The Giaour* and remarked on its publication, "Never was anything more unlucky for me than Byron's invasion of this region, . . . it will now be overrun with clumsy adventurers, and when I make my appearance, instead of being a leader, as I looked to be, I must dwindle into a humble follower—a Byronian."[81] But in dedicating *The Corsair* to Moore, Byron said of his Eastern composition: "None can do those scenes so much justice. . . . [W]ildness, tenderness, and originality are part of your national claim to oriental descent." And he later wrote to Moore, "You have caught the colors as if you had been in the rainbow and the tone of the East is perfectly preserved."[82]

Adopting the Eastern frame structure, Lalla Rookh comprises a series of verse tales told to the heroine, an Indian princess, by the handsome poet Feramorz on her journey from Delhi through the Vale of Kashmir to be married to the King of Bucharia. Love is inevitable, and at the journey's end the young poet reveals himself to be her betrothed. Lalla Rookh abounds with the fauna and bowers of the Oriental fairy tale—"places of melancholy, delight, and safety, where all the company around was wild peacocks and turtle-doves."[83] The verse tale "The Paradise and the Peri" was separately dramatized and, a sure sign of its spiritual verisimilitude, the whole book was translated into Persian.

Among the British precursors Hawthorne also encountered frequent echoes and references to The Arabian Nights in the novels of Walter Scott. The influence of the Arabian tales is particularly noticeable in The Talisman (1825), which was set in the Holy Land, near the Dead Sea, at the time of the Crusades. The Surgeon's Daughter (1827), with its Indian locales, also contributed to the Orientalism of the period.

One other English writer admired by Hawthorne should be mentioned here. Thomas De Quincey's works are laced with references to Arabia, India, Islam, Persian character, Zoroastrianism, the destruction of Palmyra, the degradation of women in Asia, and similar matter. According to Julian Hawthorne, his father was "a great reader of De Quincey's Essays." He read De Quincey aloud to his family in 1850–1851 and again after their return from England in the early 1860s.[84] Hawthorne wrote to his publisher in 1851: "You have sent me all De Quincey's writings, except the Opium Eater and the last published volume. I must, on some terms or other, have the rest of the set."[85] Although Hawthorne never met the brilliant stylist during his years in England, he surely experienced the "oriental imagery and mythological tortures" that engulfed De Quincey whenever he was in the grip of opium. The drug "transported him" into "the part of the earth most swarming with human life, the great officina gentium," with feelings of both sublimity and revulsion. "Under the connecting feeling of tropical heat and vertical sunlights," De Quincey wrote, "I brought together all creatures, birds, beasts, reptiles, all trees and plants, usages and appearances, that are found in all tropical regions, and assembled them together in China or Hindostan. From kindred feelings, I soon brought Egypt and her gods under the same law." "The mere antiquity of Asiatic things, of their institutions, histories,—above all, of their mythologies"—was so impressive to him as to overpower all sense of time and the individual.[86]

Hawthorne's English contemporaries Shelley, Keats, and Tennyson, whose works he read and admired, as well as George Meredith, Matthew Arnold, and Edward FitzGerald, all took turns at translating, imitating, parodying, or otherwise responding to the literature of Asia.[87] By mid-century England at large shared the sentiments George Eliot expressed in her review of Meredith's *The Shaving of Shagpat: an Arabian Entertainment* in 1856:

> No act of religious symbolism has a deeper root in nature than that of turning with reverence towards the East. For almost all our good things—our most precious vegetables, our noblest animals, our loveliest flowers, our arts, our religious and philosophical ideas, our very nursery tales and romances, have travelled to us from the East. In an historical as well as in a physical sense, the East is the Land of the Morning.[88]

Even the Sepoy Mutiny the following year and the termination of the East India Company did not destroy the enchantment of the Orient.

American Literary Orientalism

The enthusiasm for travel books about the East, as Mukhtar Ali Isani has shown, is as old in this country as Increase and Cotton Mather; it is not unlikely that the first set of Hakluyt's *Principall Navigations* reached the New World on the Mayflower when the British East India company was only twenty years old.[89] Even before Massachusetts, New York, and Philadelphia merchants commenced trading with the East Indies in the 1780s, American literature had begun to imitate the British and European response to the Orient. A visionary tale called "The Meditation of Cassim the son of Ahmed" appeared in the Boston *American Magazine and Historical Chronicle* as early as December 1746, and in 1779 Benjamin Franklin tried his hand at an "Arabian Tale" that was available to Hawthorne in Rufus Griswold's *The Prose Writers of America* (1847). Franklin's anecdote of the good magician Albumazar and his effort to find a philosophic justification for the existence of evil in the world suggests an acquaintance with the theodicy of Voltaire's Oriental tales as well as with the didactic fiction of the eighteenth century magazines in general.

A decade before Franklin's "Arabian Tale" a paper war between two literary societies at Princeton University produced what could be considered "the first American novel": Hugh Henry Brackenridge and Philip Freneau's *Father Bombo's Pilgrimage to Mecca* (1770). Following the fashion of mock-Oriental fiction, the authors sent their protagonist on a journey from America to Mecca disguised as a "devout musselman" and quoting Chaucer ("We jolly men passing over the Sea/For certain causes into a far countrie").[90] The novel's patina of Orientalism is mainly a matter of names and dress, Bombo's visit to Mecca is dispatched in two pages, and the work was not published until two centuries later. Nonetheless, it indicates the accessibility of the East to American writers in the generation before Hawthorne's birth. Freneau's oscillations between careers as a poet, political journalist, and East and West Indes man also foreshadowed, to some degree, Hawthorne's uncertainty about his own professional identity.

The Oriental tale became a significant genre in American fiction in the 1780s with the opening of trade in the Indian Ocean and China Sea, the proliferation of magazines, and a shift of public interest after the Revolution from political news towards lighter reading material. Well over a hundred Oriental stories appeared in the nation's magazines in the last fifteen years of the eighteenth century.[91] Which of these Hawthorne met in his retrospective browsings we can only surmise.

He was indubitably acquainted, however, with the "Mustapha Rub-a-dub Keli Khan" letters of Washington Irving, William Irving, and James Kirke Paulding (1807–1808), for he owned a copy of *Salmagundi* in which he inscribed his name in 1827.[92] The nine epistles from the "Tripolitanian prisoner of war 'at large' in New York" to "Asem Hacchem, principal slave-driver to his highness the Bashaw of Tripoli" and "Abdallah Eb'n al Rahab, surnamed the Snorer, military centinel at the gate of his highness's palace," gave new currency in America to the satirical "Eastern letters" popularized for a century by Morana, Montesquieu, Lyttelton, and Goldsmith. While it has been said that the authors of *Salmagundi* lacked the "sure sense of authority" and the coherent world view that give purpose to satire, and that they parodied a hackneyed tradition of travel writing, the Mustapha letters, nonetheless, showed "the most adept use of the Oriental observer in American literature prior to the Civil War."[93] Exposing the ridiculous in American politics and manners, Mustapha looked with wide-eyed wonder at the "infidel women" of the American "seraglios" who—though beautiful, vigorous, and scantily attired—"usurp the breeches of the men" and demonstrate the monstrousness of giving wives both a soul and a tongue.[94] Washington Irving pursued his early interest in travel literature and the imaginative possibilities of Islam during his explorations of Spain in 1826–1829, on his tour there as United States minister in 1842–1846, and in his three romantic histories of Christians and Moors: *The Conquest of Granada* (1829), *The Alhambra* (1832), which told stories and legends directly associated with *The Arabian Nights*, and *Mahomet and His Successors* (1850).

As the rage for the Orient intensified in the United States during the first two decades of the nineteenth century, abstract satiric and philosophic tales made way for more colorful adventures inspired by first-hand contacts with the East, the popularity of *The Arabian Nights*, and the verse dramas of Byron, Southey, and Moore. After its publication by H. & P. Rice of Philadelphia in 1794, *The Arabian Nights' Entertainment* became a best seller in America (selling over 40,000 copies in its first decade) and a perennial favorite for children and adults alike.[95] Irving, Longfellow, Poe, Melville, and Hawthorne all were touched by its magic.

Edgar Allan Poe was captivated by the Orient throughout his short life. All but five of the twenty-five *Tales of the Grotesque and the Arabesque* (1840) contain significant allusions or imagery drawn from *The Arabian Nights* and other Eastern sources.[96] Poe used bogus scholarly introductions to give an aura of authenticity to tales of voyages into remote and shadowy regions and glossed his texts with learned prefaces and footnotes in the manner of Robert Southey and Thomas Moore. "The Fall of the House of Usher" achieved a particularly "daring mixture of the Gothic and the Egyptian" modes of Romanticism.[97]

Whether Herman Melville had read *The Arabian Nights* by the time he was ten years old, like Byron, "the hero of his youth," we do not know, but the tales had a direct impact on his earliest published pieces, "Fragments from a Writing Desk." The "Fragments" are "permeated by an Oriental exoticism derived from Byron, Scott, and Thomas Moore."[98] Melville's major Eastern work, *Clarel* (1876), postdates the Civil War, but his *Mardi* (1849) and William Starbuck Mayo's popular *Kaloolah* (1849) reflected the diverse forms the Oriental tale had taken in America by the middle of the nineteenth century.

The growth of magazines for middle-class readers during the 1820s and 1830s and the popularity of gift books and annuals like *The Token*, where many of Hawthorne's earliest pieces appeared, created a market for works that represented the customs of the East in a diverting, decorative, yet uplifting manner. Paulding responded with some fifteen Oriental tales, mainly in the moral vein.[99] Nathaniel Parker Willis, Henry Wadsworth Longfellow, Richard Henry Stoddard, James Russell Lowell, Lydia Maria Child, William Cullen Bryant, and John Greenleaf Whittier, to name only a few others, added works of moral or emotional appeal. During the 1850s the public that had once taken to its heart the sentimental love story *Amir Khan* (1829) by child-poet Lucretia Maria Davidson was overrun with the sensationalized Eastern romances of Maturin Ballou, Sylvanus Cobb, and other hack writers. The new Biblical novel, of which Joseph Holt Ingraham's *The Prince of the House of David* (1855) is an early example, introduced another genre destined for a long life.

The most readable of the Eastern tales before the Civil War, however, were the travel narratives. Willis's lighthearted letters along his way from Italy to Greece and Turkey recorded the riches, dirt, and discomfort of the East while evincing a voyeuristic interest in the women he came across. After appearing irregularly in the New York *Mirror*, they were collected and republished in Willis's popular *Pencillings by the Way* (1835).

The most celebrated American traveler and storyteller of the generation was John Lloyd Stephens, an author, steamship executive, and victim of incurable wanderlust whose passion for ruins and lost civilizations electrified readers in the later 1830s. Stephens's *Incidents of Travel in Egypt, Arabia Petraea, and the Holy Land* (1837) was published in the same year as Hawthorne's *Twice-told Tales* and the Rev. William Ware's *Zenobia*, and his *Incidents of Travel in Greece, Turkey, Russia, and Poland* (1838) followed a year later. His travel letters from Egypt, Arabia Petraea, and the Holy Land appeared initially in the *Knickerbocker*, and Poe reviewed the book that first made him famous. Melville remembered seeing Stephens in church as a youth and wishing to follow the "wonderful Arabian traveller" home because he had lived with wild tribesmen, spent months in the valley of the Nile and among the ruins of Berenice, and journeyed from Cairo to the Holy Land dressed as an Egyptian merchant. The big eyes of Stephens long haunted Melville.[100]

While Hawthorne unquestionably knew the travel writings of Willis and Stephens, he took a greater personal interest in George William Curtis's *Nile Notes of a Howadji* (1851) and *The Howadji in Syria* (1852)—the first "a deliberately impressionistic and romantically hazy account" of a languorous journey along the Nile, the latter a more controlled narration of a "trek from Cairo across the Arabian desert to Jerusalem and thence to Damascus and Beirut."[101] Both works were based on Curtis's extended tour of Europe and the East in 1846–1850. Curtis became a resident of Brook Farm shortly after Hawthorne's departure, and when he moved to Concord in 1844 was a welcome guest at the Old Manse. This charming and quick-witted young man, who was then only twenty years old, spent many days with Hawthorne, and at least once they made a short trip together. Hawthorne probably encouraged the younger Curtis's budding interests in the East, and he later relived them vicariously when reading *Nile Notes* aloud to his family in the winter of 1850–1851.[102] The preface to *The Blithedale Romance* ends with a playful rebuke of "the brilliant Howadji" for making such a distant pilgrimage from his native land.

The "gay damsel" of Hawthorne's "The Seven Vagabonds" two decades earlier and his Oriental heroine in *The Blithedale Romance* show that he was not unresponsive to the types of scenes so passionately evoked by Curtis. Readers of the Howadji's letters to the New York *Tribune* and the resulting books were mesmerized by "that luscious expression, those gaudy alliterations, those vague allusions, those melting hues, that sadness and sweetness of the young poet's spirit."[103] Curtis's father had good reason to be disturbed by his son's visit to the Ghawazee, or dancing girls, of Egypt and his voluptuous portrayals both of the woman Kushuk, "for whom no surprises survive," and the modest Xenobi, who handed the Howadji his nargileh and "an electric chain of communication." Beneath the flowing veils "truth allow[ed] a beautiful bud-burstiness of bosom." Only after three successively more erotic chapters—"Fair Frailty," "Kushuk Arnem," and "Terpsichore"—did Curtis tear himself away from the sinuous houris of the Nile: "Farewell, Kushuk! Addio, still-eyed dove! Almost thou persuadest me to pleasure. O Wall-street! because you are virtuous, shall there be no more cakes and ales?"[104]

The next few years saw the publication of William DeForest's *Oriental Acquaintances* (1856) and Bayard Taylor's *A Journey to Central Africa; or, Life and Landscapes from Egypt to the Negro Kingdoms of the White Nile* (1854) and *The Lands of the Saracen* (1855). Although they appeared after Hawthorne's major work was done, they may have strengthened his determination to add to the literature of travel in *The Marble Faun* and *Our Old Home*. DeForest's account grew out of his observations in Asia Minor, Turkey, Palestine, and Syria beginning in 1846 and his residence in Beirut, where his brother conducted a girls' school. Unconcerned for the grand and marvelous, DeForest chatted about ordinary and even trivial affairs of the East in a tone similar to Willis's *Pencillings*.

Bayard Taylor's writings, on the other hand, were frankly escapist and steeped in physical sensation. He dedicated *The Lands of the Saracen* to

Washington Irving, who had confirmed his resolve to visit the East and "more than any other American author . . . revived the traditions, restored the history, and illustrated the character of that brilliant and heroic people."[105] Taylor's chapter "The Visions of Hasheesh" is still a gripping account of a bad narcotic trip, only slightly less terrifying than the Oriental nightmares of De Quincey's *Opium Eater*, and the following chapter, "A Dissertation on Bathing and Bodies," a memorable celebration of Circassian beauties. On the American lyceum circuit of the 1850s women swooned before Taylor's piercing glances, dashing beard, scimitar, and native Arab costume. "Doubtless many an American male gazed in the distance" after reading his description of the baths—"and drew on his cigar with a certain discontent."[106] Although there seems to have been no American equivalent to *The Lustful Turk* (1828), a blatantly pornographic novel of underground Victorian England, eroticism was a prominent element in the Eastern narratives and romances of this country too. Curtis, Taylor, and their contemporaries effectively dramatized the "sensuous, luxurious, languid and sense-satisfied spirit of Eastern life" as an antidote to the industry, bustle, and oppressive proprieties of life in the United States.[107]

While Hawthorne's retrospective readings in the periodical literature of England and America exposed him to a multitude of earlier Eastern tales, his own stories frequently appeared alongside contemporary Oriental subject matter. Robert Carter's "The Armenian's Daughter," for example, was serialized with "The Birth-mark" and "The Hall of Fantasy" in the short-lived *Pioneer* in 1843. "Drowne's Wooden Image" appeared in *Godey's Magazine* in 1844 three months after Poe's "A Tale of the Ragged Mountains" and a half year before his spoof "The Thousand-and-Second Tale of Scheherazade." The *Democratic Review*, the major outlet for Hawthorne's pieces from 1837 to 1845, regularly carried Eastern materials. Probably the busiest forum of all was the *Knickerbocker*, where Hawthorne placed "The Fountain of Youth" ("Dr. Heidegger's Experiment"), "A Bell's Biography," and "Edward Fane's Rosebud" in 1837. In nearly every issue after 1836 the New York monthly entertained its readers with correspondence, reviews, historical essays, and literary articles of all kinds on Eastern lands and life.

Publishing houses added titles and whole series on the East in response to the public's taste for travelogs and fictions. When Horatio Bridge's *Journal of an African Cruiser*, shaped and edited by Hawthorne, was printed in 1845, publishers Wiley & Putnam advertised on the back cover of the book a "Library of Choice Readings" starting with Alexander W. Kinglake's *Eothen; or Traces of Travel Brought Home from the East* and also including *The French in Algiers, Ancient Moral Tales: Evenings with the Old Story Tellers*, and Eliot Warburton's *The Crescent and the Cross*, all enthusiastically recommended by contemporary reviewers. Hawthorne reviewed five books from Wiley & Putnam's series "Library of American Books" and "Library of Choice Reading" in 1846–1847, and he published *Mosses from an Old Manse* with the firm in 1846.[108]

Essentially a Day-Dream, and Yet a Fact

The image of the "gorgeous East" that Hawthorne raised in "Fragments from the Journal of a Solitary Man" had begun to give way even in his time—under the collective influence of Asiatic societies, missionaries, German and English philologists, and in this country Ralph Waldo Emerson and the Transcendentalists—to a new myth of the "spiritual East." In the twentieth century the image of "royal" Asia has yielded even more completely to that of "mystical" Asia. "The Orient of the emperor and the spice merchant has become the Orient of the bonze and the sadhu."[109] It is clear from both his readings and his own works, however, that Hawthorne was drawn Eastward not by the Hindu scriptures and Persian love poetry of Sadi, Fergosi, and Hafiz that attracted the Transcendentalists, but by the adventure, storytelling, and exoticism that for centuries had made the "gorgeous East" the most common stereotype of Asia, and an antithesis to the West.

It is impossible fully to reawaken here the cavalcade of visionary scenes, figures, and events that drew Hawthorne's fancy to the works identified in this chapter. Models from his reading will be applied to the interpretation of individual tales and romances in the chapters following. Yet it is useful to sketch beforehand a few of the "strange landscapes" and "outlandish figures," especially those found in Hawthorne's borrowings from the Salem Athenaeum, that glimmered through the familiar walls of his chamber. Chaucer knew that "merchants are fathers of tidings and tales and that the wallets of shipmen and pilgrims are full of lies."[110] In the histories and narratives he read, Hawthorne found the same mixture of reportage and imagination that Chaucer had met on his travels and at the customs house in London. "Essentially a day-dream, and yet a fact," the East, as he later said of Brook Farm, offered Hawthorne "an available foothold between fiction and reality" (III, 2).

From the Middle Ages on, merchants and pilgrims approached the East in both fear and fascination, curiosity and censorship. For travelers by land the adventure usually began at the borders of the Ottoman Empire. Busbecq sensed the change from West to East when, venturing forth from Vienna on his embassy to Constantinople late in the sixteenth century, he was met by the Turkish horsemen and their beautifully caparisoned prancers: "a very pleasant Spectacle to a Man, unaccustomed to see such sights, for their Bucklers and Spears were curiously painted, their Sword-handles bedeck'd with Jewels, their Plumes of Feathers party-coloured, and the Coverings of their Heads were twisted with round Windings as white as Snow."[111] Two and a half centuries later, a typical pilgrim of the 1830s approached Jerusalem in a similar spirit, with "a crowd of thick-coming fancies, . . . a host of reminiscences" chasing each other through his mind. "I could scarcely believe the reality of the fact," he remarked, "that I was in that land whose wondrous history, associated with the earliest impressions of childhood, affords, year after year, new and increasing interest to those who will duly study its records."[112]

By the middle of the nineteenth century, the ease and frequency of travel had begun to demythologize the Middle East and to mechanize and commercialize its once romantic landscape. In a travel work Hawthorne doubtless knew, *Notes of a Journey from Cornhill to Grand Cairo by Way of Lisbon, Athens, Constantinople, and Jerusalem* (1846), based on an 1844 trip in the steamers of the Peninsular and Oriental Company, William Makepeace Thackeray both lauded the advances that made it possible for him to visit "as many men and cities" in two months "as Ulysses surveyed and noted in ten years" and lamented the ravages that time and technology had visited upon cultures of great antiquity: "There is no cursing and insulting of Giaours now. . . . [N]ow that dark Hassan sits in his divan and drinks champagne, and Selim has a French watch, and Zuleika perhaps takes Morison's pills, Byronism has become absurd instead of sublime. . . . The paddle-wheel is a great conqueror." Thackeray concluded, in Hawthorne-like fashion, "an allegory might be made showing how much stronger commerce is than chivalry, and finishing with a grand image of Mahomet's crescent being extinguished in Fulton's boiler."[113]

Over the next decades American literary pilgrims further deflated the image of the "gorgeous East" in satires and meditations like John Ross Browne's *Yusef* (1853), Twain's *The Innocents Abroad* (1870), and Melville's *Clarel* (1876).[114] Hawthorne's depictions of Eastern peoples and customs in the *American Magazine of Useful and Entertaining Knowledge* show that on occasion he could be just as skeptical and clear-eyed when regarding other cultures as his own. He remained inclined, however, to approach the East with the imaginative and romantic expectations that drew George William Curtis and Bayard Taylor thither in the 1840s and 1850s.

Well into the nineteenth century the historical and cultural landscape described by Eastern travelers offered a moral as well as scenic contrast to the states from which they had come. Leaving behind the democracy, comparative equality of the sexes, capitalistic individualism, and progressive ethos of the West, the accounts Hawthorne read transported him into a world unaffected by Puritan ethics of work and salvation, a world ancient, hierarchical, languid, nomadic, despotic, and luxurious—a world to be experienced, above all, through the senses. When physical hardship and predation daunted their early enthusiasm, the travelers resorted to Turkish baths, cooling sherbets, coffee, and dancing girls; nothing could be "more soothing and refreshing after a hard day's journey than a pipe and cup of coffee, which one is sure of obtaining everywhere, whatever else may be wanting."[115]

Western sojourners were continually discomposed by the lack of industry among the Turks, Persians, and Arabs. "Almost their whole Life is spent in Idleness," Joseph Pitton de Tournefort exclaimed; "to eat Rice, drink Water, smoke Tobacco, sip Coffee, is the life of a *Mussulman*." Carsten Niebuhr attributed both the vivacity and the indolence of the Arabs to climate; their laziness to the system of government. Baron de Tott wrote in a like vein: "If the climate which the Turks inhabit relaxes the Fibres, Despotism, by which they are enslaved, incites them to Violence." Yet, reflecting on the respective claims of pleasure and industry, Lady Montagu was "allmost of [the] opinion they have a right notion of Life; while they consume it in Music, Gardens, Wine and delicate eating, while we are tormenting our brains with some Scheme of Politics, or studying some Science to which we can never attain." Hawthorne might have weighed her words as she continued: "Considering what short liv'd, weak Animals Men are, is there any study so beneficial as the study of present pleasure? I dare not persue this theme; perhaps I have allready said too much. . . . [But] I had rather be a rich Effendi with all his ignorance, than Sir Isaac Newton with all his knowledge."[116]

In his note on "Turkish Idleness" in the *American Magazine of Useful and Entertaining Knowledge* for August 1836, Hawthorne's initial remark, "A Turk never works, if there is a possibility of being idle," led to further thoughts on the conduciveness of sedentary or standing postures to the mental exertions of literary men (AM, 492). His repeated castigations of his own "idleness" and the contrasts he drew in "The Custom-House" and elsewhere between literary triflers and men of real ambition and purpose gave him a natural affinity with the storytellers of the East. "Some of the voluptuous Grandees," Alexander Russell reported, "are lulled to sleep by soft music . . . or by Arabian Tales, which their slaves are taught to read, or repeat."[117] The telling of Arabian tales and recitation of Persian poetry were not a privilege only of monarchs. They were an instinctual product of the people and practiced by professional literati and the folk alike, whether in coffee shops or incidentally to daily life.

As a European infidel Carsten Niebuhr could not enter the mosques to hear "the sacred eloquence of Arabia." He did frequent "the coffee-houses in Arabia, Egypt, and Syria," however, "the only theatres for the exercise of profane eloquence," and observed poor scholars amusing their audiences with *The History of Antar* and other heroic or comic literature, all of which contained "some good morality." Mullahs of a more inventive spirit would devise their own tales and fables. Encouraged by modest rewards, they learned "to recite gracefully, or to compose tales and speeches with some success." At Aleppo Niebuhr had "heard of a man of distinction who studied for his own pleasure, yet had gone the round of all the coffee-houses in the city to pronounce moral harangues."[118] Richard Madden sent a similar report to the Earl of Blessington in 1826, observing that the "professed story tellers" of the East enjoyed "the same place in public estimation that poets do with us and that, while many of their anecdotes did not bear repetition, they usually were as pithy and pointed as Arabian proverbs. "The Arab *conversazioni*," Madden wrote, "are the very fairy reflections of 'the Arabian Nights.' . . . The Arabs of good condition assemble every evening in one another's houses; each brings his pipe and tobacco, and the gentleman of the house provides coffee and sherbet. I . . . was never more entertained."[119] The nighttime setting, the oral mode, the moral point, and the improvisational techniques of the secular storytellers of the East (also their association with the sacred eloquence of the mosque) all prefigure the design of Hawthorne's *The Story Teller*, which is discussed in Chapter 4.

The customs of the East, indeed the very architecture, cast the Western males into roles of voyeurs and Paul Prys left to imagine in the walled gardens and women's quarters of the seraglios scenes even more exotic than what greeted the eye in the marketplace. The most bizarre practices were reported. Travelers heard that the black eunuchs guarding the harems were "forc'd to use a Pipe in making Water, being depriv'd of the natural Conveyance in their Infancy." They sought and found much evidence of "Concubinage, Adultery, Bigamy, Incest, and all Vices of that Nature," including the "unnaturall sin."[120] Yet the inverted morality of the East produced a people of remarkable health and beauty. Their mixed blood seemed purer than that of the Christian, their children stronger and straighter, their tempers keener.

Long before Ingres's "Odalisque" (1825) visually transcribed Lady Mary Wortley Montagu's remarks about the inhabitants of the zenanas, or Theophile Gautier posed his famous question—"And the Women?" (1853)—Western travelers had fastened particularly on the dark-eyed houris of the East. Alexander Russell, himself a physician, found that "Medical people, whether europeans or natives, have access to the Harem, at all times when their attention is requisite."[121] Tournefort, on the other hand, excused himself from a detailed description of the wives and concubines of the seraglio, claiming "they fall no more under the Knowledge of the Senses, than so many pure spirits. These Beauties are intirely reserv'd to entertain the Sultan, and vex the miserable Eunuchs." In his official capacity as a botanist he had little reason to seek a closer acquaintance; however, he eventually rendered an account that, in similar form, runs throughout the Eastern narratives:

> The *Turkish* Women, according to the Report of our Countrymen at *Constantinople* and *Smyrna*, who see them at the Bath with liberty enough, are generally handsom and well-made. They have a delicate Skin, regular Features, and admirable Chest, and above all, black Eyes, and several of them are compleat Beauties. . . . Their Breasts are at full liberty under their Vest, without any restraint of Stays or Bodice: in a word, they are just as Nature has made them; whereas with us, by endeavouring by Machines of Iron and Whalebone to correct Nature, . . . the fine Women are frequently mere Counterfeits.

"Is it surprizing then," Tournefort queried, that the women of Europe "have Children crooked, or with false Shape?"[122]

In the 1820s Richard Madden thought the East still possessed "the loveliest women in the world": "Their beauty is particularly delicate, and the paleness of their features, and transparency of their fair complexions, are delightfully contrasted with the darkest hair, and with eyes as soft and black as the gazelle's. . . . [I]n their own figurative language, their 'eyes are full of sleep, and their hearts are full of passion.' "[123] A few years later the Egyptian wife of the British Vice Consul at Damietta perfectly satisfied her visitors' " preconceived notions of Eastern beauty—soft and languishing, with large swimming black eyes, to which the long lashes dyed at the roots with surmeh gave an extraordinary depth and brilliancy." She was arrayed in "a green velvet tunic embroidered with gold, reaching to the knees, and open in front; a petticoat of gorgeous silk resembling cloth of gold with a pattern of the gayest flowers, bound round the waist with a large Cashmere shawl; her bosom was covered with the thinnest gauze, which certainly answered no purpose of concealment."[124] The women of the East, however veiled or furtively glimpsed, prefigured the amorous, hyacinth-like virgins that Mohammed had promised to place among the magnificent palaces, the flowery fields, and the crystalline rivers of paradise.

In a medical capacity Richard Madden was privileged to look into "the *penetralia* of the harem" of the Turks, where decorum allowed him only to describe "what is fit to reach the ear, and, perhaps, a little less than met the eye." Expecting to find there nothing but misery, he was amazed to see that the apartments even of a middle-class pipe manufacturer were "furnished with costly carpets and richly covered divans." "Every thing was splendid," he announced. "Amongst the fair inmates of the harem, I could distinguish the pale Circassian from the languid Georgian, and the slender Greek from the voluptuous Ottoman." When denied access to private gardens and court-yards, travelers took their impressions of female pulchritude and bondage in the East from the slave bazaars, where they watched the inspection of "the black women of Darfur and Sennaar, and the copper-coloured beauties of Abyssinia" who were offered for sale.[125] Tournefort thought, "Nothing is so pleasant, as to see incessantly coming from *Hungary Greece, Candia, Russia, Mengrelia*, and *Georgia*, Swarms of young Wenches design'd for the Service of the *Turks*."[126] Tournefort, Madden, and their fellows described with fas-cination the scrutiny of the young women's faces, teeth, virginity, agility, sleeping postures, and naked forms, even while they condemned the Jews for their villainous trade of buying and training courtesans for the harem.

What was most remarkable to the observers from the West was that the women appeared in no way cast down after being miserably sundered from their families and countries. Their changeability and desire to serve their new lords seemed to lend some credence to the persistent, if mistaken, notion that women had no souls in Islam. The women of the East—capable of the highest devotion, chastity, and obedience; affectionate, subtle, quick-witted, civil, and ceremonious; gifted in the art of needlework and the spinet—were also capable of being "the wickedest Women in the World, Haughty, Furious, Perfidious, Deceitful, Cruel, and Impudent."[127] These lovely Fatimas enflamed even the more circumspect travel accounts read by Hawthorne, warming his bachelor chamber on many "a rainy winter's day" in Salem.

Lady Montagu defended her descriptions of the lush gardens of the East and their flower-like inhabitants by pointing out that romance was a way of life in the East, not mere poetic ornamentation. She insisted to one corre-spondent: "This is but too like (says you) the Arabian Tales; these embroi-dier'd Napkins, and a jewel as large as a Turkey's egg!—You forget, dear Sister, those very tales were writ by an Author of this Country, and (excepting the Enchantments) are a real representation of the manners here."[128] As the travelers journeyed on into Persia or Arabia and the Indies, they stepped ever

backwards into history and rediscovered, long before the gorgeous efflores-
cence of the Ottoman Turks, the ancient and simple childhood of mankind.
On entering Arabia, Carsten Niebuhr sensed at once the "liberty, independence, and simplicity" that Western man had lost by the excess of his civilization. "One can hardly help fancing one's self," he wrote, "suddenly carried
backwards to the ages which succeeded immediately after the flood. We are
here tempted to imagine ourselves among the old patriarchs, with whose
adventures we have been so much amused in our infant days." At the ex-
tremity of his travels, among the Parsee fire worshippers of Bombay, Niebuhr
felt an even greater age of days, and he speculated, two decades before Sir
William Jones arrived in Calcutta, that the examination of Indian antiquities
by Western scholars "would throw new light on those opinions and modes
of worship which were by degrees *diffused* through other parts of the east,
and *spread*, at last, into Europe."[129] Hawthorne needed to go no farther in
his search for "Faery Land."

PROVIDENCE, DESTINY, AND CHOICE OF LIFE IN THE EARLY TALES

"... with a little aid from philosophy and more from
religion, he journeyed on contentedly through life."

EARLY IN 1817, Nathaniel Hawthorne penned two quatrains to which he
gave the title "Moderate Views":

> With passions unruffled, untainted by pride,
> By reason my life let me square.
> The wants of my nature are cheaply supplied,
> And the rest are but folly and care.
>
> How vainly through infinite trouble and strife,
> The many their labours employ,
> Since all that is truly delightful in life,
> Is what all if they please may enjoy.[1]

Noting that it is "a rather extraordinary poem" for a twelve-year old, Manning
Hawthorne asked us to remember "how often this moral and sentitious [sic]
little boy had read *The Pilgrim's Progress*" and hoped that such moods were
infrequent for, if not, "he would have been an insufferable little prig."[2] Bun-

yan's seventeenth century allegory was a favorite of Hawthorne's childhood, but the association is not especially pertinent to the boy's Augustan poem of passion and reason, vain labors and simple wants. Nor, whether in private or public writings, did the author outgrow this precocious wisdom. Two decades later he wrote down the idea for a story that would dramatize the same sentiment concluding: "Moral, that what we need for our happiness is often close at hand, if we knew but how to seek for it."[3]

Reconciling oneself to the portion of life allotted by fate, seeking happiness at home, avoiding the temptation to "gather gold"—these were a consistent theme throughout Hawthorne's life and writing, whatever the ambition and acquisitiveness of his contemporaries. Before embarking on his career as a wandering storyteller, the narrator of "Passages from a Relinquished Work," "heir to a moderate competence," vows to stand "aloof from the regular business of life. This would have been a dangerous resolution, any where in the world," he observes; "it was fatal in New-England. There is a grossness in the conceptions of my countrymen; they will not be convinced that any good thing may consist with what they call idleness" (X, 407). Years later Elizabeth Hawthorne wrote of her brother's "characteristic notion . . . that he should like a competent income that would neither increase nor diminish." He turned his back on the pursuit of wealth for fear that it would "engross too much of his attention."[4]

The prescience of "Moderate Views" for Hawthorne's conduct of life is further indicated by a newly recovered number of the *Spectator*, Hawthorne's hand-lettered family newspaper, that was written in February 1822 during the winter vacation of his freshman year at Bowdoin College. His juvenile poetry particularly adumbrates the two leading essays, "On Idleness" and "On Ambition." This issue, Thomas Woodson has pointed out, shows "a higher level of intellectual and stylistic control than he could command" in August and September 1820 when preparing the first six *Spectators*, as well as "a new interest in prose moralizing." Observing "with philosophic eye, our Fellow Creatures," the essayist remarks:

Others place their hopes of happiness in gold, in the search of which they consume their lives. And having found it, they are more wretched than before. Others strive to climb the heights of literary Glory, and to bask in the sun shine of the Muses. All are employed, all are anxious, all are miserable but ourselves. Such are the advantages of Idleness.

He admits, however, that "to enjoy even Idleness, a man must have food, and food, unfortunately, cannot be obtained without Labour"—and so ends by yielding "with Patience, to the decrees of Providence."[5]

Hawthorne's measured counterpoints of reason and passion, Idleness and Ambition, with a final concession to the decrees of great Providence, are neither in the tradition of the seventeenth-century allegorists with whom he is usually linked, nor of the nineteenth-century romantics, but of the eighteenth-century essayists from Addison and Steele to Samuel Johnson and Oliver Goldsmith.[6] As the title and contents of his *Spectator* illustrate, Hawthorne fashioned his image of the profession and decorum of authorship largely after eighteenth-century models. From them he derived not only lessons in graceful and balanced discourse but themes and attitudes on religion, science, and human conduct that came to characterize a significant portion of his own tales and sketches. The control of fancy by reason, the reconciliation of solitude and society, the pursuit of wisdom, the fleeting nature of happiness, the virtues of domestic life, the governance of passion—all these propositions were imbued with life in the fictional narratives and periodical writings of the previous century. How congenial Hawthorne found the eighteenth-century synthesis of instruction and entertainment, morality and wit, and how proficient he was in its style are evident from his various prefaces, his books for children, his editorship of the *American Magazine of Useful and Entertaining Knowledge*, and his immersion in the *Gentleman's Magazine*.

While reading Johnson, Goldsmith, and the lighter English essayists of the first half of the century, Hawthorne also looked beyond the Channel to the writings of the French *philosophes*, who shared their English contemporaries' propensity for moral and philosophical fiction, their love of satire, and their early romantic spirit.[7] Hawthorne turned periodically to Rousseau's treatises on the inherent equality of man and the corrupting effects of civilization, but he made a particularly thorough study of Voltaire's *Oeuvres*. There, alongside corrosive satires on French clericalism and manners, he found a theism that reconciled rationality and belief, determinism and providence, natural religion and revelation.

Following the publication of *Les Mille et une Nuit*, the essayist-philosophers of England and France brought the Oriental tale into its Western vogue. In the abstract, the Orient offered eighteenth-century satirists an exotic but safely remote ground from which to assail the bigotry and artificialities of their societies. The more accomplished moral and philosophical tales, however—works like Samuel Johnson's *The History of Rasselas: Prince of Abissinia* and Voltaire's *Zadig*—reflected close study and specific knowledge of the history, doctrines, literature, and customs of the Eastern cultures that they introduced as foils to Western society. Bernard Picart's *Religious Ceremonies and Customs* (1731), George Sale's translation and "Historical Discourse" on the Koran (1734), and other comparativist historical and cultural studies of the time brought the practices of Western Christendom firmly before the bar of Eastern religions and creeds.

The East was a continuous factor in Hawthorne's experiences before, during, and after his years at Bowdoin. As he sought to make his choice of life, he mused over his father's shiplogs and imagined what it would be like to sail away on a Salem East Indiaman. While dropping anchor again on Herbert Street in Salem, he immersed himself in Eastern voyages and travels. We would expect his early tales to show the effects of the eighteenth-century English and French authors and their Oriental fables. Indeed, three of his first efforts drew significantly from the Orientalism of the previous century. *Fanshawe* and "The Wives of the Dead" reflect his reading, respectively, of Johnson's *Rasselas* and Voltaire's *Zadig*. "The Gentle Boy" was influenced, generally, by a convention of invidious comparisons between Muslim hospitality and Christian intolerance and, specifically, by Sir Paul Rycaut's *History of the Turkish Empire*.

Fanshawe: The Happy Valley

Like many first works, *Fanshawe, A Tale*, which Hawthorne began to write at or shortly after college, is peculiarly interesting for the transparency of the author's early life and readings. The novel is a pastiche of half-formed characters and ideas. Hawthorne paid for its publication by Marsh & Capen of Boston in 1828 but, soon feeling its lack of unity and finish, withdrew the anonymous book from circulation and refused to acknowledge it afterwards. A melodrama of villainy, stormy nights, taverns, and near rape, *Fanshawe* is most often compared to the Gothic thrillers of Charles Robert Maturin and "Monk" Lewis and to the romances of Walter Scott. The three young men who lay claim to the fair Ellen Langton—the violent and rapacious Butler, the handsome and worldly Edward Walcott, and the cloistered, scholarly Fanshawe—resemble types from the Gothic tradition while the "racing and chasing o'er Cannobie Lee" is patent Scott. According to Edward Wagenknecht, "Every feature of [Scott's] technique was dutifully imitated: his use of epigraphs, his habit of throwing the scene back into the past, his weaving back and forth from one set of characters to another, and much besides."[8]

Beyond the theatrics of Scott and his precursors, however, there are several Oriental patterns in *Fanshawe* that, once recognized, will take us still closer to Hawthorne's informing idea for the work. Martha Conant noted that, "In a study of the oriental tale in England in the eighteenth century, the high lights fall upon the *Arabian Nights*, Dr. Johnson's *Rasselas*, Goldsmith's *Citizen of the World*, and Beckford's *Vathek*."[9] Of these four, only Goldsmith's Chinese traveler fails to make an appearance in Hawthorne's first novel. The effects of *The Arabian Nights* and *Vathek* are mainly atmospheric, but Johnson's tale of the Happy Valley is central to as much meaning as the novel has.

Hawthorne's initial call to the East derived from a slightly later source. Southey's *Thalaba the Destroyer* provided the epigraph on the title page of *Fanshawe*: "Wilt thou go with me?" With this incantation a divine Damsel summoned Thalaba on his enchanted flight to Tunis, where he smote the demon hoards of Domdaniel. (To the Damsel's appeal, thrice spoken, Thalaba twice answered: "Sail on, in Allah's name!")[10] The editors of the Autograph Edition of *Fanshawe* thought this "a curiously appropriate motto for all of Hawthorne's writings; for it has a wistful, mournful cadence, and its invitation is like a beckoning hand."[11] At least it gave notice that his travelers and quests would not be limited to the soil and sunlight of contemporary New England. Hawthorne seems to have had *The Curse of Kehama* also in mind when he conceived Butler's first exchange with Ellen Langton:

'Your father,' he began—'Do you not love him? Would you do aught for his welfare?'

'Every thing that a father could ask, I would do,' exclaimed Ellen eagerly.
'Where is my father; and when shall I meet him?'

'It must depend upon yourself, whether you shall meet him in a few days or never.' (III, 361)

When the evil Oriental potentate Kehama attempted to woo fair Kailyal for his consort in Southey's Hindu romance, he did so by holding her father, Ladurlad, hostage.

Hawthorne's allusions to *Vathek* and *The Arabian Nights* serve chiefly to deepen the Gothic-Oriental twilight of his tale, especially in relation to the dark figure Butler. The "mysterious and unearthly power in Fanshawe's voice" and the "bright and steady eye" that force Butler to retire early in the novel are reminiscent of Vathek's killing stare. When he was angered, the Caliph's eye "became so terrible, that no person could bear to behold it."[12] Hawthorne showed his acquaintance also with "The Fourth Voyage of Sindbad the Sea-man" and the "Tale of the Prince and the Ogress" when he described the hags at the bedside of Butler's dying mother. Their womanly dispositions to comfort the afflicted had been "depraved into an odious love of scenes of pain, and death and sorrow. Such women are like the Gouls of the Arabian Tales, whose feasting was among tombstones, and upon dead carcasses" (III, 445).

Hawthorne interjected further symbolism from *The Arabian Nights* when Butler makes his first appearance in the guise of the "angler." The analogy to human life is obvious when Ellen muses on the fate of a famous trout: "How many pleasant caves and recesses there must be, under these banks, where he may be happy! May there not be happiness in the life of a fish?" To which Fanshawe responds: "Yes, there may be happiness, though such as few would envy;—but then the hook and the line—" (III, 354).[13] In "The History of the Young King of the Black Isles" Scheherazade tells the tale of an unfaithful queen who changed her husband's town and its inhabitants into a lake full of fish, which a poor fisherman then caught and brought before the sultan. When Hawthorne visited Samuel Johnson's childhood home dec-ades later, the Minster Pool at Lichfield reminded him of the lake in the Arabian Tales. He wrote in *Our Old Home*: "Some little children stood on the edge of the Pool, angling with pin-hooks; and the scene reminded me . . . of that mysterious lake in the Arabian Nights which had once been a palace and a city, and where a fisherman used to pull out the former inhab-itants in the guise of enchanted fishes" (V, 124).

Hawthorne's association of Samuel Johnson with *The Arabian Nights* is not capricious, for he mulled over the teachings of Johnson's most famous Oriental tale throughout his writing career. Hyatt Waggoner has associated Hawthorne's *blithe dale* with Johnson's Happy Valley, and Bernard Cohen has observed that the influence of *Rasselas* in *Septimius Felton* merits further examination, "for both works explore the vast implications of man's pursuit of happiness and the limitations of that quest."[14] At the beginning of his novel writing career, as at the end, Hawthorne drew on Johnson's Oriental tale for both an articulate setting and for the moral of his work. Behind the cluttered stage effects of ravening villains, ghoulish beldames, endangered chastity, and chases through the night the core of meaning in *Fanshawe* is the "choice of life" to be made, primarily, by Hawthorne's title character and, secondarily, by both Ellen Langton and Edward Walcott.

While considering the *Rasselas*-like setting and theme of *Fanshawe*, it is important to remember the extent of Hawthorne's affection for his English antecedent. He testified repeatedly—in his characterization in *Biographical Stories for Children* (1842), in the notebooks he kept while in England, and in the chapter "Lichfield and Uttoxeter" of *Our Old Home* (1863)—to the influence of "the great English Moralist." Hawthorne wrote in *Our Old Home* that he had become acquainted with Johnson's "sturdy English character . . . at a very early period of my life, through the good offices of Mr. Boswell," and that he seemed as familiar "to my mind's eye, as the kindly figure of my own grandfather" (V, 121-122). He was particularly moved by the story of Johnson's penance in the marketplace at Uttoxeter for his refusal, as a boy, to tend the family bookstall one day when his father was ill.

Dr. Johnson's morality, "as English an article as a beef-steak," gave a wholesome ballast to Hawthorne, whose "native propensities were towards Fairy Land." Hawthorne named only the "stern and masculine poems, 'London,' and 'The Vanity of Human Wishes,'" as productions he had cared about (V, 122-123). But there is no question of his thorough and lasting acquaintance with *Rasselas*, which long has been regarded as a prose version of "The Vanity of Human Wishes." At Bowdoin, Hawthorne joined with others in donating a set of Johnson's works to the Athenean Society library,[15] and a dozen years later, while writing a note on new "Lightning Rods" of Belgium and the Netherlands for the *American Magazine*, he "derive[d] the same moral from the result, as from the tale of the astronomer in Rasselas,— that the administration of the Elemental Kingdom would only be changed for the worse, by the interference of man" (AM, 442).

Johnson's tale of the "choice of life"—as he first thought to title *Rasselas*— appealed to Hawthorne especially in that unsettled period after the doors of Bowdoin had shut behind him in 1825, and, back home in the seaport of Salem, he struggled to choose between the workaday world of the Mannings, the Hawthornes' hereditary life at sea, and "idle" authorship. "Those, on whom the iron gate had once closed," Johnson warned of the Happy Valley, "were never suffered to return."[16] Then and afterwards the Bowdoin graduate wrestled with the same alternatives of solitude and worldly affairs, study and labor, celibacy and marriage, happiness and fame, reality and "the dangerous prevalence of imagination" that afflicted Johnson's Abyssinian prince.

Rasselas, which culminated Johnson's Oriental fictions in the *Rambler* and the *Idler*, was substantially more authoritative than the conventional periodical tales of the age. While the Eastern pundits and interrogators of eighteenth-century French and English literature often were little more than stereotypes and while Johnson, too, expounded his own philosophy of life through Rasselas, Imlac, and their fellow travelers, he did so with close knowledge of the history, topography, and legends of Abyssinia. His first book was the translation *A Voyage to Abyssinia by Father Jerome Lobo, a Portuguese Jesuit* (1735), from the French of Joachim Le Grand. Among other narratives, histories, and travels Johnson knew prior to writing *Rasselas* was Hiob Ludolf's *A New History of Ethiopia. Being a Full and Accurate Description of the Kingdom of Abessinia, Vulgarly, though Erroneously Called the Empire of Prester John* (1682). Ludolf was a renowned German scholar of the Abyssinian language, and he began his treatise by tracing the name of the nation and the origin of its natives, who "came out of that Part of *Arabia* which is called *The Happy*, which adjoyns to the *Red-Sea*: and from whence there is an easie Passage into *Africa*."[17]

When Hawthorne withdrew Ludolf's *History of Ethiopia* from the Salem Athenaeum in August 1836, he found detailed information on the mountains and rock formations of "Arabia the Happy" as well as on the political, ecclesiastical, and private affairs of its people.[18] But he already knew Ethiopia well from his reading of James Bruce's *Travels to Discover the Source of the Nile* in 1833, Richard Pococke's *A Description of the East and Some Other Countries* in 1831, and—simultaneous with his work on *Fanshawe—The Famous Voyages & Travailes of Vincent Le Blanc* in March 1827. Le Blanc's account, which authenticated the geography and customs of Ethiopia that Johnson put to use in *Rasselas*, designated two Ethiopias (one east of the Red Sea in Arabia the Happy, the other in Africa under Egypt), described the isolated monasteries of the land, and paid special attention to the seclusion of the royal princes at the carefully guarded mountain *Amara*, a place of wondrous "height, extent, beauty, and richnesse." This "terrestriall Paradise," Le Blance wrote, was "exceeding high, constituted of a rock cut like a wall, of difficult ascent, but onely by one certain way. There are Palaces and Gardens for accommodation of the Princes and their People."[19] Like the Jesuit missionaries and Portuguese navigators who had opened a road between the Ethiopian Christians and the Church of Rome, Le Blanc identified the Negus with Prester John, the legendary priest-king of the East, whose realm was rumored to be a paradise on earth, a land of peace, justice, and natural abundance where avarice and strife were unknown. Le Blanc distinguished the "lesser *India*" of his Prester John from the "high *India*" of the figure in medieval Christian legends.

Hawthorne's depiction of landscape and topography in *Fanshawe* is the most overt evidence that he had the mountain retreat of Amara and Johnson's Happy Valley in mind when constructing the novel. The obvious use of his collegiate experience and the possibility that he began the novel while still at Bowdoin have led most critics to assume, simply, "Harley College represents Bowdoin,"[20] notwithstanding the fact that Hawthorne sets the events of his tale eighty years in the past, long before the actual founding of the college in 1794. "Not only is Harley College Bowdoin," Manning Hawthorne said, "but its setting is Brunswick. The forests, the brook, the tavern—all are those of the college town in which he lived."[21] While scenic details in *Fanshawe* do celebrate Hawthorne's college haunts and experiences, the too easy equation of Harley College with Bowdoin has depreciated the moral significance of the setting Hawthorne created for his novel.

The young author made an explicit association between his "little academy" and Johnson's "palace in a valley" beginning with the second paragraph of *Fanshawe*:

> The local situation of the college, so far secluded from the sight and sound of the busy world, is peculiarly favorable to the moral, if not to the literary habits of its students. . . . The humble edifices rear themselves almost at the farthest extremity of a narrow vale, which, winding through a long extent of hill-country, is well nigh as inaccessible, except at one point, as the Happy Valley of Abyssinia. A stream, that farther on becomes a considerable river, takes its rise at a short distance above the College, and affords, along its wood-fringed banks, many shady retreats, where even study is pleasant, and idleness delicious. (III, 334)

The secluded valley, locked in interior hill country, bears little resemblance to the coastal locale of Bowdoin College. "There were no hills to break the monotony" of Brunswick, Manning Hawthorne conceded, only "the flat plains" and "pine forests."[22] Nonetheless, Hawthorne specified the *valley* setting of Harley College thirteen times in *Fanshawe*. It was not an image he used casually or otherwise associated with the New England landscape. *Valley* appears not at all in *The Scarlet Letter* or *The Blithedale Romance* and just twice in *The House of the Seven Gables*, both times in direct reference to Johnson's Happy Valley. Only after moving his setting to the Mediterranean homeland of Donatello in *The Marble Faun* did Hawthorne again employ this topographical term in his novels.[23]

Having once associated his setting with the Happy Valley, Hawthorne could have expected his readers to recognize further similarities. Above the hills the starlit heavens alternated with "Egyptian" darkness (III, 398). The "hidden wonders, of rock, and precipice, and cave" in the valley of *Fanshawe* (III, 345) have less to do with what Horatio Bridge called "the tame scenery of the Brunswick Plains" than with the unscalable walls of Amara described by Le Blanc or the "cavern in the side of a mountain" occupied by Johnson's hermit.[24] Caverns and precipices were portrayed as indigenous landforms of the East, not only in the imaginative *Arabian Nights, Vathek,* and the verse narratives of Southey, but also in the Eastern geographies and travels Hawthorne read. As in the Bible, caves were depicted there as customary habitations for thieves, prophets, and mendicants.[25] Hawthorne might also have reconfigured a favorite fishing stream near Bowdoin and the larger Androscoggin River with Abyssinia and the legendary Fountains of the Nile in mind. In both *Rasselas* and *Fanshawe* streams offer an egress to the world beyond the valley, but one blocked by cataracts. The lake that fed the verdant and fertile life of Johnson's Happy Valley "discharged its superfluities by a stream which entered a dark cleft of the mountain on the northern side, and fell with a dreadful noise from precipice to precipice till it was heard no more."[26] Similarly "the most singular and beautiful object" in the landscape at Harley

College is "a tiny fount of chrystal water, that gushes forth from the high, smooth forehead of the cliff" (III, 437–438). Nile-like, the little stream in *Fanshawe* becomes a broad and deep river, "rendered incapable of navigation" in parts of its course "by the occasional interruption of rapids" (III, 345).

By moving his little academy to a secluded valley at the headwaters of a mighty river Hawthorne, like Johnson, accentuates the contrast between a garden of innocent delights and the world beyond the mountains "where discord was always raging, and where man preyed upon man."[27] At the end of the Nile lay the populous city of Cairo, where Rasselas and his companions go to experience the vicissitudes and miseries of public life. Hawthorne makes a similar counterpoint between his lonely valley and the busy international seaport from which Dr. Melmoth brings his young charge, Ellen Langton, early in *Fanshawe*. The seaport is readily identifiable with Salem or Boston. Butler, who follows Ellen into the valley, "has felt the burning breeze of the Indies, East and West" (III, 372). "The glow of many a hotter sun than ours has darkened his brow," Edward observes, "and his step and air have something foreign in them, like what we see in sailors, who have lived more in other countries than in their own" (III, 355). Like the merchants and captains of Hawthorne's home town, Ellen's father was personally "engaged in mercantile pursuits, in a foreign country." Once he had "set his heart to gather gold," he gave up all hope of happiness, and only after the death of his wife and sister did he realize, suddenly, how much he had sacrified "in the acquisition of what is only valuable as it contributes to the happiness of life" (III, 338–339). Butler had been a protege of Mr. Langton before turning to a life of piracy on the *Black Andrew* in company with the local innkeeper Hugh Crombie.

The New England seaport plays a role in *Fanshaw* like that of Cairo in *Rasselas* as a place of envy, vice, and acquisitiveness. In Hawthorne's novel, however, the travelers' directions are reversed; here calamitous life invades the Happy Valley and seeks to remove its fairest inhabitants. The author's reluctance to send his title character out of the valley is consistent with his remark: "The students, indeed, ignorant of their own bliss, sometimes wished to hasten the time of their entrance on the business of life; but they found, in after years, that many of their happiest remembrances—many of the scenes which they would with least reluctance live over again—referred to the seat of their early studies" (III, 336).

Hawthorne's mode of characterization in *Fanshawe*, like the setting of the novel, infuses his American materials with the Orientalism of *Rasselas*. He introduces the scholarly Fanshawe through imagery appropriate to Johnson's prince-in-exile. "There was a *nobleness* on his high forehead, which time would have deepened into *majesty.* . . . The expression of his countenance was not a melancholy one;—on the contrary, it was *proud and high*—perhaps triumphant—like one who was *a ruler in a world of his own*, and independent of the beings that surrounded him" (III, 346).[28] Ellen Langton bears some resemblance to Rasselas's sister Nekayah as well as to her maid Pekuah, who was kidnapped and held for ransom by an Arab chief. Her plight in Butler's hands realizes Rasselas's romantic reveries of discovering an "orphan virgin robbed of her little portion by a treacherous lover, and crying after him for restitution and redress."[29] Believed momentarily to have been orphaned by her father's loss at sea, Ellen is set upon by the lustful Butler, who threatens to rob her of both her virginity and her inheritance until she is saved through Fanshawe's bravery.

As both the teacher and the moral guide of the young collegians placed in his care, Dr. Melmoth plays a role not unlike that of the sage Imlac, to whom Rasselas turns as "my sole director in the *choice of life*."[30] Melmoth's sedentary state at first appears far different from Imlac's life of travel through all parts of Egypt, Arabia, Palestine, Persia, and India as far as Agra and the court of the Great Mogul. Yet he is superior in worldliness to Fanshawe, was educated elsewhere, and corresponds with men of the world. Imlac's appraisal of his personal history also describes the mortal pilgrimage of Dr. Melmoth: "The life that is devoted to knowledge passes silently away, and is very little diversified by events. To talk in publick, to think in solitude, to read and to hear, to inquire, and answer inquiries, is the business of the scholar." Their experiences in the world brought the teachers to similar philosophies of life. His two decades of wandering through the East showed Imlac, "Human life is every where a state in which much is to be endured, and little to be enjoyed."[31] Twenty years of the "matrimonial yoke" taught Dr. Melmoth that "so long as the balance is on the side of happiness, a wise man will not murmur. . . . With a little aid from philosophy and more from religion, he journeyed on contentedly through life" (III, 336–337). The narrator in *Fanshawe* concurs, "That man has little right to complain who possesses so much as one corner in the world, where he may be happy or miserable, as best suits him" (III, 337).

If neither Fanshawe nor Dr. Melmoth matches the cosmopolitanism of Johnson's originals, it is partly because of the different conceptions of the two works. *Rasselas* is dialogic; the pupil and his teacher debate the various sides of such events and witnesses of life as come before them. Hawthorne, adopting a dramatic form, doubled both his master and apprentice figures. Dr. Melmoth and John Langton represent, respectively, the scholar and the man of affairs; Fanshawe and Edward Walcott, the introspective student and the well-bred socialite. The choices of life are externalized in Hawthorne's novel and the uncertainties of happiness dramatized in the pairs of characters.

While the plot of *Fanshawe* hinges on the attempted seduction of Ellen Langton by Butler and their pursuit by Edward Walcott, its meaning, finally, resides in the choice of life made by Fanshawe, whose attenuated journey from his scholastic cloister into the society of human love and sorrow reenacts the journey of experience by which Rasselas learned the ways of the world. For all his regal bearings young Fanshawe "had hitherto deemed himself unconnected with the world, unconcerned in its feelings, and uninfluenced by it in any of his pursuits." His lofty citadel of thought and his dreams of undying fame begin to yield, however, as the lovely, this-worldly Ellen stirs unaccustomed feelings in his heart. Under her influence he starts to question the years of solitude during which he "scorned to mingle with the living world" and to ask "to what purpose was all this destructive labor, and where was the happiness of superior knowledge?" Had he thrown his life away only to discover "that, after a thousand such lives, he should still know comparatively nothing?"

> But now he felt the first thrilling of one of the many ties, that, so long as we breathe the common air (and who shall say how much longer?) unite us to our kind. The sound of a soft, sweet voice—the glance of a gentle eye—had wrought a change upon him, and, in his ardent mind, a few hours had done the work of many. Almost in spite of himself, the new sensation was inexpressibly delightful. The recollection of his ruined health—of his habits, so much at variance with those of the world—all the difficulties that reason suggested—were inadequate to check the exulting tide of hope and joy. (III, 350–351)

Ellen's presence physically strengthens Fanshawe for a time. The possibility of earthly happiness brings a glow to his cheek and a reprieve from the grave even while he "reasoned calmly with himself" about the hopelessness of winning her love.

After Fanshawe resolutely saves Ellen from Butler, and gains new rights and privileges thereby, his emergence into the world reaches a crisis. "His strong affections rose up against his reason, whispering that bliss—on earth and in Heaven, through time and Eternity—might yet be his lot with her" (II, 456). Coming upon Fanshawe in a state of imagined joy, Ellen offers herself to him with gratitude and genuine affection. "Can it be misery," she asks— "will it not be happiness to form the tie that shall connect you to the world?— to be your guide—a humble one, it is true, but one of your choice—to the quiet paths, from which your proud and lonely thoughts have estranged you?" Fanshawe declines Ellen's offer with a Jamesian scruple—"I have no way to prove that I deserve your generosity, but by refusing to take advantage of it"—out of respect for Walcott's prior claim on her heart and the need to preserve his integrity in the face of a selfish passion (III, 458).

Fanshawe's triumph over the "affections" and "sensations" aroused by Ellen as well as over his dreams of immortal fame corresponds, in a degree, to Rasselas's lessened ambitions on his return to the Happy Valley. "No man," after all, as Nekayah said, "can, at the same time, fill his cup from the source and from the mouth of the Nile."[32] Fanshawe's withdrawal from the world and rededication to the killing studies that reason tells him must be his fate would seem to dramatize the eighteenth century's ethic of "happiness as virtue practiced by a saddened individual."[33] Returning to the deep recesses of one's own heart, after a wearying search for worldly riches and honor, is both a conventional theme in English Oriental tales and one firmly rooted in Eastern notions of affliction and destiny. While refusing the blessings of domestic comfort, Fanshawe still makes his choice and is content. On balance, he is presented as more the master than a casualty of his own life.

At the same time, Fanshawe's last words to Ellen, beneath their surface sentimentality, are open to more satiric interpretations. "When you hear that I am in my grave," Fanshawe beseeches her, "do not imagine that you have hastened me thither. Think that you scattered bright dreams around my pathway—an ideal happiness, that you would have sacrificed your own to realize" (III, 459). Fanshawe's quest for an *ideal happiness* has incapacitated him to accept the *real* happinesses of this world. Just how critical Hawthorne is of his young scholar it is difficult to state with assurance, but he surely knew the admonitions of Goldsmith's Chinese traveler, Hingpo, who told his allegory about the *"valley of ignorance"* to prove the futility of spending one's life in the pursuit of wisdom. "I begin to have doubts whether wisdom be alone sufficient to make us happy," Hingpo wrote. "A mind too vigorous and active, serves only to consume the body to which it is joined, as the richest jewels are soonest found to wear their settings."[34] Or as Imlac mildly admonished Rasselas: "While you are making the choice of life, you neglect to live."[35]

Is Fanshawe's refusal of earthly affections to be taken as an act of virtue or a relapse into romantic fancy? Hawthorne himself might not have been sure. The young scholar's reason for renouncing not only passion, pride, and the vain labors of the world but also the "connection" Ellen offers is never clearly explained. Whatever sensations he learns through Ellen, the experience makes no lasting change in his conduct nor stays the retreat back into his own happy valley. It could be said of Fanshawe at the end of his tale, as of Rasselas at the beginning of his, that he felt "some complacence in his own perspicacity" and received "some solace of the miseries of life, from consciousness of the delicacy with which he felt" them.[36] Insofar as Fanshawe's fate was modeled partly after Gorham Deane, the second scholar in Hawthorne's class, who died of overstudy a few weeks before the Bowdoin commencement, Hawthorne probably was inclined to treat the figure sympathetically.[37] But Fanshawe is not the author's final word, and his claims to "reason" veer perilously close to the way Johnson used the term "fancy" in his chapter "The Dangerous Prevalence of Imagination," where Imlac said of the intellectual disorders common to scholars and authors: "To indulge the power of fiction, and send imagination out upon the wing, is often the sport of those who delight too much in silent speculation."[38]

The ambiguity in Hawthorne's point of view concerning Fanshawe reflects the uncertainties found in Johnson's Oriental fable itself. Critics have come to question the once common notion that *Rasselas* simply repeated in prose Johnson's call in "The Vanity of Human Wishes" for "a healthful Mind,/ Obedient Passions, and a Will resign'd." John Aden, for instance, has read *Rasselas* as a wry, ironic demonstration that whatever little life can afford "is to be found in Cairo, the world, and not in the Happy Valley," and William Kenney has seen the tale as an argument for diversification of activities, at least, "in such a way that both satiety and its consequent withdrawal into an unhealthy solitude can be avoided."[39] While it is unlikely that Hawthorne looked for much irony in one whose "gross diet" he later contrasted so markedly with his own propensities towards Fairy Land, he hardly could have misunderstood Johnson's instructive tales of the hermit and the astronomer, which demonstrated that solitude is propitious to neither goodness nor wisdom. In his isolation Johnson's astronomer nurtured the illusion that he had the awful responsibility of governing the weather. Only the tender solicitude of Princess Nekayah and Pekuah rescued the astronomer from the "mists" of fancy and brought him to the realization: "I have purchased knowledge at the expense of all the common comforts of life: I have missed the endearing elegance of female friendship, and the happy commerce of domestick tenderness."[40] In their earlier dialogue on the consequences of domestic life, Nekayah had made the persuasive argument to Rasselas that the single life "is not retreat but exclusion from mankind"—adding, "Marriage has many pains, but celibacy has no pleasures."[41] Dr. Melmoth's domestic experiences in *Fanshawe* are a clear illustration of Nekayah's last remark. It is just such an opportunity that the practical, redemptive Ellen offers to Fanshawe and which reason might suggest he take.

While the moral dilemma of the novel hangs on Fanshawe's emergence from and return to his own Happy Valley, the final word is given to Ellen and Edward, who join in marriage four years after Fanshawe's death and embark on an "uncommonly happy" life together. "Ellen's gentle, almost imperceptible, but powerful influence, drew her husband away from the passions and pursuits that would have interfered with domestic felicity; and he never regretted the worldly distinction of which she thus deprived him. Theirs was a long life of calm and quiet bliss;—and what matters it, that, except in these pages, they have left no name behind them?" (III, 460). Nothwithstanding their implied childlessness, Ellen and Edward achieve the golden mean of reason and affection, formulated in Hawthorne's juvenile poem "Moderate Views" as well as Johnson's Oriental fable, that eludes Fanshawe.

Five years after the publication of *Fanshawe* Hawthorne brought another pair of chastened lovers down from an inland utopia. In "The Canterbury Pilgrims" (1833) the young Shakers Josiah and Miriam, with "a gift to love each other," steal away from their protected, celibate community to go "among the world's people" (XI, 122). The imprint of *Rasselas* is more diffuse in "The Canterbury Pilgrims" than in *Fanshawe* but still recognizable. Josiah and Miriam are first seen on the summit of the hills isolating the Shaker village. The connection between the valley and the outer world is marked by a crystal fountain and a stream flowing beside the road. The pilgrims they meet toiling "wearily up the long ascent" in flight from the world include a poet, a merchant (of the East Indies trade), and a family whose once kind affections have been worn away by time and care. While the world-weary pilgrims pause beside the spring, and begin to tell stories for pastime "and the benefit of these misguided young lovers," Miriam, "whose feelings were those of a nun or a Turkish lady, crept as close as possible to the female traveller, and as far as she well could from the unknown men" (XI, 123). Like Edward and Ellen before them Josiah and Miriam choose a life of "human hope and fear" over the "cold and passionless security" to which the other pilgrims are moving (XI, 131).

The transparency and conglomerate nature of *Fanshawe* gave Hawthorne some cause to distrust this youthful *jeu d'espirt*. The novel is a significant starting point, however, for exploring the author's library and dispositions and the themes and character types that run throughout his work. Ellen Langton is Hawthorne's first "snow maiden," Fanshawe begins a long line of scholars, poets, and scientists who leave their happy valleys briefly, if at all, and the three young men of *Fanshawe* establish "a psychic pattern that informs both Hawthorne's life and his successive romances."[42] It was his "Edward Walcott" self, happily, that lived and acted in the world.

"The Wives of the Dead:" Providence, Resignation, and Blessing

However important the act of choosing, the degree of choice that either Rasselas or Fanshawe has in determining his path of life is ultimately limited by the designs of all-knowing Providence as well as by the fate of his own character. The reasonable soul resigns himself to his destiny:

> MANY tears were shed over [Fanshawe's] grave; but the thoughtful and the wise, though turf never covered a nobler heart, could not lament that it was so soon at rest. He left a world for which he was unfit; and we trust, that, among the innumerable stars of heaven, there is one where he has found happiness. (III, 460)

The consolations of philosophy that Hawthorne found in the *Prince of Abissinia* were what Samuel Johnson and the writers of the eighteenth century had sought and found in the stoicism of Eastern life and religious faith. As Johnson and his contemporaries turned Eastward for instruction and models of conduct, so too Hawthorne breathed an Oriental wisdom into his raw American material. A year after the publication of *Fanshawe* this progression from original Oriental tales, through a European imitation, to native American fiction returned in "as precise and well formed a short piece as Hawthorne ever wrote": "The Wives of the Dead."[43]

Only recently have readers begun to recognize "The Wives of the Dead" as a "minor masterpiece: brief, evocative, haunting, ambiguous, inexplicable."[44] An anecdote in appearance and scarcely 2,400 words in length, this spare, inward tale is a startling contrast to the episodic *Fanshawe*. The haunting effect of "The Wives of the Dead" derives from its psychological indeterminacy and its sensitive depiction of the conflicting desires and grief of young widowhood. Its syllogistic structure, however—beginning with "premises" of scene and season, and continuing with the "precepts" of the two wives—gives it the formal coherence of a philosophic tale. Its psychological conclusions are left to the reader's imagination, but the author's intent can be made somewhat less inexplicable by considering the only explicit literary reference he makes in the tale, that is, to Voltaire's *Zadig, or Destiny: An Eastern Tale* (1747).

The admonitory and philosophic works of François-Maret Arouet de Voltaire became a dominant fact of Hawthorne's reading in the fall of 1829. He began his study of Voltaire on October 2 of that year with the first volume of the ninety-two volume Kehl edition of the *Oeuvres Complètes*.[45] On October 5, he moved immediately to Volume 56, which contains *Zadig, ou La Destinée: Historie Orientale* and other Oriental tales. Unsatisfied in the first week, he renewed the loan on October 12 and finally returned the book to the Salem Athenaeum on October 17. He continued to read uninterruptedly in Voltaire until, on December 3, 1829, he withdrew Volume 21 of the *Oeuvres*, where he found the dramas *Sémiramis* and *Le Fanatisme, ou Mahomet le prophète*, as well as the narrative *Historie de Charles XIII, Roi de Suede*, for which Voltaire had made an extensive investigation of the harems of Turkey.[46] As he read his way through the voluminous dramatic, philosophical, and historical writings of Voltaire (49 volumes by September 1831), Hawthorne encountered a major body of Orientalism that also included *Zaïre, The Orphan of China*, and apologues like "Memnon, or Human Wisdom," "The Story of a Good Brahmin," "The Princess of Babylon," "Bababec, and the Fakhirs," and "The Ghebers." The East provided a safely foreign setting from which Voltaire could satirize the French treatment of women, the arbitrary rule of kings and clergy, and quackery and cant of all kinds. But *Zadig* and his other Eastern tales also demonstrate the impressive range of specific knowledge of the Islamic, Hindu, and Christian cultures that Voltaire brought to bear for comparative discourses on passion and reason, fanaticism and toleration, imagination and nature, superstition and true religion. Reading "The Wives of the Dead" with *Zadig* in mind exposes a strong, unrecognized vein of philosophy and morality in Hawthorne's tale. Before we consider matters of meaning, however, Hawthorne's reference to *Zadig* might also help to fix his tale's date of composition.

"The Wives of the Dead" was published during the fall of 1831 in *The Token* for the following year, and it has been associated loosely with Hawthorne's plans for two early collections of stories that he failed to publish: *Seven Tales of My Native Land* in 1827, and *Provincial Tales* in 1829. He recalled the manuscript for *Seven Tales* in 1827 and burned all but one or two of the stories in disappointment. Because "The Wives of the Dead" involves experiences of land and sea in colonial New England, and because it seems both simpler and earlier than the other tales Hawthorne published in *The Token* for 1832, a few scholars have linked it tentatively to Hawthorne's earliest collection. Lea Newman thought, "It may have been written originally as part of *Seven Tales of My Native Land*, which would make its composition date considerably earlier, in 1824 or 1825." There has been more speculation that he intended to place it in *Provincial Tales*. "It was one of the tales," Newman wrote, "Hawthorne had sent to Samuel Goodrich in December 1829 in the hopes of finding a publisher for them as a collection."[47] Other scholars have excluded it from *Provincial Tales* altogether on thematic grounds as well as for lack of definitive evidence.[48] Assuming, however, that Hawthorne wrote with his study of the fifty-sixth volume of Voltaire's *Oeuvres*, containing *Zadig*, still fresh in mind, his reference locates the composition of "The Wives of the Dead" in the last quarter of 1829, several years after he wrote *Seven Tales* but in the midst of preparing his *Provincial Tales*.

Fanshawe first brought Hawthorne to the attention of the Boston publisher Samuel Goodrich, who was sufficiently interested to ask to see his next work. On December 20, 1829, Hawthorne sent Goodrich several tales, explaining in his cover letter: "These which I send have been completed (except prefixing the titles) a considerable time. There are two or three others, not at present in a condition to be sent. If I ever finish them, I suppose they will be about upon a par with the rest" (XV, 199). In his reply on January 19, 1830, Goodrich named four stories he had received. "The Wives of the Dead" was not among them.[49] Hawthorne's remark that his December submissions had been completed "a considerable time" would further remove "The Wives of the Dead" from this lot. It seems likely that it was among the "two or three other stories" he had in progress late in 1829.

The incidents of Hawthorne's schematic tale unfold in the twilight of an autumn day, a century earlier, as two comely young widows "sat together by the fireside, nursing their mutual and peculiar sorrows." Inhabiting the adjoining chambers of one residence, these "recent brides of two brothers" had received tidings on successive days of the deaths of their husbands, one "by the chances of Canadian warfare," and the other on "the tempestuous Atlantic" (XI, 192). After their consoling guests have left them alone once more, the sisters-in-law begin to manifest their respective manners of dealing with fate:

> They joined their hearts, and wept together silently. But after an hour of such indulgence, one of the sisters [named Mary], all of whose emotions were influenced by her mild, quiet, yet not feeble character, began to recollect the precepts of resignation and endurance, which piety had taught her.

She refuses to let misfortune "interfere with her regular course of duties" and begins to arrange a frugal meal. Margaret, unlike her stoical sister-in-law Mary, "was of a lively and irritable temperament." She expresses her sorrow by noisy lamentations and "childish fretfulness" (XI, 193–194).

While Mary bears her grief quietly and falls into sleep, Margaret becomes more feverish and agitated as the night advances. When a knocking at their door arouses Margaret from her troubled sleep, she learns with joy that her husband and his fellows not only have survived the Indian skirmish but are soon to return. She is hesitant to confront her grief-stricken sister with her restored personal happiness, however, and soon lapses back into a sleep of wild and delightful visions. When Mary awakes to a further knocking, she receives in her turn the glad news that, far from perishing with his ship, her husband "and three others saved themselves on a spar, when the Blessing turned bottom upwards" and are on their way home (XI, 198). Nearly overwhelmed with gladness but reluctant to arouse Margaret to "thoughts of death and woe," Mary stands above her sister-in-law until "a tear also fell upon her cheek, and she suddenly awoke" (XI, 198–199). There the tale abruptly ends giving no glimpse of the afterlife of Mary, Margaret, and their husbands.

Hawthorne's reference to Voltaire occurs when Mary is summoned to the house door and discovers there "a young man in a sailor's dress" who had wooed her unsuccessfully before her marriage. Mistaking his greeting— "Cheer up, Mary, for I seek to comfort you"—as an indelicate attack on her widowhood, she turns away in tears, for, the narrator observes, "she was no whit inclined to imitate the first wife of Zadig" (XI, 198). While introducing a superficially humorous incident from Voltaire's Eastern narrative, Hawthorne also signals at this point a broader area of philosophical accord that connects "The Wives of the Dead" to another work that, as Voltaire maintained in his introduction to Zadig, "means more than it seems to do." Like the tale of Zadig "The Wives of the Dead" is fundamentally a meditation on Providence and Destiny. Even a brief recitation of Voltaire's once universally popular tale should indicate that its significance to Hawthorne exceeded that of a mere quip.

Zadig, which is still considered after Candide to be Voltaire's most successful philosophical tale, is made up of a number of stories based on authentic Oriental narratives that the author united thematically through the life and fortunes of his title character.[50] To the twelfth-century Persian tale "The Three Princes of Serendip," the Koran, and The Arabian Nights, Voltaire added elements from later intermediaries like Montesquieu's Persian Letters. In a mock "Dedicatory Epistle" to "the Sultanah Shirah, in the Year 837 of the Hejira," the author represented the story of Zadig as originally having been written in ancient Chaldee from whence it was translated into Arabic. Assuming the guise of an editor, he claimed to have read the "manuscript, and found it, in spite of myself, curious and amusing, moral and philosophical, and worthy even of pleasing those who hate romances."[51] Zadig is presented in the tale as a rich but restrained young man of Babylon who, while seeking only the consolations of philosophy and friendship, suffered a series of abuses, imprisonment, and slavery that drove him through Syria, Egypt, Arabia, and eastward as far as Serendip (Ceylon). He first experienced the inconstancy of the world at the hands of his fiancee Semira, who although "bathed in tears night and day" abruptly married another man when she believed, erroneously, that Zadig had lost the sight of one eye while defending her from abduction. Thereafter he married Azora and "lived with her for a month in all the bliss of a most tender union." Uncertain of her fidelity, however, he charged his friend Cador with administering a test and sent servants to tell Azora of his death. "She wept, and tore her hair, and vowed that she would die," but soon allowed herself to be comforted by her husband's handsome friend and consented to take the nose from Zadig's corpse to remedy a sharp pain Cador claimed to suffer in his side. Zadig put Azora away as too unmanageable to live with and "sought for happiness in the study of nature."[52]

Several times Zadig won preferment for his sagacity and benevolence only to be deprived through human trickery or natural accident. "At last, murmurs against Providence escaped him, and he was tempted to believe that the world was governed by a cruel destiny, which oppressed the good."[53] In the crucial chapter of the tale, which is titled "The Hermit" and traceable to the Koran, Zadig witnessed the most cruel, capricious, and apparently undeserved sufferings by fire and drowning. When he was at the point of despair, however, the Hermit revealed himself as the angel Jesrad and tutored Zadig to see the benign intelligence and order behind the chaos that meets man's eyes. "There is no such thing as accident," the Hermit instructed him; "all that takes place is either a trial, or a punishment, or a reward, or a providential dispensation."[54] Educated by experience and enlightened by revelation, Zadig was then able to answer the riddles of time, life, justice, the chief good, and the art of government. He married the beautiful and virtuous Queen Astarte, was made King of Babylon, and realized the happiness of which he almost had despaired. "The queen and he together adored Providence." Each character reaped a reward commensurate with his or her character. And the tale concluded: "All men blessed Zadig, and Zadig blessed heaven."[55]

The model of *Zadig* echoes through "The Wives of the Dead" on several levels. To begin with, there is a vague foreshadowing of Hawthorne's two brides and brothers in Zadig's fiancee and his first wife and in the initial reports of his dismemberment and death, which each time are proven false. The fidelity of the young Babylonian women is tested by reports of Zadig's loss; Mary and Margaret, too, reveal their respective characters in response to their husbands' presumed deaths. More profound, however, is Hawthorne's engagement with the central theme of "The Hermit" ("the problem of evil in the universe and the doctrine of determinism") and his underlying agreement with Voltaire's theistic conclusion.[56] In the sermon of Jesrad Voltaire expounds the theodicy of Leibniz, that "there is no evil from which some good does not spring," and he vindicates the justice of God by accepting natural and moral evil as elements of an ineffable divine plan.[57] Voltaire does not imply an easy or unqualified optimism since evil is a necessary ingredient in the world and perfection exists only in the Supreme Being. *Zadig* marked a turning away in Voltaire's work from an earlier emphasis on free will and towards a new determinism.[58] He does affirm, however, a general Providence and the divine presence in temporal affairs. While the untutored, led by more passion than reason, might look only for acts of particular Providence, and become either optimists or pessimists by their bestowal, the enlightened soul blesses and seeks to live by the determinations of heaven.

In "The Wives of the Dead" Hawthorne not only probes the psychology of grief but dramatizes alternate modes of conduct in the face of destiny. The two most important terms in his tale (both conspicuous also in *Zadig*) are *blessing* and *resignation*. Hawthorne puts a not-uncommon name for a Salem vessel to symbolic use when he has Mary's husband sail on the brig *Blessing*, which "turned bottom upwards." Representing human existence as a ship tossed by turbulent seas is a venerable convention. Like Hawthorne's two brothers, all men are subject to the chances of politics and weather that slay the virtuous and the criminal alike. The brothers seemingly are modest and moral men, but their danger and release is presented neither as a punishment nor as a reward; it is a providential dispensation—and a trial for the wives. The death or survival of the brothers, indeed, is incidental to the tale inasmuch as it is beyond human control and subject to an order than man can only dimly perceive. The conduct of the sisters-in-law in the face of death, however, is of central importance, revealing both their character and their faith.

Hawthorne uses *blessing* three other times, both before and after the turning of the brig, to reveal the respective natures of the sisters-in-law. Their mutual grief and solicitude should not distract us from recognizing their considerable moral differences. The "mild, quiet, yet not feeble *character*" of Mary is the antithesis of Margaret's "lively and irritable *temperament*." Margaret's "shrieks and passionate lamentations," her "screams" and "groans" of bitterness repeat the exaggerated gestures of Zadig's fiancee Semira, who likewise "pierced the sky with her lamentations."[59] Mary recollects "the precepts of resignation and endurance, which piety had taught her," and invites her sister-in-law: "Arise, I pray you, and let us ask a blessing on that which is provided for us." Margaret, however, denies Providence, "There is no blessing left for me, neither will I ask it," and rails: "Would it were His will that I might never taste food more" (XI, 193).[60] Irrespective of the women's responses—pious or blasphemous—Providence restores their husbands. After hearing the harbinger of her husband's return, "a blessed flood of conviction" gradually swells Mary's heart. Her superior moral understanding is evident in her response to joy as in her acceptance of grief.[61]

The friends who fail to console, the loss of all that was most precious and then its providential restoration, the challenge to bless or to curse God and die—all suggest that Hawthorne also had the Book of Job in mind when writing "The Wives of the Dead." Mary's words and actions echo Job's refusal to despair: "The Lord gave, and the Lord taketh away; blessed be the name of the Lord" (Job 1:21). At the beginning of *Thalaba the Destroyer* Robert Southey argued the same proclamation of faith, after Hodeirah's death, in an exchange between "the widow'd mother and fatherless boy":

> At length collecting, Zeinab turn'd her eyes
> To heaven, and praised the Lord;
> "He gave, he takes away!"
> The pious sufferer cried,
> "The Lord our God is good!"

Zeinab rebuked her son for questioning the justice of God and prayed: "Allah, thy will be done!"[62] In a note that he appended to these verses Southey explained his rationale for putting the phrase of scripture "in the mouth of a Mahommedan": "It is a saying of Job, and there can be no impropriety in making a modern Arab speak like an ancient one. *Resignation* is particularly inculcated by Mahommed, and of all his *precepts* it is that which his followers have best observed: it is even the vice of the East."[63] As Hawthorne surely knew, *Islam* means "submission to the will of God."

The faithful wife Mary is not inclined to imitate either the exaggerated emotions or the inconstancy of Zadig's first wife. Rather, her "precepts of resignation and endurance" and her attitude of blessing reflect the Babylonian's faith in Providence. Where the unenlightened might see only blind chance or fate, Mary is able to perceive design, and by reverently bearing her sufferings she prepares herself for even more peace and felicity. The morality of "The Wives of the Dead" is as much Muslim as Christian. As George Sale observed in his discourse on the Koran, the book makes "frequent admonitions to moral and divine vertues, and above all to the worshipping and reverencing of the only true GOD, and resignation to his will; among which are many excellent things intermixed not unworthy even a *Christian's* perusal."[64]

Like Zadig, Hawthorne's "The Wives of the Dead" moves through a twilight atmosphere somewhere between daylight and dream worlds, experience and imagination. Some readers, responding to ambiguous pronoun references in the last sentence of the tale and its generally shadowy atmosphere, have argued that Mary only dreamt the news of her husband's deliverance and would wake, after the close of the tale, to a tragic truth.[65] Such a reading is discordant both with the reliability of Hawthorne's narrator and with his instructive reference to Zadig's wife. This measured, minimalist tale is too finely cut to allow such a lapse. *Zadig* lends itself to sober reflections on the precariousness of human felicity but not to tragedy.

In explaining what distinguished Hawthorne's *Twice-told Tales* from other stories of his time, a contemporary reviewer wrote of the "fine tone of sadness that pervades his best tales and sketches."[66] The narrator of "Fragments from the Journal of a Solitary Man" encouraged this popular nineteenth-century description when he said of Oberon that "a sadness was on his spirit" (XI, 313). Its pervasive *sadness* has been perhaps the most striking feature of Oriental culture to Western eyes, whether in Arab folk literature, classical Persian music, or the religion of Islam with its emphasis on martyrdom and mourning. It might be said of the author of "The Wives of the Dead," as it has of Sir Richard Burton, "His world view was Oriental in its profound sadness for the misery and sorrow of man."[67]

"The Gentle Boy": Turkish Hospitality and Natural Religion

Of all Hawthorne's short fiction "The Gentle Boy," which appeared with "The Wives of the Dead" in *The Token* for 1832, spoke most intimately to the expectations and sensibilities of his contemporaries. Equaled in length only by "Rappaccini's Daughter," "The Gentle Boy" remained Hawthorne's most popular tale throughout his lifetime. When Longfellow reviewed the expanded edition of Hawthorne's *Twice-told Tales* in 1842, he pronounced it "the finest thing he ever wrote."[68] It was one of the four tales that Hawthorne sent to Samuel Goodrich in December 1829 for his projected *Provincial Tales*. With his sure grasp of the literary marketplace Goodrich proposed to publish "The Gentle Boy" separately and on January 19, 1830, offered "$35 for the privilege" of inserting it in *The Token* for 1831.[69] Its immediate esteem on publication a year later led Goodrich to identify other tales by Hawthorne appearing in *The Token* for 1833–1837 as "By the author of 'The Gentle Boy.' " Thus this early tale has exceptional contextual as well as thematic significance.

Hawthorne's own reactions to "The Gentle Boy" were ambivalent. While he seemed uneasy about its conception and artistry, and made several deletions before republishing it, "The Gentle Boy" was the only tale of the four submitted to Goodrich in 1829 that he chose to include in the original edition of *Twice-told Tales* in 1837. He had special reason for his partiality to the tale because it had stirred the interest of the Peabody sisters and helped to open his "intercourse with the world." In 1839 Sophia Peabody provided the Flaxman-like drawing of the boy Ilbrahim that illustrated a special reissue, *The Gentle Boy: A Thrice Told Tale*. In his preface to the latter edition Hawthorne acknowledged that, perhaps, "Nature here led him deeper into the Universal heart, than Art has been able to follow."[70]

At first "The Gentle Boy" seems a straightforward attack on Puritan bigotry and an imaginative atonement for the role that the seventeenth-century progenitor William Hathorne played in the scourging, banishment, and execution of Quaker dissenters in the Massachusetts Bay Colony. The six-year-old Quaker boy Ilbrahim in Nathaniel Hawthorne's tale is first discovered at the freshly made grave of his father, who has been hanged as a heretic. The reader feels a natural sympathy not only for his mother, Catharine, who has been turned loose to die in the wilderness, but for Tobias and Dorothy Pearson, who on adopting the Quaker child "very shortly began to experience a most bitter species of persecution" from the covenanted Puritans (IX, 77).

The Quaker's all-consuming zeal, however, provides a no more life-giving theology than that of the Puritans. Catharine first appears in the tale at a Sunday church service where the congregation has just heard a smugly reasoned sermon against tolerating the Quaker heresy. Throwing back the cloak that concealed her, Catharine ascended the pulpit and released a "flood of malignity which she mistook for inspiration" (IX, 82). Her countenance, "wild with enthusiasm and strange sorrows, retained no trace of earlier beauty" (IX, 81). She acknowledged, "My heart was withered" (IX, 84). In the grip of their fanatic piety and pathology of martyrdom the Quakers sunder the "magnetic chain of humanity" and sacrifice even their own children.

In recent years Hawthorne scholarship has come to a better appreciation of the richness and complexity that, along with its heartfelt sentimentality, attracted nineteenth century readers to "The Gentle Boy." The tale is commonly seen now as a carefully balanced exposé of the "mutuality of guilt" in both Puritan bigotry and Quaker fanaticism.[71] In his subtle chapter "Nature, Virtue, and 'The Gentle Boy,' " Michael Colacurcio has concluded, furthermore, that "their assimilative reductions of the Christian Trinity" led the

Puritans and Quakers to a common, "painful, 'privative' similarity: neither side would have a doctrinal guarantee for the truth that in a fallen and pluralistic wilderness of the historical world the prime ethical imperative is *simply* loving one's neighbor as oneself." He suspected that "deficient theories of the Incarnation explain it all"—that the Puritans' restrictive covenant was fundamentally "anti-natural" and ended by denying the moral identity of all men; that in the Puritans' and Quakers' alienated pursuits of mind and instinct, creed and emotion, a world had "come apart."[72]

Even Colacurcio's sophisticated exegesis and grounding of "The Gentle Boy" in American religious history, however, has not liberated it from the essentially binary nature of earlier criticism. The dialectic of the Quakers' "ahistorical God-Within-the-Self" and the Puritans' "ahistorical God-Beyond-the-World" suggests the need for a new covenant of charity and simple love; heretofore that transcending synthesis has been given no dramatic voice within the tale itself. The only counterpoint Colacurcio adduces from outside the Puritan–Quaker dialectic is—still within the American frame—the hypothetical charity of the American Indian. When he first brings the abandoned boy to his wife, Tobias Pearson remarks: "The Heathen Savage would have given him to eat of his scanty morsel, and to drink of his birchen cup; but Christian men, alas! had cast him out to die" (IX, 75).[73]

While Tobias's nod to the more-Christian-than-we natives has had passing notice, Hawthorne's more extensive and explicit references to monotheistic Islam have been commonly dismissed as mere coloration or as evidence of a general overabundance of materials in "The Gentle Boy." After Catharine's doleful address to the Puritan congregation, and as she renewed "the wanderings of past years," the narrator concludes the third movement of the tale:

> For her voice had been already heard in many lands of Christendom; and she had pined in the cells of a Catholic Inquisition, before she felt the lash, and lay in the dungeons of the Puritans. Her mission had extended also to the followers of the Prophet, and from them she had received the courtesy and kindness, which all the contending sects of our purer religion united to deny her. Her husband and herself had resided many months in Turkey, where even the Sultan's countenance was gracious to them; in that pagan land, too, was Ilbrahim's birthplace, and his oriental name was a mark of gratitude for the good deeds of an unbeliever. (IX, 87–88)

The introduction of Muslim hospitality could not have been situated for greater effect. For the first publications of "The Gentle Boy" Hawthorne arranged his text in six movements separated by lines of asterisks. The third section, culminating in Ilbrahim's connection with the Sultan of Turkey, presents the discourses, first, of the self-congratulating Puritan minister and, then, of the grieving Quakeress. Following her wild homily, and as each held a hand of Ilbrahim, Catharine and Dorothy Pearson momentarily "formed a practical allegory; it was rational piety and unbridled fanaticism, contending for the empire of a young heart" (IX, 85). Then Catharine hearkened to the voice within: " 'Leave thy child. . . . Break the bonds of natural affection, martyr thy love, and know that in all these things eternal wisdom hath its ends'" (IX, 87). It is against this immediate background that "the followers of the Prophet" are introduced—at the structural and moral center of the tale.

The issue of Ilbrahim's Muslim birthright is intrinsic to the moral and thematic development of "The Gentle Boy." George Woodberry was on the right track when he wrote at the turn of the century: "The singularity of the tale is partly due to the fascination of the child's name, Ilbrahim, which brings before the mind an eastern background, emphasizes his loneliness, and gives a suggestion of Scriptural charm to the narrative. One almost expects to see palm-trees growing up over him."[74] In speculating about linkages of name between the gentle boy Ilbrahim and eighth-century founders of Islam, Colacurcio remarked, "How much Hawthorne knew, in the late 1820's, about the Islamic world one can only infer."[75] As has been shown in the previous chapter, inference is not necessary. He was thoroughly acquainted with the Islamic world through travel commentaries, diplomatic histories, and scriptures at the time he wrote "The Gentle Boy." With a single interruption, for example, from April 18 to June 12, 1829, Hawthorne read his way through five of the six volumes of Picart's *Religious Ceremonies and Customs*, apparently omitting only a volume on the Greeks and the Protestants. In Picart's liberal and ecumenically-minded work he encountered essays on the conformity of East Indian and Jewish customs; the religions of China, Japan, Persia, and Africa; Roman Catholicism and the Inquisition; and, apposite one another in the sixth volume, treatises on the Quakers, Anabaptists, and "Various sects of Mahometans with an appendix on the lives of Mohammed, Omar, and Ali."[76] With such eighteenth-century religious and cultural studies in his foreground some qualification must be made in the claim that "Hawthorne's own sense of comparative religion and culture came to him more powerfully from Roger Williams than from any of the Enlightenment writers with whom he was familiar."[77]

The narrator's description of Catharine's mission to "the followers of the prophet" was taken, in part, from Willem Sewel's account of the Quakeress Mary Fisher, who, after being driven from Massachusetts back to England in 1660, traveled to Adrianople and was received with honor and attention by the Sultan of Turkey. According to Sewel's *History of the Rise, Increase, and Progress, of the Christian People Called Quakers*, which Hawthorne drew from the Salem Athenaeum first in January 1828, Sultan Mahomet IV "charged her to 'speak the word she had to say from the Lord'"; and when she had done so, agreed "'that what she had spoken was truth.'" He encouraged her to stay in his country, expressing concern lest she should come to any harm in his dominions, and sought her thoughts of their prophet Mohammed. Her cautious answer—"'that they might judge of him to be true or false, according to the words and prophecies he spoke'"—the Turks acknowledged as just.[78] Sewel contrasted the stiff-necked hostility of the Puritans, who physically abused and denied food or clothing for the Quakeress during her imprisonment in Massachusetts, to the religious reverence and charity of the "in-fidels," who urged further acts of hospitality upon her.

Hawthorne reversed the sequence of the Quakeress's travels for dramatic reasons, since Massachusetts was the terminus of his tale, and added her suffering in the Catholic Inquisition. But neither Sewel's story of Mary Fisher, who was unmarried during her persecution in Massachusetts, nor the other New England histories on which Hawthorne drew for "The Gentle Boy" provided the model for the boy Ilbrahim, the focus of meaning in the narrative. It has been supposed that he was conceived simply in Hawthorne's imagination.

In fashioning and naming Ilbrahim, Hawthorne drew on one of the finest military and religious chronicles of Turkey, a work used by Edward Gibbon for his account of the Ottoman Empire: Sir Paul Rycaut's *The History of the Turkish Empire from the Year 1623 to the Year 1677*. Rycaut's long subtitle— *Containing the Reigns of the Three Last Emperours, Viz. Sultan Morat or Amurat IV. Sultan Ibrahim, and Sultan Mahomet IV. His Son, the XIII. Emperour Now Reigning*—further specifies the era of Turkish culture Haw-thorne investigated when he withdrew the history from the Salem Athenaeum on April 18, 1829, the same day he began reading Picart's *Religious Ceremonies and Customs*, and while apparently at work on "The Gentle Boy."[79]

From Rycaut's history Hawthorne knew that the regency of Mahomet IV had commenced in 1648, when his father, Ibrahim, was deposed and executed by the janizaries and the boy himself was but six or seven years old. The young Sultan was only eighteen when he received Mary Fisher in 1660 and, as described by William Sewel, manifested his charity and religious piety to the Quakeress. From Rycaut, Hawthorne learned, furthermore, that not only was Sultan Mahomet IV renowned for a wise and generous character but that his father, Sultan Ibrahim, was a tyrannous fool who during a reign of rebellion, misrule, and pusillanimity (1640–1648) threatened the survival of the Ottoman Empire. A portrait of Sultan Ibrahim and accompanying epigraph in Rycaut's history epitomized his lasciviousness and instability:

> I That of Ott'man Blood Remain Alone
> Call'd From a Prison to ascend a Throne
> My Silly Mind I Bend to soft Delights
> Hating th'unpleasant thoughts of Navall Fights
> Till Mad With Wanton Loves I Fall at First
> Slave to My Owne Then to My Peoples Lust.[80]

While the Sultan of Turkey who shows such reverence towards Catharine in "The Gentle Boy" is modeled after Mahomet IV, Hawthorne chose to use the name of the father, Sultan Ibrahim, for his young Quaker. He retained the name even after he withdrew Sewel's *History* from the Salem Athenaeum again (October 17–November 11, 1829) and reauthenticated the circumstances of Mary Fisher's barbarous handling in Boston in 1656 and her respectful reception by Mahomet IV in 1660.[81]

In composing his Quaker boy, it is possible that Hawthorne translated other features from the lives of the Ottoman sultans he read about in Rycaut's history. Mahomet IV, like Hawthorne's Ilbrahim, first appeared before the world at age six following his father's execution. During the first years of his minority he was dominated by the old Queen Mother, Kösem Sultan, a fearsome Circassian who was known for her oratorical power but eventually was assassinated through the design of Turhan Sultan, her daughter-in-law and Mahomet IV's mother. Intrigue for the dominion of their sons was the central activity of the mothers of the royal harem. This Oriental character carries over into the "militant passions," "peculiar sorrows," and "unearthly eloquence" of Hawthorne's Quaker mother and into her tangled relationship with the dependent boy.

Both Mahomet IV and Hawthorne's Ilbrahim, what is more, carried bloody stigmata on their foreheads. In a fit of displeasure with his furious queen, Sultan Ibrahim took the boy from her arms and, according to Rycaut, "with some few Curses swung him into a Cistern, where he had been certainly drowned, had not every one in that instance applied themselves to save him; at which time he received the mark or scar he wears at this day in his Forehead."[82] The Quaker boy, in turn, suffered a nearly fatal blow when he was struck on the mouth by an older playmate whom he had looked to for trust and protection; he would have died at once if elders had not saved him from the young Puritan assailants. Catharine claimed, moreover, that he had been "baptized in blood," and she exhorted Dorothy Pearson to "keep the mark fresh and ruddy upon his forehead" (IX, 86). This baptism of blood is a distortion of the Christian's baptism by water and the Spirit. But as Hawthorne also knew, the Turks believed that the time and manner of his death lay on the forehead of every man. According to Busbecq, they imagined that "every Man's Destiny is writ by God in his Forehead; so that 'tis a foolish thing in them, to think to decline or avoid it."[83]

In naming his gentle boy, Hawthorne probably avoided *Mahomet* as connotatively too strong for the delicate, sacrificial figure he wished to portray, and adopted *Ilbrahim* (or *Ibrahim*) instead because of associations with the patriarch *Abraham*, who is called *Ibrahim* in the Muslim world. He also might have alluded to the notorious Sultan Ibrahim for added satire when juxtaposing the guardians of the Christian faith, with their internecine bigotry and fanaticism, to the followers of Mohammed, with their tenets of hospitality and respect for revelation. The terms of contrast in the passage quoted earlier between "our purer religion" and the Muslim "unbeliever" in the "pagan land" of Turkey are obviously ironic. While Hawthorne was likely to write of polytheistic Hinduism as pagan and idolatrous (as he did in the *American Magazine*), he knew the fidelity and depth of Muslim faith, which repudiated the "infidels" of the West. His contemporaries in Boston and Salem—knowledgeable about their trading partners at Smyrna and the antagonists in the Greek War of Independence (1821–1829)—were better versed than we in the historical figures of the Ottoman Empire and would have felt his rebuke in honoring the name of Sultan Ibrahim. Turkey accepted the Treaty of Adrianople the same year Hawthorne submitted "The Gentle Boy" to Samuel Goodrich.

The specific affiliations between Hawthorne's Ilbrahim and the Ottoman sultans characterized by Sewel and Rycaut are less critically important, however, than the broader juxtaposition of "pure" Christians and Turkish "unbelievers" in "The Gentle Boy." At the very least Hawthorne evoked for his early readers a satiric convention practiced by Montesquieu and Goldsmith as well as in Irving and Paulding's Salmagundi.[84] Whether humorist or reformist in intent, their "Oriental letters" made Western discord and vice the foil of Eastern devotion and virtue. Like his European predecessors, Hawthorne's image of Muslim charity in "The Gentle Boy" was more than a literary flourish; it grew out of a climate of geo-cultural competition and the need to clarify the soul of the Christian nations. Christian factionalism and clerical ambition, it was thought, had been largely responsible for provoking the reforms of Mohammed in the eighth century and the zealotry that for a millennium threatened the survival of the Western states. George Sale wrote in his "Preliminary Discourse" to the Koran of the "abstrusest niceties" and "endless schisms and contentions" that "quite drove Christianity out of the world" and "gave great advantages of the propagation of Mohammedism."[85] Rycaut warned the Kings of seventeenth-century Europe of "an Universal Monarchy" of Islam unless the "Hectick Feaver" that divided the Christian community were dispelled in a new spirit of peace and concord.[86]

The French essayists and philosophers Hawthorne studied in the later 1820s held up the Turks both as a model for spiritual emulation and as a prophetic warning of the consequences of continued civil dissension. Montaigne, whose Essais Hawthorne read at various times from 1826 to 1837, reminded his countrymen that the Turks surpassed them in certain "Christian" virtues and that, whatever might be the superiority of Christian doctrine, in fact the despised Muslims could teach them lessons in justice and charity. He paid little attention to the legendary cruelty and lasciviousness of the Turks and contrasted their religious loyalty with the Calvinists' promiscuous and disputatious use of their own scriptures.[87] The "Turkish Letters" of Montaigne's contemporary Ogier Ghislain de Busbecq described both the orgies of the Christian carnival and the Turks' frugal and intelligent preparation for their own month of fasting.

The travelers and essayists Hawthorne read agreed that the Turks were far more praiseworthy than the spectres passed down by medieval Christendom. The courtesy and devotion attributed to the Sultan of Turkey by the narrator of "The Gentle Boy" were an established fact of Eastern life. "The hospitable custom," Edward Lane wrote in his notes to The Thousand and One Nights, "is observed by Muslims in compliance with the precept of their Prophet. 'Whoever,' said he, 'believes in God and the day of resurrection must respect his guest.' "[88] Zakat, an obligatory tax for the benefit of the poor, is one of the five pillars of the Islamic faith, and the Koran and Islamic tradition both stress the payment of sadagat, or charities. Even before Mohammed, hospitality was so habitual to the Arabs, George Sale wrote, "and so much esteemed, that the examples of this kind among them exceed what-ever can be produced from other nations."[89] Busbecq remarked how universal and democratic this hospitality was when he described the "hospitals" of Turkey: "There is no Man forbid the use of them, either Christian or Jew, Rich or Poor, they are open equally to all."[90] It was a sacred custom of these inns to entertain and provide food for all travelers for a period of three days.

While generally impressed with the democratic hospitality of the Oriental nations, the eighteenth and nineteenth century writers particularly noticed the Muslims' toleration of the spiritual dispensations represented in the var-ious religions and creeds. In his *Treatise Upon Religious Toleration* Voltaire claimed: "The grand seignior peacefully rules over the subjects of twenty different religions . . . Jacobines, Nestorians, Monothelites, Copthi, Christians of St. John, Guebres, and Banians; and the Turkish annals do not furnish us with one single instance of rebellion occasioned by any of these different sects." He went on to argue, "It does not require any great art or studied elocution, to prove that Christians ought to tolerate each another . . . for are we not all children of the same parent, and the creatures of the same creator?"[91] In "The Wives of the Dead" Hawthorne responded to *Zadig's* precepts of destiny, resignation, and blessing. In "The Gentle Boy" he shows a like-mindedness with Voltaire also on matters of fanaticism and toleration.[92]

Oriental hospitality and religious toleration in "The Gentle Boy" become more than a convention for satirizing American culture. The Muslim appears in Hawthorne's tale less as "the Other" (as a political-doctrinal antagonist to Puritan and Quaker Christianity) than as part of a universal worship of God. In turning from the contrarieties to the commonalities of faith, scholars of comparative religion in the eighteenth and nineteenth centuries tended to regard Islam not as the enemy of Christianity but as an affirmation of con-tinuing prophecy and revelation. Mohammed's intentions, according to George Sale, were "weeding out the corruptions and superstitions which the latter Jews and Christians had, as he thought, introduced into their religion, and reducing it to its original purity, which consisted chiefly in the worship of one only GOD."[93] Picart's "Discourse on the Mohammedans" began similarly by representing the "Religion of the *Mohametans* [as] a Compound only of the Doctrine of the Jews and the Christians" and encouraged readers to "shake of[f] the numerous Prejudices which they have received against this Reli-gion."[94] It was this reverence for the voice of the One True God that gave Mary Fisher her attentive audience with Mahomet IV at Adrianople in 1660.

In choosing to name his Quaker boy *Ilbrahim*, Hawthorne moved back through the proliferating heterodoxies and sectarianism of Muslim, Christian, and Jew to the common progenitor Abraham. While the boy's name derived most immediately from Sultan Ibrahim in Rycaut's history, its ultimate sig-nificance resides in the suggestion of the Biblical patriarch. From Abraham, through his wife Sarah, sprang Isaac and the covenanted tribes of Israel. From Abraham, through his bondswoman "Hagar the Egyptian," sprang Ishmael and the Arabian people. The gentle boy, suspended between Quaker and Puritan parents, between Muslim and Christian cultures, evokes the Biblical prophecy in Galatians 3: "And the scriptures, foreseeing that God would justify the heathen through faith, preached before the gospel unto Abraham, saying, in thee shall all nations be blessed." The final blessing he brings to his community is to terminate the diasporas and reunite the children of Isaac and Ishmael in a natural new covenant.

Pride in their exclusive covenant had closed the Puritans' eyes to the moral identity of all human souls. Hawthorne risked removing the pale erected by the covenant with Isaac and recognizing the spiritual virtue of the people of Ishmael. If he had needed precedent, he would have found it, once more, in Voltaire, particularly in the *Essais sur les Moeurs* and article "Alcoran" of the *Dictionnaire Philosophique*, where Voltaire represented Islam as being most closely related to the religion of nature.[95] What Voltaire held worthy of belief in both Christianity and Islam were the core values that are true in all religions. All men are brothers, he declared, "from Siam to California."[96] He dramatized a communion of the world's religions in a chapter of *Zadig* named, significantly, "The Supper," and he maintained a lifelong interest in the Quakers, whose practices he regarded as most consistent with the primitive Christianity of the gospels.[97]

In his consideration of "The Gentle Boy" Roy R. Male wrote of the "agonizing difficulty of finding an integrated, fruitful religious experience in America—the difficulty, that is to say, of finding a home."[98] Hawthorne's attack on religious intolerance and exclusivity led him to democratize the concept of "home" in both social and existential terms. In "The Gentle Boy" as in subsequent works he deconstructed the idea of the family as a biological and economic unit. The broken home of Ilbrahim's birth, his orphanhood, the death of Dorothy and Tobias Pearson's own children, their adoption of Ilbrahim, and the general doubling of family, mother, father, and child—these all replaced the proprietary household with a family of man knit together by love, charity, tolerance, and suffering rather than genetics. In the Eastern societies reverence for natural God-given virtue traditionally had liberalized the constitution of families and home. European travelers praised the Turks for conferring honor, office, and administrative position democratically, on the bases of merit and ability rather than birth. The Turks, Busbecq wrote, argue that "Virtue is not propagated from our Parents, but is partly the Gift of God, and partly acquired by good Discipline . . . for the Soul (they say) is not communicated with the Fathers Seed . . . but it is infus'd into his Body from the God of Heaven."[99] In the extended families of the East, tribute children and slaves rose to positions commensurate with their character and natural ability, a practice that Hawthorne and all Jacksonian America could endorse.

While the name *Ilbrahim* directed Hawthorne's readers backward to a single people of God, before there was Christian or Muslim, his narrator's original conclusion also brought the tale forward from the seventeenth century and implied a process of continuing spiritual unification. In the brief sixth section of "The Gentle Boy," following her son's death, Catharine makes a home with the Pearsons, and the gentle spirit of the departed Ilbrahim works to teach a truer religion of pity and kindness to mother as well as community. The revised version printed in *Twice-told Tales* concludes: "and when at last she died, a long train of her once bitter persecutors followed her, with decent sadness and tears that were not painful, to her place by Ilbrahim's green and sunken grave" (IX, 104–105). The original text, which Hawthorne published in *The Token* for 1832, added the sentence: "My heart is glad of this triumph of our better nature; it gives me a kindlier feeling for the fathers of my native land; and with it I will close the tale."[100] The moral philosophy Hawthorne expressed here is, like Voltaire's, ultimately melioristic.[101]

The main effect of the Orientalism in "The Gentle Boy" is to universalize and unify the family of man. But Hawthorne also introduced two other elements in the tale that complement the Turkish hospitality and piety that have been discussed. First, like the narrator himself, the Quaker boy possessed the gift of storytelling.

> [A] faculty which he had perhaps breathed in with the air of his barbaric birthplace . . . was that of reciting imaginary adventures, on the spur of the moment, and apparently in inexhaustible succession. His tales were of course monstrous, disjointed, and without aim; but they were curious on account of a vein of human tenderness, which ran through them all, and was like a sweet, familiar face, encountered in the midst of wild and unearthly scenery.

Ilbrahim had inherited the gifts of Scheherazade, and the "moral obliquity" of a young Puritan boy who heard his romances "grated very harshly against Ilbrahim's instinctive rectitude" (IX, 91). Hawthorne was not alone at his time in noting the "monstrous" tendencies of the Eastern tales but was peculiarly ready, it seems, to credit veins of human tenderness. Just as the followers of the Prophet made a triad with the Puritans and Quakers of the tale, so too Ilbrahim's "romances" offered a rhetorical alternative to the inhuman homilies of the Puritan minister and the ravings of Catharine. In young Ilbrahim the worlds of mind and instinct, rectitude and tenderness, come together again.

The other particularly Oriental characteristic of "The Gentle Boy" is its theme of pilgrimage. When "the traveller" Tobias Pearson first takes up the fatherless Ilbrahim, Hawthorne's label appears merely incidental to Pearson's journey from town to his "home" (IX, 74). In the course of the tale, however, the major characters all emerge as pilgrims on the path of life, traveling between birth and death, East and West, until, like the angelic hermit in *Zadig*, they cross to the other side. As "Ilbrahim's brief and troubled pilgrimage drew near its close," his grieving family considered "the departing traveller's reception in the world whither he goes."

While Dorothy Pearson watched over Ilbrahim's final hours, he "led her by the hand, in his quiet progress over the borders of eternity." She "almost imagined that she could discern the near, though dim delightfulness, of the home he was about to reach" (IX, 102–103). Edwin Fussell cited this passage and other borderland experiences in Hawthorne's tales as consequences of his encounter with the American frontier.[102] Read in its full context, however, "The Gentle Boy" must be seen as crossing frontiers not only of colonial Massachusetts and the unsettled wilderness, nineteenth-century America and its Puritan past, but of original and new covenants, American culture and the Eastern cradle of religions. The Oriental tradition of pilgrimage, with the collateral notion of the travail of life, is more ancient than Bunyan or Chaucer and the Crusades.

Travelers and the difficulty of "finding a home" in America generally abound in the tales that Hawthorne sent to Goodrich in 1829. The "wounded traveller" Reuben Bourne made "his solitary pilgrimage" in "Roger Malvin's Burial." When Robin journeyed from his backwoods home to the metropolis of Boston in "My Kinsman, Major Molineux," he mused, "Strange things we travellers see!" (XI, 220). Hawthorne's young sojourners seek their destinies out in the world no less than the philosophic travelers of Johnson and Voltaire or the voyagers and explorers whose accounts Hawthorne continued to read. Appropriately, when Robin entered a public inn in search of his kinsman:

> The only guests to whom [his] sympathies inclined him, were two or three sheepish countrymen, who were using the inn somewhat after the fashion of a Turkish Caravansary; they had gotten themselves into the darkest corner of the room, and heedless of the Nicotian atmosphere, were supping on the bread of their own ovens, and the bacon cured in their own chimney smoke. . . . Robin felt a sort of brotherhood with these strangers (XI, 213).

Hawthorne was well acquainted with the democratic caravansaries of Turkey, where travelers lodged, supped, and made their beds with their carriages, camels, and horses close at hand. "There is nothing done in secret," wrote Busbecq; "there all is open, and every Body may see what another does, unless the darkness of the night do hinder him"—a forthrightness that naturally attracted Robin in the frustrated quest for his kinsman.[103]

Young Ilbrahim's Oriental faculty for storytelling, the signs of pilgrims and travelers, and the fellowship of a caravansary all carried forward into the two volumes of tales Hawthorne wrote for his next projected work, *The Story Teller*.

THE STORY
TELLER

"... not to mention my prototypes in the East"

BY THE END OF 1830 Hawthorne had abandoned plans for two collections of stories conceived thematically. *Seven Tales of My Native Land*, composed shortly after his graduation from Bowdoin, reportedly was accepted by a Salem printer but recalled and then mostly burned by the author in exasperation over a long delay in publication. According to Hawthorne's sister Elizabeth the tales, whimsically named after Wordsworth's poem "We Are Seven," dealt with witchcraft and with pirates and privateers. *Provincial Tales*, which Hawthorne first submitted to Samuel Goodrich late in 1829, apparently was planned "along lines not essentially different from those of the earlier group."[1] It also comprised stories of colonial and early revolutionary New England. Hawthorne continued for a time to seek the publication of *Provincial Tales* as a whole, but by early 1831 he consented to let Goodrich use four of the tales mentioned in the previous chapter—"The Gentle Boy," "The Wives of the Dead," "My Kinsman, Major Molineux," and "Roger Malvin's Burial"— anonymously in *The Token* for 1832.

The miscarriage of the first two collections and the piecemeal appearance of his stories neither drove Hawthorne into the ranks of mere periodical writers nor deterred him from further efforts at book publication. While *The Scarlet Letter*, his first acknowledged full-length romance, appeared when Hawthorne was in his mid-forties, from the beginning he regarded the profession of authorship as the writing of books that would stand on their own spine. Instructed by the failure of his first two attempts, however, Hawthorne's third book of stories marked a radical departure from *Seven Tales* and *Provincial Tales* in technique as well as subject matter. Over a period of two or three years, almost certainly beginning as early as 1831, he committed himself wholly to a new, more ambitious and complex cycle of sketches, essays, and tales he came to call *The Story Teller*. This work, which eventually contained as many as three dozen framing and internal pieces, was arranged along a journey from a New England coastal town by land, canal boat, and lake steamer to Niagara Falls (thence to Detroit) and return in the 1830s, and was unified by "the conception of a travelling story-teller, whose shiftings of fortune were to form the interludes and links between the separate stories."[2]

The Story Teller departed from the two preceding collections in at least three respects. First, although several of the internal tales looked back to the history and folklore of colonial times, the occasion and narrative cast of *The Story Teller* were primarily contemporary. Secondly, as suggested by its title, the work was to be integrated and to derive its significance from a narrator-persona new to Hawthorne's writing. Thirdly, in this latest work Hawthorne explicitly adapted and applied models of Eastern storytelling, learned through years of reading, to his native American materials. While the Oriental element had remained muted and situational in the tales of the late 1820s, it figured prominently in the origin, structure, and themes of *The Story Teller*.

Despite the failure of the two earlier collections, Hawthorne pursued his new idea—combining personal experience, reading, and imagination, the historical and the contemporary, the East and the West—in the conviction that he had his hands on an original and timely work. "That third of Hawthorne's early attempts to assemble a fully organic collection of tales," Michael Colacurcio has written, might provide "our most credible metaphor of significant literary intention in Hawthorne's early phase. It may even afford us our one most legitimate opportunity to consider how Hawthorne might have presented himself to posterity if certain merely bibliographical conditions of his career had been otherwise."[3] *The Story Teller* was narratively organic, however, to a degree unapproached in the earlier gatherings, and given the author's avowed intention, as well as the apparent architecture of the work, it might be misleading to label it, at all, as a mere "collection."

Early in 1834 Hawthorne sent the bulky manuscript for a two-volume book to Samuel Goodrich in Boston with the hope of securing a publisher. How aggressive the self-interested Goodrich might have been on behalf of the talented but still anonymous contributor to his *Token* is unknown. Apparently through Goodrich's offices the work came into the hands of the editors of the *New-England Magazine*, who began to publish it serially. Two installments, titled "The Story Teller No. I" and "The Story Teller No. II," appeared in the November and December 1834 issues. For reasons that can only be speculated, the editors discontinued their serialization of the text Hawthorne had presented and dashed his hopes of seeing it published as a whole. Stripped of their narrative framework, interior stories and other pieces of *The Story Teller* appeared in the *New-England Magazine* almost monthly throughout 1835, until Park Benjamin, who had assumed editorial control in

1834, amalgamated the publication with his *American Monthly Magazine* of New York. Benjamin continued to publish components from *The Story Teller* there as late as 1837. Goodrich apparently also reserved several choice tales for *The Token*.[4]

Hawthorne was grievously disappointed in the fate of *The Story Teller*. Years later he wrote to Elizabeth Peabody, "[I]t was Park Benjamin, not Goodrich, who cut up the 'Storyteller.'" According to his sister-in-law, once the book has been torn apart, "he cared little for the stories afterwards, which had in their original place in the 'Storyteller' a greater degree of significance."[5] Obviously disspirited, Hawthorne did no creative work for some time after the dismantling of *The Story Teller* and until the appearance of *Twice-told Tales*, which was underwritten without the author's knowledge by his friend Horatio Bridge. Major elements of *The Story Teller* later appeared in his popular miscellanies *Twice-told Tales*, *Mosses from an Old Manse*, and *The Snow-Image*, but while these three collections mark the general progress in Hawthorne's career, it is difficult to read them as either topically or narratively unified works. *The Story Teller* was the most innovative and intricately designed of Hawthorne's books of stories. Even after the success of *The Scarlet Letter*, *The House of the Seven Gables*, and *The Blithedale Romance*, he remembered *The Story Teller* materials as "written quite up to the usual level of my scribblings"—and "no bad stuff."[6]

Although Goodrich and Park Benjamin apparently mined all the discrete travel sketches, essays, and imaginative tales that feasibly could be offered for readers of their annuals and monthlies, some amount of narrative and connective tissue has been irretrievably lost. Disagreement also continues concerning the inclusion and place within the original *Story Teller* structure of several works published from 1833 to 1838.[7] Nevertheless, the effort of reconstruction is sufficiently advanced to demonstrate now that Hawthorne intended to introduce modes of storytelling and to develop themes derived from Eastern literature and travels. We can start with the outermost frames that inaugurated and concluded *The Story Teller*: "The Seven Vagabonds," "The Story Teller No. I," "The Story Teller No. II," and "Fragments from the Journal of a Solitary Man."

The Narrative Frame: "The Seven Vagabonds"

"The Seven Vagabonds," which appeared in *The Token* for 1833 and thus had been written by the summer of 1832, has been regarded as both a forestudy and as an abandoned introduction to *The Story Teller*. The narrator of "The Seven Vagabonds," recalling an incident "in the spring of my life and the summer of the year" when he was a youth of eighteen with "an elastic foot, as tireless as the wing of the bird of Paradise," introduces himself as one of the "idle travellers" of the world (IX, 350, 359). No motive is given for his wandering other than an innate penchant for travel, even if only over the hills and lakes to Canada. Seeking shelter from a summer rain in the wagon of an itinerant showman, the young man came into the company of six other travelers, all of whom, it happened, were en route to ply their arts and trades at a camp-meeting in Stamford.

The narrator was particularly attracted by a "damsel of gay attire," a rosy-faced, rainbow-hued gypsy, whose light figure "seemed calculated to traverse the whole world without weariness." Through her diorama showbox, the foreign maid took him on imaginative trips to the great cities of the world, in whose streets he "had long yearned to tread." "But there was one scene," he relates, "which charmed my attention longer than all those gorgeous palaces and churches, because the fancy haunted me, that I myself, the preceding summer had beheld just such an humble meeting house, in just such a pine surrounded nook, among our own green mountains." While this vow of affection for the native soil, and its village church, anticipates the theme of homecoming that pervaded *The Story Teller*, the narrator still sighs in regret, "none but myself, I thought, should have been her companion in a life which seemed to realize my own wild fancies, cherished all through visionary boyhood to that hour." He envies the damsel and her male companion, "whose happy home was throughout all the earth!" (IX, 357–359).

Led by the combination of events and his own wayward fancy, the narrator's spirit of adventure soars beyond New England and Canada to the farthest East. The majority of mankind might be resigned to wear out all their tomorrows amidst the same dull surroundings. "But there were some, full of the primeval instinct, who preserved the freshness of youth to their latest years by the continual excitement of new objects, new pursuits, and new associates; and cared little, though their birth place might have been here in New England, if the grave should close over them in Central Asia" (IX, 364). Determining to join the other six vagabonds on their "pilgrimage," the narrator is challenged by the old showman to say how he will earn his bread, for even vagabonds require a vocation. Earlier the young man had toyed with the idea of becoming a traveling bookseller. Now he announces his calling:

> My design, in short, was to imitate the story tellers of whom Oriental travellers have told us, and become an itinerant novelist, reciting my own extemporaneous fictions to such audiences as I could collect.
> 'Either this,' said I, 'is my vocation, or I have been born in vain.' (IX, 366)

Before the seven pilgrims can embark on their motley *hadj* to the religious revival at Stamford, word reaches them that the camp-meeting has broken up, and the travelers disband. Having found his vocation, however, and in a mood ambiguously pensive and joyous, the narrator allies himself with a wandering Penobscot Indian and sets forth towards Boston.

"The Seven Vagabonds" brings together in skeletal form themes that would pervade Hawthorne's tales and romances, ever more dramatically, for the next quarter century. Of principal importance are the travel motif (with special emphasis on "pilgrimage"), the vacillating fidelity of the narrator to his native ground, and a tension between the dull but serene orderliness of New England life (epitomized by the country church) and the wilder gayety and color emanating from the land of gypsies and storytellers. This tension would be embodied particularly in Hawthorne's famous "dark" and "light" maids, who summoned the wavering fancy of his male travelers forth and back in the later romances.

The narrator of "The Seven Vagabonds," significantly, attributes his knowledge of Eastern storytelling not to the secondary models of the Augustan moralists, nor to the romances of Byron, Southey, or Scott, but to the authentic Oriental travelers Hawthorne knew so well. When this tale first appeared in *The Token*, Hawthorne referred to "Eastern travellers" rather than "Oriental travellers."[8] The revision made when republishing "The Seven Vagabonds" in *Twice-told Tales* removed any possible misunderstanding about *which East* Hawthorne meant.

Precisely when Hawthorne's natal instinct for travel, reflected in the repeated musings over his father's logbooks, began to express itself in the form of an "itinerant novelist" is uncertain. "Once a year or thereabouts" after his return to Salem in 1825, he later recalled, "I used to make an excursion of a few weeks, in which I enjoyed as much of life as other people do in the whole year's round."[9] On summer trips through New England and New York state he sometimes accompanied his uncle Samuel Manning, who bought horses for the family's coachlines. He was with his uncle in Concord and Canterbury, New Hampshire, in August 1831, for instance, and alluded in letters at the time both to the surly inhabitants of Maine and to the unlikelihood of reaching Canada. Although it has been suggested that the idea for *The Story Teller* might have occurred to Hawthorne first while on this trip, its roots certainly reached down to the Eastern travels and voyages he read throughout 1827.[10] His excursion in 1831, however, seems to have given Hawthorne's continuing passion for travel a new literary focus as he withdrew the Salem Athenaeum's copies of *Asiatic Researches* and the accounts of John Cochrane, Sir John Chardin, Alexander Russell, Jonas Hanway, and Richard Pococke in close succession from October through December 1831. "The Seven Vagabonds" was an early product of an evolving design.

The truncated close of "The Seven Vagabonds"—the end of the summer showers, word that the camp meeting had "broke up," the dispersion of the company, and the young man's abrupt departure with the Penobscot Indian—suggests that the author had clarified and enlarged his purpose while in the act of writing "The Seven Vagabonds" and so quickly tied it up in the summer of 1832 for an independent publication in *The Token*. On June 28, 1832, Hawthorne wrote to Franklin Pierce of his latest travel plans:

> I was making preparations for a northern tour, when this accursed Cholera broke out in Canada. It was my intention to go by way of New-York and Albany to Niagara, from thence to Montreal and Quebec, and home through Vermont and New-Hampshire. I am very desirous of making this journey on account of a book by which I intend to acquire an (undoubtedly) immense literary reputation, but which I cannot commence writing till I have visited Canada. I still hope that the pestilence will disappear, so that it may be safe to go in a month or two.[11]

Two and a half months later Hawthorne was on the road. He wrote to his mother from Burlington, Vermont, on September 16 that he had passed through the White Mountains, had climbed Mount Washington, and "might be in Canada tomorrow if I thought proper."[12]

After his multiple encounters with the formal and thematic possibilities of Eastern travel writing, Hawthorne became a literary traveler himself no later than the summer of 1832. There is solid internal as well as circumstantial evidence that his design for *The Story Teller* was amplified and brought into focus, if indeed not inspired, by his reading of Eastern voyages and travels. If "The Seven Vagabonds" proved too narrow for Hawthorne's final plan, it nevertheless announced the themes and genre of the larger work and established the narrative posture of a wearied traveler who, worn by experience, returns years later to his home community.

The Narrative Frame: "The Story Teller"

The rudimentary structure and themes of "The Seven Vagabonds" were recast and elaborated in the first two installments of *The Story Teller* that appeared in the *New-England Magazine* at the end of 1834: "The Story Teller No. I" (containing the narrative frames "At Home," "A Flight in the Fog," and "A Fellow-Traveller") and "The Story Teller No. II" (containing "The Village Theatre" and, in its original setting, "Mr. Higginbotham's Castastrophe").[13] "The idea of becoming a wandering story teller," Hawthorne's speaker remarks, "had been suggested, a year or two ago before, by an encounter with several merry vagabonds in a showman's wagon, where they and I had sheltered ourselves during a summer shower." The narrator proposes, in his retrospective book, to give "a picture of my vagrant life, intermixed with specimens . . . of that great mass of fiction to which I gave existence, and which has vanished like cloud-shapes."

First, however, the narrator explains the motives for his setting out. Until he fled from home, the wayward fancy of the young man had grated against "the stern old Pilgrim spirit" of his guardian, Parson Thumpcushion, with disagreement on a thousand points. "Heir to a moderate competence," he had suffered "an orphan's fate." The crux of the conflict with his guardian, however, was no lack of affection but rather the latter's determination that, like his own sons, the young man should adopt a particular profession in medicine, the ministry, commerce, law, or farming and the youth's equal resolve to remain "aloof from the regular business of life" (X, 406–407).

The resemblances of the narrator to his author are many, but nowhere is the connection more explicit or significant than in this respective exhortation and reluctance to embrace a useful occupation. As early as March 1821, in a letter to his mother concerning his preparation for college, Hawthorne systematically discounted the ministry, law, and medicine before he raised the idea of "becoming an Author, and relying for support upon my pen."[14] Seven years later, after graduating from Bowdoin and while on a trip to New Haven with Samuel Manning, Hawthorne impatiently set aside a younger relative's suggestion that he consider "the Pulpit, the Bar and the Pill Box." When asked what he would do with himself, he reportedly answered: "I wish to God I could find out."[15] Hawthorne's anxiety of vocation and the low regard in which the community of Salem held literary triflers are best known through "The Custom-House" essay years later in *The Scarlet Letter.* The choice of life, however, adumbrated in *Fanshawe,* becomes the motive behind the flight of the Story Teller, who felt himself ranked at home "with the tavern-haunters and town-paupers." "The consequence of all this, was a piece of light-hearted desperation"—the decision already expressed in "The Seven Vagabonds" to imitate the storytellers of whom Oriental travelers had told (X, 407–408).

In pursuit of his ignominious calling, the young Story Teller gives up his home in a state of "delicious excitement" and takes "the whole world in exchange." "Not to mention my prototypes in the East"—the outsetting Story Teller also claims the example of Childe Harold and Don Quixote, of the wandering orators and poets he has heard with his own ears, and of the "illustrious itinerant in the other hemisphere," Oliver Goldsmith. He commits himself to *viva voce* performance and claims the peculiar mental and personal qualifications necessary for the undertaking (X, 408, 410). He prides himself both on the difficulty of his trade and on the prodigious talents and cultivation that are required: "[E]very thing, indeed, was requisite; wide observation, varied knowledge, deep thoughts, and sparkling ones; pathos and levity, and a mixture of both, like sunshine in a rain-drop; lofty imagination, veiling itself in the garb of common life; and the practised art which alone could render these gifts, and more than these, available" (X, 416).

The narrator particularly relishes the dramatic potential of his undertaking, which would enable him to unite the characters of both the novelist and actor. In addition to occasions that offer a financial reward, he intended to exercise his narrative faculty and test the strong points of his stories wherever an audience might gather. As the occasions of storytelling would require, he "manufactured a great variety of plots and skeletons of tales, and kept them ready for use, leaving the filling up to the inspiration of the moment" and providing "two or more commencements and catastrophes to many of the tales" (X, 416–417). When the Story Teller rose to deliver his first evening recitation, "Mr. Higginbotham's Catastrophe," the tale was "as yet an unfilled plot; nor, even when I stepped upon the stage," he says, "was it decided whether Mr. Higginbotham should live or die" (X, 418).

In its original context, "Mr. Higginbotham's Catastrophe," which is presented in "The Village Theatre," introduced the tale-within-a-tale structure and the dramatic connection between narrative frame and interior tales that were to characterize *The Story Teller.* The pun on the word *catastrophe* refers not only to the uncertain fate of the title character, who is narrowly saved from a hanging, but to Yankee tobacco pedlar Dominicus Pike's search for a *denouement* to his premature and misinformed accounts of Mr. Higginbotham's demise. As Hawthorne's Story Teller seeks to fill out the plot of the story he tells, on stage and through the inspiration of his audience, so too Dominicus Pike bumbles towards the resolution of *his* story, and decides its outcome. In "A Flight in the Fog" Hawthorne's narrator declared his determination "not to enter on my profession within a hundred miles of Home" lest Parson Thumpcushion should "put an untimely catastrophe to my story" (X, 411). Through the layering of *catastrophes* and other parallelisms the dramatic relationship between Hawthorne's narrator as vagrant youth, the narrator as performing artist, and the protagonists of the tales he tells is made complete. "Mr. Higginbotham's Catastrophe" is a story told by one storyteller about another; and behind it all stands a third storyteller—the author.

Hawthorne's narrator represents *The Story Teller* as being a *post facto* written account of a series of such extemporaneous oral performances. To unify the occasional presentations and to organize the relationship between the itinerant narrator and the tales he invented, the Story Teller promises to give with each specimen "a sketch of the circumstances in which the story was told. Thus my air-drawn pictures," he continues, "will be set in frames, perhaps more valuable than the pictures themselves." Hawthorne's three-dimensional structure originally included: an autobiographical account of the Story Teller's itinerant life; specimens of "that great mass of fiction" to which he gave existence; and circumstantial frames connecting the fictions to the villages, fields, and scenery of his native land. The whole, finally, was prepared for a didactic purpose. "I write the book," says the narrator, "for the sake of its moral, which many a dreaming youth may profit by, though it is the experience of a wandering story teller" (X, 408–409).

As Hawthorne takes pains to inform his reader—first declaring his intention "to imitate the story tellers of whom Oriental travellers have told us," and then evoking his Eastern "prototypes"—the formal characteristics of his artistry as well as the vocation itself derive from the interlocking tale-tellers and Chinese-box structure of the Eastern story cycles. "Telling stories within stories is a very old narrative convention," Barbara Hardy has reminded us, and from the time of *The Arabian Nights* "prose narrative has delighted in the presentation of individual narrators." Charles Dickens learned his dramatization of narrative largely from *The Arabian Nights*, whose tales delighted him throughout his life.[16] *The Story Teller* shows a similar acquaintance with the craft of Scheherazade, who faced the challenge of extemporizing a successful entertainment each night (or losing her head) and in the process developed a multi-tiered set of picaros and tale-tellers the ilk of Sindbad, Ali Baba, and Aladdin. In the immediate foreground the handsome poet Feramorz of Thomas Moore's *Lalla Rookh* recited his stories of the East along the wedding processional from Delhi through Kashmir. When Hawthorne read James Morier's *Adventures of Hajji Baba of Ispahan* in July 1827, he sampled another three-dimensional work that was introduced by a putative translator, recounted the life of an itinerant youth in search of a vocation, and told tales—both sacred and profane—by dervishes, the *Kessehgou* (storyteller), and Hajji Baba himself.

The pattern of Hawthorne's borrowings from the Salem Athenaeum late in 1831 suggests that he was intentionally weighing the models of the Eastern travelers. Although he could have found suitable guidelines at many points, Alexander Russell's account of the storytellers of Aleppo in the mid-eighteenth century is so prescriptive for "Mr. Higginbotham's Catastrophe" as to suggest there was no great distance, either in time or in intention, between Hawthorne's reading of *The Natural History of Aleppo* in November 1831 and the inception of *The Story Teller*. "The recitation of Eastern fables and tales," according to Russell, is by nature "a dramatic performance." The stories are animated by the manner and actions of the speaker, who, "by combining the incidents of different tales, and varying the catastrophe of such as he has related before, gives them an air of novelty."

> He recites walking to and fro, in the middle of the coffee room, stopping only now and then when the expression requires some emphatical attitude. He is commonly heard with great attention, and, not unfrequently, in the midst of some interesting adventure, when the expectation of his audience is raised to the highest pitch, he breaks off abruptly, and makes his escape from the room, leaving both his heroine and his audience, in the utmost embarrassment. Those who happen to be near the door endeavour to detain him, insisting on the story being finished before he departs, but he always makes his retreat good; and the auditors, suspending their curiosity, are induced to return at the same hour next day, to hear the sequel. He no sooner has made his exit, than the company, in separate parties, fall a disputing about the characters of the drama, or the event of the unfinished adventure. The controversy by degrees becomes ferious, and opposite opinions are maintained with no less warmth, than if the fate of the city depended on the decision.[17]

The Eastern storytellers set a high standard, but one Hawthorne was quick to emulate. The story of Mr. Higginbotham "was originally more dramatic" in its oral form than in its written form, according to the narrator, "and afforded good scope for mimicry and buffoonry; neither of which, to my shame, did I spare." His audience, drawn into the fabrication of the story, was "ineffably delighted, and gave way to such a tumult of approbation, that, just as the story closed, the benches broke beneath them." As he made his escape, "from pit and boxes there was now a universal call for the Story Teller" (X, 420).[18]

Since the time of Nelson F. Adkins's essay "The Early Projected Works of Nathaniel Hawthorne" (1945), critics have assumed that *The Story Teller* was influenced in some large measure by Washington Irving's *The Sketch Book of Geoffrey Crayon*.[19] It is equally reasonable to believe that Hawthorne was inspired by the more proximate models of Longfellow's *Outre-Mer*, preliminary sketches of which appeared in the *New-England Magazine* from July 1831 to February 1833 under the title *The Schoolmaster*, and by Nathaniel Parker Willis's *Pencillings by the Way*, which began to appear in the New York *Mirror* in February 1832. In *The Schoolmaster* Longfellow also planned a framework for his sketches and began with a first person confession to the reader: "My childhood was passed at my native village in the usual amusements and occupations of that age; but as I grew up I became satiated with the monotony of my life. A restless spirit prompted me to visit foreign countries. I said, with the cosmopolite, 'The world is a kind of book in which he who has seen his own country only has read but one page.' "[20]

Irving, Longfellow, and Willis anticipated to varying degrees the fictionalized narrator, the mapped trip, the dramatic frame-and-tale structure, the oral presentations, and the moralizing of *The Story Teller*. All three, moreover, demonstrated in Hawthorne's own time the artistic, as well as the commercial, rewards of Easterly travel and storytelling—Willis through his personal pilgrimage to Greece and Turkey, Longfellow through the inspiration derived from Mandeville and *Childe Harold*, Irving through a fondness for travel and the Moors that only strengthened with the years. When introducing *The Sketch Book*, Irving confessed to a boyhood passion for "books of voyages and travels" that distracted him from his schoolwork: "How wistfully would I wander about the pier heads in fine weather, and watch the parting ships, bound to distant climes. With what longing eyes would I gaze after their lessening sails, and waft myself in imagination to the ends of the earth."[21] That Hawthorne thought of Irving, Longfellow, and Willis as of-a-kind is evident from his juxtaposition of the three writers in the first printing of "The Hall of Fantasy" (*Pioneer*, 1833). In a section dropped when the sketch was collected in *Mosses from an Old Manse* Hawthorne first mentioned Willis, who "looked so much like a man of the world, that he seemed hardly to belong" in the Hall—then Sprague, Pierpont, Longfellow, Irving, and "the renowned Geoffry Crayon" (X, 635–636).[22]

Hawthorne's secondary roads to the storytellers of the East also ran backwards through Washington Irving's favorite author, Oliver Goldsmith. Irving confessed that Goldsmith's writings "were the delight of my childhood, and have been a source of enjoyment to me throughout life," and in 1849 he published a full-scale biography of Goldsmith that he had begun a quarter century earlier.[23] Like his contemporaries, Irving tended to read the adventures of Goldsmith's philosophic vagabonds autobiographically, and the fruits of Goldsmith's Continental tour in 1755, presented in *The Traveller* and *The Vicar of Wakefield*, no doubt influenced Hawthorne's strategies for *The Story Teller* as well. Nevertheless, for Goldsmith, as for his American admirers, the experience of European travel was a paler reflection of the adventure and knowledge waiting in the East. "He had," Irving wrote, "always a great notion of expeditions to the East, and wonders to be seen and effected in the oriental countries."[24] *The Citizen of the World* was one result of this curiosity. While Hawthorne moved the locus of the traveling storyteller wholly onto the American soil, the structure, the storytelling techniques, and the didactic purpose of his work, too, were inspired by their Eastern originals.

In allying himself with Oriental models, Hawthorne's Story Teller chose a structure, well known to readers in the 1830s, that would accommodate a wide variety of materials. In its essay "Tales" in 1832, the *Encyclopedia Americana* noted that "the natives of the East have long been celebrated for their tales or stories, founded on familiar incidents and comic scenes, or on wild legends of good and bad spirits," and cited numerous "specimens of the wealth of the Eastern story-tellers" out of which flowed, in successive eras, the Milesian tales of the Asiatic Greeks, the *Gesta Romanorum*, and the narratives of Italy, France, and England.[25] From India, Persia, and Arabia came tales of high adventure and fantasy, picturesque legends, and religious allegories. Characterization in the Eastern tales was slight and inclined towards the abstract. The tales typically were strung along a cord of narrative and held together by their framing device. As later commentators have continued to point out, the molecular structure of the classical Arabic tales demanded attention from the audience only in short bursts, and in his "nighttime conversations" the Eastern fabulist carried the listener's mind easily from topic to topic.[26] The framing circumstance devised by Arabic and Medieval storytellers made it possible to combine quite autonomous materials. This flexible format, one in which tales could be manipulated at random with little change in overall effect, no doubt has bothered modern critics looking for unity of subject matter and a consistent point of view far more than it did audiences in the 1830s.

The coherence of the Eastern tales, moreover, lay less in their characters and material than in the effort of the storyteller to abstract wisdom from the multiplicity of life and to teach his fellows the consolations of an inscrutable yet all-powerful God. Even the Eastern tales in which the elements of pure fantasy and adventure predominated tended to serve moral and didactic ends. Drama may have been proscribed in Islam as a representational art, and fiction (in the form of novels) interdicted as a species of lying, but story literature (in the form of fables and apologues) was tolerated and even flourished. Most stories "preached by illustrating the success and joy that was available to the 'good' man and by conveying a sense of the terror and misery that was in store for the wayward."[27]

From the late eighteenth century onwards, American literary critics praised Eastern storytellers for combining dramatic narrative with moral instruction. In its essay "Benevolence; Or, the Good Samaritan," the new *Massachusetts Magazine* in 1789 emphasized the figurative and metaphorical style of the Eastern nations:

> This method is particularly adapted to inculcate truths, that in themselves are disagreeable and unpleasing. Such truths delivered in plain and direct language, would disgust, and the hearer would close his ears against instruction. But when the same truths are disguised in parables, or fables, a man may be surprized into attention—truth may seize the heart, and force convictions on the mind, before prejudice takes the alarm, or has time to make opposition. Our Saviour himself adopted this mode of instruction.[28]

John Neal, whom Hawthorne particularly relished while a student at Bowdoin,[29] went to the heart of the same matter in his essay "Story-Telling" in the *New-England Magazine* for January 1835, a month after the appearance there of Hawthorne's "The Story Teller No. II." Considering the "very language of the East, that other world, out of whose glorious fragments and august ruins, our world has been slowly and gradually and most laboriously put together," Neal asked: "what is it but a series of profound apothegms and significant allusions, each a story of itself and heavy with the fine gold of ancient wisdom, and bright with the half-smothered sunshine of Past Experience."[30]

Hawthorne apparently intended to dramatize the secular and sacred forms of storytelling in the performances, respectively, of the Story Teller and the diffident young New England holy man Eliakim Abbott, who joins him in "A Fellow-Traveller." For a week or two before encountering Eliakim, the Story Teller "travelled almost at random" (X, 411), but in company with his new companion his wanderings take on the purposefulness of a pilgrimage.[31] Together the odd pair determine to move from village to village, quickening the dull spirits of the land with their religious homilies by day and imaginative tales by night. Hawthorne's earnest but dry-as-dust cleric, unfortunately, has mastered none of the skills of the mullahs who attracted large audiences and invented a popular religious prose by interpreting verses from the Koran. While we do not know which pieces of *The Story Teller* originally were written for Eliakim, the contents of the work as a whole reflect both the secular adventures and the moral cast of mind of the outsetting storytellers.

The appearance of Eliakim, whose name means "God raises up," introduces a special element of Eastern fatalism and destiny to *The Story Teller*. At their first meeting the narrator accepts his offer of bread with the pious expression: "A pilgrim, such as I am, must not refuse a providential meal." "We are all pilgrims and wanderers," Eliakim replies; "but it is strange that we two should meet." Lest the reader miss the nuance of their exchange, the narrator then adds:

> I inquired the meaning of this remark, but could obtain no satisfactory reply. But we had eaten salt together, and it was right that we should form acquaintance after that ceremony, as the Arabs of the desert do; especially as he had learned something about myself, and the courtesy of the country entitled me to as much information in return. I asked whither he was travelling.
> "I do not know," said he; "but God knows." (X, 413–414)

Eliakim's response, like the Bedouin life to which the singular couple commit themselves, embodies a popular notion of Eastern fatalism. As Edward Lane noted in his contemporary edition of *The Arabian Nights*: "The phrase 'God is all-knowing,' is generally used by an Arab writer when he relates anything for the truth of which he can not vouch; and Muslims often use it in conversation, in similar cases, unless when they are uttering intentional falsehoods."[32] That Hawthorne regarded the Arabs as archetypal wanderers, in need of God's benign Providence, is evident from other references in his works,[33] and he knew the ceremonial significance of salt as a bond of friendship from several sources. Baron de Tott, for instance, wrote an account that Hawthorne had read in 1827: "The Turks think it the blackest ingratitude, to forget the Man from whom we have received Food; which is signified by the Bread and Salt" in their ceremonies.[34] The language of this Eastern custom became so natural to Hawthorne that in 1850 he wrote to his irrascible relative

Horace Conolly, who had sought to turn him out of the Salem Custom House: "and at the close of all I find myself eating bread and salt and getting corned with you, and just as kindly as if nothing had happened."³⁵

While in "The Seven Vagabonds" Hawthorne's pilgrims join company en route to a religious site, the camp-meeting at Stamford, in the original design of The Story Teller his itinerant novelist and Eliakim become part of the endless caravan that wended towards the tourists' Mecca of the New World, Niagara Falls, upon the opening of the Erie Canal in 1825. After eating salt with his companion, the Story Teller embarks on a circular pil-grimage that includes historical, legendary, and scenic locales along the Erie Canal, Lakes Erie and Ontario, the St. Lawrence River, Lake Champlain, and the White Mountains of New Hampshire.³⁶ His exact itinerary has not been established, but the Story Teller's primary destination undoubtedly is Niagara Falls, which possessed much of the same romance of the foreign and distant particularly associated at the time with explorations for the headwaters of the Nile.³⁷ In "Monsieur du Miroir," a sketch probably composed in connection with The Story Teller, the writer follows his alter ego to ever farther and more sublime bodies of water:

> I have leaned from a precipice that frowns over Lake George—which the French called Nature's font of sacramental water, and used it in their log-churches here, and their cathedrals beyond the sea—and seen him far below, in that pure element. At Niagara, too, where I would gladly have forgotten both myself and him, I could not help observing my companion, in the smooth water, on the very verge of the cataract, just below the Table Rock. Were I to reach the sources of the Nile, I should expect to meet him there. Unless he be another Ladurlad, whose garments the depths of the ocean could not moisten, it is difficult to conceive how he keeps himself in any decent pickle. (X, 163–164)

Hawthorne's narrator tries "to be poetical about the Grand Canal. In [his] imagination, De Witt Clinton was an enchanter, who had waved his magic wand from the Hudson to Lake Erie, and united them by a watery highway, crowded with the commerce of two worlds, till then inaccessible to each other."³⁸ The romance of travel, however, inevitably points beyond the native font at Lake George, and the falls at Niagara, to the springs by the Happy Valley of Abyssinia and the oceans of Southey's Hindu romance.

The Narrative Frame: "Fragments from the Journal of a Solitary Man"

Altered to a degree yet unknown from Hawthorne's original text, the con-clusion of The Story Teller appeared in the American Monthly Magazine for July 1837 in "Fragments from the Journal of a Solitary Man."³⁹ After years of travel, the Story Teller, who left home in "lighthearted desperation," re-enters his New England village a sadder, a wiser, and perhaps a dying man. Although only some twenty-four years of age, he returns from his journeying with "wasted frame and feeble step" (XI, 326).

The weakened state of Hawthorne's solitary man is far more than a maudlin, Byronic affectation. The disease, enervation, and casualties of travel,
whether undertaken for knowledge, profit, or adventure, were all too well
known in the Hawthorne family and in the journals of other real travelers
from Thomas Coryat to Samuel Shaw. In "The Custom-House" Hawthorne
contrasts the hardy figure of the "outward-bound sailor," in search of a position, with "the recently arrived one, pale and feeble, seeking a passport to
the hospital" (I, 6). An essay titled "Pilgrimage to Mecca" that appeared in
the *American Magazine of Useful and Entertaining Knowledge* shortly after
Hawthorne's tenure as editor drew a conventional sketch of the cost of travel,
contrasting the splendor of a caravan departing Cairo with the depleted pilgrims who reached the holy shrine:

> Alas, how different was the appearance of this same caravan, after a long
> and fatiguing march across the desert, on its arrival at *Mecca!* Wan, pale, and
> worn down with fatigue and thirst, incrusted with a thick coat of dust and
> perspiration, they who composed it seemed scarcely able to crawl to the place
> of their destination. . . . One had almost lost his sight by the sand and dust;
> another preserved but a remnant of intellect, and a third in consequence of
> great fatigue and constant alarms and fears, had become subject to spasmodic
> movements, and he held his head fast by the ears to prevent its turning round
> like a top.[40]

If Eliakim did not perish in the course of their travels, like Carsten Niebuhr's
fellow travelers to Arabia in the 1760s, he apparently separated from the Story
Teller before the latter's return.

There is no evidence that the Story Teller and his companion ever left
their native land and the Canadian shores of the Great Lakes, yet he coaxes
the reader to experience their journey under the species of world travel. The
Story Teller introduced himself to Eliakim by remarking: "To be sure, there
was a certain place which I called home; but I have resolved not to see it
again, till I have been quite round the globe, and enter the street on the east,
as I left it on the west" (X, 414). At the end of his journey he laments the
modesty of his accomplishments in these words:

> The time has been when I meant to visit every region of the earth, except the
> Poles and central Africa. I had a strange longing to see the Pyramids. To Persia
> and Arabia, and all the gorgeous East, I owed a pilgrimage for the sake of their
> magic tales. And England, the land of my ancestors! . . . Yet, with this home-
> sickness for the father-land, and all these plans of remote travel,—which I yet
> believe that my peculiar instinct impelled me to form, and upbraided me for
> not accomplishing—the utmost limit of my wanderings has been little more
> than six hundred miles from my native village. Thus, in whatever way I consider
> my life, or what must be termed such, I cannot feel as if I have lived at all.
> (XI, 315)[41]

It is important to notice that even in painful retrospect the Story Teller
does not regret his *choice to travel*, and to earn his way as an itinerant novelist,

but rather his *failure to travel far enough*. He has been suspended, irresolutely, somewhere between the domestic felicity of his native village and those consummating experiences for which Eastern travelers gladly risked disease and death. The narrator's language in "The Canal-Boat" illustrates his droll but unavailing effort to evoke a cosmopolitan "voyage" and the experiences of a "traveller" from "the dismal swamps and unimpressive scenery" along the Erie Canal: "Bound to a distant port, we had neither chart nor compass, nor cared about the wind, nor felt the heaving of a billow, nor dreaded shipwreck, however fierce the tempest, in our adventurous navigation of an interminable mud-puddle" (X, 430). Simultaneously committed to the world views of the Eastern travelers yet inhibited by the scope of the author's own inland experiences, Hawthorne's Story Teller was doomed from the outset to the realm of unrealized dreams.

While failing to realize the ambitions of his elastic youth, the Story Teller also has forsworn in their pursuit "the settled, sober, careful gladness of a man by his own fireside, with those around him whose welfare is committed to his trust and their guidance to his fond authority." The gay damsel and her male companion in "The Seven Vagabonds"—"Blessed pair"—were able to reconcile the two great adventures of love and travel, and to establish a "happy home . . . throughout all the earth!" But domestic as well as foreign delights elude the Story Teller. For all his "vagrant fantasies," he writes, "I have never truly loved, and perhaps shall be doomed to loneliness throughout the eternal future, because, here on earth, my soul has never married itself to the soul of woman." Unlike Fanshawe a few years earlier, the solitary man finally comes to believe, with the philosophical mind of Johnson and Goldsmith, that, "The truly wise, after all their speculations, will be led into the common path, and, in homage to the human nature that pervades them, will gather gold, and till the earth, and set out trees, and build a house" (XI, 314).

From the beginning the Story Teller declares an intention to write his book "for the sake of its moral, which many a dreaming youth may profit by, though it is the experience of a wandering story teller" (X, 409). The interior tales of *The Story Teller* cycle contribute their own several morals, sometimes implicitly but often, as characteristic of the genre, with a final formulated statement. Finally in "My Home Return" (the only separately titled section of "Fragments from the Journal of a Solitary Man") the narrator draws the composite moral to which all the others have led:

> "He shall be taught," said I, "by my life, and by my death, that the world is a sad one for him who shrinks from its sober duties. My experience shall warn him to adopt some great and serious aim, such as manhood will cling to, that he may not feel himself, too late, a cumberer of this over-laden earth, but a man among men. I will beseech him not to follow an eccentric path, nor, by stepping aside from the highway of human affairs, to relinquish his claim upon human sympathy. And often, as a text of deep and varied meaning, I will remind him that he is an American." (XI, 326–327)

The parting injunction emphasizes the extent to which his sympathies and calling alienated the Story Teller from his native land.

Storytellers and Pilgrims

In his discerning essay "The Storyteller" Walter Benjamin traced the origins of the genre to two prototypes: the seafaring merchant, who introduced the lore of faraway places, and the settled cultivator, who "stayed at home, making an honest living, and who knows the local tales and traditions." The former brought to storytelling the romance of the geographically remote; the latter contributed "the lore of the past, as it best reveals itself to natives of a place." Each sphere, Benjamin observed, has produced its own tribe of storytellers. The full historical development of storytelling "is inconceivable without the most intimate interpenetration of these two archaic types," and the storyteller reaches his "full corporeality" only by fusing them.[42]

The twin currents of storytelling came together in the manuscript Hawthorne completed in 1834.[43] The "tension between the traveller and the stay-at-home" is fundamental not only to understanding the overall structure of *The Story Teller* but to appraising individual tales within the work and much of Hawthorne's subsequent writings. While his frame narrative transports the reader outward to distant places, such interior tales as "Young Goodman Brown," "The Gray Champion," and "The Ambitious Guest" frequently carry the listener backwards into American history and folklore. It is tempting to find a similar tension at work, biographically, between Hawthorne's maternal relatives, the Mannings, with their sedentary ways, and the paternal Hawthornes, who for three generations and more had ventured forth on ever farther seas. Keeping account books for the Mannings' New England coachlines while imitating entries in his father's East India logs, Hawthorne embodied within himself the doubleness of the storyteller.

Benjamin made a moral as well as an aesthetic distinction between the modern novel, which is written by a single, uncounseled individual, and the oral tale, in which the experience of the storyteller and his audience meets. "The nature of every real story," according to Benjamin, is that "it contains, openly or covertly, something useful. The usefulness may, in one case, consist in a moral; in another, in some practical advice; in a third, in a proverb or maxim. In every case the storyteller is a man who has counsel for his readers." The rise of the novel and the dissemination of the printed word heralded the decline of the personal art of storytelling and the wisdom it conveyed.[44] This process of secularization is evident in Hawthorne's career both through the experience of the Story Teller, whose initially spontaneous tales are frozen in print for the sake of "the book," and through the author's subsequent shift in genre from "oral" tales to the long prose romances of the 1850s.[45] Understanding the prototypes and narrative intentions of *The Story Teller* might temper the impatience some critics have shown towards Hawthorne's efforts to extract wisdom from the fabric of life.

The twin streams of storytelling described by Benjamin are closely related to the two forms of literature that Percy Adams has juxtaposed in *Travel Literature and the Evolution of the Novel*: "the domestic narrative and the adventure narrative, the static and the dynamic."[46] The central fact in the personal destiny of Hawthorne's Story Teller is his oscillation between these poles. The tension of travel and the native village, adventure and domesticity, is also the chief theme of the tales he invents, whether explicitly in "Young Goodman Brown," "The May-Pole of Merry Mount," "Wakefield," and "The Great Carbuncle," or more subtly in "Little Annie's Ramble" and "The Village Uncle."

The journey motif is fundamental both to Hawthorne's earlier tales and to his later romances. The diverse nature of the journeys undertaken by his protagonists, in *The Story Teller* and elsewhere, has not been thoroughly explored, nor is this the place for a taxonomy of his travelers. Before proceeding, however, it is useful to consider what kind of traveler the Story Teller might be. To refine the critical usage of the term Dan Vogel has distinguished five species of *journey*—the Wandering, the Quest, the Pilgrimage, the Odyssey, and the Going-Forth—which are characterized principally by the motives and goals of the traveler. These modes are not mutually exclusive and may well appear at successive stages of a single account. Hawthorne's Story Teller, for example, represents himself as a purposeless wanderer until he announces his career as an "itinerant novelist" (in "The Seven Vagabonds"). After he joins with Eliakim (in "The Story Teller"), his journey takes on the nature of a pilgrimage, by his own avowal, and aspects of a quest. His flight from home also reflects the conditions of a Going-Forth, where the hero "feels stirred only by possibility, not by a preconceived vision of his goal."[47]

Pilgrimage would appear to be the form of journey most broadly applicable to *The Story Teller* inasmuch as the Story Teller lays explicit claim to the title "pilgrim" and directs his journey towards the natural shrine of Niagara Falls.[48] Within its framework of pilgrimage, however, *The Story Teller* relates a variety of individual quests. Whatever the cause of a hero's departure from home, the continuation of his journey, Percy Adams has noted, "nearly always involve[s] some kind of quest." Seven types common to both the novel and the travel narrative are quests involving "religion, war, a golden or social utopia, exploration, monetary gain, a person, and knowledge of the world or oneself."[49] Eliakim Abbott's quest obviously is of the first type; he searches for souls to save, if not from paganism, then at least from spiritual inertia. The Story Teller explicitly repudiates the search for monetary gain. In lieu of material objectives, he embarks on a quest of exploration (combining adventure and vocation) that, in due course, evolves into a quest for knowledge of himself. The stories he invents and tells along his way are species of his own quest to know his place in the world. Most specifically, the quest theme that runs throughout Hawthorne's work from 1829 to 1838 focuses on the meaning and discovery of "home."[50] Considering the biography of the author, it is not surprising to find an occasional search also for father figures.

The *catastrophe* of Hawthorne's solitary man—a product of the tales he invented as well as of his six years' travel—is not entirely typical of the genre. The conventional traveler, according to Adams, "whether a questor from the start or perhaps turning from a motiveless going forth to a quest or pilgrimage,

... finally turns home, the conqueror of great forces, wiser, perhaps sadder, but invariably master of the world he started from as well as all those worlds he encountered during his heroic or adventurous or knowledge-seeking years of wandering."[51] The travelers from Salem, however, did not always return, and those that did, not invariably as masters of their own fate.

Travelers Home

The dominant theme of the tales told by the Story Teller is one of journeying forth and homecoming. In psychological terms, this tension between the foreign and the domestic reflected the doubleness in the author's own heritage. In aesthetic terms, the antithesis between a wandering fancy and fidelity to the native land expressed his problematic search for materials and perspectives suitable to writing American romance. In moral terms, the pilgrims populating the tales in *The Story Teller* mirrored the narrator's quest, foreshadowed in the novel *Fanshawe*, for a reasonable choice of life. It would be impractical and unnecessary to evaluate each of the interior tales of *The Story Teller* even if there were consensus on their identity. A look chiefly at "An Ontario Steamboat," "The Great Carbuncle," "The Village Uncle," "Little Annie's Ramble," "Young Goodman Brown," and "The Threefold Destiny" should illustrate sufficiently the dramatic prefiguring of the Story Teller's own destiny in the tales he enacts.

The reflective sketch "An Ontario Steamboat," which Hawthorne published in the *American Magazine of Useful and Entertaining Knowledge* for March 1836, almost certainly was first written for *The Story Teller*. What position it occupied in the original work we cannot tell, but when Hawthorne used this account of American pilgrimage in his first issue of the *American Magazine*, he placed it immediately after his history of the holy city "Jerusalem" and its successive Eastern monarchs. Together "Jerusalem" and "An Ontario Steamboat" bracketed the march of civilization from Sosotris, King of Egypt, to immigrant travel and tourist cruises on "the Steam-boats on the Canadian lakes."[52]

The precincts of Hawthorne's steamboat, bound westward from Ogdensburgh to the other end of Lake Ontario, serve the classical purposes of a pilgrim's caravan "for studying the characteristics of different nations, and the peculiarities of different castes." While the narrator holds a ticket among the aristocracy in the "grand cabin," his sympathies, like Robin's predilections for his simple countrymen's caravansary in "My Kinsman, Major Molineux," direct him to the "male and female multitude on the forward deck." There he is attracted by the slender girls "preparing to repose their maiden-like forms on the wide, promiscuous couch of the deck," and particularly by one "young woman, who had a babe at her bosom." Hawthorne's observations while traveling in the fall of 1832 were instructed by the Oriental travelers he had read late the previous year. He may have remembered at this point, for instance, John Chardin's remarks on a woman with a child at her breast bought by a Greek merchant while crossing the Black Sea from Constantinople to Persia in 1671. "Indeed," Chardin wrote, "I never saw more lovely Nipples, and a rounder Neck, nor a smoother Skin; which created both Envy and Compassion."[53]

After peering into the lives of the promiscuous multitude on the forward deck, the narrator of "An Ontario Steamboat" fastens upon a single family of "very straightened circumstances" but such obvious "moral strength" that, he says, "it did me good to look at them."

> In one sense, they were homeless, but in another, they were always at home; for domestic love, the remembrance of joys and sorrows shared together, the mutual anxieties and hopes, the united trust in Heaven, these gave them a home in one another's hearts; and whatever sky might be above them, that sky was the roof of their home.

The narrator's sober pleasure in this scene echoes the quiet envy felt by the seventh vagabond while in the presence of his gypsy damsel and her male companion. The moral drawn by the author, however, as he considers the homeless exiles' "passage through the world" rings closer to Eliakim's characteristic resignation to Providence: "As we had all our destined port, and the skill of the steersman would suffice to bring us thither, so had each of these poor wanderers a home in futurity—and the God above them knew where to find it."

The family grouping in "An Ontario Steamboat"—"a father and a mother, and two or three children"—carrying their household with them, is unusual among Hawthorne's pilgrims. Dramatic economy, if not indeed psychological considerations, encouraged him to focus typically on the first two pillars of the domestic establishment, man and wife, just prior to or after the time of marriage. Furthermore, while the new wives for a time accompanied their husbands on excursions from home, his young women eventually became associated with the immobile household gods. With rare exceptions like Mary Wortley Montagu and Emma Roberts, the voyagers and travelers Hawthorne read were male. The instinct of men, he believed, was to travel; the instinct of women, to remain at home. "No doubt," Hawthorne wrote in another *American Magazine* essay:

> The unhappiness of female emigrants may be largely attributed to the innate character of the sex. Women were not meant to be wanderers, as men are. . . . A wise Providence has given woman a nature unfitted for change of place, that she may be like a warm, domestic light, beaming from a cottage window, to lure man homeward, who would otherwise roam far and wide, nor ever settle down, till his limbs were too stiff to bear him further. (AM, 476)[54]

It became increasingly evident in Hawthorne's work that, against his roaming, unsettled nature, a man's "careful gladness" was to be found "by his own fireside." In his successive works of the 1830s and afterwards Hawthorne's fair-haired New England maids are identified almost indissolubly with the American lares and penates.

In the course of his travels Hawthorne's Story Teller offered his countrymen a series of parables and precautionary tales building, in the composite, to the final admonition "not to follow an eccentric path" nor to forget "that he is an American." Two of the tales associated with *The Story Teller*, "The Canterbury Pilgrims" and "The May-Pole of Merry Mount," find the "warm, domestic light" from interestingly opposite points of departure.[55] In the former tale, as mentioned in the previous chapter, Josiah and Miriam flee the Shaker utopia at Canterbury to begin life together outside the Happy Valley. Of the pilgrims they meet laboring in the other direction, the most sobering are a family of parents and children whose love and patience, unlike the cheerful household on the Ontario steamboat, have been worn away by the vicissitudes of the world. While the young couple in "The Canterbury Pilgrims" exchange a sexless Eden for the real world of passions and the flesh, Edgar and Edith, the Lord and Lady of "The May-Pole of Merry Mount," readily allow themselves to be retrieved by Endicott and his somber Puritans from the erotic fairyland into which they had wandered. Such possibilities for happiness as the world offers are found not in utopias, either ascetic or sensual, but among the common sufferings and sympathies of home.

Traveling newlyweds are the central characters also in "The Great Carbuncle: A Mystery of the White Mountains," which the Story Teller apparently narrated on his way through New Hampshire. Like the two earlier couples, Matthew and Hannah are surrounded by a lively company. But while Josiah and Miriam, Edgar and Edith, are depicted rather statically in their moments of transition, Matthew and Hannah actively engage with six other travelers in searching for a fabulous gemstone. Hawthorne's seven vagabonds made common cause when planning their pilgrimage to the camp meeting at Stamford. The eight travelers of "The Great Carbuncle" are competitors for a prize that, presumably, only one can attain.

"The Great Carbuncle" has been labeled by Patrick Morrow as one of a "Pilgrimage Group" of tales that ran throughout Hawthorne's short story writing career.[56] While the narrator refers more than once to the "pilgrims of the Great Carbuncle," it is more accurate to read this as a tale not of common *pilgrimage* but of individualized *quests* with the eight adventurers respectively seeking riches, or fame, or knowledge of self and the world.[57] The Seeker, Doctor Cacaphodel, Ichabod Pigsnort, the Cynic, the Poet, and Lord Devere all are killed, blinded, or otherwise confounded in their search for the radiant gem. Matthew and Hannah alone escape untouched. Their original purpose, unlike their "selfish and solitary" rivals, is an innocent one: to light their humble cottage with the luminous stone and admire one another's face in its glow. As they ascend the Crystal Hills, it is true, "nature herself seemed no longer to keep them company," and in the actual radiance of the red stone they seem "changed to one another's eyes." But they stop at the brink of fatal enchantment, vowing instead to "kindle the cheerful glow of our hearth, at eventide, and be happy in its light," and never again to "desire more light than all the world may share with us" (IX, 160–163). Eschewing the alien stone, they drink a simple communion of lake water from the hollow of their hands and return to "peaceful years" and "length-ened lives" at home. Rejected by the simple, wise young couple, the gem begins to lose its splendor and, reportedly, falls from the cliff where it was embedded.

Beyond its generic similarity to "the dreamer awakes" theme in *The Ara-bian Nights* two elements of "The Great Carbuncle" particularly evoke Haw-thorne's prototypes in the East and their moralizing tales. One is the carbuncle itself, which although ostensibly discovered in the folklore of the American Indians, was particularly associated at the time with the caverns and alchemy of the East—a matter that will be discussed in the next chapter. The other concerns Dr. Cacaphodel, the second character introduced in the tale, "a little elderly personage . . . who had wilted and dried himself into a mummy, by continually stooping over charcoal furnaces, and inhaling unwholesome fumes, during his researches in chemistry and alchymy" (IX, 151).

Dr. Cacaphodel seeks the elusive stone not for wealth or personal adorn-ment but for scientific analysis and the purposes of a learned dissertation he hopes to write. Hawthorne seems to have derived both his doctor's name and occupation from the cuckolded apothecary "Dr. Cacafogo" in Letter XIX of Goldsmith's *Citizen of the World*, titled "From Lien Chi Altangi, to Fum Hoam, first president of the Ceremonial Academy at Pekin, in China [The English method of treating women caught in adultery. The Russian method]."[58] The marital infidelity suffered by Goldsmith's Dr. Cacafogo, and Lien Chi Altangi's instructive report on modes of punishing faithless wives in India, Persia, Turkey, and China, could have served as a caution to Matthew and Hannah. More importantly, though, Hawthorne intended the name itself, *caca-phodel*, as a warning against following eccentric paths in life. The prefix has a plainly excrementary connotation, and *phodel* probably derived from the obsolete verb *fode*, which according to the *Oxford English Dictionary* means: "To entertain with delusive expectations; to encourage or confirm a foolish purpose or opinion, soothe in fancied security." True to his name and to the motif at the heart of Hawthorne's tale, Dr. Cacaphodel, like his fellow pilgrims of the Great Carbuncle, embarked on a delusive quest leading him far from home. Dr. Cacaphodel is little more than a type character in "The Great Carbuncle," but the rumors that he conducted experiments with his own blood are premonitory, and from this germ proceeded a school of outlandish scientists and magicians in Hawthorne's works, frequently given Eastern mannerisms, that includes Aylmer, Rappaccini, Chillingworth, and Westerveldt.

Not all the marital tales in *The Story Teller* end in such unambiguous felicity as Matthew and Hannah share, nor could Hawthorne's Story Teller have played this single chord endlessly without wearying his audience. "Wake-field," for example, imagines the psychological circumstances of "the strangest instance, on record, of marital delinquency." The narrator tells of a placidly married man of London who, "under pretence of going a journey," bids his wife adieu and returns to the fireside only after twenty years of watching her, from a distance, grieve and grow old. The conclusion of "Wakefield" holds a lesson for the Story Teller and for all species of wanderers from Young Goodman Brown to Ethan Brand: "[B]y stepping aside for a moment, a man exposes himself to a fearful risk of losing his place forever. Like Wakefield, he may become, as it were, the Outcast of the Universe" (IX, 140).

One of the least known but more intriguing tales Hawthorne composed in 1833–1834 is "The Village Uncle: An Imaginary Retrospect," which originally appeared under the title "The Mermaid; A Reverie" in *The Token* for 1835.[59] "The Village Uncle" seems at first to be a simple reminiscence by an elderly New England fisherman on the domesticating influence of his late wife, Susan. Its subtitle, however, opens the possibility that Hawthorne's Story Teller, towards the darkening end of his journey, imagines for himself an alternative to the itinerant novelist's life that became his fate. The Village Uncle, raised in a coastal town whose sons sailed as far as the East Indies and told "narratives that might startle Sinbad the sailor," once possessed a heart by nature like a "chill and lonesome cavern, hung round with glittering icicles of fancy" (IX, 315–316). A half century earlier the rugged old man was a pale, solitary figure, locked in a hermitage of his own mind, "a scribbler of wearier trash" than even the volumes he read, "a man who had wandered out of the real world and . . . hardly knew whether he lived, or only dreamed of living" (IX, 311). Then Susan's "simple and happy nature" mingled itself with his own, and while he "taught her to love the moonlight hour" and lent her mind a contemplative turn, she "kindled a domestic fire" within his heart and made him feel "a deeper poetry" (IX, 316–317). The quiet tale of wooing and home ends without apparent regret: "Be this the moral, then. In chaste and warm affections, humble wishes, and honest toil for some useful end, there is health for the mind, and quiet for the heart, the prospects of a happy life, and the fairest hope of Heaven" (IX, 323).

"The Village Uncle" casts a wistful but unembittered retrospect down the road not taken. "Little Annie's Ramble," which also may have been told by the Story Teller in the lonely years at home following the conclusion of his journey, shows the narrator in a more troubled and regretful state of mind.[60] This little regarded tale begins with a seemingly aimless excursion through the streets of a coastal town by an adult male attired in black and a sprightly five-year-old girl he has taken from her father's doorstep. The child, with "that longing after the mystery of the great world" (IX, 121) that he had felt in his own boyhood, delights at the simple color and variety of shop window and street side. In the course of their ramble images of the East are subtly but schematically juxtaposed to homely products. The "turbaned Turk, threatening us with his sabre, like an ugly heathen as he is," is safely immobilized behind glass next to "a Chinese mandarine," toy soldiers, and a wooden doll (IX, 124). The circus has brought its great elephant to town and a haughty tiger who "was wont to leap forth upon such inferior animals [as man], from the jungles of Bengal." In an adjoining cage, "a hyena from Egypt, who has doubtless howled around the pyramids, and a black bear from our own forests, are fellow-prisoners, and most excellent friends. The narrator moralizes, "Are there any two living creatures, who have so few sympathies that they cannot possibly be friends?" In this spirit of cultural harmony, where East and West lie down together, even the chimney sweep's voice sounds forth "like that of a muezzin from the summit of a mosque" (IX, 126–128).

In the end, however, the momentary accord of age and youth, of the errant man and the "sinless child," of the foreign and the native is broken by a peal of alarm. The same town crier who at the start of the tale announces "that an elephant, and a lion, and a royal tiger, and a horse with horns, and other strange beasts from foreign countries, have come to town" broadcasts the disappearance of young Annie (IX, 121). If this were a tale of the twentieth century, the narrator would be accused of child molestation. The solitary man, however, has taken the innocent child in hand only to see the world again through eyes for which Turks and tigers and muezzins are still part of the great untold mystery. He prays for her: "Forget not to thank heaven, my Annie, that after wandering a little way into the world, you may return at the first summons, with an untainted and unwearied heart, and be a happy child again. But I have gone too far astray for the town crier to call me back!" In his wanderings, had he become "some monstrous beast more horrible than any in the caravan?" (IX, 128–129).

Lost and Found: "Young Goodman Brown" and "The Threefold Destiny"

As he laments in "Fragments from the Journal of a Solitary Man," the Story Teller realized neither of the two great opportunities available to him. He "never truly loved." Nor did he satisfy his "peculiar instinct" to visit the wondrous East. The two goals, as Hawthorne had observed in his own family history, must have seemed mutually exclusive. But the tension between them provided the continuing drama within and between the tales and sketches of *The Story Teller*. The domestic triumphs of "The Canterbury Pilgrims," "The May-Pole of Merry Mount," and "The Great Carbuncle" became ever harder to sustain in the course of the Story Teller's travels. "The Village Uncle" finally has the spectral and intangible air of a seafarer's reverie. The naivete of "Little Annie's Ramble," built on the purloined consciousness of a child, crumbles before the irredeemable *alienation* of the traveler.

Whatever the original sequence of its parts, and their present critical reputation, the dramatic design of *The Story Teller* eventually inspired a tale that is recognized to be one of Hawthorne's most acute explorations of human darkness and light, estrangement and faith. "Young Goodman Brown," which appeared in the *New-England Magazine* for April 1835, has been praised autonomously for its superior fusion of psychological romance and the folklore of American witchcraft. Yet its place in the narrative and thematic structure of *The Story Teller* is also immediately apparent. Hawthorne's protagonist is a younger "traveller" (he repeats the label) who, after three months of marriage to his homey maiden, still must embark on a "journey" (also repeated) away from the village of Salem and into a strange part of the world to find his "nature" and his "destiny" (X, 86). Like many of the Arabian tales Hawthorne's story concerns a night pilgrimage and is pursued in a dreamlike atmosphere. "My journey, as thou callest it, forth and back again," Young Goodman Brown tells his wife, "must needs be done 'twixt now and sunrise" (X, 74). Unlike Josiah, Edgar, and Matthew, however, Young Goodman Brown is unaccompanied by his young bride, or so he first believes. And unlike the outsetting Story Teller, who is joined by the godly if ineffectual Eliakim, Young Goodman Brown finds his "fellow-traveller" is the devil. While Eliakim may have someways protected his secular companion, the new wayfarer leads Young Goodman Brown directly into temptation.

There are few explicit references to the East in "Young Goodman Brown," only that the devil's rod had formerly been lent "to the Egyptian magi." But the witch's coven in the forest—lighted by four burning pine trees and filled with frightful sounds—the baptism of blood, the polluted hearts and obscene crimes all evoke the concatenation of evil in a number of Oriental tales, most notably the Hall of Eblis in Beckford's *Vathek* and Thalaba's descent to Domdaniel and the caverns of hell in Southey's romance.

The same temptation from which Young Goodman Brown finally recoils—"to penetrate, in every bosom, the deep mystery of sin, the fountain of all wicked arts" (X, 87)—was offered to the horrible sorceress Princess Carathis and to her son the Caliph. Like Hawthorne's young traveler, Vathek intended to renounce god (or Mahomet) and adore the powers of earth only long enough to learn the divine secrets, and he vowed to return to the arms of Nouronihar after visiting the Palace of Subterranean Fire.[61] Young Goodman Brown and his Faith are as Puritan and American as Beckford's pair are erotic and Oriental. Nonetheless, both tales involve an underworld of sex and magic, and their outcome is nearly identical. By the end, in Beckford's words, the hearts of the young travelers had "burst into flames"; "they lost the most precious gift of Heaven, *hope!*"; and they became "horrors" to themselves, and to the world around them.[62]

Hawthorne also may have had Robert Southey's "Champion of the Lord ... against the race of Hell" in mind, but if so, he dramatically inverts, or at least complicates, the intentions of the hero. The object of Thalaba's quest was to avenge his father's and siblings' murder, and after some vacillation he found himself the warrior of good against the forces of hell. Young Goodman Brown, on the other hand, not only flees the witches' sabbath at the end but carries away devastating doubts about the goodness of his ancestry. On his way "to root from earth the Sorcerer brood," Thalaba asked his guardian angel, "Tell me the needful Talisman!" He was answered, "The Talisman is Faith."[63] His Faith saved him at the last minute when he was tempted by the transparent garments and "harlot limbs" of the dancing girls.

> With earnest eyes the banqueters
> Fed on the sight impure;
> And Thalaba, he gazed,
> But in his heart he bore a talisman,
> Whose blessed alchemy

> To virtuous thoughts refined
> The loose suggestions of the scene impure.
> Oneiza's image swam before his sight,
> His own Arabian Maid.
> He rose, and from the banquet room he rush'd,
> Tears coursed his burning cheek;
> And nature for a moment woke the thought,
> And murmur'd, that, from all domestic joys
> Estranged, he wander'd o'er the world
> A lonely being, far from all he loved.
> Son of Hodeirah, not among thy crimes
> That momentary murmur shall be written![64]

Because death had rent Oneiza from his side in the very hour of marriage, Thalaba could enjoy his virginal bride only after passing through the gates of death, and then but with the spiritual senses. Young Goodman Brown's Faith is a more problematic woman. Whether she hears, or heeds, the husband's pleas—"Faith! Faith! . . . Look up to Heaven, and resist the Wicked One!"—is unanswered (X, 88). Matthew and Hannah, together, shunned the Great Carbuncle and drank pure water from their cupped hands. Does Young Goodman Brown's Faith, alone, drink blood from the hollowed rock? Once his Faith leaves home, the young man's dying hour is bound to be "gloom." Young Goodman Brown learns, too late, the risks of travel.

While it has become one of his most often anthologized tales, Hawthorne did not choose to republish "Young Goodman Brown" until Mosses from an Old Manse in 1846. By contrast, the now neglected "The Threefold Destiny: A Faery Legend," which first appeared in the American Monthly Magazine for March 1838, was collected almost immediately in the second edition of Twice-told Tales in 1842 and given the privileged position at the end of the volume. The relation between these tales is interesting not only because of Hawthorne's apparent fondness for the latter but for the parallelism between the two. Read together, they are mirror images, "The Threefold Destiny" a point-by-point refutation of the dour fate of Young Goodman Brown and an affirmation of the redemptive homecomings of the associated tales.

The connection of "The Threefold Destiny" with The Story Teller has not been confirmed. Although it was published a year or more after the other installments, the fact that it appeared in Park Benjamin's American Monthly Magazine at all suggests a possible relationship. It obviously is consistent with the preceding tales in its layered narrative, its Eastern experience and theme of existential quest, and its concern for teaching "many a dreaming youth" the need to foreswear a life of travel and fancy for a useful vocation at home. Alfred Weber saw in the tale an extraordinarily clear and detailed mirroring of The Story Teller frame and regarded its use of Oriental storytelling as a further link. Weber further suggested that "The Threefold Destiny" translates the life story of Hawthorne's Story Teller into a didactic fairy tale, with the reservation, which is an important one, that the Story Teller does not share Ralph Cranfield and Faith Egerton's happy fate.[65] The tone of this fairy legend and the destiny of its young couple, indeed, are diametrically opposed to the fate both of the Story Teller and of Faith and Young Goodman Brown. For the pariahhood of the traveling Story Teller, and his gloomy detachment from the realities of the world, "The Threefold Destiny" substitutes a roseate ending and an unprecedented conversion to the beatitudes of hearth and marriage.

If the tale had been written first for *The Story Teller*, it was thoroughly recast before Benjamin published it in March 1838. More likely it was an entirely new work that Hawthorne wrote about the same time he was preparing the biographical sketch of Thomas Green Fessenden that appeared in the January 1838 issue of Benjamin's magazine. An apparent germ for the story appears in Hawthorne's notebooks between August 22 and October 7, 1837:

> A young man and girl meet together, each in search of a person to be known by some particular sign. They watch and wait a great while for that person to pass; at last some casual circumstance discloses that each is the one whom the other is waiting for. Moral, that what we need for our happiness is often close at hand, if we knew but how to seek for it.[66]

Even more significant to the theme and characterization of the tale are the providential events that befell Hawthorne beginning in 1837 and permanently changed the direction of his life: the appearance of *Twice-told Tales* in March 1837; his acquaintance with the Peabody sisters starting in November 1837 (and the interest in the ethereal Sophia that began to manifest itself in his notebooks early the next year); and his "great moral enterprise," encouraged by Elizabeth Peabody, to create "a new literature for the young."[67] Writing "The Threefold Destiny" late in 1837 or early the following year, Hawthorne reemployed the Oriental tale to dispel the gloom of "Young Goodman Brown." As he came before the world in his own right, Hawthorne may have intended this fable as a refutation—abbreviated in size, identical in form and moral, but opposite in personal result—to the wearied resignation of *The Story Teller*.

"The Threefold Destiny" is a cogent paradigm of both Hawthorne's imaginative life and his art. The first paragraph, as Buford Jones has pointed out, "is literally a miniature critical preface and the second a fictional representation of the journey-to-fairy-land theme."[68] At the outset the narrator declares his intention to combine "the spirit and mechanism of the faery legend . . . with the characters and manners of familiar life" in a manner that will cast a "subdued tinge of the wild and wonderful" over the New England scene. Rather than telling a story of "real" events, however, he wishes to speak through "an allegory, such as the writers of the last century would have expressed in the shape of an eastern tale," yet infused with more warmth than those "fanciful productions."

To achieve this effect, the storyteller describes the homecoming one twilight summer eve of "a tall, dark figure, over which long and remote travel had thrown an outlandish aspect." In his ten years of world-wandering, Ralph Cranfield experienced at first hand the realities of those remote lands which the narrator of "Night Sketches Beneath an Umbrella" visited only through the literature of travel.

> The staff, on which this traveller leaned, had been his companion from the spot where it grew, in the jungles of Hindostan; the hat, that overshadowed his sombre brow, had shielded him from the suns of Spain; but his cheek had been blackened by the red-hot wind of an Arabian desert, and had felt the frozen breath of an Arctic region. Long sojourning amid wild and dangerous men, he still wore beneath his vest the ataghan which he had once struck into the throat of a Turkish robber. (IX, 472–473)

At every step the world-wanderer "had lost something of his New-England characteristics" and taken on new peculiarities so that when he reentered his native village he excited "the gaze and curiosity of all" (IX, 473). His first night in the remembered chamber where he had slumbered away his child-hood is wilder than any he ever spent "in an Arab tent"; in the clear light of the next day he confuses the familiar features of a village squire with those of the visionary sage who "had looked forth upon him from the Pyramid of Cheops" thinking that the same form had beckoned among the colonnades of the Alhambra and "mistily revealed itself through the ascending steam of the Great Geyser" (IX, 477–480).

As a young man Cranfield had expected three marvelous events to mark his destiny: the discovery of a beautiful maid wearing a talismanic jewel in the shape of a heart; the revelation of a hidden treasure; and the power to influence and sway his fellow creatures. Worn by his ungratified search, he chose, at last, to "lay aside the pilgrim's staff" and seek to regain "somewhat of the elasticity of youth in the spot where his threefold fate had been fore-shown him" (IX, 475). There, at his own doorstep, his destiny is accomplished. Cranfield finds the jeweled emblem that eluded him throughout the East in the common quartz arrowhead that he had placed in the bosom of his child-hood playmate Faith Egerton, and cries, clasping her in his arms: "Faith! Faith! ... you have interpreted my wild and weary dream!" (IX, 481). He discovers the treasure sign—"the Latin word *Effode—Dig!*"—carved by his own hand, on a tree at the door of his mother's dwelling (IX, 474). And the three venerable wisemen materialize as the worthy fathers of the village, come to offer him an office equal to kings and potentates, the village schoolmaster-ship.[69] The very breath of the village cattle, Cranfield realizes, is sweeter "than the perfume which was wafted to our ship from the Spice Islands" (IX, 480).

> Yes; the wild dreamer was awake at last. To find the mysterious treasure, he was to till the earth around his mother's dwelling, and reap its products! Instead of warlike command, or regal or religious sway, he was to rule over the village children! And now the visionary Maid had faded from his fancy, and in her place he saw the playmate of his childhood!

The narrator concludes his allegory by apotheosizing the happiness of those who read the riddle of existence "without a weary world-search" or spending a lifetime in vain: "Would all, who cherish such wild wishes, but look around them, they would oftenest find their sphere of duty, or prosperity, and happiness, within those precincts, and in that station where Providence itself has cast their lot" (IX, 481–482).

The "dreamer awakes" is a recurrent motif in Eastern tales, as in Irving's *Alhambra*, and one that Laurence would call to mind at the close of Hawthorne's sixth story of "Famous Old People" (VI, 107). The author also seems to have had Southey's *Thalaba the Destroyer* in mind once more when establishing an atmosphere of hazardous journeys in the East. Twice Thalaba, who like Cranfield (and Hawthorne) was left fatherless, heard the command: "*Remember, Destiny hath mark'd thee from Mankind!*" The first summons came from the Death-Angel, who decreed that he pursue the peculiar destiny left him by the death of his father. The second was delivered by Oneiza, the maid whose fairy form eluded Thalaba until his quest was accomplished.[70] "The Talisman is Faith" for both Thalaba and Cranfield on their journeys, and both characters achieve their maids only after annihilating the surreal worlds in which they have wandered. Hawthorne, however, inverts Thalaba's fate. Thalaba redeemed his Faith only after a spectacular transcendence of this life through death, while Cranfield, chasing away the fantasies of his twilight journeys, finds Faith to be a chaste goddess of the fireside.

To reach the conclusion that "nowhere else in all his writings is the Spenserian basis for the techniques of his craft so frankly explained" as in "The Threefold Destiny" one must first overlook a great deal of evidence that Hawthorne knew and cultivated in his own way the fairy legends of the East.[71] A closer analogy to Hawthorne's tale than the *Faerie Queene* would be the Rev. Russell Conwell's famous "Acres of Diamonds" speech, which the American Baptist minister delivered over six thousand times in the half century following the Civil War. Conwell began his inspirational address with the parable of an ancient Persian farmer who roamed the world in search of riches from the Indus River to Golconda and the Mountains of the Moon. The parable concluded: "Had Al Hafed remained at home and dug in his own cellar or in his own garden, instead of wretchedness, starvation, poverty and death in a strange land, he would have had 'acres of diamonds'—for every acre, yes, every shovelful of that old farm afterwards revealed the gems which since have decorated the crowns of monarchs."[72]

"The Threefold Destiny" is a richer blend of adventure, psychology, and wisdom than one is likely to realize if armed only with the models of Bunyan and Spenser. Restored to its original context in Hawthorne's life and works, and seen in a dramatic relationship with other tales like "Young Goodman Brown," "The Threefold Destiny" is less easily dismissed as a "pat, little moralized legend," and more likely to be seen, through the eyes of the younger Henry James, as evincing "in a degree distinctly appreciable . . . an original element in literature."[73] The maidens' symbolic name *Faith* (ambiguous in "Young Goodman Brown," unquestioned in "The Threefold Destiny") is only one of the counterpoints linking the two tales. Young Goodman Brown embarks on his journey at nightfall; Ralph Cranfield returns home before dark. The ministers, magistrates, and father figures of Salem lead Young Goodman Brown astray by promising to show him "your nature and your destiny"; Cranfield seeks his "Messenger of Destiny" throughout the East before discovering him at home. While the earlier tale wonders problematically, "Had Goodman Brown fallen asleep in the forest, and only dreamed a wild dream of a witch-meeting?" (X, 89), in the latter tale the wild dreamer awakes at last. And while their search in "The Great Carbuncle" is a delusion (a *phodel*) for all the "pilgrims" except Matthew and Hannah, Cranfield's *effode* ends with a general consecration of family, community, and occupation.

"The Threefold Destiny" can be read as Hawthorne's spiritual homecoming—a testament of love to New England maidenhood, a farewell to the damsels and fancies of the Orient that had warmed his chamber in Herbert Street for a dozen years. But the reconciliations between home and travel, duty and fancy, were not absolute. Hawthorne wrote in his notebook during July 1838 in anticipation of an extended vacation from Salem: "[Ladurlad], in the Curse of Kehama—on visiting a certain celestial region, the fire in his heart and brain died away for a season, but was rekindled again on returning to earth. So may it be with me, in my projected three month's seclusion from old associations."[74] Ralph Cranfield, happily, saw the world before marriage while Young Goodman Brown began his journey only after three months in wedlock. In "Rappaccini's Daughter" and Hawthorne's romances of the 1850s the Oriental maidens would wax ardent and sensual as confessions of love for the homegrown, fair-haired mermaids following Susan and Faith grew increasingly pallid and strained.

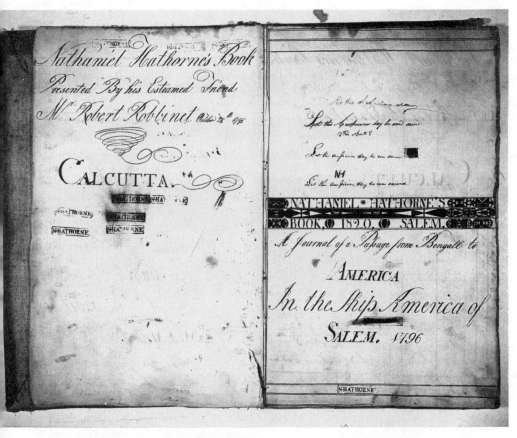

Hawthorne's appropriation of his father's logbook for the *America* (1795–1796). Courtesy of The Essex Institute, Salem, Massachusetts.

"Ahmad bin Na'aman, Emissary from Muscat to the United States, Friend of Salem Merchants," portrait by Edward Mooney (1840). Peabody Museum, Salem, Massachusetts.

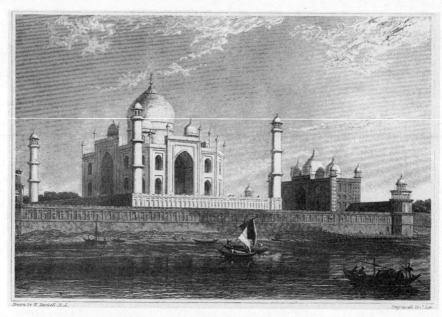

"The Taje-mah'l at Agra," *The Oriental Annual* (1834). Courtesy of
The Huntington Library, San Marino, California.

"The Favorite of the Haram," *The Oriental Annual* (1835).
Courtesy of the Huntington Library, San Marino, California.

Sultan IBRAHIM Emperour of the Turkes *Anno Dom.* 1640

I That of Ottman Blood Remain Alone
Call'd From a Pryson to ascend a Throne
My Silly Mind I Bend to Soft Delights
Hating th'unpleasant thoughts of Nauall Fights
Till Mad With Wanton Loues I Fall at First
Slaue to My Owne Then to My Peoples Lust.

Hiram Powers, *The Greek Slave* (1843). Yale University Art Gallery. Olive Louise Dann Fund.

Harriet Goodhue Hosmer, *Zenobia in Chains* (1859). Wadsworth
Atheneum, Hartford. Gift of Mrs. Josephine M. J. Dodge.

William Wetmore Story, *Cleopatra* (1869 [original, 1858]). The Metropolitan Museum of Art. Gift of John Taylor Johnston, 1888. (88.5 a-d)

THE FAIRY-LAND
OF HAWTHORNE'S
ROMANCE

"Visits to Castles in the Air—Chateaus en Espagne &c—
with remarks on that sort of architecture"

ON JULY 9, 1842, the thirty-six-year-old author's life took an irrevocable turn. That day Nathaniel Hawthorne was married to Sophia Peabody in Boston and, as he wrote to his sister on July 10, moved "straight to Paradise" at the Manse in Concord.[1] Particularly during their first year of marriage the Hawthornes celebrated life at the Manse as "a perfect Eden." The relation of the New Adam and Eve was never far offstage in the twenty-one stories and sketches Hawthorne published during his three years in Concord and in the two-volume *Mosses from an Old Manse* (1846).

Because sketches in *Mosses from an Old Manse* show a heightened interest in contemporary social problems, they have been taken to represent Hawthorne's "attempt to develop a more fully realistic strain in his art." J. Donald Crowley has called *Mosses* "an epitome of Hawthorne's continuing efforts to reconcile the claims of the life of the imagination with those attaching to an active involvement in the real world."[2] The new collection, however, by no means brought an end, or even a suspension, to the author's pilgrimages to the lands of wonder. Some of the pieces that went into *Mosses*—e.g., "Young Goodman Brown" and "Passages from a Relinquished Work"—were written for *The Story Teller* and demonstrate motifs consistent with Hawthorne's conception of that story cycle, but even the tales written in the early 1840s manifest the author's continuing penchant to leave the actualities of home for imaginative explorations.

Hawthorne struggled for some time to create an introduction for his *Mosses* that would present the newly assembled pieces in the proper atmosphere. He wrote to Evert Duyckinck in July 1845: "It was my purpose to construct a sort of frame-work, in this new story, for the series of stories already published, and to make the scene an idealization of our old parsonage, and of the river close at hand, with glimmerings of my actual life—yet so transmogrified that the reader should not know what was reality and what fancy."[3] "The Old Manse" is the first in the series of prefaces Hawthorne would offer over the next decade and a half in an effort to define what he referred to in "The Custom-House" as "a neutral territory, somewhere between the real world and fairy-land, where the Actual and the Imaginary may meet, and each imbue itself with the nature of the other." Most critics have fastened on the temporal rather than the geographical dimensions of Hawthorne's search for the *neutral territory*, noting his preceding remark in "The Custom-House" that "moonlight ... is a medium the most suitable for a romance-writer to get acquainted with his illusive guests" (I, 35–36) and the hypnagogic twilight settings of "Young Goodman Brown," "My Kinsman, Major Molineux," "The May-Pole of Merry Mount," "The Threefold Destiny," "Ethan Brand," and other tales. "The white sunshine of actual life" that Hawthorne speaks of in "The Hall of Fantasy" could be transcended by turning to the hours between day and night or, historically, by revisiting the old times. Yet Hawthorne also knew the imaginative possibilities of spatial distance, and beginning with *Mosses from an Old Manse* his prefaces took a turn away from the dusty highways of American life and towards the origins of the romance.

Once having left the public thoroughfare and turned down the wheel-track leading from the "gate-posts of rough-hewn stone" to the door of the Manse, readers of "The Old Manse" were invited to suspend the associations of their mundane lives. "The glimmering shadows, that lay half-asleep between the door of the house and the public highway, were a kind of spiritual medium, seen through which, the edifice had not quite the aspect of belonging to the material world" (X, 3). The Manse, like all of Concord, already was tinctured by the Orientalism of the Transcendentalists. Emerson had written *Nature* in Hawthorne's little nook of a study, "for he was then an inhabitant of the Manse, and used to watch the Assyrian dawn and the Paphian sunset and moonrise, from the summit of our eastern hill" (X, 5). The longer passage in *Nature* that Hawthorne is paraphrasing here gave a global formula of civilization and romance: "The dawn is my Assyria; the sunset and moonrise my Paphos, and unimaginable realms of faerie; broad noon shall be my England of the senses and the understanding; the night shall be my Germany of mystic philosophy and dreams."[4] For Emerson, and for Hawthorne too, the Assyrian and Paphian provided a fairy-land between the common sense of noonday and the dreams and mysticism of night. Herman Melville confirmed the exactness of this metaphor when he cited it in his review "Hawthorne and His

Mosses" in 1850. Although Hawthorne found the walls of his study blackened with smoke, "and made still blacker by the grim prints of Puritan ministers that hung around," a cheerful coat of paint and gold-tinted wallpaper soon brightened the small apartment (X, 5). And when memories of boating on the Concord river with Ellery Channing came back to him, he "could have fancied that this river had strayed forth out of the rich scenery of my companion's inner world;—only the vegetation along its banks should then have had an Oriental character" (X, 22).

Hawthorne brought to the Manse ideas and impressions of the East that, unlike Emerson's, were influenced more by the adventures of historic travelers and Arabian tales than by Indian philosophy or Persian poetry. He approached the bound volumes in the library of the Manse with "a superstitious reverence," for they had, he wrote, "a charm in my eyes, similar to what scraps of manuscript possess, for the good Mussulman. He imagines, that those wind-wafted records are perhaps hallowed by some sacred verse; and I, that every new book, or antique one, may contain the 'Open Sesame'—the spell to disclose treasures, hidden in some unsuspected cave of Truth" (X, 21). At the end of "The Old Manse" the author invites the reader to imagine himself a guest in the same cheerful study, where he will "take forth a roll of manuscript, and intreat his attention to the following tales" (X, 35).[5]

The Manse was Nathaniel and Sophia Hawthorne's first home, both a momentary Eden and a domestic refuge of the kind that his Story Teller, a decade earlier, had sought in vain. Nevertheless, by reason of his professional and financial needs the Bedouin life had become an established tradition that even Hawthorne's faithful marriage could not end. "In fairy-land, there is no measurement of time," Hawthorne wrote, "and, in a spot so sheltered from the turmoil of life's ocean, three years hastened away with a noiseless flight." But when the time came for them to recross the spiritual medium before the door of the Manse, to pass between the tall stone gate-posts and re-enter the thoroughfare of life, they did so "as uncertain as the wandering Arabs where our tent might next be pitched" (X, 33).

The wandering Arab was not a capricious metaphor. It enjoyed some currency between the Hawthornes and was particularly useful in portraying their loss of Eden. After his distant cousin Horace Conolly, late in 1838, told Hawthorne the story of a young French Canadian couple in Acadie who were separated on their wedding day, he reportedly brooded over the story of the "wandering Arab girl" before finding he could make nothing of it. Afterwards Hawthorne allowed the tale to be repeated to Longfellow, who turned it into *Evangeline*.[6] In a letter to Sophia late in 1844, while she was staying with the Peabodys in Boston, he referred twice to the multitude in her mother's "Caravanserai."[7] Two years later Sophia wrote congratulating their friend Horatio Bridge on his marriage: "It seems to me that human beings are wretched Arabs until they find central points in other human beings around which all their brightest and richest sentiments shall revolve."[8]

On other occasions during the Old Manse years both Hawthornes evoked imagery from *The Arabian Nights* to signify the fairy-land they inhabited between plain reality and sheer imagination. While her husband was working on "The Old Manse" in July 1845, Sophia wrote to Bridge: "I have often thought it would be enchanting to be an Aladdin's lamp, & astonish people with unexpected pearls & diamond houses."[9] In "A Virtuoso's Collection," which appeared in the *Boston Miscellany* in May 1842, shortly before the Hawthornes' marriage, the visitor to the Virtuoso's *Wunderkammer* put "the day of wild wishes" in the past and foreswore anything "that may not come in the ordinary course of Providence," including apparently the antique brass lamp.

> "It is a thousand years," [the Virtuoso said] "since the genius of this lamp constructed Aladdin's palace in a single night. But he still retains his power; and the man who rubs Aladdin's lamp, has but to desire either a palace or a cottage."
> "I might desire a cottage," [the visitor replied] "but I would have it founded on sure and stable truth, not on dreams and fantasies. I have learned to look for the real and the true." (X, 481)

"Aladdin and the Magic Lamp" was one of Hawthorne's favorite Arabian Nights entertainments. He referred to it on several occasions and as late as February 1858 wrote in his Italian notebooks of the white sunshine coming through the unpainted windows of Saint John Lateran in Rome: "It is like the one spot in Aladdin's palace which he left for the king, his father-in-law, to finish, after his fairy architects had exhausted their magnificence on the rest; and the son, like the king, fails in the effort" (XIV, 75).

The visitor's nonchalance to the offer of Aladdin's lamp in "The Virtuoso's Collection" and his preference for the real and true in lieu of dreams and fantasies would support the observation that Hawthorne's "Mosses" seek to reconcile flights of imagination with engagements in the real world. At the same time, the sketches of the Old Manse period dramatize and elaborate, as nowhere else in his work, the locale and architecture of the imagination. "The Hall of Fantasy" (1843) especially manifests Hawthorne's focus on the pleasure domes and fairy castles of the East as prototypal settings for tales of wonder and fancy. Its long opening paragraph mentions a number of competing architectural styles but speculates that the hall built from a visionary Moorish design is likely to outlive all other structures.

> IT HAS happened to me, on various occasions, to find myself in a certain edifice, which would appear to have some of the characteristics of a public Exchange. Its interior is a spacious hall, with a pavement of white marble. Overhead is a lofty dome, supported by long rows of pillars, of fantastic architecture, the idea of which was probably taken from the Moorish ruins of the Alhambra, or perhaps from some enchanted edifice of the Arabian Tales. The windows of this hall have a breadth and grandeur of design, and an elaborateness of workmanship, that have nowhere been equalled, except in the Gothic cathedrals of the old world. Like their prototypes, too, they admit the light of heaven only through stained and pictured glass, thus filling the hall with many-colored radiance, and painting its marble floor with beautiful

or grotesque designs; so that its inmates breathe, as it were, a visionary atmosphere, and tread upon the fantasies of poetic minds. These peculiarities, combining a wilder mixture of styles than even an American architect usually recognizes as allowable—Grecian, Gothic, Oriental, and nondescript—cause the whole edifice to give the impression of a dream, which might be dissipated and shattered to fragments, by merely stamping the foot upon the pavement. Yet with such modifications and repairs as successive ages demand, the Hall of Fantasy is likely to endure longer than the most substantial structure that ever cumbered the earth.

Like the Hall of Kings in *Vathek*, Hawthorne's edifice is ringed with effigies of "rulers and demi-gods" chosen from "the realm of imagination, and its kindred regions." Says a friend of the narrator: "All who have affairs in that mystic region, which lies above, below, or beyond the Actual, may here meet, and talk over the business of their dreams" (X, 172–173).

The fairy precincts visited in numerous tales of the Old Manse period are redolent with what Sir Richard Burton called "the dreamy tranquillity, the airy castle-building," of Asia.[10] Taking their cue from *The Arabian Nights*, travelers both before and after Hawthorne's period looked for and found a ready-made *fairy-land* in the East. In the twentieth century the celebrated woman traveler Freya Stark began her study of Arabic "in hopes that . . . it might lead me . . . to some sort of fairy-land of my own."[11] Nor was it necessary in Hawthorne's own time, like Bayard Taylor, to employ the visions of hasheesh in order to quicken "those finer senses, which occupy a middle ground between our animal and intellectual appetites."[12] The description of "The Mahal, or Palace-Tomb, Of the Emperour Shah Jehan's Wife" that Hawthorne offered in the *American Magazine of Useful and Entertaining Knowledge* found the objective correlative sought by the romantics of the 1830s and 1840s. The passage he reprinted from Emma Roberts's *Scenes and Characteristics of Hindostan* begins:

> The reader of Eastern romance may here realize his dreams of fairy land, and contemplate those wondrous scenes so faithfully delineated in the brilliant pages of the Arabian Nights. . . . the Taaje rises, gleaming like a fairy palace. . . . No description can do justice to this shining edifice, which seems rather to belong to the fanciful creations of a dream than to the sober realities of waking life—constructed of gathered moonbeams or the lilies which spring in paradise. . . . Nothing can be more beautiful or more chaste; even the window-frames are of marble; and it would seem as if a part of Aladdin's palace had been secured from the general wreck, and placed in the orange groves of Agra.

Before the Taj Mahal Miss Roberts felt "that the gorgeous palaces, the flowery labyrinths, the orient gems, and glittering thrones so long classed with ideal splendours, were not the fictitious offspring of romance" (AM, 425).

Origins of the Romance: "The Arabian System"

Hawthorne's reference in "The Hall of Fantasy" to "a wilder mixture of styles" than even the American architect of the 1840s would permit—"Grecian, Gothic, Oriental"—means less to modern readers than it did to his contemporaries. The twentieth-century reader will appreciate the distinction between the Classical and the Romantic styles, and might sense a difference between Gothic and Oriental influences, but is unlikely to bring a very specific understanding of the roles the three traditions played in the formulation of American literature. Scholarship on American literary Gothicism and on literary Orientalism in Britain and France is quite well developed. We do not yet have, however, a full appreciation of the part that the East played, both directly and through European intermediaries, in the cultural melting pot of the new nation during Hawthorne's era. Most Oriental studies undertaken by scholars of the American Renaissance have focused on the importance of Indian scriptures and mythologies to the Transcendental poets and essayists. Less attention has been paid to the impact of the Near and Middle East, and their traditions of storytelling, on writers of the American prose romance.[13]

To restore the original drama and color of Hawthorne's works it is vital to remember the ferment of romantic nationalism that swept the Western world in the late eighteenth and early nineteenth centuries and the intimate relation of the new nationalism to folklore and storytelling. The concepts of romance practiced by scholars of American literature today are more restrictive than the ideas held a century and a half ago in an age of universal histories, biblical archaeology, and comparative religions. Hawthorne showed just how broad his contexts were when he claimed his purpose in *Peter Parley's Universal History* was "a clear, vivid and continuous tale of the great human family."[14] America's quest for a national literature occurred simultaneously with like developments in Germany and Scotland as everywhere the decorum of classicism gave way to a new spirit of feeling and adventure built upon primitive models. The new Americans were quick to appropriate cultural materials from the Orient as well as from Europe and the Mediterranean.

In the British isles the romantic ferment was incited by Thomas Percy's *Reliques of Ancient English Poetry* (1765) and by James Macpherson's translation—or invention—of third-century Gaelic poetry and tales. To a significant extent, however, the search for the origins of storytelling and romance turned Eastward, producing an active essay literature in periodicals like the *Gentleman's Magazine* on the authenticity of *The Arabian Nights* and other Oriental tales. By the end of the century the English Romantics were ready to embrace the heroic figures and the pastoralism of the East as a counterweight to the industrializing culture of the West. Byron signaled the equations his contemporaries were drawing between their nationalist movements and the East in 1814 when he dedicated *The Corsair* to Thomas Moore, who was then at work on *Lalla Rookh*. "The wrongs of your own country [Ireland], the magnificent and fiery spirit of her sons, the beauty and feeling of her daughters," can all be found in the East, Byron wrote. "Your imagination will create a warmer sun, and less cloudy sky; but wildness, tenderness, and originality are part of your national claim of oriental descent, to which you have already thus far proved your title more clearly than the most zealous of your country's antiquarians."[15] When American audiences devoured the books of the wonderful Arabian traveler John Lloyd Stephens, and his majestic descriptions of the ruined civilizations and noble tribesmen of Egypt, Arabia, and the Holy Land, they were drawn by a similar contrast to the nervous commercialism of their native land.

The significance of the East in the evolution of Western romance is strongly illustrated by the controversy surrounding the "Arabian system" that Thomas Warton promoted in *The History of English Poetry* (1774–1781). Warton's dissertation "Of the Origin of Romantic Fiction in Europe" began:

> That peculiar and arbitrary species of Fiction which we commonly call Romantic, was entirely unknown to the writers of Greece and Rome. It appears to have been imported into Europe by a people, whose modes of thinking, and habits of invention, are not natural to that country. It is generally supposed to have been borrowed from the Arabians. But this origin has not been hitherto perhaps examined or ascertained with a sufficient degree of accuracy.

Warton proposed to make a more extended inquiry into the time and manner by which the Arabian influence entered "the popular belief, the oral poetry, and the literature, of the Europeans." It generally was assumed that Arabian fictions were introduced to the Western imagination by means of the Crusades beginning in the eleventh century. Warton argued, however, that these fantasies appeared some three centuries earlier when the Saracens erected their royal seat at Cordova and began the religious and cultural conquest of Spain. "The ideal tales of these Eastern invaders, recommended by a brilliancy of description, a variety of imagery, and an exuberance of invention, hitherto unknown and unfamiliar to the cold and barren conceptions of a Western climate, were eagerly caught up, and universally diffused." They quickly passed by commercial channels through the ports of Toulon and Marseilles into France and Italy.[16]

Warton traced the legend of King Arthur to the contact of Welsh bards with the Arabian tales circulating in Armorica and linked the Holy Grail to a miraculous cup from the East found in fictions of Breton and Provence. In opposition to the case Percy made for the primacy of the Gothic bards, Warton claimed that the Gothic and Skaldic inventions had merely eased the way for the Arabian fables, which in the ninth century largely superseded them. "The Arabian fictions were of a more splendid nature, and better adapted to the increasing civility of the times. Less horrible and gross, they had a novelty, a variety, and a magnificence, which carried with them the charm of fascination." Warton argued that the Goths and Skalds enriched their fables from "this new and fruitful source of fiction, opened by the Arabians in Spain, and afterwards propagated by the crusades." From these beginnings "that singular and capricious mode of imagination arose, which at length composed the marvelous machineries of the more sublime Italian poets, and of their disciple Spenser."[17]

Warton's "Arabian system" was immediately and roundly attacked, but without denying that the Arabic cultural environment of Andalusia conveyed the warmth and richer fantasy of Islamic culture to medieval Europe. Exaggerated and contentious as some aspects of his long dissertation might be, "its very existence and acceptance throws a strong light on the ideas with which his age was imbued."[18] Clara Reeve cited and summarized Warton's thesis with approbation in *The Progress of Romance* (1785), which was published together with her adaptation *The History of Charoba, Queen of Egypt*, which in turn inspired Walter Savage Landor's *Gebir*. Nineteenth-century critics found Percy's case for the Northern sagas and Warton's claims for Oriental fables both inaccurate in so far as they operated exclusively of each other. Walter Scott preferred to locate the foundations of these fables "deep in human nature" and wrote in his "Essay on Romance" (1824) that romance was "like a compound metal, derived from various mines, and in the different specimens of which one metal or other was alternately predominant." Nevertheless, he too credited the Arabian tales with a great "vivacity of invention" and a stronger "tendency to the marvelous" than the Northern fictions.[19]

Hawthorne found similar distinctions between the lamentational tone of the peoples inhabiting the borders of the Northern ocean and the lighter spirit of the Arabian and Persian fictions when he read Frederick Schlegel's *Lectures on the History of Literature, Ancient and Modern* in 1828.[20] Henry Wadsworth Longfellow also gave considerable attention to the Orientalization of Spain in his inaugural lecture "Origin and Growth of the Languages of Southern Europe and of Their Literature" as professor of Modern Languages at Bowdoin College in September 1830. Longfellow emphasized the "oriental pomp and magnificence of expression" that characterize the Spanish language, traced the origins of French drama and the Romances of Chivalry to Oriental sentiments, and found the influence of the Troubadours and Arabian poetry at work in the pastorals and amatory ballads of Italian literature.[21] None of Hawthorne's contemporaries, however, so completely caught the spirit of the Moorish world as Washington Irving in his collection of tales and sketches *The Alhambra*. During his sojourn in the Alhambra Irving lived, he said, "in the midst of an Arabian tale" and shut his eyes to everything that called him "back to everyday life."[22]

By the time the *Encyclopedia Americana* began to appear in 1829 the influence of Arabia in the development of European literature was an accepted fact. It would be difficult to find a more comprehensive and scholarly representation of Americans' knowledge of the world in the first half of the nineteenth century than in the thirteen volumes of Frances Lieber's *Encyclopedia*, which was one of Hawthorne's main references.[23] In the *Americana's* essay "Arabian Literature and Language" he could have read:

> What Bagdad was to Asia, the high school at Cordova was to Europe, where, particularly in the 10th century, the Arabians were the chief pillars of literature. . . . There is no doubt that they had . . . a powerful effect on modern European poetry; for no small share of the romantic poetry of the middle ages belonged to the Arabians. The adventurous, chivalrous spirit, the tales of fairies and sorcerers, and perhaps, also, rhyme, passed from the Arabians to our western poetry.[24]

In other essays the encyclopedia called attention to the Moorish storytellers at the Royal court in Provence, with its "mirthful, soft and luxurious life," and stated simply: "The native land of this fairy mythology is Arabia, from whence it was brought to Europe by the Troubadours." It played an important part in the romances of chivalry and was "naturalized in England before the time of Chaucer and Spenser."[25]

This emphasis on the Arabian channels of romance into medieval Europe did not exclude the fables of Persia, India, and the farthest East. The *Americana's* article "Arabian Nights" began by declaring:

> The East is the ancient and native country of fabulous histories. The ever-active fancy of the people, their love of adventures, their belief in spirits, and their fondness for lively stories, are attested by numerous travellers. This character appears in the amusements of their coffee-houses and caravansaries. It gave rise (perhaps first in India and Persia) to those thousand fables, which, contrary to Mohammed's express command, found in Arabia a second home, and were spread, with alterations and improvements, first separately, and afterwards in large collections, through all Europe. Many of them found their way thither in the time of the crusades or sooner.

The essayist called attention to the textual labors of French, Danish, and German philologists and embraced Von Hammer's opinion that "these fables sprung up in the soil of India, were afterwards transplanted to Persia, and finally made Arabian property by a translation into that language, in the time of the caliph Al Mansur, about 30 years before the time of Haroun al Raschid, the contemporary of Charlemagne."[26]

As mentioned in the preceding chapter, the *Americana* followed the legacy of the Eastern storytellers into the Milesian tales of the Asiatic Greeks and the fourteenth-century *Gesta Romanorum*, a compilation of "classical stories, Arabian apologues, and monkish legends" from which "the Italian novelle, the French *contes* and *fabliaux*, and the English tales, were derived." Boccaccio's *Decameron* and Chaucer's *Canterbury Tales* developed from the same original or intermediate sources.[27] In all cases the genealogical line ran backwards through Southern Europe to Arabia and on to Persia and India. While a distinction was commonly made between *arabesque* and *grotesque* forms in painting, literature, and the decorative arts, the latter, presumably more indigenous European form also was linked to the former. The *Americana's* essay "Grotesques," which Hawthorne quoted entire in the *American Magazine of Useful and Entertaining Knowledge* for June 1836, noted: "The origin of these fantastic compositions is traced, by Boettinger, to the carpets of Persia and India, adorned with all the wonders of Oriental fable." The arabesque maintained its more floral and air-drawn imagery while "the taste for grotesques has, in part, degenerated into the monstrous and unnatural."[28]

The classical discipline of the Renaissance temporarily pushed the East into the background. But by the time of Galland's translation of *The Arabian Nights* in 1704, European colonization and the descriptions of Persian and Indian life by Olearius, Le Blanc, Chardin, and a host of other travelers had prepared a climate favorable to rediscovering the wonderland of the Orient. In the 1830s the study of Oriental literature was the cutting edge of scholarship, "a vast field of learning," the *Americana* observed, "cultivated, in recent times, with great zeal." Five Asiatic societies had been established by Europeans for the investigation of Oriental literatures and cultures. Silvestre de Sacy's *Grammaire Arabe* (Paris, 1810) opened the study of the Arabian language directly, and Persian and Hebrew indirectly, and Terrick Hamilton's translation of the Arabian romance *Antar* into English in 1819–1820 was greeted as a great event.[29]

Europeans and Americans turned repeatedly to Arabia for models of pristine culture and folk identity. "The Arabians are still," the *Americana* claimed, "as in the most ancient times, Nomades, of patriarchal simplicity."[30] Washington Irving compared the "stern, simple, and enduring" character of the native American Indian with the Arab.[31] Carsten Niebuhr captured the same primitive, romantic type—free of the refinements and excesses of civilization—when beginning the second volume of his *Travels into Arabia*. "If any people in the world afford in their history an instance of high antiquity, and of great simplicity of manners, the Arabs surely do," Niebuhr wrote. "We are here tempted to imagine ourselves among the old patriarchs, with whose adventures we have been so much amused in our infant days."[32] It was its depiction of Arabian pastoralism that made "Antar, A Bedoueen Romance" such a celebrated text among Hawthorne's contemporaries. *The Arabian Nights*, *Antar*, and Eastern stories in general were essentially a product of the people and possessed in a superlative degree the adventure, practical wisdom, human understanding, and core of morality so indispensable to a popular literature.

Their folkloristic quality and identification with children's literature have kept the ever-popular Arabian Nights tales mostly outside the pale of modern-day criticism. *The Arabian Nights*, however, was not only a favorite reading for several generations of English writers from Scott and Byron to Dickens. It also has been a continuous pastime and model for American storytellers from Irving and Longfellow to William Porter (O. Henry), who turned New York City into a "Baghdad by the Subway."[33] Like his contemporaries, Hawthorne went to the fountainhead of fairy legend and story even while tapping the successive eruptions of the Eastern spirit from Boccaccio to Spenser and Robert Southey. When he put his hand on the town pump in Salem, and a rill gushed forth as far as India, he completed a historical cycle.

The Architecture of Fairy-Land: Cloud-Castles and Caverns

Tracing the Gothic and Oriental strains in Western literature proceeded hand-in-hand in Hawthorne's time with a similar exploration of architectural traditions. Mediterranean, Indian colonial, and Far Eastern forms have been practiced widely in American domestic architecture during the twentieth century, but American builders were also seized by a mania for Egyptian, Islamic, and Asian styles in the mid–1800s. By the 1830s "the Egyptian was recognized as the monumental style supreme," and house designs incorporating Oriental motifs appeared in American books of architecture in the 1840s.[34] For a time the Oriental was an active contestant to Classical and Gothic styles, and when Greek Revival eventually emerged as *the* American style of the first half of the nineteenth century, it was infused with Eastern as well as Hellenic elements.

Two entries in Hawthorne's notebooks show his awareness of the Classical, Gothic, and Oriental currents in architecture and his interest in building imaginary castles of the most suitable materials. He wrote between September 1 and October 25, 1836: "[T]he architecture of a country always follows the earliest structures. . . . The Egyptian is so of the cavern and mound; the Chinese of the tent; the Gothic of over-arching trees. Greek a cabin."[35] Seven years later he jotted down his notion to write a tale based on "Visits to Castles in the Air—Chateaus en Espagne &c—with remarks on that sort of architecture" (VIII, 242).[36] By the time he made the latter entry, Hawthorne already had published "The Hall of Fantasy," whose architecture derived "from the Moorish ruins of the Alhambra, or perhaps from some enchanted edifice of the Arabian tales," and had noted that while the structure could be entered in waking moments, it was more accessible "by the universal passport of a dream" (X, 172–173).

Early the next year he returned to the same fairy architecture and with a wave of the pen built a cloud-castle for "A Select Party" (1844). The sketch begins:

> A MAN of fancy made an entertainment at one of his castles in the air, and invited a select number of distinguished personages to favor him with their presence. The mansion . . . was . . . of a magnificence such as is seldom witnessed by those acquainted only with terrestrial architecture. Its strong foundations and massive walls were quarried out of a ledge of heavy and sombre clouds. . . . Perceiving that the general effect was gloomy—so that the airy castle looked like a feudal fortress, or a monastery of the middle ages, or a state-prison of our own times, rather than the home of pleasure and repose which he intended it to be—the owner, regardless of expense, resolved to gild the exterior from top to bottom. Fortunately, there was just then a flood of evening sunshine in the air. This being gathered up and poured abundantly upon the roof and walls, imbued them with a kind of solemn cheerfulness; while the cupolas and pinnacles were made to glitter with the purest gold, and all the hundred windows gleamed with a glad light, as if the edifice itself were rejoicing in its heart. (X, 57–58)

Before a thunderstorm blew out the lights of the departing guests, the man of fancy hosted an entertaining company of ideal and romantic figures. His hall, like others that Hawthorne built at the Manse in Concord, had the lighter qualities associated with the tiled courtyards, latticed marble screens, and Moorish arches of Arabia, Persia, and India. The author would invoke those spiritualized structures again at key points in his romances of the 1850s, for instance, in Pearl's transformation of the Governor's Hall in *The Scarlet Letter.*

As implied by the passages from Hawthorne's notebooks, a distinction was popularly made between the imaginative, aspiring styles of Arabia and the farther East and the monumental and cave-like buildings of the Egyptians. The cavernous Egyptian style was thought particularly appropriate for memorials, prisons, tombs, and cemeteries and was copied extensively in the 1830s and 1840s, notably in the gateways to Grove Street Cemetery in New Haven, Connecticut, and Mount Auburn Cemetery in Cambridge, Massachusetts. Melville's Bartleby took his secret to the grave in the "Tombs" prison of New York City.

The equations Hawthorne made in his 1836 notebook entry between the earliest structures of the Egyptians, Chinese, Goths, and Greeks and the architectural styles of their developed civilizations were not incidental. At the same time he copied the formulaic remark on architecture in his notebooks, he also was writing this comment on architecture for the second volume of *Peter Parley's Universal History*:

> 2. Architecture appears to have been one of the earliest inventions, and its works have been regulated by hereditary imitation. Whatever rude structure the climate or materials of any country forced the first inhabitants to construct, the same form was kept up in after years by their more refined posterity.
> 3. Thus the Egyptian style of building derived its origin from the *cavern* and *mound*; the Chinese from the *tent*; the Grecian from the wooden *cabin*, and the Gothic from the *bower* of trees.[37]

Hawthorne lifted Peter Parley's eight-paragraph overview of architecture from the *Encyclopedia Americana's* essays "Architecture" and "History of Architecture" preserving not only the wording but the italics of the original.[38] When he borrowed the Salem Athenaeum's copy of the *Gentleman's Magazine* for 1835, he would have found the same formula repeated in a review of Thomas Hope's *An Historical Essay on Architecture*. The review stated the identical principles, namely: "in China . . . the original tent remains in the form and disposition of the building to which it gave way"; "the buildings of Egypt and India" share a "cavern-like" quality; and the temples of Greece "preserv[e] the form, and imitat[e] the construction, of the primitive hut." Thus, added the *Magazine*, "the tent, the cave, and the hut, survive in the pagoda and the kiosk, the massy temples of Egypt, and the more elegant ones of Greece."[39]

In the wake of *The Arabian Nights* caves and caverns became a standard trapping of European Oriental tales as the locale of hidden treasure and terrifying confrontations. Southey's Domdaniel in *Thalaba the Destroyer* and the hellish caverns of *Vathek* led to the less horrendous cave in which Ellen Langton is held captive in *Fanshawe*. That Hawthorne continued to associate caves with the landforms and tales of the East is apparent from his English notebooks. In 1857 he compared the Greek Cavern at Bath, England—"a very dirty, sordid, disagreeable burrow, more like a cellar gone mad than anything else"—unfavorably with his idea of the real thing. "I rather think my idea of the cavern," he wrote, "is taken from the one in the Forty Thieves, or in Gil Blas; a vast, hollow womb, roofed and curtained with obscurity."[40]

The cavern stands high on any list of Hawthorne's symbols as an emblem of the mysteries of the human heart. During his years at the Manse he set down his most thoughtful definition of this symbol:

> The human Heart to be allegorized as a cavern; at the entrance there is sunshine, and flowers growing about it. You step within, but a short distance, and begin to find yourself surrounded with a terrible gloom, and monsters of divers kinds; it seems like Hell itself. You are bewildered, and wander long without hope. At last a light strikes upon you. You press towards it yon, and find yourself in a region that seems, in some sort, to reproduce the flowers and sunny beauty of the entrance, but all perfect. These are the depths of the heart, or of human nature, bright and peaceful; the gloom and terror may lie deep; but deeper still is this eternal beauty. (VIII, 237)

In writing his psychological romances Hawthorne integrated the imagery of the cavernous heart—illuminated by the fiery carbuncle and embraced by adamantine walls—with more narrative subtlety than most contemporary authors, but his use of cavern imagery never strayed far from the allegorical associations of its time.

Hawthorne drew on both the lighter, magical figure of caverns in *The Arabian Nights* and the more loathsome, infernal forms they took in the Gothic Oriental tales. "The Village Uncle" (1835) and "The New Adam and Eve" (1843) especially exemplify the former treatment. Until the simple fisherman's daughter Susan kindles a domestic fire within the narrator's heart in the previous tale, "that chill and lonesome cavern [was] hung round with glittering icicles of fancy" (IX, 316). He builds a joyful cottage for this Daughter of the Sea and yet cannot keep from wondering whether his blissful home might all be illusion. He imagines "precisely how a magician would sit down in gloom and terror, after dismissing the shadows that had impersonated dead or distant people, and stripping his cavern of the unreal splendor which had changed it to a palace" (IX, 322–323).

"The New Adam and Eve," which appeared in the *Democratic Review* for February 1843, is an unabashed valentine to the new bride Sophia Hawthorne and an offshoot of the Edenic imagery that filled the author's notebooks during their first year of marriage.[41] In this tale an innocent young couple wander amazedly into a world of Boston from which all inhabitants have been removed. The streets and business signs, "with their unintelligible hieroglyphics," are of no use in explaining the relics from the now dead civilization or the riddle of the couple's own destiny (X, 249). In time they enter a bank vault and muse over the "huge packages of bank notes, those talismanic slips of paper, which once had the efficacy to build up enchanted palaces, like exhalations, and work all kinds of perilous wonders." The wonderment of the new-made couple before the world's treasures causes the narrator to think: "How like is this vault to a magician's cave, when the all-powerful wand is broken, and the visionary splendor vanished, and the floor strewn with fragments of shattered spells" (X, 261). Because this is a moral tale, Adam and Eve's pilgrimage inevitably leads them to the graveyard—not to just any cemetery, however, but to Mount Auburn.

Mount Auburn Cemetery, which was situated on a tract of rolling land near the road from Cambridge to Watertown and incorporated in 1831, inspired the rural cemetery movement in America. Hawthorne would have been particularly interested in this undertaking not only because of the spon-sorship of the Massachusetts Horticultural Society, and the prominent roles played by Joseph Story, Daniel Webster, Edward Everett, and other North Shore dignitaries, but also for the examples of Grecian, Gothic, and Oriental architecture found along the wooded paths and meadows that lay behind the Egyptian gateway designed by Jacob Bigelow.[42] As they tread the winding lanes of the cemetery, Hawthorne's Adam and Eve pass "among marble pillars, mimic temples, urns, obelisks, and sarcophagi, sometimes pausing to contem-plate these fantasies of human growth, and sometimes to admire the flowers wherewith Nature converts decay to loveliness." The idea of death, the riddle behind the hieroglyphics and talismans around them, is never far off. But if he were to choose the symbol for death, the narrator declares, he would seek it not among the Egyptian sarcophagi and tombs, but rather in the white marble monument of a "Child asleep, with soft dreams visible through her transparent purity" (X, 266–267).[43]

Hawthorne's explorations occasionally reached the "eternal beauty" and repose at the depths of the human heart, but his more disturbing tales usually leave the traveler stranded some distance inside, amidst the "terrible gloom and monsters of divers kinds." "The Christmas Banquet" (1844), which he wrote for his projected "Allegories of the Heart," is a case in point. The tale of an annual feast for ten of the world's most miserable persons, it is narrated by Roderick Elliston, the haunted protagonist of "Egotism; or, The Bosom Serpent" (1843). As he unfolds his manuscript and prepares to read, Roderick comments: "My former sad experience, as you know, has gifted me with some degree of insight into the gloomy mysteries of the human heart, through which I have wandered like one astray in a dark cavern, with a torch fast flickering to extinction" (X, 284). Roderick's remark evokes images of the archaeologists and treasure seekers who plundered the ruins of Karnak and Luxor. Nor had the stewarts at his Christmas banquet forgotten "the fantasy of the old Egyptians, who seated a skeleton at every festive board, and mocked their own merriment with the imperturbable grin of a death's-head," for just such a shrouded visitor graces the head of Roderick's table (X, 286).

The dense cave imagery in "The Man of Adamant: An Apologue" (1837) several years earlier also evoked a decidedly Eastern atmosphere. The cavern in "the heart of a rocky hill" where Richard Digby guards his religious de-lusions, "at first sight, reminded him of Elijah's cave at Horeb, though perhaps it more resembled Abraham's sepulchral cave, at Machpelah" (XI, 162). When the "dreamlike spirit" of Mary Goffe is unable to dispel the enchantment of his religious bigotry, Digby's body petrifies and he remains frozen in a personal hall of the dead. Although there are cases of enchantment and petrification in *The Arabian Nights*, a more striking analogue is Beckford's Hall of Eblis and its pre-Adamic sultans. Like them, "This repulsive personage seemed to have been carved in the same gray stone that formed the walls and portals of the cave" (XI, 168). The following stanza from Book Five of *Thalaba the Destroyer* also prefigured the fate of Digby and the response of the farmer whose children discover his petrified corpse a century later:

> No eye of mortal man
> If unenabled by unenchanted spell,
> Had pierced those fearful depths;
> . . .
> The affrighted countrymen
> Call it the mouth of Hell;
> And ever when their way leads near,
> They hurry with averted eyes,
> And dropping their beads fast,
> Pronounce the Holy name.[44]

"The cave of horrors" to which Mohareb introduced Southey's hero anticipates the imagery that Hawthorne would deploy in characterizing the inner state of his own figures. After recovering from his initial fascination with the horrid cave, the farmer in "The Man of Adamant" heaps stones into its mouth, and his wife and children add their pebbles and sod until all evidence is removed, except for the marvelous legend itself. Hawthorne adopted the conventional imagery of the Oriental fabulists but realized more fully what they had partially understood: that the beast is most hideous when raging in the breast of men.

Further Eastern Symbols

Besides his rolled manuscripts, cloud-castles, and caverns a number of Hawthorne's other symbols have a particularly Oriental resonance. Like his pervasive veil imagery Hawthorne frequently used *hieroglyphics* and *talisman* in connection with the riddles that lay between his protagonists and their destiny. The allegorists and moral tales of the East assumed an emblematic view of life. The excavation of tombs, temples, and pyramids and the removal of Egyptian antiquities to England and France in the first decades of the nineteenth century inspired a particularly heated scholarship on the secrets of hieroglyphic writing. Champollion demystified the symbols to some extent when he discovered in 1821 that the hieroglyphics were phonetic and represented an arbitrary assignment of human sounds to pictures rather than an immediate link of natural objects with underlying truths. Despite this linguistic explanation the term *hieroglyphics* ("sacred engraving") maintained its metaphysical signification on both sides of the Atlantic. In summarizing Clarkson's lecture on Egyptian hieroglyphics in 1831, the *Gentleman's Magazine* noted his skepticism about Champollion's strictly alphabetical approach and summarized the speaker's description of three stages of hieroglyphical languages: the anaglyphic ("a species of improved picture-writing, shrouding religious rites, records, and mysteries, under compound symbols beautifully combined"); the ideological ("pure hieroglyphics, representing ideas by characters imitative . . . or figurative"); and the phonetic ("the step from symbolical to alphabetic writing").[45]

In Hawthorne's time the Egyptian hieroglyphics signified both the foundations of language and the mysteries of the East. John Neal asked in 1835: "And the very characters in which the earliest doings and the best feelings of our race are perpetuated, the hieroglyphics, what are they but so many abridgments—types—the concentrated essence—the very *otta* of all that was worth preserving in the history of many a forgotten empire?"[46] Hawthorne's use of "hieroglyphics" is most conspicuous in reference to Hester and Pearl in *The Scarlet Letter*, but it runs throughout his writings from the essay on "The Egyptian Papyrus" in the *American Magazine of Useful and Entertaining Knowledge* for April 1836 to his French and Italian notebooks in 1858 and *Septimius Felton*.[47] When trying to read the reflected image in his sketch "Monsieur du Miroir," the author speculated that the shifting expression of eyes and countenance was perhaps the "visible hieroglyphics" of his modulated breath; yet while the lips were seen to move, the image kept its secrets (X, 160).

The term *talisman* appears as frequently as *hieroglyphics* in Hawthorne's writings and with a related meaning. Hawthorne's use of the talisman has been linked generally with his concern for the revelation of truth. Richard D. Rust noticed that Hawthorne applied the word "most frequently to an object, person, or idea with preternatural power to increase health, reveal character, or permit intuitive understanding," and cited an entry in the American notebooks late in 1841: "A man with the right perception of things—a feeling within him of what is true and what is false. It might be symbolized by the talisman, with which, in fairy tales, an adventurer was enabled to distinguish enchantments from realities" (VIII, 222).[48] The significance of this thought to Hawthorne is substantiated by its appearance, verbatim, also in an earlier notebook for 1840 (VIII, 186). His closer association of both the talisman and truth-telling with Eastern sources, however, seems not to have been pointed out.

This was a popular figure in Hawthorne's time, providing the title for Walter Scott's *The Talisman*. Its connections in the early nineteenth century, however, were fundamentally Oriental. The lengthy note "Talisman" in the *Encyclopedia Americana* in 1832 began by noting its derivation from the Arabic word for *figure* and proceeded to mention its uses among the Egyptians, Arabs, and Turks (who adopted sentences from the Koran as talismans), as well as the Greeks and Romans, and its conveyance to Europe through the medical sciences of the Middle Ages.[49] In *Lalla Rookh* Thomas Moore borrowed his image of "the Mountain of the Talisman" as a figure of the unattainable from Sir John Macdonald Kinneir's geographical accounts of the Persian Empire. Kinneir reported "a curious hill, Koh Talism, the Mountain of the Talisman, . . . of [which] according to the traditions of the country no person ever succeeded in attaining its summit."[50] As early as 1791 a tale published in the *Massachusetts Magazine* called "The Talisman of Truth" made the link for American writers with the Eastern sources of wisdom.[51]

The first of the "three fatalities" that Ralph Cranfield sought in the East was "the discovery of the maid, who alone, of all the maids on earth, could make him happy by her love." The token for recognizing her would be a heart-shaped jewel, "of pearl, or ruby, or emerald, or carbuncle, or a changeful opal, or perhaps a priceless diamond" (IX, 473). Hawthorne did not use the term *talisman* in this instance, but Cranfield's effort to solve the riddle of his existence in the East, before his providential discovery of Faith at home in Massachusetts, is representative both of the talismanic devices in eighteenth-century Oriental tales and of the experience of the author's "wandering Arabs" from *The Story Teller* into "The Old Manse."

Wherever effusions of gemstones appear in Hawthorne's writings they are likely to lend an Eastern coloration. In complaining about the circumscribed literary world of Massachusetts, Nathaniel P. Willis wrote to his mother from England in 1835: "The mines of Golconda would not tempt me to return and live in Boston."[52] For Hawthorne, too, Golconda was the antipode of New England. His essay "Rubies" in the *American Magazine* for April 1836 noted the superstitious value set upon rubies by the Burmese, who would prize a single stone as highly as a kingdom. Throughout his twelve years of imprisonment, a deposed king of Pegu "held continually in his hand a lump of pitch, which was supposed to be a charm or a talisman" but contained his most magnificent crown jewel (AM, p. 336).

Of the Oriental gems scattered throughout Hawthorne's works the *carbuncle*—as rubies and garnets were more poetically known—has the most thematic significance.[53] Hawthorne first introduced his legend "of the Great Carbuncle of the White Mountains" in "Sketches from Memory" (1835), which was part of the framework of *The Story Teller*. This inestimable jewel, guarded by a jealous spirit, enthralled all beholders with "an unutterable yearning to posses it" that led them to wear their lives away in a vain search. "On this theme," the narrator wrote, "methinks I could frame a tale with a deep moral" (X, 428). Both "The Threefold Destiny" and "The Great Carbuncle: A Mystery of the White Mountains" end when the young questors turn their backs on exotic, foreign gems and find a clear light in the common materials of their native land. Among the seekers of the Great Carbuncle in Hawthorne's story is one who "had listened to a traveller's tale of this marvelous stone, in his own distant country" (IX, 152).

Although Hawthorne acknowledged his source to be James Sullivan's history of Maine, the legendary carbuncle illuminated many contemporary Oriental tales.[54] There, as Master Ichabod Pigsnort allows for his fellow Bostonians, "the quest for the great Carbuncle [was] deemed little better than a traffic with the evil one" (IX, 155). In *Vathek*, for instance, the promise of possessing the great Carbuncle of Giamschid lured the innocent Nouronihar away from her betrothed, Gulchenrouz, and brought her under the Caliph's deadly influence. Byron mentioned the stone in *The Giaour*, and Southey used it in both *Thalaba the Destroyer* and *The Curse of Kehama* to throw a surreal light through mansions of diabolic splendor. "The living carbuncle" hung "self-suspended . . . in air,/As its pure substance loathed material touch" in evil Shedad's palace of pride.[55] When Ladurlad visited the Hall of Death, he beheld:

> Each in his own alcove, and on his throne,
> The kings of old were seated: in his hand
> Each held the sceptre of command,
> From whence, across the scene of endless night,
> A carbuncle diffused its everlasting light.[56]

While fabulous gems appeared in Eastern travelers' accounts mainly as signs of Oriental opulence, the European Romantics infused the carbuncle with some of the uncanny psychological quality that distinguishes Hawthorne's tales.

Like *carbuncle* the ubiquitous symbol *adamant* also appeared with special frequency in the Oriental tales. Since it is impervious to any force, *adamant* was often used as a synonym for diamond. In *The Arabian Nights* furious storms drove ships to their destruction against the black mountains of adamant. Throughout the popular Oriental tales gates, walls, and mountains of adamant barred the spiritual traveler's way to the sanctums of paradise or hell. "Two adamantine doors/Closed up the cavern pass" that Thalaba approached on his way to scourge the dens of Domdaniel. Smiting "the gates of adamant" with his hand, he "past/The threshold, over which was no return," and wended downward into the vaults of hell.[57] Padalon, the Hindu hell of Southey's *The Curse of Kehama*, likewise was built on a rock of adamant. Its dungeons were partitioned by thick walls of adamant, and the infernal city of Yamenpur was solid diamond.[58] Southey's source was the Koran, where the Mahometan hell is described as being encircled by a wall of adamant. In "The Vision of Mizra" (1711), Addison's hero looked down from the highest hill of Bagdad upon the stream of men passing over the bridge of life. Those who fell off, as all sooner or later must, were either carried towards the islands of the blest or borne beyond the rock of adamant. Hawthorne put this familiar symbol to work in "The Man of Adamant" as an image of the imprisoned soul and the impenetrable walls that can make a hell of the heart.

Other symbols widely found in the Oriental tales appear in Hawthorne's writings. Though they sometimes have an allegorical function, their significance often is more decorative than thematic. One such device is the magic mirror which, as in *The Arabian Nights*, helps to reveal true character in "Dr. Heidegger's Experiment" (1837), "Peter Goldthwaite's Treasure" (1838), "Old Esther Dudley" (1839), and "Feathertop: A Moralized Legend" (1852). Threadbare, fanciful Peter Goldthwaite allows that, "as for castles in the air, mine may not be as magnificent as that sort of architecture," but he dreams nonetheless of erecting a jeweled palace where his dilapidated old ruin stood and discovers a number of talismans and magic objects in the process of dismembering it: a piece of parchment, a key, a bound chest, and a brass lamp, which he tells his companion Tabitha is "not Aladdin's lamp, though I take it to be a token of as much luck" (IX, 383, 397). "Peter, the Destroyer," as Hawthorne calls him—hinting at Southey's Thalaba—eventually learns that all buried treasures are dross and that true wealth is the love of friends, but only after tearing down his own house. The idea for "The Snow-Image" (1850) also might have come from Southey, for in *Thalaba* Laila's playmates are men and women made of snow—given motion, life, and sense by her father Okba but chilling to the touch and ever melting away at night.

In a few cases Hawthorne counted on Eastern associations for light satire or parody. When the husband in "Mrs. Bullfrog" (1837) becomes aware that he has married an ogre ("two rows of orient pearls gleaming between her parted lips"), he recalls "the tale of a fairy, who half the time was a beautiful woman, and half the time a hideous monster" (X, 134–135). In "The Vision of the Fountain" (1835) Hawthorne drew on the image of "an enchanter, who kept the mysterious beauty imprisoned in the fountain" (IX, 215). A likely source in Washington Irving's "Legend of the Rose of Alhambra." Hawthorne replaced the supernatural enchantment of Irving's beautiful Zorahayda, who was released by the tears of her lost lover's descendant, with a natural explanation based on the reflected image of the village squire's daughter, who was home from boarding-school. "If I transformed her to an angel," the young man moralizes, "it is what every youthful lover does for his mistress. Therein consists the essence of my story" (IX, 219). Seymour Gross has interpreted the tale as a parody of sentimental gift-book fiction that lost its meaning when removed from the framework of *The Story Teller*.[59] "The Vision of the Fountain" is a slight piece, but it complements the more serious tales of *The Story Teller* by presenting the alternate attractions of fanciful and homey maidens.

Medicine, Alchemy, and the Elixir of Life

The symbols of caverns, carbuncles, and adamant were frequently interconnected in the Oriental tales and associated there with the magical arts. To the people of Hawthorne's time the East was a fount of nostrums, drugs, and healing potions of all kinds. To the scholar the Orient, and especially Arabia, was the birthplace of medicine, pharmacology, and alchemy.

Hawthorne related potent drugs to the East both before and after publication of *Mosses from an Old Manse*. In his early sketch "Dr. Bullivant" (1831) the narrator pays a visit to the shop of a "gay apothecary" where, if one desires "some hot, Oriental drug, it is accompanied by a racy word or two that tingle on the mental palate." Dr. Bullivant's wit is well suited to the substances he prescribes. While "a phenomenon" in his community, his character illustrates important changes beneath the surface of New England society in the later seventeenth century, "modified as it became by new ingredients from the eastern world, and by the attrition of sixty or seventy years over the rugged peculiarities of the original settlers." The colonists traded "with the whole maritime world" and "could not remain entirely uncontaminated by the extensive intermixture with worldly men." As in *The Scarlet Letter*, the severity and gloom of the earliest Puritans are colored in "Dr. Bullivant" by the presence both of American Indians and of sailors from the Spanish Main. "Bearded Saracens" appear next to other figures on the commercial signs of the town, which are "not a barren record of names and occupations . . . but images and hieroglyphics, *sometimes typifying* the principal commodity offered for sale, though generally intended to give *an arbitrary designation* to the establishment."[60] Dr. Dolliver in Hawthorne's late unfinished work is a decayed specimen of the same type. The patchwork gown which he habitually wore "had an eastern fragrance, too, a smell of drugs, strong-scented herbs, and spicy gums, gathered from the many potent infusions that had from time to time been spilt over it; so that, snuffing him afar off, you might have taken Dr. Dolliver for a mummy" (XIII, 454).

When she introduced the smallpox inoculation to England and extolled the science of the Turks, Lady Montagu confirmed a respect for the healing arts of the East dating back to the famous philosopher, physicist, and physician Avicenna (980–1037). According to Max Meyerhof, "the Middle Ages in medicine and science" did not come to an end until the sixteenth century, and with it the direct Arabian influence. The struggle between "Hellenism" and "Arabism" persisted in Northern Italy until both eventually were crushed by the modern scientific method. Even more significant in this context, however, is the fame Arabia enjoyed as the home of alchemy (*al-kimiya*), which from the time of Jabir in the early tenth century exercised a profound influence upon the subsequent course of the chemical sciences in Europe. Mystic practitioners subsequently turned the search for the Philosopher's Stone into a matter of superstition and fraud, but in the hands of Jabir alchemy was an experimental science.[61]

The distinctions between science and magic, chemistry and alchemy, medicine and quackery were romantically imprecise in the East. Richard Pococke wrote of Egypt in the late 1730s: "They have a great notion of the magic art, have books about it, and think there is much virtue in talismans and charms."[62] Carsten Niebuhr reported the claims of "respectable Mahometans" that among the valuable treasures in Mohammed's tomb at Medina was "the philosopher's stone, or a large quantity of powder for converting other metals into fine gold." Niebuhr saw "such a mixture of fable in the account" that he did not know what to think, but he acknowledged that the Arabs were "passionately addicted to this science" and that there were more "votaries" to the philosopher's stone in Arabia than he had expected. "The idea of the philosopher's stone is originally oriental," he wrote, "and has been brought westward, like many other foolish tales."[63] In 1827 Richard Maden confirmed the continuing practice of magic by the Arabs, including the use of the magic circle, and distinguished the "puerile" witchcraft of the English from the "magical fictions of the Orientals," who greeted their practitioners with honor and "affected to have no league with demons." In the East, Madden continued, "astronomy and astrology, magic and medicine, were synonymous words for general science."[64]

The apothecaries and alchemists in Hawthorne's tales—Dr. Cacaphodel, Aylmer, Dr. Rappaccini, Dr. Heidegger—derive from this tradition and dedicate themselves, likewise, to transubstantiating the Actual into the Ideal. In his ambivalent status between science and magic, the alchemist is akin both to the Romantic artist (in his neutral territory somewhere between daytime and night) and the wayfarer (suspended between the foreign and the domestic). Each travels by imagination beyond the limits of verifiable experience in his search for heightened awareness, beauty, truth, or immortality—for a substance capable of turning base into pure metals, for a key to the hieroglyphics of life.

The finest of Hawthorne's alchemical tales, "The Birth-mark," first appeared in the *Pioneer* in March 1843 and was placed strategically in his *Mosses* between "The Old Manse" and "A Select Party," where it brilliantly introduces the struggle between the gross materialism of earth and the artist-scientist's aspirations for a higher state of being. In order to remove from his bride's cheek the tiny birthmark that she thought a "charm," and other suitors found a "fairy touch," but which he saw as "the symbol of imperfection," Aylmer transports Georgiana from the daylight world "into a series of beautiful apartments" of arabesque splendor like the tower apartment of Lady Rowena in Poe's "Ligeia."

> The walls were hung with gorgeous curtains, which imparted the combination of grandeur and grace, that no other species of adornment can achieve; and as they fell from the ceiling to the floor, their rich and ponderous folds, concealing all angles and straight lines, appeared to shut in the scene from infinite space. For aught Georgiana knew, it might be a pavilion among the clouds.

The fragrance of a burning pastille and perfumed lamps filled the air as "airy figures, absolutely bodiless ideas, and forms of unsubstantial beauty, came and danced before her." Confident in his science, Aylmer "felt that he could draw a magic circle around her, within which no evil might intrude" (X, 43–44). In return, like the houris of the Prophet's paradise, "she poured out the liquid music of her voice to quench the thirst of his spirit" (X, 50). In the intervals of his study and research Aylmer gave Georgiana "a history of the long dynasty of the Alchemists, who spent so many ages in quest of the universal solvent, by which the Golden Principle might be elicited from all things vile and base" (X, 46).

Like the cloud-pavilions in "The Hall of Fantasy" and "A Select Party," Georgiana's apartments are a realm of romantic sensibility where ideal types can be imagined. "The scene around her looked like enchantment." Its purpose is to break the spell of another "charm," the birthmark. His quest to spiritualize matter raises Aylmer from the practice of science into alchemy and art. But in the hot and sooty laboratory where his potions are made another being is at work, his earthy assistant Aminadab, whose behavior suggests the efrits and jinns who threaten travelers in the Oriental tales. The magic circle Aylmer would draw around Georgiana is not proof against the baser world, and in seeking to transport her soul out of its imperfect sphere and into the realm of gold, he destroys the thing he loves.

Aylmer believed that it was "altogether within the limits of possibility" to discover the universal solvent for eliciting the Golden Principle and intimated that, if it were not for the discord it would produce in nature, he might even concoct the Elixir Vitae. Like the philosopher's stone images of the elixir (from the Arabic *al-iksir*, "the stone"), and of the Fountain of Youth, ran through the fables of the East and emerged in Hawthorne's tales.[65] The fountain of youth appears in "Edward Fane's Rosebud," "The Hall of Fantasy," "A Select Party," and "Dr. Heidegger's Experiment," and Hawthorne struggled to bring the Elixir of Life to a dramatic focus in his unfinished manuscripts for *Septimius Felton* and *The Dolliver Romance*. The elixir and the fountain of youth tempted adventurers in *The Arabian Nights* and the *Travels of Sir John Mandeville*. The temptation they pose for Hawthorne's characters was foreshadowed, too, in *The Curse of Kehama*. Kehama offered Kailyal the "Amreeta-cup of immortality" if she would be his bride, and then swallowed the potion to his own lasting torment.[66]

Both the philosopher's stone and the elixir of life also appear among the Oriental curiosities in "A Virtuoso's Collection," with which Hawthorne concluded his *Mosses*.[67] The philosopher's stone is described in terms like the Great Carbuncle as "a crystalline stone, which hung by a gold chain." The narrator asks of the Virtuoso: "And you have the Elixir Vitae, which generally accompanies it?" Like Kailyal in Southey's Hindu drama, the narrator is asked to drink of the magic elixir, but he refuses the temptation, explaining: "No, I desire not an earthly immortality. . . . Were man to live longer on the earth, the spiritual would die out of him. The spark of ethereal fire would be choked by the material, the sensual" (X, 489). Elsewhere in the sketch the narrator confessed that for a time he "knew not which to value most, a Roc's egg as big as an ordinary hogshead, or the shell of the egg which Columbus set upon its end" (X, 491). At last, though, he is a faithful American and returns from the hall of fantasies to the sunny thoroughfares of his home town.

The Children's Stories

The taste for storytelling, myth, and the magical fictions of the East that drew Hawthorne's fancy to *The Arabian Nights*, Southey's Oriental dramas, and the tales of real travelers also came to his aid when writing for juvenile audiences. Four years after *Peter Parley's Universal History* he re-entered the children's market with three short volumes of historical tales and legends from New England, called *Grandfather's Chair*, *Famous Old People*, and *Liberty Tree*, that were published in 1841 and collected the following year as *The Whole History of Grandfather's Chair*. The grandfatherly narrator of this cycle of stories reflects the author's prior experience both as the garrulous Peter Parley and as the itinerant novelist of *The Story Teller*. Like the exemplary Scheherazade, Grandfather's challenge is to sustain his listeners' interest through a series of instructive and entertaining stories told in the magic hours before bedtime. When little Alice falls asleep, Laurence is reminded "of the story of the enchanted princess, who slept many hundred years, and awoke as young and beautiful as ever" (VI, 107). Also like the vizier's daughter, Grandfather ends his tales with tantalizing promises of more to come. His chair is a flying carpet of sorts, transporting his audience from the everyday world of the framing tales to the imaginative stories within. Its purpose, according to the author, is to carry the reader back and forth between a "substantial and homely reality" and "the shadowy outlines of departed men and women" (VI, 5).

The *Whole History of Grandfather's Chair* reappeared as part of *True Stories from History and Biography* in 1851. That year Hawthorne also completed a longstanding plan by writing *A Wonder-Book for Girls and Boys*, where the Greek legends are "taken out of the cold moonshine of classical mythology, and modernized, or perhaps gothicized, so that they may be felt by children of these days."[68] The light atmosphere and fanciful touches of the *Wonder-Book* reflect his satisfaction upon completing *The Scarlet Letter* and *The House of the Seven Gables* and what Roy Harvey Pearce saw as the "sense of idyllic closeness to his wife and children" Hawthorne felt while living at Lenox in western Massachusetts.[69] Although the author wrote that he had "perhaps gothicized" the classics, his disposition at the time tended towards the more gorgeous life of the East. The furnishings of the Hawthornes' house at Lenox that Sophia described to her mother in June 1850 suggest an atmosphere of delicacy and romance. Beginning with "the beautiful antique ottoman, the monument of Elizabeth's loving-kindness, covered with woven flowers," Sophia also named a "fairy tea-table," a carved chair with a "tapestry of roses," and "the beautiful India box, and the superb India punch-bowl and pitcher, which Mr. Hawthorne's father had made in India for himself."[70] It was an ideal setting for storytelling. Sophia wrote again that while he was "a stoic about all personal comforts," her husband "should like a study with a soft, thick Turkey carpet upon the floor, and hung round with full crimson curtains so as to hide all rectangles."[71] It has been said that "the straight line, the acute angle, the rectilinear room" were all anathema to Edgar Allan Poe because they implied a faculty of sober reason that is antithetical to the imagination.[72] Like the merchant grandees of Salem Hawthorne, too, sought to soften and warm the rigid corners of New England life with products of the East.

In constructing the *Wonder-Book* Hawthorne carried forward some of the principal techniques of his *Grandfather's Chair*: an imaginative storyteller, the framed narrative, evening and morning settings, and a passage back and forth between real and legendary worlds. While regaling the children of Tanglewood, Eustace Bright boasts of truly Oriental powers of storytelling. " 'It would be a great pity,' said he, 'if a man of my learning (to say nothing of original fancy) could not find a new story, every day, year in and year out, for children such as you' " (VII, 9). Eustace's interplay with the children and his progress in his college studies set each Greek legend within a flexible structure of introduction and epilog. When he called his young auditors' attention to Monument Mountain, on the other side of Tanglewood lake, Eustace compared it to "a huge, headless Sphinx, wrapped in a Persian shawl; and, indeed," the writer agrees, "so rich and diversified was the autumnal foliage of its woods, that the simile of the shawl was by no means too high-colored for the reality" (VII, 36).

Hawthorne's friends and critics were quick to notice the more delicate colorings that entered his work at Lenox. Melville found in *The House of the Seven Gables* "rich hangings, wherein are braided scenes from tragedies" and "indolent lounges to throw yourself upon."[73] When Robert Carter, editor of the *Commonwealth*, wrote to Hawthorne in February 1853 praising the achievement of *A Wonder-Book*, he chose *The Arabian Nights* as the appropriate model for a book of tales that aimed to become timeless. The new book, Carter wrote, had thrown him "into a tumult of delight, almost equal to that of the first perusal of 'Robinson Crusoe' or the 'Arabian Nights.'" He believed it would "mark an era in fiction" as did the translation of the Arabian tales. He thought, however, that the classical tales were superior to the "Mahometan mythology" in intellectual as well as moral interest and took Hawthorne to task for his light tone, intrusive speakers, and contemporary New World setting. He hoped that if Hawthorne chose to continue the book, he would reconcile the tone and setting of the parts so that "it will be read in the future as universally as the 'Arabian Nights,' and not only by children."[74]

Roy Harvey Pearce has speculated that Carter's letter might have contributed to the narrative simplicity of Hawthorne's sequel, *Tanglewood Tales*, which appeared later in 1853 with a solitary introduction.[75] The new book, however, continued to show touches of fairy-land. The author apologized in his introduction that the poor little hillside behind his Wayside at Concord, "with its growth of frail and insect-eaten locust-trees," could not treat Eustace Bright to the grandeur he had enjoyed in the Berkshires. He feared it was all a bore to his "airy guest," that is, until he led Eustace to "my predecessor's little ruined, rustic summer-house, mid-way on the hill-side," which, "evanescent as a dream," was "a true emblem of the subtile and ethereal mind that planned it." This kiosk, which was left to the Hawthornes by Bronson Alcott, apparently is the same one that George William Curtis likened upon visiting the Wayside in 1853 to "the hanging gardens of Semiramis."[76] The fairy structure impressed Eustace as an ideal locus for storytelling, "the work of magic" and "full of suggestiveness" (VII, 176–177).

In his children's books Hawthorne sought to transmute both the stern, granite-like characteristics of New England and the cold, indestructible beauty of the Greek legends into warm, human stories. In *A Wonder-Book*, he said, the classical legends had "perhaps assumed a Gothic or romantic guise" (VII, 4). The respective claims of the Classical and the Gothic on Hawthorne's sensibility became a main theme in his thought later in the decade when he toured the cathedrals and museums of Europe and worked out his aesthetic perceptions in the French and Italian notebooks. The Oriental commonly has been subsumed within the Gothic in discussing nineteenth-century American literature, and Hawthorne was liable to merge the two traditions when making contrasts to the Classical mode.[77] But like his contemporaries, and his family, he was inclined also to make distinctions.[78] As early as "An Old Woman's Tale" (1830), with its motif of magic sleep and buried treasure, a lighter arabesque quality offset the grotesque in Hawthorne's writing, and his allegories, fairy legends, and apologues steadily followed an Eastern vein. He cogently limned his historical tastes when visiting the Crystal Palace in 1855:

> The Indian, the Egyptian, and especially the Arabic courts are admirably done. I never saw nor conceived anything so gorgeous as the Alhambra. There are Byzantine, and medi-aeval representations, too ... that gave me new ideas of what antiquity has been. ... There is nothing gorgeous now. We live a very naked life. This is the only reflection I remember making, as we passed from century to century through the succession of classical, oriental, and medi-aeval courts, adown the lapse of time.[79]

The course of European literature was profoundly affected by the poetry and prose of the East, both in the medieval period and in the eighteenth century, when the tales of Arabia and poetry of Persia returned to challenge the dominant classicism. "The Greek appeals through beauty to the intellect, the Arab or Persian through richness of colour to the senses and the imagination," H. A. R. Gibb wrote. "Where the Muslim writer excels is in clothing the essential realism of his thought with the language of romance."[80] The East offered the rich colors, natural passions, and mysterious incidents that Hawthorne and his fellow Romantics tried to evoke from the history and myths of their own new nations.

If the darker elements in Hawthorne's work are also attuned to the climes of Northern Europe, his fairy-land is better suited to tropical latitudes. As we will see in the next chapter, the neutral territory of The Scarlet Letter intermixes the fairy-land of the East with the real world of seventeenth-century New England. Were it not for the frame of golden thread woven around the grim emblem of her sin, the story of Hester Prynne would have remained just such an unrelieved tale of the Actual as the entry Hawthorne jotted in his notebooks in 1844–1845: "The life of a woman, who, by the old colony law, was condemned always to wear the letter A, sewed on her garment, in token of her having committed adultery" (VIII, 254).

Philologists and lexicographers of the late eighteenth century attempted to connect the word *fairy* with the Persian *peri*.[81] Closer examination disallowed an etymological link but did not lessen the figurative association in Hawthorne's time. The standard definition of *peri* still offers an impressive formula for the nature and story of Pearl in The Scarlet Letter: "*Persian folklore: a male or female supernatural being like an elf or fairy but formed of fire, descended from fallen angels and excluded from paradise until penance is accomplished, and orig. regarded as evil but later as benevolent and beautiful.*"[82] Hawthorne's college nickname *Oberon*, which he applied to the subject of "The Devil in Manuscript" and elsewhere, derives not only from Shakespeare's figure but earlier from the King of Fairies who, according to legend, came from Northern India to Scandinavia to dance by the light of the moon.

HAWTHORNE'S ORIENTAL WOMEN: THE FIRST DARK LADIES

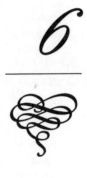

6

"richer than a garden of Persian roses"

NO FEATURE IN HAWTHORNE'S romances of the 1850s is of greater psychological and cultural interest than his remarkable heroines. "The problem of *The Scarlet Letter*," according to one critic, "is really the problem of how to interpret Hester." Another has declared more sweepingly, "The question of women is *the* determining motive in Hawthorne's works, driving them as it drives Hawthorne's male characters."[1] The last great act in Hawthorne's career was the evolution of the female type that culminated in Miriam of *The Marble Faun*. For a half century his "dark lady" has been celebrated as "the most resplendent and erotically forceful woman in American fiction" and "a dream-image of sexual bliss."[2] The Edenic state of Hawthorne's "New Adam and Eve," written in his first year of marriage, was both static and temporary. Eve soon had to struggle for place in his fiction against Adam's "first wife"—the demonic Lilith.[3]

Interpretations of Hawthorne's dark heroines have tended to move in two directions. First are the efforts to situate them within a convention of resolute, dark-haired, tragically sexual women reaching forward in the American Romance from Julia Franklin in Susanna Rowson's *Charlotte Temple* and Martinette de Veauvais in Charles Brockden Brown's *Ormond*. Even the exponents of this generic approach have recognized, however, that while of all American writers he took most seriously "the conflict of the ideal woman and the romantic woman," Hawthorne's dark ladies go "far beyond the regular romantic conception."[4] More contentious, but also more illuminating of the dangerous undercurrents in his fiction, have been the psychoanalytic explorations of the last couple decades, which have stopped just short of claiming that Hawthorne found his first dark lady, at home, in the person of his older sister Elizabeth.[5]

The backgrounds to the present study are more cultural and biographical than psychological. Yet the evolution of Hawthorne's female types after his marriage to Sophia Peabody in July 1842 inevitably raises questions of emotional attachment and the imagination. Ralph Cranfield's repudiation of the Oriental maid who haunted his dreams and his embrace of the salvific Faith Egerton never quite achieved the "life-like warmth" that the author sought to give "The Threefold Destiny." It was still the product of theory rather than realized experience. The declaration Hawthorne made six years later, however, in "Rappaccini's Daughter," suggests that he soon reached a profounder level of personal and sexual knowledge: "Blessed are all simple emotions, be they dark or bright! It is the lurid intermixture of the two that produces the illuminating blaze of the infernal regions" (X, 105). By 1844 the traveler had begun to stretch his elastic foot once more and to dream of pleasures away from home.

In *The Education of the Senses* Peter Gay has portrayed the marriage of Nathaniel and Sophia Hawthorne at some length as "an ecstatic union of two kindred spirits, as gratifying physically as it was mentally."[6] Early in their engagement, in July 1839, Hawthorne wrote to his "blessed Dove" that he never took up her sacred letters without first washing his hands (after a day spent measuring salt and coal at the Boston Custom House).[7] By January 1842, he was writing more fervidly that they had left behind "such expression as can be achieved with pen and ink" and that their spirits would soon demand more adequate expression than even "pressures of the lips and hands, and the touch of bosom to bosom. . . . Then we shall melt into one another, and all be expressed, once and continually, without a word—without an effort."[8]

As Gay observes, upon their engagement to marry Sophia could "permit herself and her fiancee erotic liberties, apparently short only of intercourse itself." They "found the married state a license for deeply felt . . . erotic pleasures."[9] Hawthorne wrote to his bride in March 1843 that after so many years of seclusion from society, this sole relationship satisfied all his desires. "The longer we live together," he confessed, "the deeper we penetrate into one another, and become mutually interfused—the happier we are" (VIII, 366). Yet Sophia's remark the following month that the "inward thought alone" makes the body "either material or angelical" also foreshadows the enigma of "Rappaccini's Daughter." Is this miraculous form "the temple of the living God" or "the den of the archfiend"? Before their marriage, she wrote to her husband, "I knew nothing of its capacities, & the truly married alone can know what a wondrous instrument it is for the purposes of the heart."[10]

During the first year and a half of marriage Hawthorne's physical and spiritual desires were reconciled and incarnate in his new bride. His references at the time to his "naughty Dove" and "naughty little wife" show his appreciation of this happy paradox (VIII, 363). In Sophia he finally possessed the "gay damsel" glimpsed in "The Seven Vagabonds." Courtship and marriage seem to have resolved, at least momentarily, what Philip Rahv called Hawthorne's and the New World's "problem of experience."[11] That he felt himself launched on a voyage of discovery is evident from the imagery of a note to his "Dearest Love" on the first anniversary of their marriage: "Methinks this birth-day of our married life is like a cape, which we have now doubled, and find a more infinite ocean of love stretching out before us" (VIII, 390).

Inevitably, the consubstantiation of the Romantic woman with the Ideal woman succumbed to the realities of time and married life. Sophia's pregnancy and the birth of the Hawthornes' first child in March 1844 marked a particular change in the relationship of the New Adam and Eve. In lieu of her earlier private raptures on the temple of the body, Sophia's letter to her sister-in-law Louisa on February 4, 1844, was preoccupied with details of sewing "little nightgowns, more shirts & petticoats, & more nightcaps & other garments for myself"—and only then with her husband, who seemed withal "as inexhaustible in riches & wonders as Aladdin's lamp or any magician's instrument."[12] Following the birth of their daughter Una and during the period when poverty drove the Hawthornes back to their respective family homes in Boston and Salem, their letters and notebooks took on a regretful tone witnessing the loss of their Edenic freedom. "References to 'my little wife' and 'my kingly husband' . . . thinned out as their carrot-haired child of immortality intruded."[13] From the beginning Hawthorne showed an unsentimental recognition that his own life would be permanently changed. The birth of a child, he wrote to George Hillard, "ought not to come too early in a man's life—not till he has fully enjoyed his youth—for methinks the spirit can never be thoroughly gay and careless again, after this great event." It called this trifler out of the "cloud-region" where he had wandered "preposterously long" and gave him "business on earth."[14]

During their honeymoon at the Old Manse Hawthorne found his wife both "a *woman* and an angel," but with the birth of their child she assumed the more formal role imposed by maternity as well as the decorum of the time.[15] Even without the much-thumbed evidence of Sophia's expurgations of the earthier passages in her husband's letters and notebooks, her greater emotional control would be expected. Hawthorne might still have been fretting at the changes in his life when he wrote two decades later in *Our Old Home*: "Those words, 'genteel' and 'ladylike,' are terrible ones and do us infinite mischief" (V, 286).

When outlandish figures again thrust themselves within the sacred precincts of Hawthorne's hearth in 1844, and foreign damsels beckoned once more, his imagination was charged with physical knowledge and the ambiguities of love as he had experienced it in this world. For a season his marital experience might have brought fairy-land almost within his grasp, but the world he knew was never able quite to provide the woman of his dreams. Years later William Dean Howells gave a revealing report of his meeting with Hawthorne in 1860: "With the abrupt transition of his talk throughout, he began somehow to talk of women, and said he had never seen a woman whom he thought quite beautiful. In the same way he spoke of the New England temperament, and suggested that the suppression of emotion for generations would extinguish it at last."[16]

"Drowne's Wooden Image": The Dark Lady of Fayal

On Sunday, March 3, 1844, Hawthorne wrote to his sister Louisa of the birth that day of his daughter Una, "after being ten awful hours in getting across the threshold. I have not yet seen the baby," he added, "and am almost afraid to look at it." The next letter in Hawthorne's surviving correspondence, written eight days later, transmitted the manuscript of "Drowne's Wooden Image" to John Frost in Philadelphia for publication in the July issue of Godey's Magazine and Lady's Book.[17] These products of Sophia's and Nathaniel's simultaneous parturitions offer an unusual opportunity to speculate about the convergences of the author's domestic and his imaginative experiences. Although "Drowne's Wooden Image" has received far less attention than his other artist stories, it is perhaps "the clearest statement in all of Hawthorne's fiction of how the creative artist creates," and has been called one of his "undiscovered masterpieces."[18]

Writing under the impression that the Hawthornes' first years in Concord were a period of unswerving domestic felicity, Neal Frank Doubleday thought it difficult to understand why anyone would suppose the "tale of an unconsummated love especially appropriate to the Old Manse period" and surmised that it probably was conceived earlier in Hawthorne's career.[19] Millicent Bell, on the other hand, found "this delicate and tender little piece in which the claims of life and art are not antithetical, but identical," particularly apt "to Hawthorne's honeymoon in the Old Manse."[20] In light of Hawthorne's pressing need for money and the nature of his other writings early in 1844, the period of Sophia's lying-in seems the most likely time for the composition of "Drowne's Wooden Image." Doubleday's distraction by the theme of unconsummated love and Bell's attribution of a muse-like role to Sophia during the blitheful "honeymoon" both overlook the change that two years of marriage and a child evidently wrought in the Hawthornes' relationship.[21]

As the author would demonstrate in his major romances, there always was "a secret snare" to falling in love with one of his fair New England maidens. The creative power of his protagonists waned in the presence of the "domestic marvels," Gloria Erlich noticed: "Holgrave gives up his wizardry for Phoebe. Kenyon notices that he is less of an artist under the influence of Hilda, and Hollingsworth goes off with Priscilla a broken man."[22] Nor do we have to look forward into the 1850s for evidence that a New England matron and her buxom child were more provocation than an inspiration. "The Artist of the Beautiful," which appeared in the *Democratic Review* for June 1844, coincides with "Drowne's Wooden Image" not only in time but in theme. Hawthorne wrote of his frustrated artist in this tale with telling circumlocution: "Owen Warland's story would have been no tolerable representation of the troubled life of those who strive to create the Beautiful, if, amid all other thwarting influences, love had not interposed to steal the cunning from his hand." For a time fair Annie gave a visible shape to Warland's spiritual aspirations. "Of course he had deceived himself; there were no such attributes in Annie Hovenden as his imagination had endowed her with" (X, 464).[23]

The source of inspiration in "Drowne's Wooden Image" is an *other* type of woman than either Annie Hovenden or the new madonna Sophia Hawthorne. In 1838 Ralph Cranfield came in from his realm of "wild and weary dreams" to find happiness with his childhood playmate. Six years later, in "Drowne's Wooden Image," a visionary maid such as Cranfield had sought in Spain and Turkey, Arabia and India, appeared on the shores of colonial Massachusetts, transported thence by a merchant ship like those Hawthorne himself had weighed and measured in Boston and so often sailed in reverie. The genealogy of Hawthorne's "dark lady" begins in earnest with the voluptuous "young Portuguese lady of rank" he introduced in July 1844 (X, 320).

Nowhere in Hawthorne do the archetypes of storytelling described by Walter Benjamin face each other more squarely than in the opening paragraph of "Drowne's Wooden Image," where, "in the good old times of the town of Boston," the young woodcarver named Drowne is approached by a Captain Hunnewell, who has just brought his brig *Cynosure* back from her maiden voyage to Fayal. The local artisan exhibited an inborn "knack" for rendering the human figure in whatever materials came to hand, from the child's snow statues to the warmer pine and oak "images of king, commander, dame, and allegory" carved by the adult craftsman. Until the seafaring merchant commissions him to create a figurehead for his ship, however, all of Drowne's progeny had a kindred aspect, the sign not of deficient skill but of the absence of a deep quality of soul or intellect that "would have made Drowne's wooden image instinct with spirit" (X, 306–310).

As he labors upon his great block of native oak, the secret link between the carver and the captain manifests itself in the figurehead of a fantastically attired woman whose complexion was "much deeper and more brilliant than those of our native beauties." "In the dark eyes, and around the voluptuous mouth, there played a look made up of pride, coquetry, and a gleam of mirthfulness." The flowers adorning her head—"Strange rich flowers of Eden"—certainly "never grew in the rude soil of New England" (X, 312–314). It becomes obvious that during his long, secluded hours of carving Drowne has worked from a living model, an exotic dark lady brought from her home in the Azores under the temporary protection of Captain Hunnewell. Drowne's hand takes fire from her tropical warmth, and the native American wood yields as never before the hamadryad within. Under her spell the Massachusetts Pygmalion realizes the full sensuality of the original. Shunning the artist John Singleton Copley's advice to preserve the simplicity of the wood, he paints the habiliments and countenance of his sculpture with nature's full colors and fills his townsmen with sensations both of reverence and of fear, "as if, not being actually human, yet so like humanity, she must therefore be something preternatural." Her air and expression induce the query: "who and from what sphere this daughter of the oak should be" (X, 314).

This question of origin is not a trivial one. At the time of the story, in the early 1770s, Massachusetts merchantmen could not yet claim the firsthand experience of their Portuguese precursors with the warm beauties of the East Indies. However, they were regular visitors to the Portuguese island of Fayal and knew its darker tropical charms. From the 1780s onwards Massachusetts vessels would mark their destinations with names like *Canton*, *Bengal*, and *Hindu*. Hunnewell's *Cynosure* points to the most exotic destination commonly available to New England sailors of the 1770s, a halfway station along the searoad from the West to the East.

The main elements of "Drowne's Wooden Image" are congruent with Hawthorne's better known tale "The Artist of the Beautiful": a New England craftsman creates, once in his life, a living work of art; native maidens are not a sufficient inspiration; in the end, both his artistic creation and the woman are taken from him (fair Annie Hovenden by Robert Danforth, the dark lady of Fayal by Captain Hunnewell). However, while Owen Warland eventually transcends the inspiration of woman entirely and takes his vision directly from nature, the departure of the lady of Fayal leaves Drowne's visage devoid of "the light of imagination and sensibility, so recently illuminating it." Captain Hunnewell has the further pleasure of escorting his foreign lady back to her home island, and the artist Copley, who appears in the story as an informed commentator on Drowne's art, would leave Boston himself in 1774 for the richer artistic climate of England. Only Drowne is left behind, with the ghost of his departed dream, "again the mechanical carver that he had been known to be all his lifetime." He later hews a figure of the Captain, "holding a telescope and quadrant," but apparently never steers forth again from his harbor, even in imagination (X, 319).

Despite Doubleday's observation that this tale "is not a treatise in aesthetic theory," it seldom is read as anything more.[24] Its psychological underpinnings and its place in the movement of Hawthorne's imagination just prior to the Salem Custom House years deserve attention. Hawthorne hardly could have overlooked the application to his own life of the contrast between the homebound wood carver and his globe-trotting townsmen. Drowne's dream-world creativity and his dulled sensibility on awakening echo the troubled spirits of the narrator in "Night Sketches Beneath an Umbrella" after many a day spent with a book of Eastern travels.

Captain Hunnewell's island lady is the first in a succession of ever more Easterly beauties that would inspire the author and tempt his male protagonists. Millicent Bell nicely projected the implications of the dark lady's fleeting appearance in "Drowne's Wooden Image" when she wrote:

> She is a true sister of Zenobia . . . an image of feminine allure that held Hawthorne first and last and created his most memorable female characters—Beatrice Rappaccini, Hester, Zenobia, and Miriam. And being like them, she suggests experience, that night journey which the man who would be an artist must take. She suggests knowledge, the ambiguous fruit gained only through experience, which is the creative intellect's desire. And she suggests, too, sin, the moral cost of experience and knowledge, which is the artist's peril.[25]

One wonders in what spirit Sophia Hawthorne first heard or read her husband's tales of 1844, with their darker fantasies. But then, he had warned her amidst the raptures of courtship "that he had depths which not even she could plumb."[26] And she wrote to her mother from their Concord paradise on September 3, 1843: "No two minds were ever more completely different and individual than Mr. Hawthorne's and mine. It would be impossible to have intercourse with one another, if our minds ran into one another."[27]

"Rappaccini's Daughter": The "Poison-Damsel"

An occasional reference point for treatises on "Rappaccini's Daughter" has been the following quotation, which Hawthorne set down in his notebooks during 1839:

> "A story there passeth of an Indian King, that sent unto Alexander a fair woman, fed with aconites and other poisons, with this intent, either by converse or copulation complexionally to destroy him."
>
> Sir Thomas Browne.[28]

Hawthorne was seldom so specific in quoting or citing sources for his notes as in this passage from Sir Thomas Browne's *Pseudodoxia Epidemica, or, Enquiries Into Very Many Received Tenents, Commonly Presumed Truths* (1646). Since the publication in 1978 of his lost notebook for 1835–1841, it has been obvious that the deletion of the phrase "either by converse or copulation" from Mrs. Hawthorne's *Passages from the American Note-Books*, and all subsequent editions, was due not to the author's self-censorship but to the delicacy and refinement of his wife. The bowdlerization lends a certain rationale to Henry Fairbanks's flamboyant judgment that Sophia "carried her nice airs into every nook of his being like a disinfectant."[29] It is remarkable, given the host of Biblical, Ovidian, Dantean, and Miltonic approaches to "Rappaccini's Daughter" and its explicit theme of physical and moral poison, that no one has paid any appreciable attention to the manifestly Eastern origins of the "poison-damsel" or read Hawthorne's tale in a context more foreign and distant than old Italy.

The accuracy of Hawthorne's transcription and his wider acquaintance with Browne and his celebrated contemporary and commentator Sir Kenelm Digby make it reasonable to think that he was acquainted with at least the immediate contexts of the passage he excerpted from Browne's work.[30] Editions of *Pseudodoxia Epidemica* published in Hawthorne's time appeared with the footnotes of Dean Christopher Wren, including this remark on the lines copied by Hawthorne:

> Hee that remembers how the Portuquez mixing with the women in the eastern islands founde such a hot overmatching complexion in them, that as the son puts out a candle, soe itt quentcht their hot luste with the cold gripes of deathe; may easilye conceive, without an instance, what a quick effect such venemous spirits make by a contagious transfusion.

"The loathsome copulation with those bodyes," Wren reported, indeed the very touch of them, was as deadly as the bite of a rabid dog.[31]

Early in 1844, in "Drowne's Wooden Image," the dark lady of Fayal drew the fancies of New England merchants and craftsmen as far eastward as the Azores. By the end of the same year, in "Rappaccini's Daughter," the exotic damsel was beckoning from the farthest Indies with Circe-like spectres of what Western adventurers, from the Macedonians to the Portuguese, had found there. Years later the author's sister recorded his captivation by a "mermaid" of Swampscott during a summer sojourn in the early 1830s. "At that time he had *fancies* like this whenever he went from home," Elizabeth Hawthorne said.[32] When his tale of the poisonous maid appeared in the *Democratic Review* for December 1844, the new father was ready to leave home again despite the earlier admonition of his Story Teller "not to follow an eccentric path" or to forget, as a text of deep meaning, "that he is an American."

The story's vexing, ambivalent conclusion makes it all too easy to overlook Hawthorne's preface to "Rappaccini's Daughter" and the conventions to which it pays allegiance. In presenting his "translation" of "*Beatrice; ou la Belle Empoisonneuse*," "From the Writings of [M. de] l'Aubépine," the author adopts the same guise of the commentators and translators who conveyed to Western audiences the legends and literature of the East. The preface to "Rappaccini's Daughter" imitates not only introductions to volumes of authentic scholarship but the satirical forewords to works like Voltaire's *Zadig*, Morier's *Hajji Baba of Ispahan*, and Walpole's *Hieroglyphic Tales*. The Eastern and Moorish inflection of the narrator's preface is further enriched by references to Aubépine's " '*Le Culte du Feu*,' a folio volume of ponderous research into the religion and ritual of the old Persian Ghebers, published 1841," and " '*La Soirée du Chateau en Espagne*,' I tom. 8vo. 1842." The narrator says of Aubépine (whose name is *hawthorn* in French) that his "inveterate love of allegory" was likely to invest his fictions, whether historical or timeless, "with the aspect of scenery and people in the clouds" (X, 91–93).

Although set in the city of Padua "very long ago," "Rappaccini's Daughter" achieves its romantic distance less through separation in time than in space and culture. Hawthorne's contemporary readers would have been quick to appreciate the screens he sets up between the American audience, a French storyteller, and the city in Italy, but the movement Eastward is far more dynamic than has been generally noticed. Not only does young Giovanni Guasconti move from the southern and western coast of Italy to the city of Padua in the northeast; the characters and culture he confronts there are redolent of a still farther East. In Aubépine's tale the buccolic young man from Naples travels for "the first time out of his native sphere" and encounters the strange sights that all Hawthorne's travelers see (X, 93). The theme of travel, and of encounter with Eastern maidens, is particularly apparent when Giovanni first enters Beatrice's garden: "[S]he became gay, and appeared to derive a pure delight from her communion with the youth, not unlike what the maiden of a lonely island might have felt, conversing with a voyager from the civilized world" (X, 112). Like Ralph Cranfield before him, Giovanni associates the Eastern maiden with the secret of his life. "The Threefold Destiny" concluded: "Happy they *who read the riddle* without a weary world-search, or a lifetime spent in vain!" (IX, 482; italics added). Similarly, Giovanni's pulse "throbbed with feverish blood, at the improbable idea of an interview with Beatrice, and of standing with her, face to face, in this very garden, basking in the Oriental sunshine of her beauty, and snatching from her full gaze *the mystery which he deemed the riddle* of his own existence" (X, 109-110; italics added).

The city of Padua and its thirteenth-century university, where Sir Thomas Browne himself had studied medicine, provided Hawthorne a convenient crossroads to the East. Lying only a few miles inland from the entrepot of Venice, Padua was among the first European cities to feel the effects of Arabian science and philosophy and to benefit from the cultural diaspora that accompanied the fall of Constantinople.[33] The minaret-like cupolas and bell tower of St. Anthony's Basilica and the Byzantine elements and gilded domes of the city still give it an Oriental atmosphere.

From its first mention as the "pleasure-place of an opulent family" (X, 94) the garden of Doctor Rappaccini is described formulaically in terms suitable to the palaces of the East, and especially to the *Haram* (the place of "forbidden things"). If the narrator's ambiguous references to Adam and Eve are likely to evoke Christianized notions of the Garden of Eden, his pervasive Oriental imagery and characterizations connote even more vividly the sensuous *Jannat al Ferdaws* ("Garden of Paradise") of Islam. Koranic descriptions of the happy mansions of Paradise and their ravishing, unpolluted female inhabitants had inspired earthly replications in the enclosed gardens, pavilions, and harems of the faithful from Granada to Agra.[34]

Hawthorne found prototypes for Rappaccini's garden throughout the Eastern commentaries he read. Lady Mary Wortley Montagu's description of a Turkish harem of the early eighteenth century began typically by emphasizing the extreme rarity of a Christian's admission into the house of a man of quality, and the customary exclusion from the women's apartments, which were built backwards and had "no other prospect than the Gardens, which are enclos'd with very high Walls." Lady Montagu continued:

> In the midst of the Garden is the Chiosk, that is, a large Room, commonly beautify'd with a fine fountain in the midst of it. It is raised 9 or 10 steps, and enclos'd with Gilded Lattices, round which, Vines, jess'mines, and Honey suckles twineing make a sort of Green Wall. Large Trees are planted round this place, which is the Scene of their greatest Pleasures, and where the Ladys spend most of their Hours, employ'd by their Music or Embrodiery.[35]

Describing the harems of Aleppo in the mid-eighteenth century, Alexander Russell took similar note of the courtyard, basin, fountain, and flowering plants, and added: "Where the size of the court admits of a larger shrubbery, temporary divans are placed in the grove; or arbours are formed of slight latticed frames, covered by the vine, the rose, or the jasmine: the rose shooting to a most luxurient height, when in full flower, is elegantly picturesque."[36]

The Gardens of Paradise, which were a popular subject of illustrative art as well as landscape architecture in Europe and America in the eighteenth and early nineteenth centuries, find a complement in Rappaccini's garden with its exclusive walls, its hidden entrance, its paths and luxuriant shrubbery, and especially its marble fountain, in the midst of which stands a resplendent shrub "that bore a profusion of purple blossoms, each of which had the lustre and richness of a gem" (X, 95). The blossoms are indistinguishable from jewels, and the plant itself is the vegetable sister of beautiful Beatrice. "The purple gems" of Beatrice's magnificent plant and the "gem-like brilliancy" of her fantasies—"as if diamonds and rubies sparkled upward among the bubbles of the fountain"—reflect the customary imitation of flowers by jewels in the East (X, 113). Lady Montagu was enraptured by the Turks' profuse ornamentation of clothing and their dressing of hair with precious stones. "[T]he most general fashion," she wrote, "is a large Bouquet of Jewels made like natural flowers, that is, the buds of Pearl, the roses of different colour'd Rubys, the Jess'mines of Di'monds, Jonquils of Topazes, etc., so well set and enammell'd tis hard to imagine any thing of that kind so beautifull."[37]

The entrance into Rappaccini's garden revealed by the ogrish housekeeper also has its model in a number of Eastern histories and fictions. When Giovanni forces himself "through the entanglement of a shrub that wreathed its tendrils over the hidden entrance" and on into Beatrice's garden, he repeats the escapades of amorous swains who explored the penetralia of the harems in many earlier accounts. Joseph Pitton de Tournefort observed in his *Voyages into the Levant* that "the extreme Constraint with which they are guarded" made the Turkish women "go a great way in a little time"; and that, notwithstanding all precautions, handsome young fellows, disguised like female slaves, were often introduced to their apartments.[38] The Hajji Baba's glimpse of the raven-haired Zeenab filled him with such passion that he "felt a great desire to leap over the wall and touch her," setting in motion an intrigue in the harem of her master that eventually led to the death of the beautiful Curdish slave.[39]

The most significant feature of Rappaccini's "pleasure-place," of course, is the gorgeous Beatrice herself, whose "experience of life had been confined within the limits of that garden." Like her sisters of the Eastern zenanas, she was "half-childish and half woman-like," with sudden moments of "queen-like haughtiness" (X, 104, 112). Accounts of the houris of the East, compounded as much from rumor and male fantasy as from the privileged observation of physicians and female travelers, gave the Western world an ambivalent cluster of images combining sexual appetite with childlike innocence, high nobility with mere silliness. In the face of her opulent naivete Giovanni responds to Beatrice "as if to an infant" (X, 113). Her voice, "as rich as a tropical sunset," made him think of "deep hues of purple or crimson, and of perfumes heavily delectable" (X, 96–97). Beatrice inhales the perfumes of the garden plants "as if she were one of those beings of old classic fable, that lived upon sweet odors" (X, 102). The latter reference carries us beyond Mohammed's Paradise, with its maids of pure musk, to that ultimate land of fable recorded by Pliny the Elder, whose account of the "Astomes" Hawthorne paraphrased in the *American Magazine of Useful and Entertaining Knowledge*, where he wrote: "In the farthest part of India towards the East, near the source of the river Ganges, there is a nation that have no mouths and do not subsist by eating and drinking, but by inhaling sweet perfumes through their nostrils" (AM, 490).[40] Similarities between "Rappaccini's Daughter" and the Indian drama *Shakuntala*, particularly the sisterhood of Shakuntala with the blossoming Madhavi-creeper, suggest that the author was acquainted, too, with Kalidasa's seven-act fairy tale.[41] Hawthorne's characterization of Beatrice overall owes much more to her Eastern prototypes than to the Eve of Christendom.

"The Oriental sunshine" of Beatrice's beauty comes to a darker focus finally on her sexual being. Arrayed as splendidly as the flowers, Beatrice "looked redundant with life, health, and energy; all of which attributes were bound down and compressed, as it were, and girdled tensely, in their luxuriance, by her virgin zone" (X, 97). Lady Montagu was struck by the girdle, "of about 4 fingers broad, which all [the Turkish women] that can afford have entirely of Diamonds or other precious stones."[42] Hawthorne's heavily punctuated, breathless depiction of Beatrice's deep and vivid bloom and his attention, ultimately, to her "virgin zone" evoke not only this characteristic item of dress but also its problematic association with female chastity.

The gorgeous flowers of Rappaccini's garden, and especially "the magnificent shrub, with its purple gems clustering all over it," plainly represent Beatrice's ripened sexuality (X, 101). The code of the flowers Giovanni and Beatrice present to one another, and their potentially fatal consequences, was a well established part of Eastern intrigue. A passerby instructed the sometimes slow-witted Hajji Baba in its signification after he had caught a glimpse of an unveiled beauty and she had thrown down her flower.

'Are you such a novice,' answered the old woman, 'not to know what that flower means? Your beard is long enough, you are not a child, and your dress proclaims that you have travelled; but you have travelled to little purpose, if you know not what a lady means when she gives you an almond flower.'

'O yes,' said I, 'I know that *fistek* almond rhymes to *yastek* pillow; and I know that two heads upon one pillow have frequently been compared to two kernels in one almond; but my beard is long enough to remind me also, that such things do not happen without danger, and that the heads may be cut off, as well as the kernels swallowed up.'[43]

Beatrice's relation with her purple gems is initially autoerotic. "Approaching the shrub, she threw open her arms, as with a passionate ardor, and drew its branches into an intimate embrace; so intimate, that her features were hidden in its leafy bosom, and her glistening ringlets all intermingled with the flowers" (X, 102). In her solitude Beatrice could only nurture her own sexuality. When the handsome male traveler enters her world, however, the islanded maiden forgets her inward-directed passion in the freedom of meeting the young man. As Doctor Rappaccini finally makes clear, the purpose of all this sensual cultivation is to bring Giovanni to the purple flower. He bids his daughter at the end, "Pluck one of those precious gems from thy sister shrub, and bid thy bridegroom wear it in his bosom" (X, 127).

In Beatrice beauty and sexuality are frighteningly mixed. Earlier, lying on his couch, Giovanni "dreamed of a rich flower and beautiful girl," who were "different and yet the same, and fraught with some strange peril in either shape." The gorgeousness of Rappaccini's flowers "seemed fierce, passionate, and even unnatural" to Giovanni; Beatrice, the richest of them all, was "to be touched only with a glove, nor to be approached without a mask" (X, 97–98, 110). Once his fantasies become incarnate in Beatrice, it matters not to Giovanni "whether she were angel or demon." Leaving his native sphere behind, he is drawn "irrevocably within her sphere, and must obey the law that whirled him onward, in ever lessening circles, towards a result which he did not attempt to foreshadow" (X, 109). When Hawthorne celebrated his Sophia as "*woman* and angel" in March 1843, he threw himself happily into a vortex of physical and spiritual sensations. The whirlpool that engulfs young Giovanni Guasconti is more ominous. The mystery of Beatrice and the riddle of Giovanni's existence are inextricably rooted in the gorgeous purple gem, simultaneously seductive and loathsome, of her sex. Through Beatrice's flower Hawthorne evokes an apparition of the same deadly sexuality that Dean Wren's "Portuguez" sailors had found when "mixing with the women in the eastern islands" and that Hollywood moguls would recreate in the sultry Theda Bara, whose name was an acronym for "Arab Death."

In "Rappaccini's Daughter" Hawthorne tapped into an archetypal struggle that carried him far outside the waters of American propriety. When he read the still incomplete manuscript to his wife in the fall of 1844, she asked him: "But how is it to end? . . . Is Beatrice to be a demon or an angel?" He reportedly answered with some emotion, "I have no idea!" Julian Hawthorne wondered whether the story did not suffer artistically from the brighter alternative chosen by his father, which shifts perspective three-quarters through the tale from Giovanni's anxiety at Beatrice's impoisoned nature to the author's omniscient assertion of her purity of soul.[44] The drama of the story moves in one direction; the moral abruptly turns in another. Is Beatrice poisonous, sexual, and demonic? Or pure, spiritual, and angelic? She is both. It is for Giovanni to solve the riddle. Although learned in the sciences, Beatrice remains as spiritually naive as conventional depictions of the women of the harem. Unlike the more complex Hester, Zenobia, and Miriam, she is uneducated by sin, neither moral nor immoral, but essentially amoral, a creature of wizardry and a mystery to the explorer.

At this point Hawthorne's notebook entry of 1839 concerning the Indian woman sent to Alexander becomes particularly relevant. Alexander's campaign to Northern India in 327 B.C. was the first major Western penetration into the mysterious East, and it heralded the symphony of exploration, sex, death, and encounter with the Other that would mark all subsequent invasions of the Orient. According to Plutarch, the Macedonian army took some seventy towns in India. As a means of solidifying control in the Eastern empire, Alexander compelled his officers to intermarry with women of the conquered provinces and himself took the Bactrian princess Roxana, reputed to be one of the most beautiful virgins of Asia, as a wife. His vision of thrusting all the way to the Ganges was frustrated, in part, by rebellion against his policy of intermarriage and his Orientalizing ways. The history of Alexander's march through Persia, Afghanistan, and the Punjab into India was well known to Hawthorne through Pliny the Elder and Plutarch's *Lives* as well as the schoolbooks of the last century.[45] Beatrice's first sight of Giovanni's beautiful head— "rather a Grecian than an Italian head, with fair, regular features, and a glistening of gold among his ringlets"—signals the arrival of just such a Western conqueror (X, 104).

Giovanni, of course, is hardly a world-class explorer, and even after he finds his way into Beatrice's garden and walks side-by-side with her, they do not consummate their love. "They had looked love . . . they had even spoken love . . . and yet there had been no seal of lips, no clasp of hands, nor any slightest caress, such as love claims and hallows." His perception of her vacillates between "the mysterious, questionable being, whom he had watched with so much awe and horror," and "the beautiful and unsophisticated girl, whom he felt that his spirit knew with a certainty beyond all other knowledge" (X, 115-116). When Giovanni grows too secure in his spiritual knowledge of Beatrice, however, the scientist Baglioni offers him an instructive tale:

> "I have been reading an old classic author lately," said he, "and met with a story that strangely interested me. Possibly you may remember it. It is of an Indian prince, who sent a beautiful woman as a present to Alexander the Great. She was as lovely as the dawn, and gorgeous as the sunset; but what especially distinguished her was a certain rich perfume in her breath—richer than a garden of Persian roses. Alexander, as was natural to a youthful conqueror, fell in love at first sight with this magnificent stranger. But a certain

sage physician, happening to be present, discovered a terrible secret in regard to her."

"And what was that?" asked Giovanni, turning his eyes downward to avoid those of the Professor.

"That this lovely woman," continued Baglioni, with emphasis, "had been nourished with poisons from her birth upward, until her whole nature was so imbued with them, that she herself had become the deadliest poison in existence. Poison was her element of life. With that rich perfume of her breath, she blasted the very air. Her love would have been poison!—her embrace death! Is not this a marvellous tale?" (X, 117)

Giovanni nervously rejects Baglioni's tale as "a childish fable," but the narrator is not so dismissive. Baglioni goes on to observe that Rappaccini "tinctures his medicaments with odors richer than those of Araby," and to warn that in the lovely Beatrice, "That old fable of the Indian woman has become a truth" (X, 118-119). Baglioni's fable, like Holgrave's tale of Alice Pyncheon in *The House of the Seven Gables* and Zenobia's tale of the veiled lady in *The Blithedale Romance*, holds the key to the larger work in which it appears. Furthermore, it is clear from the greater detail in Baglioni's account, particularly his reference to the sage physician and the Indian woman's ever more deadly breath-love-embrace, that Hawthorne's acquaintance with the story of Alexander and the poison-damsel was more comprehensive than what he had found in Sir Thomas Browne.

The primary European version of this poison-damsel legend appeared in the *Secretum Secretorum, or, De Regimine Principum*, which purportedly was "a collection of the most important and secret communications sent by Aristotle to Alexander the Great when he was too aged to attend his pupil in person."[46] The *Secretum* derived from Arabic and Greek manuscripts and was first translated into Latin in the twelfth century. While not considered today the authentic writings of Aristotle, it became "the most widely read work of the Middle Ages," was translated into most of the European languages, and played a significant role in the development of Western literature.[47] In his fascinating treatises *Poison-Damsels and Other Essays in Folklore and Anthropology*, N. M. Penzer wrote of the *Secretum*:

According to the text, Aristotle is warning Alexander against entrusting the care of his body to women, and to beware of deadly poisons which had killed many kings in the past. He further advises him not to take medicines from a single doctor, but to employ a number, and act on their unanimous advice. Then, as if to prove the necessity of his warnings, he recalls a great danger which he himself was able to frustrate. "Remember," he says, "what happened when the King of India sent thee rich gifts, and among them that beautiful maiden whom they had fed on poison until she was of the nature of a snake, and had I not perceived it because of my fear, for I feared the clever men of those countries and their craft, and had I not found by proof that she would be killing thee by her embrace and by her perspiration, she would surely have killed thee."[48]

The *Secretum* provides both the "physician" not mentioned by Browne (Aristotle taught Alexander philosophy, medicine, and science from ages thirteen to sixteen) and the "embrace" of death. It also mentions the serpentine associations of the poison and an admonition for the student-king not to trust himself to a single doctor. Hawthorne's references to the snake-like creepers in Beatrice's garden do little more than embellish the theme of fallen Eden, but Giovanni commits a fatal error in accepting medicine from a single doctor (Baglioni himself) rather than combining, if that were possible, the advice of both Doctors Rappaccini and Baglioni.

The parallels between the story of Alexander and "Rappaccini's Daughter" are economical and precise: the Indian King and Rappaccini; Alexander and Giovanni; the beautiful maiden fed up on poison and Beatrice; Aristotle and Baglioni. In both cases the young woman is a pawn in a struggle of dominion between three men. Hawthorne's tale, of course, becomes much more than this as he democratizes the roles of the sexes and dramatically imagines the moment of contact between the Western man and the Eastern maid. Yet recognizing the historical and folkloric paradigm for Hawthorne's drama may also redeem it from overly allegorical or clinical interpretations. It has been suggested that Hawthorne might have derived his poison-damsel from the *Gesta Romanorum*, which did much to spread the motif in Medieval Europe.[49] Baglioni's tale is closer to the Eastern original, however, and Hawthorne does not strive for a Christian moral in the vein of the *Gesta* tales. He could have found other accounts of poisonous inoculation, too, in Pliny the Elder's story of Mithridates, Varthema's report of the Sultan of Cambaia (included in *Purchas His Pilgrimes*), the *Travels of Sir John Mandeville*, and the writings of Sir Thomas Warton.

The few discussions of Hawthorne's poisonous maiden that have noticed the European versions of the Alexander story have overlooked the origination of a parallel legend of the *visakanya* ("poison-damsel") in the Punjab during the reign of the last Nanda kings, who controlled the major portion of the Ganges valley as well as a considerable territory to the south at the time of Alexander's invasion. The legend of the poison-damsel appears at various points in Sanskrit literature, most notably in Visakhadatta's seventh-century political drama the *Mudra-Rakshasa* (or *Signet-Ring of Rakshasa*) and in Somadeva's eleventh-century classic *Katha-Sarit-Sagara* (or *Ocean of Story*), which appeared in India around the same time as the Latin translation of the *Secretum Secretorum* in Europe. Visakhadatta's play deals with the formation of the great Maurya Empire in 313 B.C. and with its founder, Chandragupta Maurya, who reconquered the territories taken by Alexander and, through his grandson Asoka, inaugurated the unbroken chain of Indian history. In the *Mudra-Rakshasa*, as in the Western story of Alexander and Aristotle, the king (Chandragupta) is saved by his minister (Chanakya) from the deadly effect of a *visakanya* sent by the Nanda king. As Penzer demonstrates, this motif can also be traced in the literatures of Persia, Mesopotamia, Arabia, Syria, and Asia Minor. The legend of the poison-damsel originated in India before the Christian era, "travelled slowly westwards, and received its greatest impetus by becoming attached to the Pseudo-Aristotelian myths of medieval Europe."[50] How much of the original Eastern legendry of the *visakanya* Hawthorne was acquainted with is unknown. Such tales might have circulated orally in the Massachusetts ports during Hawthorne's youth, and German Orientalists began to publish a Western translation of Somadeva's Sanskrit classic in 1839, the same year Hawthorne copied out his note from Browne's *Pseudodoxia Epidemica*. In any case, it does not assume too much to read "Rappaccini's Daughter" within this wider context.

According to Penzer, four successively more lethal forms of contact are common to the *visakanya* tales in their Eastern and Western versions: the look, the breath, the touch, and copulation. Of the whole *ars amoris indica* intercourse is "the most obvious and successful way of passing on the poison."[51] In Hawthorne's tale the relationship of Giovanni and Beatrice is projected against these same four stages of intimacy. Doctor Rappaccini continues to mask his face and glove his hands against the poisonous breath and touch of his plants, but Giovanni becomes sympathetically imbued with Beatrice's poison to the point that they can "look love" and "speak love" together. The logical end of their mutual inoculation would be to move through the third stage (touch) and on to the fourth (copulation). The imagery of the tale and Beatrice's tensely girdled zone all point in this direction. But while Giovanni, like Beatrice, develops a breath that kills insects and a touch that withers normal flowers, he stops short of the ultimate connection with the Eastern woman.

Penzer discounts the factual existence of the "poison-damsel" pointing instead to a variety of pharmacological phenomena, psychological fears, and superstitions that, he concludes, creative storytellers wove into their legend of the beautiful but poisonous woman. The self-inoculation of snake charmers against the venom of their serpents and the deadly *el-bis* plant of India played their part, but equally significant to the legend, and perhaps to "Rappaccini's Daughter," were the real experience of venereal disease among sailors, the myth of the *vagina dentata*, and recurrent fears surrounding the first act of intercourse. In Indian lore the maiden could poison only once and, like the cobra, would spend her accumulated poison in the first embrace.[52] The imaginative credibility that the *visakanya* still has in the East is illustrated by the straightforward treatment it received in a recent book on *Secret Services in Ancient India*, where it is described as a peculiar mark of Indian genius and an "institutionalized . . . intelligence technique" that was given up in the post-Gupta period.[53]

In neither the Eastern nor the Western accounts of the poison-damsel is any moral judgment levied upon the girl herself. Her body, nurtured on poisonous plants from the crib upwards, is a tool for the intrigues of others; her soul does not come under consideration. Even in the *Gesta Romanorum*, where the "envenomed beauty" is presented as an exemplum of the poisons of Luxury and Gluttony, the girl herself remains essentially innocent. After her kiss kills a malefactor who is given her for a test, Alexander just returns the maid to her mother.[54]

While Hawthorne psychologizes the legend in "Rappaccini's Daughter," and enriches the primary sexual encounter through shades of romantic love, Beatrice does not greatly transcend the moral neutrality of her prototypes. The author makes a late effort to intertwine her poison and her purity, but the demonic and the angelic continue to occupy their separate spheres, the former of the body, the latter of the soul. As Baglioni's antidote takes effect, eradicating the poison from Beatrice's system, her physical life is consumed.[55] The soul might be innocent but it has no resting place.

The fascinating ambiguities of "Rappaccini's Daughter" are as much matters of culture as of morality. As in the legends of Chandragupta, Alexander, and the poison-damsels, Hawthorne's focus remains primarily upon the survival of the young male adventurer in his confrontation with another species of being. Giovanni finds the islanded maid simultaneously desirable and repulsive, splendid and lethal. He crosses farther over the borders of daylight and night, rationality and imagination, the known and the unknown, the West and the East than Hawthorne's protagonists had gone before. But he stops short of a final exchange of persons. Giovanni will not surrender himself to Beatrice's world, yet by seeking to bring her into conformity with his destroys the very thing that enchanted him. It is not an unusual experience in inter-cultural romance.

The Scarlet Letter: "Doth the universe lie within the compass of yonder town?"

What if Giovanni *had* taken the purple flower offered to him? Hawthorne might have asked himself this question more than once over the fallow years following his departure from the Old Manse in 1845, while he looked seaward from the Custom House in Salem and another "small troglodyte [a son named Julian] made his appearance" at home.[56] His answer was *The Scarlet Letter*, written upon his dismissal from the surveyorship of customs in 1849. In his new work Hawthorne pursued the "lurid intermixture" of light and darkness to a dramatic conclusion for both the Eastern maid and her male visitor. Overcoming his earlier scruples, in *The Scarlet Letter* Hawthorne risks letting the Rev. Arthur Dimmesdale actually know the dark beauty Hester Prynne. Again, he does not depict the act of sexual coupling; instead, he presents the fruits of such knowledge, the elf-child Pearl, "whose innocent life had sprung, by the inscrutable decree of Providence, a lovely and immortal flower, out of the rank luxuriance of a guilty passion" (I, 89).

Hawthorne's engagement with the passionate Hester, like Drowne's creative affair with the dark lady of Fayal, inspired his ultimate artistic achievement. This adventure into the unknown was not without cost, however. Five years later Thackeray's coolness in the face of his own adversity caused Hawthorne to remember "my emotions when I read the last scene of the Scarlet Letter to my wife, just after writing it—tried to read it, rather, for my voice swelled and heaved, as if I were tossed up and down on an ocean, as it subsided after a storm." He continued, "I think I have never overcome my own adamant in any other instance."[57] Hawthorne's imagery is especially portentous. If he and Sophia had rounded the "cape" and entered a "more infinite ocean of love" by the first anniversary of their marriage, the encounter of Hester and the Puritan minister steered him into even more storm-tossed seas. Perhaps not even in his most intimate moments with Sophia had Hawthorne emerged so far from the cave where he, like Richard Digby in "The Man of Adamant," had immured himself.

At first *The Scarlet Letter* appears to be the most authentically *American* of all Hawthorne's major works. The journey on which the author invites his reader in "The Custom-House" is neither upward into Arabesque halls of fantasy, nor away to Padua, but backwards into the town of Boston in 1642–1649. The dense native character of *The Scarlet Letter*, however, is achieved largely by contrasting the sombre Puritanism of seventeenth-century New England to the luxuriant, exotic figure of Hester Prynne, and by distinguishing "the links that [once] united her to the rest of human kind—links of flowers, or silk, or gold"—from "the iron link of mutual crime" that binds her to the Puritan minister (I, 159–160). When he revived a "class of susceptibilities" that had lain dormant within him, and recovered the "neutral territory, somewhere between the real world and fairy-land, where the Actual and Imaginary may meet," Hawthorne wove a brilliant Oriental motif into his New World tale of sin and punishment (I, 36).

American critics, impressed by the role of the *wilderness* in Puritan homilies and by the "Forest Walk" of Hester, Dimmesdale, and Pearl, have tended to forget that Boston, like Britain's and Europe's other colonies, faced distinctively seaward. When Hester finally persuades her lover to flee with her, their path leads not into the Western wilderness but eastward across the ocean. The wildest figures in "The New England Holiday" at the end of the novel, indeed, are not the barbarians of the American forest but the "rough-looking desperadoes, with sun-blackened faces" and "broad-brimmed hats of palm-leaf," from the Spanish Main (I, 232). Recognizing a kindred spirit, their captain throws his gold chain to Pearl. In the seventeenth century Massachusetts Bay already was an intersection on the highways of the world.

As Hawthorne works his way backwards in "The Custom-House" through nearly two centuries of time, he creates an atmosphere of the foreign and the remote. Like the framework to *The Story Teller*, "The Old Manse," and the inter-sections to his children's stories the author's long introduction to *The Scarlet Letter* prepares his audience for a wonderful tale to follow. He recalls the "marvellous gifts as a story-teller" of one veteran shipmaster in his service (Captain Stephen Burchmore) and regrets the obliviousness of their fellow officers to "all the world's wonders which they had witnessed with their youthful eyes" (I, 16). As the author again exerts his "fancy, sluggish with little use, to raise up from these dry bones an image of the old town's brighter aspect," he thinks first of the time "when India was a new region, and only Salem knew the way thither" (I, 29). When he finally uncovers the talismanic letter A and the faded manuscripts of Surveyor Pue, he takes them up with the same Mussulman-like reverence he had felt when turning over the old books at the Manse in Concord and so begins his search for the deep meaning behind that "mystic symbol."

Mark Van Doren wondered in 1949 where, "if not in the New England of his time, Hawthorne unearthed the image of a goddess supreme in beauty and power." A quarter century earlier D. H. Lawrence already had laid his hand on Hester's "rich, voluptuous, oriental characteristic" when evoking "the dark, phallic principle" in America.[58] Despite Lawrence's poetic celebration of Hester's dark force, however, her foreign and especially her Eastern origins have not been well understood.

The struggle of passion, prophecy, and puritanism took on Eastern colorations in Hawthorne's writings as early as his portrayal of Catharine in "The Gentle Boy" and his sketch of Anne Hutchinson in the *Salem Gazette* for December 7, 1830, who caused him to think that when a woman answers the impulse of genius, she should "obey the inward voice with sorrowing reluctance, like the Arabian maid who bewailed the gift of prophecy."[59] Like Catharine and Anne Hutchinson, Hester is an alien in seventeenth-century Massachusetts; and like Giovanni Guasconti, Arthur Dimmesdale is lost when he travels beyond his native sphere. Traditional moral, historical, and symbolist readings of *The Scarlet Letter*, and even the latter-day psychoanalytic and feminist approaches to Dimmesdale and Hester, have not sufficiently realized the cultural and archetypal dialectic of Puritan pastor and his "Oriental" Other, or their failure, in the end, to make a *universe* of their separate *spheres*.

Although Hester had come to Massachusetts Bay in the same migration that transported her fellow colonists from Holland and England, Hawthorne's characterizations make it apparent from the beginning that she is different in kind from the coarse "wives and maidens of old English birth and breeding" who await her appearance at the prison door. The tall young woman who stands before them, with her "figure of perfect elegance, on a large scale," her "dark and abundant hair," her rich complexion, and her "marked brow and deep black eyes," is equally distinguished from her bold and rotund contemporaries and from the fair, delicate generations that evolved in America from these ancestresses (I, 50–53). Like the provincial brats in "The Gentle Boy," "the little Puritans" of this community intuitively perceive "something outlandish, unearthly . . . in the mother and [her] child" (I, 94). As in Hawthorne's uses of the term in "The Gentle Boy," *The Blithedale Romance*, and elsewhere, the *outlandishness* of Hester and Pearl implies their non-Western character. He applies the adjective in its original sense of "not native, foreign," and weaves a pattern of geographical-cultural images to represent Hester's alienation from the people of Boston. By the time she meets the Rev. Mr. Dimmesdale in the forest and convinces him to sail off with her, Hester "had habituated herself to such *latitude* of speculation as was altogether *foreign* to the clergyman. . . . Her intellect and heart had their home as it were, in *desert places*. . . . For years past she had looked from this *estranged* point of view at human institutions. . . . The scarlet letter was her *passport into regions* where other women dared not tread" (I, 199; italics added). The borders that Hester invites Dimmesdale to cross require real as well as symbolic passports.

One of the more significant images by which Hawthorne defines the relationship of Hester and Dimmesdale is *sphere*. However threadbare the term has become in the late twentieth century, in Hawthorne's time and in his seafaring milieu it bore stronger geographical connotations. Neither the Western nor the Eastern hemisphere was fully known in the 1840s, not to itself, and certainly not to the other. Throughout *The Scarlet Letter* Hester is enclosed in a "sphere" of her own nature that excludes her and Pearl from the community of Boston as effectively as the walls of Doctor Rappaccini's garden removed Beatrice from the world of Padua. When Hester first appears in the Market Place, the scarlet letter, "so fantastically embroidered and illuminated upon her bosom . . . had the effect of a spell, taking her out of the ordinary relations with humanity, and inclosing her in a sphere by herself" (I, 53–54). At the end of the novel it is still "usually the case wherever Hester stood, [that] a small, vacant area—a sort of magic circle"—forms around her (I, 234).

Hester is not disciplined simply because of the sin of adultery. The alienation runs far deeper. The scarlet letter signifies less a single rash deed that has made her an outcast from the Puritan community than a character for whom, and a sphere in which, the Christian commandments are not authoritative. The actions of the New England townsmen leave her "as much alone as if she inhabited another sphere, or communicated with the common nature by other organs and senses than the rest of human kind" (I, 84). Like Beatrice Rappaccini, who might have lived upon sweet odors, Hester is another species of woman than the early Bostonians were habituated to.

Hester speaks more truly than is often realized when she answers Pearl's question about the meaning of her letter: "What know I of the minister's heart? And as for the scarlet letter, I wear it for the sake of its gold thread!" (I, 181). So lurid is the contrast between the sable field of the novel and the scarlet A glowing upon it that it is easy to forget that the threads of gold in which Hester frames the letter are as representative of her as the scarlet letter itself. Hester is characterized by the "elaborate embroidery and fantastic flourishes of gold thread" surrounding the letter A even before her large figure, dark hair, and deep black eyes are described in "The Market-Place." Her needlework here and afterwards manifests "much fertility and gorgeous luxuriance of fancy" (I, 53). *Gorgeous* has a typical Oriental resonance here for Hawthorne. Hester's sewing, especially her fantastic embroidery in flowers, silk, and gold, provides more than a means of livelihood for herself and a vicarious sensual outlet for the community. It identifies her with the opulent, imprisoned sisterhood of the seraglios for whom needlework, along with the care of their children, provided an almost exclusive form of imaginative expression. Hester "had in her nature a rich, voluptous, Oriental characteristic,—a taste for the gorgeously beautiful, which, save in the exquisite productions of her needle, found nothing else, in all the possibilities of her life, to exercise itself upon." It was her "mode of expressing, and therefore soothing, the passion of her life" (I, 83–84).

Hawthorne encountered similar characterizations of Eastern women repeatedly in his reading. The author of *Three Weeks in Palestine and Lebanon* called attention to the dress of a British consul officer's stunning Egyptian wife in the 1830s: "a green velvet tunic embroidered with gold, reaching to the knees, and open in front; a petticoat of gorgeous silk resembling cloth-of-gold, with a pattern of the gayest flowers."[60] In adorning her Pearl, Hester likewise allows "the gorgeous tendencies of her imagination their full play; arraying her in a crimson velvet tunic, of a peculiar cut, abundantly embroidered with fantasies and flourishes of gold thread." It was, indeed, "the scarlet letter endowed with life!" (I, 101-102). Hawthorne would have remembered especially Lady Montagu's long and lush descriptions of the needlework in the harems of Constantinople during the eighteenth century—the heavily embroidered brocades, satins, and velvets; the silk handkerchiefs; the waistcoats and caps ornamented with golden fringes and tassels.

While her exquisite embroidery soothes her passion and fills the solitary years spent with Pearl, Hester also develops "a tendency to speculation" focusing particularly on "the opposite sex" and the fate of womanhood. Such thought is not native to her, though, nor was it thought characteristic of her Eastern sisters. The travel accounts read by Hawthorne varied considerably in their appraisals of the beauty, pride, and grace of the female inhabitants of the seraglio, but they were generally agreed about the lack of education and mental discipline found there. Hester's speculations only cast her adrift in a Gothic-Oriental wilderness. She "wandered without a clew in the dark labyrinth of mind; now turned aside by an insurmountable precipice; now starting back from a deep chasm" (I, 166). Notwithstanding the effects of the scarlet letter, Hester's "impulsive and passionate nature" continues to manifest itself, and even while she seeks to reconnect with the father of her child, she imagines throwing off her shackles as a "life-long bond-slave" (I, 57, 227).

Before the novel begins, Hester and Dimmesdale had *known* one another; their spheres had merged. Twice more in the course of the novel their respective worlds of Oriental passion and Puritan conscience seem about to become one. The novel, indeed, is constructed on the possibility of this reunion. The first connection, in the chapter titled "The Pastor and His Parishioner," brings Dimmesdale to Hester in the forest. As their chill hands touch, taking "away what was dreariest in the interview," they feel themselves, "at least, inhabitants of the same sphere" (I, 190). Their meeting in the forest-dell warms but also bewilders the minister. As the title of a following chapter, "The Minister in a Maze," suggests, Dimmesdale temporarily loses himself amidst the precipices and labyrinths of Hester's world. Physically transformed by their encounter, "He leaped across the plashy places, thrust himself through the clinging underbrush, climbed the ascent, plunged into the hollow ... with an unweariable activity that astonished him" (I, 216). He yields "with deliberate choice, as he had never done before, to what he knew was deadly sin" (I, 222).

By the time Hester and Dimmesdale meet again, at the climactic Election Day sermon, the clergyman has poured his passions back into the form of

Puritan homiletics. As Hester watches the young divine proceeding towards the church and remembers the pledges they made in the forest, she imagines that "one glance of recognition" must pass between them. A great dreariness comes over her when she senses that Dimmesdale is, again, "so remote from her own sphere, and utterly beyond her reach." "How deeply had they known each other then! And was this the man? She hardly knew him now!" (I, 239). It appears briefly that their worlds yet might become one when, after his inspired sermon, Dimmesdale calls Hester and Pearl to join him beside the pillory in the market place. However, just as Dimmesdale could not yield to Hester, except momentarily in their forest walk, so now Hester cannot enter wholly into Dimmesdale's world.

The circumstances of Hester's life and the action of the scarlet letter do turn her "in a large measure, from passion and feeling, to thought" (I, 164). But by her nature Hester can never overcome the feeling that, "What we did had a consecration of its own" (I, 195)—and that they would spend their "immortal life together." Dimmesdale, on the other side, fears to his dying hour that when they transgressed their reverence for each other's soul, it became vain to hope they could meet hereafter "in an everlasting and pure reunion" (I, 256). Many years later, when Hester is laid in the grave, a space still intervenes, "as if the dust of the two sleepers had no right to mingle" (I, 264).

Hester and Dimmesdale both strive to bring their worlds into alignment, she by venturing into regions of thought, he by leaving his study to explore realms of passion. But after the consummation that started the life of little Pearl, they are not to be one again. The rounding of their universe is possible only through Pearl, the "connecting link between these two" (I, 154). When Hester and the Puritan minister gave Pearl her existence, they broke "a great law . . . and the result was a being, whose elements were perhaps beautiful and brilliant, but all in disorder." At the moment of her conception Pearl drew together from her mother and her father "the deep stains of crimson and gold, the fiery lustre, the black shadow, and the untempered light" (I, 91). The fractured law is not simply a commandment against adultery but a taboo against mingling the known and the unknown, the native and the outlandish, the sad-colored world of New England and the gorgeous East. The language Hawthorne uses to establish Pearl's role in the novel signifies the bridge she offers between these two worlds. Hester's scarlet letter is "the talisman of a stern and severe, but yet a guardian spirit" (I, 181). Her daughter, the scarlet letter imbued with life, is presented in language equally nuanced with the Orient. Pearl is "the living hieroglyphic, in which was revealed the secret they so darkly sought to hide,—all written in this symbol,—all plainly manifest,—had there been a prophet or magician skilled to read the character of flame!" (I, 207).

Hawthorne's depictions leave no doubt that for seven years Pearl is truly her mother's daughter. She is characterized as "an infant princess," and "a wild, tropical bird, of rich plumage," brilliantly picturesque in her "adornment of flowers and wreathed foliage" and "gorgeous robes which might have extinguished a paler loveliness" (I, 90, 111, 208). Pearl's character particularly stands forth in "The Governor's Hall," where the author attests to her deep and luxuriant beauty, bright complexion, and "hair already of a deep, glossy brown, and which, in after years, would be nearly akin to black" (I, 101). Pearl's spirit transfigures Governor Bellingham's mansion. As sunshine falls across the face of the edifice, whose stucco walls are intermixed with fragments of glass, "it glittered and sparkled as if diamonds had been flung against it by the double handful." Its brilliancy, the author adds, "might have befitted Aladdin's palace, rather than the mansion of a grave old Puritan ruler" (I, 103). A union of the Puritan and the Oriental seems imminent at this moment.

The struggle for Pearl's soul, however, is not so easily won. So long as she inhabits only her mother's world, she is a prisoner of her own circle of radiance. Only through Dimmesdale's acknowledgment of his fatherhood is the enchantment lifted. Dimmesdale seeks to enter her circle in the forest scene through a kiss that he hopes "might prove a talisman to admit him into the child's kindly regards" (I, 212). Pearl impatiently washes it off at the brookside. She later bestows the talisman herself when the minister reveals his own scarlet letter in the final scaffold scene. "Pearl kissed his lips. A spell was broken" (I, 256). In Pearl the worlds of Hester and Dimmesdale finally become one. While she would never lose "a trait of passion, a certain depth of hue," she also takes on her father's soul, and the tears that fall upon his cheek are "the pledge that she would grow up amid human joy and sorrow, nor for ever do battle with the world, but be a woman in it" (I, 90, 256).

The figure Pearl enabled Hawthorne to transcend without denying the ultimate alienation of Hester Prynne and Arthur Dimmesdale. In the absence of such a synthesis, he would have ever greater difficulty resolving the dialectics of his next three romances. Through Pearl, however, The Scarlet Letter closes with the world wholly in order. The answer to Hester's question of Dimmesdale—"Doth the universe lie within the compass of yonder town?"—is definitely "no!" (I, 197). While New England eventually becomes the place of "a more real life for Hester Prynne," Pearl retreats from the ragged Western edge of empire and marries into the European aristocracy. The "armorial seals" upon her letters to Hester, "of bearings unknown to English heraldry" (I, 262), suggest a Mediterranean house like the palace of the Paduan noble where Giovanni Guasconti took residence and which exhibited over its entrance "the armorial bearings" of an ancient family. It is a rightful habitation for this hybrid flower of Oriental passion and Puritan creeds.

The House of the Seven Gables: Suzerains and Turbans

From 1844 to 1850 Hawthorne's efforts to read the riddle of the Oriental woman became ever more intimidating. Although the dark lady of Fayal momentarily sent Drowne's wooden spirit into the realm of fancy, the Massachusetts artisan stayed safely becalmed at home when the dream vanished. In Beatrice Rappaccini, Giovanni confronted such an intermixture of love and horror as stirred "the illuminating blaze of the infernal regions." When he was unable to bring Beatrice "rigidly and systematically" within the realm of his own experience, and unwilling to risk a closer knowledge, Giovanni left the poison-damsel die in her own pleasure-place (X, 105). *The Scarlet Letter* brought the voluptuous Oriental characteristic to full life but only with the death of the male lover. By knowing Hester, Dimmesdale came alarmingly close to losing his way. It was the last time Hawthorne would seriously risk the life of his male protagonist in the arms of the dark lady.

Both Nathaniel and Sophia Hawthorne were emotionally shaken by the conclusion of *The Scarlet Letter*. It lacked sunshine, he wrote Horatio Bridge in February 1850. "It is a positively h-ll-fired story, into which I found it almost impossible to throw any cheering light."[61] Hawthorne was determined not to put himself and his reader through the same trauma again and went immediately to work on an antidote, a romance filled with "sunshine" and "cheering light." In *The House of the Seven Gables* (1851) he returned to a theme he had mined heavily from *Fanshawe* through *The Story Teller* and "Ethan Brand," the meaning and rediscovery of *home*. In his new novel, as in "The Threefold Destiny," finding one's destiny in the girl next door also means foreswearing the visionary maids of the Orient. In lieu of the rich, full-figured Hester, Hawthorne now presents Phoebe, a goddess of light, by everyone's consent, including her own, "a cheerful little body," "a nice little housewife," "a brisk little soul," a "little figure of the cheeriest household-life" (II, 74, 77, 82, 140). Phoebe is not devoid of sensual interest. "All her little, womanly ways, budding out of her like blossoms on a young fruit tree," sometimes cause her cousin Clifford "to tingle with the keenest thrills of pleasure" (II, 141). But her virginal buds are a tamer species than either Beatrice's purple gems or, later, Zenobia's exotic flower.

In *The House of the Seven Gables* Hawthorne paid homage to his redeeming wife. He gave Phoebe his pet name for Sophia, and he probably adopted the cognoman *Holgrave* (holograph?) as a clue to his own role within the novel. Like the author, Holgrave has written for *Godey's* and *Graham's* magazines. His love interest is no longer a problem of "angel or demon," but resolutely both angel and woman. On publishing the novel, Hawthorne wrote to Bridge in July 1851: "I think it a work more characteristic of my mind, and more *proper* and natural for me to write, than the Scarlet Letter."[62]

While Holgrave's speculative occupations included some travel as a supernumerary on a packet ship, *The House of the Seven Gables* steers clear of any and all entanglements with gorgeous dark women. Similarly, the Orientalism in this domestic comedy is the least substantial or emotionally disturbing of Hawthorne's long romances. In place of the life-and-death confrontations of the preceding romances *The House of the Seven Gables* is embroidered with lighter designs borrowed from the fairy-world of *The Arabian Nights*: necromancers, talking pictures, magic fountains and mirrors, a "hieroglyphic" document holding the key to a secret treasure, and of course an enchanted maiden. The chief "Oriental" thread in the novel still concerns the relation of men and women but with a sharp change of emphasis from *The Scarlet Letter*. Male dominion over women provides most of the dramatic interest in the novel as Hawthorne replaces the potent, statuesque Hester and her vacillating Puritan lover with patterns of sexual enslavement and liberation more suggestive of an abduction from the seraglio.

From their seventeenth-century progenitor down to the current generation the males of the Pyncheon tribe display appetites like those popularly associated with the lords of the harem. The Puritan Colonel Pyncheon "had worn out three wives" and sent them to their graves through "the remorseless weight and hardness of his character in the conjugal relation." While losing some of his ancestor's sexual hegemony, Judge Jaffrey Pyncheon gave his single lady "her death-blow in the honey-moon" when he "compelled her to serve him with coffee, every morning, at his bedside, in token of fealty to her leige-lord and master" (II, 123). Jaffrey Pyncheon's sensual endowments, if less productive, are more voluptuous than any of his ancestors. He flourishes "a gold-headed cane of rare, oriental wood," and it was said of him, "in reference to his ogre-like appetite, that his Creator made him a great animal, but that the dinner-hour made him a great beast" (II, 116, 275). Jaffrey's rough-bearded, dark physiognomy might not have been unpleasant to a woman with the space of a room between, but Phoebe is repelled when her kinsman first seeks to kiss her. "The man, the sex, somehow or other, was entirely too prominent in the Judge's demonstrations of that sort" (II, 118). In the latest generation even poor Clifford, wearing his faded damask dressing gown after thirty years in prison, demonstrates a decayed appetite for opulence and beauty.

The other male line in The House of the Seven Gables, descending from the original Matthew Maule, also exerts an Eastern sovereignty over the women of the novel, in this case, however, not through the sexual proprietorship of the seraglio but through the psychic enchantments of the wizard. The Maules' power to enslave is dramatized in Holgrave's tale of Phoebe's ancestress, the beautiful, gentle, yet haughty Alice Pyncheon. Once Gervayse Pyncheon had given his daughter Alice to the second Matthew Maule, a carpenter and mesmerist, to use as his medium in searching for the lost title-deed to the Pyncheon territory in Maine, she became "Maule's slave, in a bondage more humiliating, a thousand-fold, than that which binds its chain around the body" and was constrained to do his "grotesque and fantastic bidding" (II, 208).

The Eastern atmosphere of Holgrave's legend of Alice Pyncheon and its applicability to the developing relation of Holgrave and Phoebe are equally apparent. Like its precursors in The Story Teller, this tale-within-a-tale conveys a lesson that many a dreaming youth, and the storyteller himself, might learn by. Among his many marvellous gifts, Holgrave tells Phoebe, is "that of writing stories." When Phoebe laughingly asks for a sample, Holgrave opens "his roll of manuscripts" and begins the tale of Alice Pyncheon (II, 186). In so doing, he adds the guise of the Eastern storyteller to the Maules' hereditary wizardry. At the conclusion of his tale, which ends with the spiritual subjugation and physical death of Alice Pyncheon, Holgrave observes that a "certain remark-able drowsiness . . . had been flung over the senses of his auditress." Phoebe's drooping lids and measured breathing demonstrate in Holgrave, "as he rolled up his manuscript," the same "lawful magic" attributed to the coffee-house literati at Aleppo and points farther East. His achievement particularly an-ticipates the magician Westervelt and Zenobia's tale of "the veiled lady" in *The Blithedale Romance*. As Holgrave completes his tale, "A veil was beginning to be muffled about [Phoebe], in which she could behold only him, and live only his thoughts and emotions" (II, 211).

Unlike Westervelt and his own great-grandfather Matthew Maule, how-ever, Holgrave forebears enslaving the body and soul of his young maid. He could have completed his mastery over Phoebe's virgin spirit with a wave of the hand, but he "had never lost his identity" amidst his personal vicissitudes and years of wandering, and he permits Phoebe's influence to bring him back within the laws and peaceful practices of their society (II, 177). "Your poise will be more powerful than any oscillating tendency of mine," he tells her (II, 307). Holgrave is a more compliant American than either Ethan Brand or Ralph Cranfield, who had lost some pieces of his New England character at every stage in his ten years' journeying to and in the East.[63]

At first sight the deterioration of the Pyncheons' sultan-like dominion appears not much more than a matter of costume. It is, however, associated with a theme of eugenics that runs throughout the novel. Both in "The Custom-House" in 1850 and in *The House of the Seven Gables* the following year Hawthorne lamented the thinning of physical and mental bloodlines that results from a too exclusive mixing with one's own kind. "Human nature will not flourish," he wrote in "The Custom-House," "any more than a potato, if it be planted and replanted, for too long a series of generations, in the same worn-out soil" (I, 11-12). He vowed that his children would set their roots into new earth. Hawthorne puts a similar horticultural-zoological met-aphor in Holgrave's mouth in *The House of the Seven Gables*:

> "To plant a family! This idea is at the bottom of most of the wrong and mischief which men do. The truth is, that, once in every half-century, at longest, a family should be merged into the great, obscure mass of humanity, and forget all about its ancestors. Human blood, in order to keep its freshness, should run in hidden streams, as the water of an aqueduct is conveyed in subterranean pipes. (II, 185)

The Pyncheon breed had not thrived through the generations, the author remarks; "it appeared rather to be dying out" (II, 24). With the sole exception of Phoebe's budding branch, the latter shoots of the Pyncheon family tree are few, withered, and sterile—only the epicene Clifford and the decrepit Hepzibah, "a gaunt, sallow, rusty-jointed maiden, in a long-waisted silk-gown, and with the strange horror of a turban on her head!" (II, 41).

That Hepzibah's dry, sexless figure is intended as a droll parody of Oriental splendor and fecundity is suggested by the repeated references to her turban. Hawthorne establishes an identity through this symbol no less sharply than through Hester's scarlet letter or Zenobia's flower or Faith Brown's pink ribbon. *Turban* (or *turbans, turbaned*) appears eight times in *The House of the Seven Gables*, always with direct reference to Hepzibah, and nowhere else in Hawthorne's five completed romances. Each time Hepzibah's turban stands as a gay, queer contradiction to the perpetual scowl that contorts her brow. The aesthetic Clifford is particularly repulsed by the "uncouthness of a turban on her head" (II, 109). The confusions of her character and dress are brought out most sharply in the chapter "The Scowl and Smile," where Hepzibah is depicted as "the East-Wind itself, grim and disconsolate, in a rusty black silk-gown, and with a turban of cloud-wreaths on its head!" (II, 223).

Hawthorne's use of the turban as an emblem of Oriental majesty is further dramatized through the stunted Pyncheon hens, whose distinguishing mark was "a crest, of lamentably scanty growth ... but so oddly and wickedly analogous to Hepzibah's turban, that Phoebe ... was led to fancy a general resemblance betwixt these forlorn bipeds and her respectable relative." The Pyncheon hens once were a noble, vital breed reaching almost the size of turkeys, and fit for a prince's table, but are "now scarcely larger than pigeons. ... It was evident that the race had degenerated, like many a noble race besides, in consequence of too strict a watchfulness to keep it pure" (II, 88–89). Where the barnyard sultan formerly ruled a fertile harem, Chanticleer now possesses only two wives, who yield scarcely an egg. Holgrave points out to Phoebe that the peculiar plumage and funny tuft that adorn her "feathered riddle" betoken "the oddities of the Pyncheon family, and that the chicken itself was a symbol of the life of the old house" (II, 152).

While Hepzibah's horror of a turban can be regarded in part as a spinsterly grab at fashion, it is even more a sign of her decayed dreams of a "harlequin-trick of fortune" from the East. She muses that "an uncle—who had sailed for India, fifty years before, and never been heard of since—might yet return ... and adorn her with pearls, diamonds, and oriental shawls and turbans, and make her the ultimate heiress of his unreckonable riches" (II, 64).[64] One of her proudest family possessions is "a China tea-set, painted over with grotesque figures of man, bird, and beast, in as grotesque a landscape" (II, 76–77). Closer at hand, Hepzibah also dreams of an invitation to rejoin the English branch of the family. Nevertheless, while her ideas of escaping her cent-shop through the lavishments of the East or an English patrimony are equally made of air, the latter seems to be the less promising of the two. The gene-pools of England were even more stagnant than those of Salem. At Leamington Spa a few years later Hawthorne savored first the delights of permanency, but as his love of change again asserted itself, he became "sensible of the heavy air of a spot where the forefathers and fore-mothers have grown up together, intermarried, and died, through a long succession of lives, without any intermixture of new elements, till family features and character are all run in the same inevitable mould" (V, 59).

Like his other remarks on cultural and genetic intermixture, Hawthorne's perceptions in *Our Old Home* were affected no doubt by his uncle Robert Manning's renowned experiments in the breeding and propagation of fruits. Holgrave's tribute to the subterranean mixture of blood in *The House of the Seven Gables*, however, is more pertinent to the harems and society of the Ottoman Turks, which were a popular subject for amateur eugenicists into the nineteenth century. The practice of *devsirme* (child tribute) periodically stripped the villages of the Ottoman territories of the brightest, strongest youths, who were then trained for the elite Janissary corps and the civil administration. Simultaneously, the most beautiful Circassian, Georgian, and Greek women, as well as the black and copper beauties of Darfur and Abyssinia, were offered in the slave bazaars for sale as concubines and wives. At the height of its imperial glory, under Soleiman the Magnificent in the mid-sixteenth century, all eight grand viziers of the Ottoman Empire were humble-born Christians first brought to Turkey as slaves, and Soleiman's beautiful queen Roxelana (or *Hürrem*, "the laughing one"), whom he married after his accession, entered his harem as a slave.[65] In contrast to Europe's artificial aristocracies of birth and wealth, preferment in the golden age and extended families of the Ottoman Empire was based on merit and talent. The Eastern world had a long history of merging its families "into the great, obscure mass of humanity," of abandoning ancestry, and of freshening its blood through hidden springs. Busbecq, Tournefort, and other travelers in the Ottoman Empire continually remarked that the mixing of races from all parts of Africa, Asia Minor, and the Eastern Mediterranean had produced a people of exceptional physical and spiritual fibre—including, no doubt, many an elf-child like Hester's Pearl.

The intermixing that concludes *The House of the Seven Gables* is of a light sort, consistent with Hawthorne's determination to write a cheerful story. The betrothal of Phoebe and Holgrave and the mingling of aristocratic and plebian, mercenary and magicians' blood suffice to solve the ancestral riddle, lift the enchantment from Phoebe's ancestress, and generally disspell the gloom of the novel. On transplantation from the dismal old House of the Seven Gables to their new country estate, Chanticleer and his two hens begin "an indefatigable process of egg-laying" (II, 314). The ghost of Alice Pyncheon is freed from the web of psychic and sexual sorcery spun around her by Matthew Maule and floats heavenward in celebration of Holgrave and Phoebe's union. Alice's Poesies erupt from their long dormancy into full bloom. Maule's Well once more pours forth its kaleidoscopic pictures. Instead of holding Phoebe in the kind of bondage that Matthew Maule imposed on Alice Pyncheon, compelling her as an ultimate humiliation to prepare his bride for the nuptial bed, Holgrave releases Phoebe from thralldom to his mesmerizing will and, like Soleiman's raising up of the beautiful slave Roxelana, takes her for his wife.

Hawthorne's subtle Oriental motifs in *The House of the Seven Gables* play at some of the dark edges of his engagement with the East. For the most part, however, he resolutely subordinates his darker psychological tendencies to the fairy-tale-like objectives of this work, domesticating his females and restraining the traveler's desire to know them too well. When Holgrave produces his roll of manuscript, he begins to read, not at night, but "while the late sunbeams gilded the seven gables," and he concludes in a mixture of moonshine and lingering daylight (II, 186). Despite the putative solidity of Holgrave and Phoebe's new country house, the edifices in *The House of the Seven Gables*, as the author confesses, are built of "materials long in use for constructing castles in the air" and have "a great deal more to do with the clouds overhead, than with any portion of the actual soil of the County of Essex" (II, 3).

It is interesting that Hawthorne interrupted his reading of *The Seven Gables* manuscript to Sophia on the night of January 15, 1851, to read aloud instead from Southey's *Thalaba the Destroyer*. He apparently had decided that day to revise the last three chapters of the romance.[66] If Hawthorne usually turned to Southey's Oriental dramas for other-worldly adventures, in this case the poet laureate helped him in some small way to lift the shades of darkness following his derisive, haunted portrait of the dead Jaffrey Pyncheon. The same foil-like function that the Pyncheon hens serve for the sexually arid Hepzibah, little Ned Higgins serves for the hungry beast Judge Pyncheon. "This remarkable urchin," Hepzibah's most demanding client for circus crackers, "was the very emblem of old Father Time, both in respect of his all-devouring appetite for men and things, and because he, as well as Time, after engulfing thus much of creation, looked almost as youthful as if he had been just that moment made" (II, 115). The caravan of camels, elephants, dromedaries, and whales that disappear into the cavernous stomach of little Ned spoofs the ogrish appetite of the Pyncheon males. In the ensemble of felicity at the end of the novel Hepzibah gives her earliest and staunchest customer enough silver "to people the Domdaniel cavern of his interior with as various a procession of quadrupeds, as passed into the ark" (II, 318). By the close of the novel the demonic is safely confined to the precincts of a child's stomach.

HAWTHORNE'S ORIENTAL WOMEN: THE FEMALE SOVEREIGNS

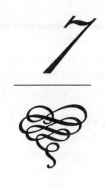

"Thus, between two countries, we have none at all, or
only that little space of either, in which we finally lay
down our discontented bones."

ONE OF THE MOST PROVOCATIVE cultural images created by an American in the nineteenth century was Hiram Powers's *The Greek Slave* (1843), which was shown in his studio in Florence, Italy, before going on display at the International Exhibition in London in 1851 and then touring America. The subject of Powers's sculpture, as described in a contemporary broadside, was "a GRECIAN MAIDEN, made captive by the TURKS, and exposed for sale in the Bazaar of Constantinople."[1] Manacled with chains, her head turned chastely from the viewer's gaze, and very, very naked, Powers's white marble figure at once aroused and arrested the passions of her audience. For male viewers she offered an opportunity to enjoy, safely frozen in stone, the pleasures of the Turkish sultans and merchants. For more than a few female viewers, perhaps, the statue projected fantasies of self-display and submission free of social stigma.[2] Even the Protestant clergy approved the statue, for Powers had laid a Christian cross upon the clothes piled beside the maiden.

Like Powers's first nude, *Eve Tempted* (1839–1842), *The Greek Slave* is a stunning witness to the cultural and psychological confrontation of East and West at mid-century. Despite the approbation of his *Slave* by clergymen and critics, the sentiments she aroused were not quite proper for mixed company. "None but ladies and families" were admitted during the afternoons at one of her exhibitions in America.[3] Hawthorne's fellow Salemite Clara Crowninshield remarked while touring Europe with Henry Wadsworth Longfellow that it *was* "an awkward thing to contemplate naked statues with young gentlemen."[4] Beneath the cold, neo-classical surface of the marble *Slave* one could still feel the moist clay from which the original Adam and Eve were formed.

Notwithstanding Hawthorne's praise for Powers a couple years later as both "a great man" and "a great artist,"[5] he saw "little beauty or merit" on first beholding *The Greek Slave* at the Egyptian Hall in London in August 1856. "It seems to me time to leave off sculpturing men and women naked," he wrote in his notebooks.[6] Hawthorne criticized the nudity of *The Greek Slave* on aesthetic rather than on moral grounds, however, objecting to the imposition of classical models upon contemporary figures. He was not noticeably concerned by the bondage and fate of the Greek slave, and it is likely that the moral revulsion towards her Turkish captors attributed to audiences of the 1850s has been somewhat exaggerated by later generations. The enslaving of Greeks, Circassians, and Georgians by the Turks, after all, was nothing new or unexpected in the world. Bible-reading audiences of the nineteenth century were thoroughly versed in Old Testament prototypes of masters and slaves and could trace an unbroken line of bondage in the East down into the modern age. On beholding "a Circassian Slave" in the studio of C. G. Thompson at Rome in February 1858, Hawthorne found the painting "voluptuously beautiful, and a noble womanhood stirring within her" (XIV, 72). As the celebrated abduction of Aimee Dubucq de Rivery by Algerian corsairs in 1784 illustrated, the fate of a Christian slave in the Turkish seraglio was not necessarily a mean one and, indeed, could become the instrument in a greater Providence. Seized on her way home to Martinique from a convent school in Nantes, the beautiful Mdme. de Rivery, a cousin of the Empress Josephine, was given as a present to the Sultan of Turkey and became " 'the French Sultana,' mother of Sultan Mahmoud II, The Reformer, whose sweeping changes laid the first foundations of the new Turkey." The sentiment might be repugnant to late twentieth-century sensibilities, but a significant number of Hawthorne's contemporaries would have agreed with a modern biographer of the French Sultana that, even in the Seraglio, she had "considerably more freedom to be essentially a woman than many women now enmeshed in the complex mechanism of our economic civilization."[7]

The East provided only one of several historical and mythological themes for American artists and sculptors in Hawthorne's time, but it was a theme of particular interest to the author. After the interlude of *The House of the Seven Gables*, in his last two finished romances—*The Blithedale Romance* (1852) and *The Marble Faun* (1860)—Hawthorne shaped female heroines as richly

Oriental as Hester in *The Scarlet Letter*, and more. He called attention in the preface of *The Marble Faun* to Harriet Hosmer's "noble statue" of the Syrian Queen Zenobia, and he gave special importance in the novel to William Wetmore Story's statue of Cleopatra. Hosmer's *Zenobia in Chains* (1859), which was displayed at the International Exhibition in London in 1862, depicts a dignified figure who, although manacled like *The Greek Slave*, is fully clothed. Story's *Cleopatra*, which also was exhibited in London in 1862, stands between his earlier modest, fully clothed works and the bold nudity of his later *Salome* and *Delilah*. *Cleopatra* exposes just one breast. The female sovereigns in *The Blithedale Romance* and *The Marble Faun*, however clad, left Hawthorne—and Coverdale and Kenyon—something to wonder about.

Competing images of female sovereignty and subjugation became increasingly commonplace in Western culture from the 1830s onwards, particularly with reference to the problematic status (queen or slave?) of the women of the East. The longest chapter of Anna Jameson's *Memoirs of Celebrated Female Sovereigns* (1831), which Hawthorne may have read early in 1835, was that on Queen Zenobia of Palmyra.[8] Like the ambiguous figure of Eve, both *Urmutter* and source of sin, Zenobia, Cleopatra, Semiramis, and other female sovereigns from the East were regarded with mixed feelings of fear and desire. But however they might have dominated their weaker sisters of the same sex, they were destined to be vanquished in the end by a superior male force. Female "bondage and attendant chains, manacles, ropes, and such" were prominent trappings of American sculpture in the 1840s and 1850s.[9] Their social and psychological equivalents are an important aspect of Hawthorne's handling of women in his major romances.

In *The Blithedale Romance* and *The Marble Faun* Hawthorne found new means of dealing with the tension that had left his male protagonists suspended, first, between the "angel or demon" within Beatrice Rappaccini and, then, between the darker and lighter forces dramatized alternately in Hester Prynne and Phoebe Pyncheon. In the last two full-scale romances Hawthorne allowed his dark female heroines to display their large physical and emotional prowess but each time brought them to their knees at last before male authority. He also achieved a new dramatic control over the central problem of his long fictions by multiplying his cast of characters and counterpointing elements that previously had been more complexly intermixed. The enigma of woman and angel, body and soul, demon and fireside goddess is played out dramatically in *The Blithedale Romance* through the half-sisters Zenobia and Priscilla and in *The Marble Faun* through Miriam and Hilda. The male role, simultaneously, divides into three parts: the man who had once known the Oriental beauty (Westervelt and Miriam's model); the man who newly possesses her (Hollingsworth and Donatello); and the author's vacillating spokesman (Coverdale and Kenyon), who enviously imagines his fellow travelers' experience of the dark woman even while pledging allegiance to his safe, spiritual, brown-haired homebody.

In Hawthorne's major romances, as in the neo-classical sculptures of his age, the male artist eventually immobilizes the passionate Oriental female in stone. Seventeenth-century Boston magistrates turned Hester Prynne into a "majestic and statue-like" being that Love would no longer seek to dwell upon or Passion "ever dream of clasping in its embrace" (I, 163). In *The Blithedale Romance* Zenobia's body assumes a grotesque and rigid form in death by drowning. At the close of *The Marble Faun* Miriam, though physically free, is condemned to a social imprisonment no less cruel than Donatello's. Hawthorne's Pygmalion wielded the power not only to create a dark lady out of native wood but to reverse the process and, when her voluptuous Oriental characteristic became too potent, to turn the Other back into a statue again.

The Blithedale Romance: "Zenobia! Queen Zenobia!"

A half year before setting seriously to work on *The Blithedale Romance* Hawthorne wrote to thank his erstwhile fellow utopian George William Curtis for a copy of the sensational and sensual *Nile Notes of a Howadji* (1851). He had read Curtis's book aloud to his wife and reported: "[B]oth she and I have felt that we never knew anything of the Nile before. There is something beyond descriptive power in it. You make us feel almost as if we had been there ourselves. And then you are such a luxurious traveller!" Although he did not explain why the fragrance of Curtis's chibouque was "a marvellous blessing" to him, Hawthorne confessed, "I felt a little alarm, as I penetrated the depths of those chapters about the dancing-girls, lest they might result in something not altogether accordant with our New England morality." Those passages were "gorgeous, in the utmost degree," and at the time of his writing he hardly knew whether he and his wife "escaped the peril, or were utterly overwhelmed by it."[10]

Hawthorne's reading of *Nile Notes of a Howadji* and *The Howadji in Syria*, which appeared the following year, was not the first time he had shared an Oriental flight of fancy with his younger friend. While they were communitarians together at Brook Farm a decade before, the drudgery of their New England agricultural life occasionally was suspended for a day's amusement like the masquerade depicted in *The Blithedale Romance*. According to the memoir of an onlooker, the central figure on such a day ("the observed of all observers") was a young woman named Ora—said to be one of the few who broke through Hawthorne's customary reserve—who appeared "free and graceful in white Turkish trousers, a rich oriental head-dress, and Charles Dana's best tunic, which reached just below her knee." At a fancy-dress ball sometime later friends of Brook Farm arrived attired as dervishes and Greek girls. Anna Shaw "was superb as a portly Turk in quilted robe, turban, moustache, and cimeter, and bore herself with grave dignity."[11] That these figures were not altogether accordant with "New England morality" was precisely the point.

It is obvious that Hawthorne did not entirely escape the peril either of Brook Farm or of the gorgeous narratives of The Howadji. *The Blithedale Romance* can be read as a response to the imaginative and profitable genre of travel writing that George William Curtis so luxuriously represented albeit without straying from the precincts of their native land. The preface of Hawthorne's romance closes with the instructive remark: "Even the brilliant Howadji might find as rich a theme in his youthful reminiscences of Brook Farm, and a more novel one—close at hand as it lies—than those which he has since made so distant a pilgrimage to seek, in Syria, and along the current of the Nile" (III, 3). The author's strategy in his new romance is reminiscent of his endeavor in *The Story Teller* two decades earlier to send a curious traveler (now in the guise of a "Minor Poet") on a fancy-filled quest to a native shrine. While the taverns and muddy streets of Boston and the coarse common sense of Silas Foster lend a certain native ballast to the story, *The Blithedale Romance* resumes Hawthorne's movement away from the cultural and imaginative landscape of New England.

In introducing *The Blithedale Romance* Hawthorne stated his concern "to establish a theatre, a little removed from the highway of ordinary travel, where the creatures of his brain may play their phantasmagorical antics, without exposing them to too close a comparison with the actual events of real lives." He had contrasted his imaginative flights to ordinary travel several times before, notably in "The Old Manse," where he invited his auditor to leave "the public highway" and pass with him through a "spiritual medium." His latest work in 1852, however, sounded his strongest lament yet at the absence in America of a "Faery Land, so like the real world, that, in a suitable remoteness, one cannot well tell the difference." What the American romancer needs, Hawthorne declared, is "an atmosphere of strange enchantment, beheld through which the inhabitants have a propriety of their own." George William Curtis exploited the ready-made fairy-land he found in Egypt, Palestine, and Syria, with all its strange enchantments and exotic proprieties. The nearest approximation in Hawthorne's experience was his old home at Brook Farm, "certainly the most romantic episode of his own life—essentially a day-dream, and yet a fact—and thus offering an available foothold between fiction and reality" (III, 1-2).

Of all Hawthorne's longer works *The Blithedale Romance* offers the most fertile field for speculation about the origins of his fairy-land and is also the richest in Oriental characteristics and themes. In his hands the community of Brook Farm (or Blithedale) becomes a middle ground between the plain moralities of New England and the gorgeous possibilities of the East. The search for a proper foothold between reality and fiction runs throughout the work, particularly with reference to Coverdale and Priscilla. Coverdale's hermitage—an arabesque configuration of tendrils and grape vines binding four native white-pine trees together in a "knot of polygamy" (III, 98)—provides an imaginative habitat above the hue and cry of the world not unlike the Moorish edifices in "The Hall of Fantasy" nine years earlier or Donatello's Aladdin-like tower in *The Marble Faun* eight years later. Coverdale's resolution to follow his "day-dream" to its natural consummation echoes the narrator's assurance in the earlier tale that his cloud-castles of fantasy would outlive any structure built of coarser materials. What if one's day-dream should never materialize, Coverdale asks: "Its airiest fragments, impalpable as they may be, will possess a value that lurks not in the most ponderous realities of any practicable scheme" (III, 11).

The borderlands between day-dream and fact, enchantment and reality, are especially marked by the pervasive veil imagery in the novel, which focuses most intensely on the spiritual medium Priscilla. When Priscilla is enshrouded in her silvery veil, "slight and ethereal as it seems, the limitations of time and space have no existence" for her. Then, Westervelt claims, "She beholds the Absolute!" (III, 201). Despite the obvious legerdemain, Westervelt sends his medium into an ideal, visionary state like that of the romantic poet at his moment of highest receptivity. The rude noises of the real world, "the roar of a battery of cannon would be inaudible to the Veiled Lady"; nevertheless, were Westervelt to will it, "she could hear the desert-wind sweeping over the sands, as far off as Arabia; the ice-bergs grinding one against the other, in the polar seas; the rustle of a leaf in an East Indian forest" (III, 202). The Arabian and East Indian imagery are no more than one would expect from a showman like Westervelt, tricked out in the garb of an Oriental wizard. Yet in this impressively layered romance, Priscilla's experiences on both sides of the veil are symbolic also for the fate of Coverdale and the Blithedale community at large. Like Westervelt willing the spirit of the Veiled Lady between the polar seas and the desert wind, Hawthorne makes a point of juxtaposing frigid and tropical zones and sending his travelers forth and back between them.

The extent to which *The Blithedale Romance* taps into the popular genre of travel literature has not been sufficiently appreciated. Hawthorne could not draw upon the same first-hand experience with the foreign that produced a *Childe Harold's Pilgrimage,* or *Omoo* and *Typee,* or Curtis's *Nile Notes,* but in his well-trained imagination the few scant miles between Boston and West Roxbury, where George Peabody had purchased two hundred acres and founded Brook Farm, took on world proportions. *The Blithedale Romance* is his only novel to be told in the first person, and it is likely that Coverdale's narrative role was suggested by a long caravan of real and legendary travelers from Sir John Mandeville to Lady Mary Wortley Montagu and The Howadji who, like Coverdale, returned to tell, more or less, what they saw and felt behind the veil of the East.

In an earlier time and more adventurous spirit Coverdale once quit his "comfortable quarters, and plunged into the heart of the pitiless snow-storm, in quest of a better life" (III, 10). Like the fogbank through which Hawthorne's outsetting Story Teller had passed from one world to another, the snow storm veils the world of home from that which Coverdale and his fellow pilgrims are seeking. "Sometimes, encountering a traveller," they push on to their "journey's end," feeling upon arrival at Blithedale that they have "transported ourselves a world-wide distance from the system of society that shackled us at breakfast-time" (III, 12–13). When Hollingsworth's knock is first heard on the door at Blithedale, Coverdale announces in the same spirit, "There is one of the world's wayfarers!" (III, 25). The wretched cold Coverdale suffers from his travel and the feverish dreams that ensue might have been suggested by the severe headcold Hawthorne contracted on his first nine-mile walk from Boston to West Roxbury in April 1841. But in the novel they also set off his two hemispheres of experience. The language Coverdale employs to describe his readings during a slow recuperation further accentuates the communal sense of travel, exploration, and conquest in the name of civilization. The prophets studied at Blithedale were like "some solitary sentinel, whose station was on the outposts of the advance-guard of human progression." Their utterances were well suited "to pilgrims like ourselves, whose present bivouâc was considerably farther into the waste of chaos than any mortal army of crusaders had ever marched before" (III, 52).

When life even at Blithedale becomes routine, Coverdale's taste for novelty fills him with thoughts of "going across the Rocky Mountains, or to Europe, or up the Nile—of offering myself a volunteer on the Exploring Expedition—of taking a ramble of years, no matter in what direction, and coming back on the other side of the world." After that he might throw aside his "pilgrim-staff and dusty shoon" and adopt Blithedale as a permanent home (III, 140). Instead, he puts on his city clothes, which now seem "strange and outlandish," and returns to Boston, where his "sensations were those of a traveller, long sojourning in remote regions, and at length sitting down again amid customs once familiar" (III, 137, 145). Rather than feeling himself securely at home there, however, Coverdale experiences the same disorientation felt earlier by travelers like Ralph Cranfield and later by Kenyon in *The Marble Faun*. Suspended between the old and the new, the known and the unknown, he began "to lose the sense of what kind of world it was" (III, 140). Coverdale's return visit to Boston concludes with Westervelt's exhibition of the "veiled lady"; not surprisingly, when Coverdale reenters Blithedale, he is swept up in another masquerade and wonders whether the whole affair is anything "but dream-work and enchantment" (III, 206).

It has been suggested that *The Blithedale Romance* inverts the story of *Rasselas*—with the young male seeker returning to the real world in Boston after his excursion in a fool's paradise, rather than retreating to the Happy Valley after an unsatisfying sojourn in Cairo.[12] However enduring were Samuel Johnson's effects on Hawthorne, the literary associations of *The Blithedale Romance* with nineteenth-century travel romances appear even stronger. Coverdale's long return visit to Boston in the middle of the novel does not plant him on familiar, solid ground once more. The most "Oriental" of the Blithedalers reappear in the port city, and Coverdale's hotel room looks across a sheltered courtyard of grape-vines and trellises directly into the boudoir shared by Westervelt, Zenobia, and Priscilla. Blithedale at first view had struck Coverdale as a most fanciful place. Now, upon paying a call to Zenobia's drawing room, he is introduced to a realm of still greater mystery, luxury, and passion than could be found among the rustic communitarians. "In the gorgeousness with which she had surrounded herself—in the redundance of personal ornament, which the largeness of her physical nature and the rich type of her beauty caused to seem so suitable—"Coverdale beholds the true character of

Zenobia: "passionate, luxurious, lacking simplicity, not deeply refined, incapable of pure and perfect taste" (III, 164-165). Expecting to find himself among familiar surroundings, Coverdale travels into ever more mysterious realms. The glow of an astral lamp, "penetrating mistily through the white curtain" that Zenobia let fall between the damask draperies of her drawing room, casts the shadow of a passing figure now and then "upon this medium." The outline is too vague, however, for even Coverdale's "adventurous conjectures to read the hieroglyphic that it presented" (III, 161-162).

Coverdale's role at Blithedale is that of wayfarer and raconteur. Like the author's own father embarking from a snow-swept Massachusetts harbor for Madeira and Hindostan, Coverdale travels from one geo-cultural sphere into another. The same antithetical worlds of polar icebergs and Arabian sands that the Veiled Lady could visit by an act of spirit characterize Miles Coverdale's first trip from Boston to Blithedale in the midst of an April snowstorm. On reaching Simon Foster's farmhouse, he expostulates: "Paradise, indeed! Nobody else in the world, I am bold to affirm—nobody, at least, in our bleak little world of New England—had dreamed of Paradise, that day, except as the pole suggests the tropic" (III, 9-10). The brutal climate, as might be expected, sends the mind of the company gathered before Foster's blazing hearth in search of the antipode to the harsh materiality of their lives. The snow drifts sweeping past the window call forth thoughts of tropical figs and pineapples, breadfruit and coconuts. Some favor naming their institution " 'The Oasis,' in view of its being the one green spot in the moral sand-waste of the world"; others wish to defer for a year's time before choosing whether to name it "The Oasis" or "Saharah" (III, 37).

Hawthorne had used a similar antithesis of the frozen north and the warm tropics in "Drowne's Wooden Image," where the native chill of his Boston woodcarver melted for one inspired moment before the tropical beauty of Fayal. The author had also contrasted the depths of a Massachusetts winter with the heat of love four years earlier in a letter to Sophia Peabody: "How strange, that such a flower as our affection should have blossomed amid snow and wintry winds—accompaniments which no poet or novelist, that I know of, has ever introduced into a love-tale."[13] These earlier dialectics come to full flower in The Blithedale Romance in clusters of associations with New England (the grim reality of work, a hardening of intellect) and the tropics (idleness, wit and love) that Arnold Toynbee might have included in an environmentalist critique of society and civilization. In Hawthorne's own time philosophers of history and literature were also inclined to explain the character and genius of people by their climatic location. The author of the essay "Progress of Literature in Different Ages of Society" in the Gentleman's Magazine for 1821, for example, noted: "It has been supposed that the luxuriant and indulgent inhabitants of Eastern countries had, nevertheless, a more elevated cast of genius, a greater turn for brilliant expression, and a superior talent for fine imagery, than nations of a Western hemisphere, or peoples more approximating the poles." According to a Dr. Gillies:

"The rigorous severity of European skies gave strength and agility to the limbs, and hardy boldness to the mind—but chilled the fancy, and benumbed the finer feelings of the soul."—These superior advantages of the East were supposed to be the effects of a mild atmosphere,—of a clear and cloudless sky,—of a fertile soil, and all the genial accompaniments of such latitudes.

The Arabs and Persians were reputed to "have always been the greatest Poets of the East, and among them, as amongst other nations, Poetry was the earliest vehicle of all their learning."[14] As a model for the reformation of American society, Blithedale might have been a fool's paradise, but as a cultural excursion, it pushed on towards the latitudes of poetry and romance.

The hieroglyphic figures that Zenobia, Priscilla, and Westervelt cast onto the curtain veiling their Boston apartment from Coverdale's eyes suggest the seraglio-like world that lies behind. When Coverdale makes his way into Zenobia's drawing room, fresh from the homely furnishings of the old farm house at Blithedale, he is struck "that here was the fulfilment of every fantasy of an imagination, revelling in various methods of costly self-indulgence and splendid ease." The queen of this harem was arrayed with an opulence and gorgeousness suitable to her setting; "those costly robes which she had on, those flaming jewels on her neck, served as lamps to display the personal advantages which required nothing less than such an illumination, to be fully seen" (III, 163–164). Zenobia and Priscilla present opposing sides of the same essential riddle, the riddle of womanhood, to the eyes of their beholder. Coverdale describes Zenobia as merely a "public name"—"a sort of mask" in which the woman appeared before the world, "a contrivance, in short, like the white drapery of the Veiled Lady, only a little more transparent" (III, 8). Penetrating this mask and deciphering "the mystery of your life," Coverdale confesses to Zenobia, become the main object of his exploration.

The Oriental configuration of Hawthorne's characters is particularly apparent in the boarding house where Westervelt holds both Zenobia and Priscilla in a mysterious captivity, but it pervades the novel. While the "intolerable bondage" that enthralls Priscilla is of a mesmeric sort, the "miserable bond" that enslaves Zenobia to Westervelt is originally sexual in nature (III, 190, 104). Whenever Westervelt is presented—whether on his arrival at Blithedale, or as the necromancer in Zenobia's legend of "The Silvery Veil," or as the mesmerist at the Village Hall in Boston—he is characterized as an Oriental wizard. In the first instance he is arrayed in a gold chain and fiery gem and carries the staff of a magi carved in vivid imitation of a serpent. In the latter cases he appears "in an Oriental robe, with a dark beard"—"looking like one of the enchanters of the Arabian Nights" (III, 114, 199). In Zenobia's story of the silvery veil the dark lady assisted the "terrible magician" in bringing the pale maiden under his power. She threw the veil ("a powerful enchantment") around her, "and she was his bond-slave, forever more!" (III, 115–116).

The legend with which Zenobia entertains her fellow Blithedalers is one of the most explicitly Oriental devices in this romance. Nowhere else in

Hawthorne's fiction are the mysteries of the veil more conspicuously redolent of the East. The veil imagery in *The Blithedale Romance* is readily traceable to contemporary and historical accounts of the silvery shrouds that concealed the women of the East from the world beyond the harem walls. Busbecq's remark that they were "so hooded and veil'd, as if they were Hobgoblins or Ghosts" appeared, in one form or another, in many places.[15] Baron de Tott explained: "A Turk marries his neighbour's daughter, or widow, without knowing her. He has no other method of determining his choice, than from the report of his other wives, or of some medatrix."[16] The matter of *knowing*, in a metaphysical and psychological as well as a physical sense, what lies behind the veil is the root of Coverdale's desultory quest.

In the course of the novel the hegemony that the Oriental Westervelt exercises over both Zenobia and Priscilla is transferred to the Western reformer Hollingsworth. Whether Hollingsworth redeems the "snow-maiden" Priscilla before or after the loss of her virtue is ambiguous. Zenobia describes her as existing "on the sunny side of experience" and Coverdale thinks of peeking beneath her still-folded petals; however, there are signs that Priscilla might already have been initiated into the world of sensuality that had engulfed Westervelt and Zenobia (III, 60). Coverdale catches the scent of "a weed of evil odor and ugly aspect" that Zenobia planted among Priscilla's "fragrant blossoms" at the May Day masquerade (III, 59). The most explicit "symbol of Priscilla's own mystery," which presumably is related to her chastity, is the silk purse that she weaves and Moodie peddles surreptitiously in the streets. It is almost impossible "that any uninitiated person should discover the aperture; although, to a practised touch, [it] would open as wide as charity or prodigality might wish" (III, 35). The relation between Zenobia and Priscilla in *The Blithedale Romance* is not unlike that of the voluptuous, full-blown rose Kushuk Arnem in Curtis's *Nile Notes of a Howadji* and the "still-eyed Xenobi"—a modest "dove of a Ghazeeyah, a quiet child, the last born of Terpsichore." Kushuk Arnem had "the air of a woman for whom no surprises survive."[17] Zenobia similarly manifests herself to Coverdale as no girl, but rather "a woman to whom wedlock had thrown wide the gates of mystery" (III, 47).

It is academic which of the two women, Zenobia or Priscilla, wins Coverdale's heart inasmuch as, like Theodore in Zenobia's tale, he does not have the courage to strip the veil or the mask from either face. His stuttering confession in the final line of the novel ("I—I myself—was in love—with—Priscilla!") jerks the story back into accordance with New England mores and dutifully restates Hawthorne's perpetual theme of homecoming (III, 247). But his assertion of love for Priscilla—after Hollingsworth has torn away the veil and revealed "a household, fireside joy" rather than a monstrous visage—carries little dramatic conviction, however much Coverdale insists this fact is "essential to the full understanding of my story" (III, 114, 247). The propriety of such love fools neither Coverdale nor the reader about the greater allure of her dark half-sister.

Coverdale's fancy is most captivated by the dark and tragic Zenobia, whose nom de plume, martial bearing, regal beauty, and intellectual strength identify her immediately with the Syrian queen who took the reigns of government into her own hands following the death of her husband Odenathus in A.D. 267 and determined to make Palmyra the mistress of the Roman Empire. Her occupation of Egypt and invasion of Asia Minor so threatened the hegemony of Rome in the East that Aurelian destroyed the city of Palmyra and its inhabitants in A.D. 272 and led the vanquished queen back to Rome in chains. Queen Zenobia claimed descent from Cleopatra and the Macedonian kings of Egypt, and Aurelian was not about to risk the embarrassment that Julius Caesar and Marc Antony had suffered in the arms of her progenitrix three centuries earlier.

In the course of Coverdale's narration, Zenobia's stance as a proud, independent feminist, a writer, and an intellectual gradually succumbs to the fatality of her type. Zenobia often has been regarded as a mask for Margaret Fuller, who frequently visited Brook farm and drew a host of young women "slaves" in her train. Coverdale surmises that Priscilla, too, had come to Blithedale "with the one purpose of being [Zenobia's] slave" (III, 33). Hawthorne most consistently characterizes Zenobia, however, in terms befitting an Oriental queen. Deriving from the larger pattern of Oriental beauties the author had encountered in his readings, Zenobia gives full expression to the female type that inspired Beatrice Rappaccini and Hester Prynne. "Any passion would have become her well," Coverdale remarks, "and passionate love, perhaps, the best of all" (III, 102). Coverdale is first struck by her fine intellect but comes to perceive in the morbid sensitivity of his sickness that there is "no severe culture in Zenobia." Like Hester Prynne, her moral and intellectual development was incomplete, her mind "full of weeds" (III, 44).

Likewise, the simple "American print" in which she first appears ill-suits the gorgeous female. A spacious and "admirable figure of a woman," Zenobia seems "rather indolent" in her quiet moods, "but when really in earnest, particularly if there were a spice of bitter feeling, she grew all alive, to her finger-tips." Her playful remark that she would not assume the "garb of Eden" until after May Day causes Coverdale to imagine "that fine, perfectly developed figure, in Eve's earliest garment." She often has the effect upon him "of creating images which, though pure, are hardly felt to be quite decorous, when born of a thought that passes between man and woman." Such paragons of *woman* existed in the East. However, Coverdale continues, "We seldom meet with women, now-a-days, and in this country, who impress us as being women at all; their sex fades away and goes for nothing, in ordinary intercourse. Not so with Zenobia" (III, 15-17). When illness and exhaustion break down Coverdale's usual inhibitions, "the flesh-warmth over her round arms, and what was visible of her full bust," move him deeply. "Zenobia's sphere impressed itself powerfully" on Coverdale and transforms him during the period of his weakness "into something like a mesmerical clairvoyant." She would have been a fit subject for either painters or sculptors, but Coverdale prefers the latter representation, thinking "the cold decorum of the marble would consist with the utmost scantiness of drapery, so that the eye might chastely be gladdened with her material perfection, in its entireness" (III, 44, 46).

Above all, Zenobia is characterized by the exotic flower that newly adorns her hair each day. While at Blithedale, Zenobia puts up her abundant dark hair "soberly and primly, without curls, or other ornament," except for a single flower, which manifests the same unrepentant sexuality symbolized by Hester's scarlet letter (III, 15). Zenobia's flower stands forth even in the midst of a New England winter. It is "an outlandish flower—a flower of the tropics, such as appeared to have sprung passionately out of a soil, the very weeds of which would be fervid and spicy." It might be that in Coverdale's feverish fantasies this "floral gem" looks "more gorgeous and wonderful than if beheld with temperate eyes" (III, 45). After the delirium of Coverdale's illness has passed, however, he continues to regard her "invariable flower of the tropics" as "a subtle expression of Zenobia's character" and "a talisman" (III, 59, 45). The flower strikes deep root into his memory; even in retrospect he can "both see it and smell it" (III, 15). In Boston Zenobia replaces the natural flower, which wilts from the heat of New England fireplaces, with a jeweled imitation, and the full gorgeousness with which she arrays herself when away from Blithedale nearly overpowers the circumspect Coverdale. "The splendor of those jewels on her neck, like lamps that burn before some fair temple, and the jeweled flower in her hair" help Coverdale realize her consummate womanliness (III, 191).

Zenobia's tropical flower, which "assimilated its richness to the rich beauty of the woman," is no less Eastern and sexual in nature than Beatrice Rappaccini's purple gem (III, 45). As often as his mind reverts to the subject, Coverdale knows that "Zenobia has lived and loved! There is no folded petal, no latent dew-drop, in this perfectly developed rose!" (III, 47). The petals that another man might turn are not for his hands, however. Coverdale survives seeing and smelling the fragrant flower but, like Giovanni Guasconti, he does not risk a more intimate contact.

Zenobia both exhibits and rails against the sexual determinism of woman. "How can she be happy," Zenobia protests, "after discovering that fate has assigned her but one single event, which she must contrive to make the substance of her whole life? A man has his choice of innumerable events." To which Coverdale replies sardonically: "A woman, I suppose, . . . by constant repetition of her one event, may compensate for the lack of variety" (III, 60). Their exchange echoes Julia's famous lament in the first canto of *Don Juan*:

> 'Man's love is of his life a thing apart,
> 'Tis woman's whole existence; . . .
> Man has all these resources, we but one,
> To love again, and be again undone.'[18]

But it also touches a deeper social and theological issue discussed in the Eastern commentaries Hawthorne read. It was an extraordinary point of Koranic doctrine, Lady Montagu wrote, that: "Any Woman that dyes unmarry'd is look'd upon to dye in a state of reprobation. To confirm this beliefe, they reason, that the End of the Creation of Woman is to encrease and Multiply." Birth and care of children "are all the Virtues that God expects from her." Byron's Julia took refuge in a convent, but the redemption of an Eastern woman was, if she had lost one master, immediately to replace him with another. Lady Montagu challenged the vulgar notion that the Islamic people "do not own Women to have any Souls"; nevertheless, she conceded that the form of eternal bliss destined for women of the good sort was still inferior to the paradise appointed for men.[19]

In *The Blithedale Romance* Coverdale laments that Hollingsworth's "masculine egotism" would deprive woman "of her very soul, her inexpressible and unfathomable all, to make it a mere incident in the great sum of man" (III, 123). Like the Western emperor Aurelian, Hollingsworth figuratively, if not literally, vanquishes the proud Eastern queen and brings her home in chains. When Coverdale comes upon Hollingsworth, Zenobia, and Priscilla in their climactic menage a trois, "she represented the Oriental princess, by whose name [they] were accustomed to know her. Her attitude was free and noble, yet, if a queen's, it was not that of a queen triumphant, but dethroned, on trial for her life, or perchance condemned, already" (III, 213). Spurning the Eastern enchanter Westervelt and rejected in turn by the New England reformer, Zenobia realizes too late that, despite her crusade for women's rights, she too is "an hereditary bond-slave"—weak, vain, impulsive, and passionate. Emancipated but unfree, she drowns herself.[20]

The recovery of Zenobia's rigid and bleeding corpse, cruelly wounded in the breast, drew upon Hawthorne's memory of a suicide that he had beheld in Concord in 1845 as well as Margaret Fuller's death by drowning in 1849. Again, however, the character and tragedies typically associated with Eastern women came to his aid in imagining the fatality to which Zenobia's beauty, wealth, and passion impelled her. In spite of their presumed seclusion, Baron de Tott had told in 1744 of spirited Turkish "women of a higher condition, who are hurried away by an ungovernable passion, and escape clandestinely from their prisons. These unfortunate women always carry off their jewels, and think they can possess nothing too precious for the man who receives them. The fatal inclination which leads them astray, prevents them from perceiving, that it is to these very riches they owe their ruin." Zenobia, too, seeks to buy Hollingsworth's love with her wealth, although it is rationalized on both sides as aid to social reform, and she is ruined when her fortune and Hollingsworth's love both are transferred to Priscilla. De Tott continued about the Turkish women: "One often sees the naked bodies of these unfortunate wretches floating in the harbour, under the windows of their murderers."[21]

It has been suggested that Hawthorne killed off Zenobia (like Beatrice Rappaccini earlier) because he was afraid of his powerful female creations and had no way finally of reconciling their passion with the restraint of his male protagonists. When Coverdale first sees Zenobia, he imagines the Creator offering her to Adam with the words: "Behold Eve, here is a woman!" (III, 17). But Coverdale is no Adam. His fantasies of submitting to a government by women—"how sweet the free, generous courtesy, with which I would kneel before a woman-ruler!"—are a weak foil to Hollingsworth's clearer perception of the nature of sexual power (III, 121). Hollingsworth is ready to call upon his own sex if necessary "to use its physical force, that unmistakeable evidence of sovereignty, to scourge [the petti-coated activists] back within their proper bounds!"—although he trusts "the heart of true womanhood knows where its own sphere is" and would not stray beyond it (III, 123). Zenobia concedes to Hollingsworth's authority with humility and grief, though not anger, and Coverdale's confirmed bachelorhood largely neutralizes his own erotic fantasies about the woman.

Coverdale's return to bachelor comforts in Boston, and his narration a dozen years later of the opportunity that once had been his to become quite another man, call to mind the history of Hawthorne's Story Teller. In the tales of the 1830s the two great adventures in life—love and travel—eluded the young man, leaving him to die in obscurity. To be sure, Coverdale suffers neither the Story Teller's despair nor his ignominious end. His social commitments on returning to Boston fall somewhere between Oberon's ineradicable alienation and Ralph Cranfield's hearty embrace of Faith and America. Nevertheless the termination of The Blithedale Romance brought a new desolation to Hawthorne's romances. In The Scarlet Letter the earnest struggle of the American minister with the voluptuous dark woman ended in his death but also gave life to the beautiful Pearl. The union of Holgrave and Phoebe in The House of the Seven Gables touched off a general burst of fecundity. Neither The Blithedale Romance nor The Marble Faun, however, gives indication that a brighter day is to follow. If Hawthorne's earlier men had been wounded too severely in affairs of the heart to risk seriously engaging Coverdale with Zenobia, the redemptive powers of Priscilla and the fair-haired maidens to whom the author officially paid homage had also begun to fade.[22]

In The Blithedale Romance Hawthorne not only domesticated the Eastern travel narrative represented by The Howadji but also brought to the American soil one of the most potent Oriental figures of the age. Next to Cleopatra, Queen Zenobia may have been the most celebrated Eastern woman in the literature of the eighteenth and nineteenth centuries. She was the object of a plethora of historical essays, poems, plays, and romantic novels.[23] Among the many historical sources Hawthorne is known to have used, he could have found essentially the same account of the legendary queen in John Harris's Navigantium atque Itinerantium Bibliotheca, Pierre Bayle's Dictionary Historical and Critical, and Edward Gibbon's History of the Decline and Fall of the Roman Empire. Robert Southey appropriated the name Zeenab for Thalaba's mother, adding in a footnote, "It may be worth mentioning, that, according to Pietro della Valle, this is the name of which the Latins have made Zenobia."[24] Hawthorne might have been familiar, too, with stories of Lady Hester Stanhope (1776–1839), the eccentric "Queen of Palmyra," who left England for the Levant in 1810, encamped for a time among the ruins of Palmyra, and set up her own despotic principality on the slopes of Mount Lebanon. While he was measurer of salt and coal at the Boston Custom House, he could have seen the ship *Zenobia* embark in June 1839 on a voyage to the East Indies and China.[25]

Most important, perhaps, was Hawthorne's acquaintance with William Ware's acclaimed historical romance *Zenobia; or, The Fall of Palmyra*, which first appeared serially in the *Knickerbocker* magazine in 1836–1837 under the title "Letters of Lucius M. Piso, from Palmyra, to his Friend Marcus Curtius, at Rome."[26] Ware's work was received with enormous enthusiasm and reprinted throughout the 1840s and 1850s. Its author was praised for having "*saturated* his mind with the very spirit of the past. He has rolled back the tide of time," a contemporary reviewer remarked, "and placed us in Palmyra, the magnificent capital of the East, and caused all her glories to pass palpably before us, as if we were gazing upon a moving panorama."[27] When Hawthorne had his usual struggle to find a title for his new romance in May 1852, he tried out various possibilities on Edwin P. Whipple including: " 'The Blithedale Romance'—that would do, in lack of a better. 'The Arcadian Summer'—not a taking title. 'Zenobia'—Mr. Ware has anticipated me in this."[28] Ware might have prevented Hawthorne from naming the novel after his queenly figure; he noways deterred him from reworking the historical prototype for his own purposes.

In writing *The Blithedale Romance* Hawthorne would assume his contemporaries' familiarity with both classical and latter-day treatments of the Palmyrene empire and its militant queen. The alternate names the Blithedalers first consider for their new community in the American desert—"Oasis" or "Saharah"—epitomize the before and after conditions of the Syrian city-state that lay in a vast sandy desert midway between Aleppo and Damascus. An article "Palmyra, or Tadmor" in the February 1836 *American Magazine of Useful and Entertaining Knowledge* extolled the wealth and magnificence of this once great and pacific kingdom (the "city of palms") and expressed the astonishment of nineteenth-century visitors, in view of its location, "that such a magnificent city should ever have been built, where Palmyra once stood." Quoting Pliny, the *American Magazine* continued, "Palmyra is finely located; it is well watered, and the soil is rich; but it is surrounded on all sides by a sandy desert, which separates it from the rest of the world."[29] The traditional images of the Queen of Palmyra to which William Ware and Nathaniel Hawthorne both responded are best encapsulated in Edward Gibbon's account:

> But if we except the doubtful achievements of Semiramis, Zenobia is perhaps the only female whose superior genius broke through the servile indolence imposed on her sex by the climate and manners of Asia. She claimed her descent from the Macedonian kings of Egypt, equalled in beauty her ancestor Cleopatra, and far surpassed that princess in chastity and valor. Zenobia was esteemed the most lovely as well as the most heroic of her sex. She was of a dark complexion. . . . Her voice was strong and harmonious. Her manly understanding was strengthened and adorned by study. She was not ignorant of the Latin

tongue, but possessed in equal perfection the Greek, the Syriac, and the Egyptian languages.[30]

Queen Zenobia's utopian kingdom came to an end, according to the *Encyclopedia Americana* in 1833, when Aurelian, "disgusted at the usurpation of the richest provinces of the East by a female, determined to make war upon her" and razed the city.[31] The tropical oasis of Blithedale and the independence of its queen are likewise doomed by the politics of Zenobia and Hollingsworth.

In his romantic novel Ware praised Queen Zenobia's "marvelous union of feminine beauty, queenly dignity, and masculine power" while giving her a softer beauty of emotions and sentiments than was found in the historical original.[32] Among other changes Ware made for his fictionalized history were reducing Queen Zenobia's number of sons and daughters and emphasizing the fair Julia, a less-spirited offshoot whose slavish dependence on her mother prefigures the Zenobia-Priscilla relationship in *The Blithedale Romance*. "Without Zenobia, what should I be?" Julia asks. "I cannot conceive of existence, deprived of her, or of her regard." Queen Zenobia, in her turn, trusts Julia "as a sister."[33] The storyteller of Ware's epistolary novel is a young Roman senator named Lucius M. Piso, who journeys from Rome to Palmyra to seek the help of Queen Zenobia in freeing his brother Calpurnius from captivity at the court of the king of Persia. This once effected, Lucius remains in Palmyra, shows an interest in the beautiful, warrior-like Fausta but proposes marriage instead to Princess Julia (whom Queen Zenobia intends to marry to Hormisdas of Persia for a political alliance), and observes the sack of Palmyra by Aurelian's troops. While his hotter-blooded brother marries Fausta and stays behind in the devastated oasis of Palmyra, Piso finally returns to the cosmopolitan city of Rome, where he awaits permission of the now dethroned queen to marry her daughter Julia.

The parallels of incident and character between Lucius Piso and Miles Coverdale suggest that Hawthorne may have been responding to the kindred nature of Ware's traveler when he developed his own first-person narrator. Neither male is willing to commit himself entirely to the cause of which he becomes a part, and both withdraw in the end from their "tropical paradise" to a capital city. Like Piso at Palmyra, Miles Coverdale at Blithedale is a commentator, a "calm observer," "the Chorus in a classical Play" (III, 97). Although Piso says he is "not unwilling to adventure where I shall mix with a greater variety of my own species, and gain a better knowledge of myself by the study of others," he typically views the scene around him with detachment, "as a man and a philosopher."[34] If anything, Coverdale shows an even greater resistance to self-surrender than Piso, for while Coverdale rejects out of hand Hollingsworth's demand that he participate in the reform of criminals, "a purpose in life, worthy of the extremest self-devotion—worthy of martyrdom, should God so order it!" (III, 133)—Piso stands at the brink of conversion to Christianity, an act which he acknowledges "insists upon an undivided sovereignty over the whole character and life of the individual."[35]

Coverdale's surprised disclosure of love for Priscilla at the end of *The Blithedale Romance* might also have been influenced to some extent by Piso's half-hearted attempts to win the hand of Julia. Coverdale would affirm, "I should not, under any circumstances, have fallen in love with Zenobia," but it is only *she* whom he envisions in the garb of Eve, and he manifests his tardy affections for Priscilla only after proving unequal to the mystery of Zenobia (III, 48). So also with Lucius Piso, who is much enamored with Fausta, a warmer alter ego of Queen Zenobia, until he is discouraged at last by her unbreachable devotion to the queen. Piso then turns his attention to Julia: a being who "lives in her affections" and cannot "become part of the world abroad"; who first appears in the novel hidden "in the folds of her veil" and "seems too ethereal for earth."[36]

Most interesting, though, are both the parallels and the dissimilarities of Hawthorne's Zenobia with her prototypes. Like the queen described by Edward Gibbon, Hawthorne's Zenobia makes "no scruple of oversetting all human institutions" and lifts her voice "in behalf of woman's wider liberty" (III, 44, 120). Zenobia possesses the "strong and harmonious" voice of her historical model: "What girl had ever spoken in her mellow tones!" Coverdale wonders (III, 47). "With the living voice, alone," Zenobia seeks to "compel the world to recognize the light of her intellect" (III, 120). Queen Zenobia was noted for marching miles on end at the head of her troops; Hawthorne's Zenobia, too, needs "a large amount of physical exercise," particularly by walking (III, 156). Her salient traits—her "bloom," her "health," her "vigor"— and especially her final struggle with Hollingsworth all represent the martial character of the queen who, after the death of Odenathus, led her husband's troops in the conquest of Syria, Egypt, and all of Asia Minor. In Ware's romance Queen Zenobia is presented as anything *but* "a patient household drudge."[37] Hawthorne's narrator likewise declares, "Nature certainly never intended Zenobia for a cook" (III, 48). She is "Zenobia! Queen Zenobia!" (III, 211).

However numerous the connections between Hawthorne's figure and the typical presentations of Queen Zenobia, his innovations are still more significant. Although Queen Zenobia poignantly symbolized the fate of large-minded and heroic women at the hands of men throughout the ages, her personal fortune was not a hard one either in history or in Ware's historical romance. "Aurelian was far from treating her with severity," John Harris wrote in the 1740s. After a fatiguing parade through the streets of Rome, where her strong frame was burdened with a great weight of jewels, "she had a Country-house given her near the Tiber, where she lived many years, with her family, in great honour, and perfect tranquillity."[38] Ware's deposed queen speaks of herself as surviving, like Palmyra, "in ruins," and reproaches herself for her errors, but she never comes to the point of despair.[39] In the accounts of both Gibbon and Ware, Queen Zenobia "broke through the servile indolence imposed on her sex by the climate and manners of Asia" and prefigured the feminists of 1840s America. Van Wyck Brooks dubbed her "a true New England woman born too soon."[40] Hawthorne, on the other hand, begins with a New England advocate for the rights of the female sex but then, one-by-one, strips away the veils concealing the indolent, passionate, complex and tragic woman beneath.

The historical figure, according to John Harris, "was indeed, in all respects the most accomplished lady of her time, and equally remarkable for her unblemished chastity, her extensive learning, her masculine courage, and her deep policy."[41] In William Ware's historical romance Queen Zenobia steadfastly upholds her love for glory and institutions and spurns the weakness of tying herself to a man. She declares: "Love is a delirium, a dream, a disease." When the loved object "is attained, it is then oftener like the ocean heaving and tossing from its foundations, than the calm, peaceful lake, which mirrors friendship. And when lost, all is lost, the universe is nothing. Who will deny it the name of madness?"[42] Hawthorne's Zenobia, neither chaste nor independent, dramatizes all too well the truthfulness of this admonition. In the end Hollingsworth extracts a far greater humiliation from Zenobia than Aurelian had imposed upon the Syrian queen in her public display at Rome.

In Ware's popular story Queen Zenobia aptly expresses the two-fold Otherness that Hawthorne embodies in his own voluptuous Oriental figures. "But forget not," she admonishes Lucius Piso, "that I am an Oriental and— a woman. This double nature works at my heart with more than all the power of the schools."[43] The allure of Ware's heroine and his romance for the nineteenth-century reader was just this intermixed struggle of empire and sex as the romantic, passionate East succumbed to a classical, Western hegemony and the great female principle was subjugated to male authority. When Coverdale, Hollingsworth, and Silas Foster recover Zenobia's body from the stream, its rigor mortis gives the sensually and politically threatening dark woman of the East a statuesque pose that can be beheld without further threat to New England moralities.

The Marble Faun: "Were you not afraid to touch her?"

It is fitting that when Hawthorne embarked from the Boston Harbor on July 6, 1853, in company with his wife, three children, and publisher William D. Ticknor, the Cunard paddle-wheeler carrying him eastward to his new consular post was named Niagara, for the Niagara Falls had been the primary objective of his pilgrimage westward into America by canal boat and steamer two decades earlier. In the seven years before the Hawthornes again set foot in their native land the romanticist brought both of his parallel careers to a culmination. First, as United States Consul to Liverpool he held perhaps the most lucrative and prominent of political appointments related to America's maritime trade, the reward for writing his campaign biography of Franklin Pierce. Then, after an extended residence in Italy, he addressed his Gentle and Benevolent Reader with the longest of his romances: The Marble Faun.

By all testimony Hawthorne's practical service to American travelers through the port of Liverpool would have made his grandfather "Bold Daniel" Hathorne proud of him. There he was in daily contact with sailors' yarns like those that a half century later would inspire the psychological novels of

Joseph Conrad, and there, in 1854, Commodore Matthew Perry invited him to edit his journals of the Japan expedition. In *Our Old Home* Hawthorne recalled particularly listening to the tales of a Captain Walter M. Gibson. "Many of his scenes were laid in the East, and among those seldom visited archipelagoes of the Indian ocean, so that there was an Oriental fragrance breathing through his talk and an odor of the Spice Islands still lingering in his garments." What Hawthorne said of Gibson's "Oriental fantasies" typifies the melding of the Actual and the Imaginary that he had found for so many years in the travel literature of the East. He accepted the captain's fantasies "not as matters of indubitable credence, but as allowable specimens of an imaginative traveller's vivid coloring and rich embroidery on the coarse texture and dull neutral tints of truth" (V, 22–23).[44] During his consulship in England he exercised again the habits of mind and imagination that once had compelled the adolescent to muse over his dead father's East India logs. His extensive, well-researched answer to the U.S. Secretary of State's list of queries about British maritime activities and regulations manifested both his grasp and his interest in matters of world-wide commerce.[45]

In England Hawthorne was exposed even more immediately than in the United States to the Orientalism that grew out of European colonization in South Asia and commercial and military adventures in the Levant. One of the most haunting passages in Hawthorne's English notebooks is his protracted description of the beautiful Jewess he met in August 1856 at a Lord Mayor's banquet in London, which was held in the brilliantly lighted Egyptian Hall of the Mansion House. The ambivalence and hesitancy of Hawthorne's description—the rhythm of advance and withdrawal, desire and repugnance—suggest that he still did not know what to think about the Oriental Other, or what it was *proper* to think.

My eyes were mostly drawn to a young lady who sat nearly opposite me, across the table. She was, I suppose, dark, and yet not dark, but rather seemed to be of pure white marble, yet not white; but the purest and finest complexion, (without a shade of color in it, yet anything but sallow or sickly) that I ever beheld. Her hair was a wonderful deep, raven black, black as night, black as death; *not* raven black, for that has a shiny gloss, and her's [sic] had not; but it was hair never to be painted, nor described—wonderful hair, Jewish hair. Her nose had a beautiful outline, though I could see that it was Jewish too; and that, and all her features, were so fine that sculpture seemed a despicable art beside her; and certainly my pen is good for nothing. If any likeness of her could be given, it must be by sculpture, not painting. She was slender, and youthful, but yet had a stately and cold, though soft and womanly grace; and, looking at her, I saw what were the wives of the old patriarchs, in their maiden or early married days—what Rachel was, when Jacob wooed her seven years, and seven more—what Judith was; for, womanly as she looked, I doubt not she could have slain a man, in a good cause—what Bathsheba was; only she seemed to have no sin in her—perhaps what Eve was, though one could hardly think her weak enough to eat the apple. I never should have thought of touching her, nor desired to touch her; for, whether owing to distinctness of race, my sense that she was a Jewess, or whatever else, I felt a sort of repugnance, simultaneously with my perception that she was an admirable creature.[46]

Hawthorne's remark about his desire "to touch," or not, apparently revealed more of the "Inmost Me" than was seemly to his wife, who omitted that reference from her edition of Passages from the English Note-Books.

Just as remarkable as Hawthorne's passionate evocation of the young Jewess was his hateful decription of her elderly husband, the Lord Mayor's brother. Excited by envy, he reviled the man in the meanest terms. "He must have been circumcised as much [as] ten times over," Hawthorne wrote. "I never beheld anything so ugly and disagreeable, and preposterous, and laughable."[47] Both images continued to vex him. When he set to work on The Marble Faun, this "miraculous Jewess" became the prototype of Miriam and, less specifically, her husband provided the original of Miriam's model.

The year and a half Hawthorne spent in Rome and Florence after leaving England early in 1858 marked the farthest extent of his world travels and the nearest realization of his oft-expressed wish to trot around the world and visit "all the gorgeous East." Notwithstanding his friendly chastisement of The Howadji for making his literary pilgrimage to Syria and along the Nile, the romance Hawthorne began in Italy brought him squarely into the genre of travel reportage. Hawthorne chose a contemporary and foreign setting for his new work, no doubt, both in response to the fresh stimuli of the historical landscape before him and the success other writers and artists of the time were enjoying through their exploitation of exotic cultures. The Marble Faun; or, the Romance of Monte Beni completed an evolution from the earliest American historical past in The Scarlet Letter to the present-day but geographically and culturally remote.

In his preface to The Blithedale Romance Hawthorne still declared his intent to find richer and more novel themes at home than abroad. By the time he wrote his introduction to The Marble Faun, the native land had become intractible. "No author," he declared, "without a trial, can conceive of the difficulty of writing a Romance about a country where there is no shadow, no antiquity, no mystery, no picturesque and gloomy wrong. . . . Romance and poetry, like ivy, lichens, and wall-flowers, need Ruin to make them grow." He justified his choice of Italy for the new romance as affording him "a sort of poetic or fairy precinct, where actualities would not be so terribly insisted upon, as . . . in America." Most critics subsequently have read The Marble Faun as Hawthorne's "Italian romance," a novel of American expatriate experience amidst the fauna and ruins of the Italian peninsula.

Approaching The Marble Faun strictly as an Italian romance, however, and regarding Italy as a self-sufficient fairy precinct, limits rather than enriches our understanding of the cultural drama that takes place there. It is more instructive to think of Italy as a cultural crossroads—"where the Actual and the Imaginary may meet"—somewhere between the real world of America and the fairy-land of the farther East. Italy serves Hawthorne here, as in "Rappaccini's Daughter," as a jumping-off place for the fancy. There is abundant evidence that Hawthorne regarded Rome in particular not as the eternal city but as a middle moment in the chronicle of civilization that began in the ancient East. As seen by the story of Aurelian and Queen Zenobia, Rome might be an arena to which the Oriental woman was brought, bound and manacled, from the East, but it was not her birthplace.

When Kenyon looks down from Donatello's tower and seeks to read the majestic landscape spread before him, he feels his best thoughts "are only expressible by such grand hieroglyphics as these around us" (IV, 258). Likewise, the relics of empire met everywhere in the city of Rome are significations for what lay beyond. Kenyon is particularly moved by "the red granite obelisk—eldest of things, even in Rome—" which rises in the center of the Piazza del Popolo. More than any other icon the obelisk fixes the spatial and cultural location of the novel:

> All Roman works and ruins (whether of the Empire, the far-off Republic, or the still more distant Kings) assume a transient, visionary, and impalpable character, when we think that this indestructible monument supplied one of the recollections, which Moses, and the Israelites, bore from Egypt into the desert. Perchance, on beholding the cloudy pillar and the fiery column, they whispered awe-stricken to one another—"In its shape, it is like that old obelisk which we and our fathers have so often seen, on the borders of the Nile!"—And, now, that very obelisk, with hardly a trace of decay upon it, is the first thing that the modern traveller sees, after entering the Flaminian Gate! (IV, 106)[48]

Rome is situated in the Mediterranean between North and South, East and West. The hot, dry "Sirocco" off the deserts of North Africa steals strength from the invalids who throng there, and the "Tramontana" from beyond the Alps stabs them through and through (IV, 369). The red-trousered French soldiers encountered in the streets of the city are equally likely to bear the "medals of Algiers" and of the Crimea (IV, 100). In Hawthorne's time Rome was a historical juncture to which "hordes of Anglo-Saxons" from the North came annually in search of a glimpse of mirth and carnival and Paradise (IV, 437).

As the only major character in The Marble Faun indigenous to Italy, Donatello's origins and moral development reflect the mysteries of the civilization he inhabits. The Monte Beni family, according to legend, originated among the Pelasgi in prehistoric times, "the same noble breed of men, of Asiatic birth, that settled in Greece; the same happy and poetic kindred who dwelt in Arcadia" (IV, 233). It would be as difficult to trace "the stream of Donatello's ancestry to its dim source," the narrator avers, "as travellers have found it, to reach the mysterious fountains of the Nile. And, far beyond the region of definite and demonstrable fact, a romancer might have strayed into a region of old poetry" (IV, 231). The marble saloon of the family's castle is adorned with pillars of "Oriental alabaster" and "frescoed with ornaments in arabesque" (IV, 279). The interminable vista of apartments within the castle reminds Kenyon of "the hundred rooms in Blue Beard's castle, or the countless halls in some palace of the Arabian Nights" (IV, 219). The myth of

Donatello's origins—like Hawthorne's earlier legends of the poison-damsel, Alice Pyncheon, and the silvery veil—points backwards in time and outward in space, more or less explicitly, to Eastern prototypes.

The symmetries of *The Marble Faun* with the preceding romances are particularly apparent in the arrangement of characters. For the tragic queen Zenobia we now have Miriam; for the ethereal Priscilla, the angelic Hilda; for the minor poet and too-cautious swain Coverdale, the sculptor Kenyon; for the wizard-lover Westervelt, Miriam's model; and, less certainly, for the un-imaginative reformer Hollingsworth, the not altogether human Donatello. The "self-concentrated philanthropist" and the Arcadian faun at first could not seem more unlike; however, they provoke the same response from the author's spokesmen—surprise and disappointment for having unworthily claimed the love of the female sovereign. In both *The Blithedale Romance* and *The Marble Faun* the dark woman has been known sexually by one man before submitting herself to another, leaving first Coverdale and then Kenyon to content themselves as best they can with her paler sisters.

Donatello, Miriam, Kenyon, and Hilda are arranged along a continuum of character from the Eastern-exotic to the American-domestic. Miriam's origins are no less mysterious than Donatello's; it is obvious that the bloodlines that came together in creating this passionately original woman flowed through subterranean aqueducts. Of the several rumors that circulate concerning her breeding, the most prominent, that she is "the daughter and heiress of a great Jewish banker," is suggested by the "rich Oriental character in her face" (IV, 22). Her "deep, dark eyes" and "the large and bounteous impression" that she makes manifest the same Orientalism that the author had bestowed upon Hester Prynne and Zenobia and are emblematic of "Miriam's rich, ill-regulated nature" (IV, 78, 23, 280). Hawthorne mines a wide vocabulary of Oriental imagery in bringing Miriam to life. The queenly figure relieves "what would otherwise be a dangerous accumulation of morbid sensibility" through the practice of her needlework (IV, 40). Her secret is associated with the mysteries of the cavern. "If her soul was apt to lurk in the darkness of a cavern, she could sport madly in the sunshine before the cavern's mouth" (IV, 83). Her secret is "no precious pearl." "My dark-red carbuncle," she confesses, "red as blood—is too rich a gem to put into a stranger's casket!" (IV, 130). The gem she typically wears on her bosom, crystallizing everything that is passionate and glowing in her disposition, is "not a diamond, but something that glimmered with a clear, red lustre, like the stars in a southern sky" (IV, 396). And the murder of the model, with Miriam's consenting glance, instantly engraves itself "in the eternal adamant" (IV, 171).

While Miriam is a more mysterious and complex character than the tragic queen of *The Blithedale Romance*, she shares Zenobia's need to submit to male authority and a corresponding will to rule over her lesser sisters. The impression that Miriam had knelt before the model suggests to Kenyon a terrible thralldom. "Free as she seemed to be—beggar as he looked—the name-less vagrant must then be dragging the beautiful Miriam through the streets of Rome, fettered and shackled more cruelly than any captive queen of yore, following in an Emperour's triumph" (IV, 108). Hawthorne's image probably was suggested by Harriet Hosmer's statue *Zenobia in Chains*, which he praises in the preface to the novel.[49] But whereas Hosmer's *Zenobia* wore her manacles lightly as bracelets, and the third-century queen had lived the rest of her life as an independent matron in a villa outside Rome, it is Miriam's nature to exchange one form of bondage for another. Kenyon marvels that "this proud and self-dependent woman" would willfully fling herself into a new subjection and, in Donatello, fix her passion on an object "which, intellectually, seemed far beneath her" (IV, 280, 283). At the same time, Miriam has the compressed heat and tiger-like deadliness of her Egyptian prototypes. Like the Roman tabby that stretches itself out on the altar of the Pantheon—"the first of the feline race," Kenyon remarks, "that has ever set herself up as an object of worship, in the Pantheon or elsewhere, since the days of ancient Egypt" (IV, 458)—Miriam is potentially dangerous to the "doves" of Rome.

The "slender, brown-haired, New England girl" Hilda, tending her vestal flame in a dove-cot high above the turbid city of Rome, is little more than a stereotype of "purity and rectitude" throughout the novel (IV, 7, 383). Her "light brown ringlets, her delicately tinged, but healthful cheek, her sensitive, intelligent, yet most feminine and kindly face" all characterize her as a good little soul from America, "a delicate wood-anemone from the western forest-land" (IV, 63, 334). There is no confusion about angel or demon, or even angel or woman, concerning Hilda. "As an angel, you are not amiss," Miriam informs Hilda; "but, as a human creature, and a woman among earthly men and women, you need a sin to soften you!" (IV, 209).

Hawthorne characterizes his major figures less through authorial description than by association with the works of art each produces. *The Marble Faun* is as much an "artist story" as "Drowne's Wooden Image" or "The Artist of the Beautiful." The peculiar fixations of Miriam, Hilda, and Kenyon reveal themselves most vividly through the topics of their paintings, sketches, and sculptures, and the trio communicate with each other most expressively through their art. To some degree the Eastern subject matter of Miriam's paintings and Kenyon's sculptures reflects a general Oriental transfusion in the Greek Revival of the mid-nineteenth century and the popular fascination with the East that expressed itself in the odalisques of Jean Auguste-Dominique Ingres and in Eugene Delacroix's romantic history paintings of North Africa and Turkey.[50] But the prophetic pictures of Miriam and Kenyon also bring to a climax Hawthorne's lifelong engagement with the Orient.

Consistent with her character, Miriam works in the richest and liveliest art as a painter in oils. Over and over again her sketches and paintings depict "the idea of woman, acting the part of a revengeful mischief towards man." Her lethal beauties, what is more, are obsessively of Biblical and Eastern origin: Salome receiving the head of John the Baptist; Judith contemplating the head of the Babylonian general Holofernes; "Jael, driving the nail through the temples of Sisera" (IV, 43–44). In each case Miriam began with a conception "of perfect womanhood, a lovely form, and a high, heroic face of lofty beauty" before converting her heroine into a "vulgar murderess." As Donatello immediately senses, Miriam's masterwork, for which each of the others appears a mere forestudy, is essentially a self-portrait:

> She was very youthful, and had what was usually thought to be a Jewish aspect; a complexion in which there was no roseate bloom, yet neither was it pale; dark eyes, into which you might look as deeply as your glance would go, and still be conscious of a depth that you had not sounded, though it lay open to the day. She had black, abundant hair, with none of the vulgar glossiness of other women's sable locks; if she were really of Jewish blood, then this was Jewish hair, and a dark glory such as crowns no Christian maiden's head. Gazing at this portrait, you saw what Rachel might have been, when Jacob deemed her worth the wooing seven years, and seven more; or perchance she might ripen to be what Judith was, when she vanquished Holofernes with her beauty, and slew him for too much adoring it. (IV, 48)

The portrait on Miriam's easel has a remarkable effect upon Kenyon. Like Hawthorne's heavily monitored description of his marvelous Jewess in 1856, every phrase in his description of Miriam's portrait is driven home: "she seemed to get into your consciousness and memory, and could never afterwards be shut out, but haunted your dreams, for pleasure or for pain; holding your inner realm as a conquered territory, though without deigning to make herself at home there" (IV, 47–48).

Each of Hawthorne's three dark heroines of the 1850s—Hester, Zenobia, and Miriam—bears the name of an Eastern queen or prophetess and holds in her hands the lives and destiny of men. The Biblical Hester (or Esther) became the bride of King Athasuerus of Persia, whose kingdom extended from India to Ethiopia, when he cast out Queen Vashti for refusing to love and honor her lord. He intended to set an example that every man should be the ruler of his own kingdom; yet in the Book of Esther the heroine became the power behind the throne and destroyed the tribe of Haman in order to preserve her own people, the Jews. Esther's triumph is celebrated in the feast of Purim. Although Queen Zenobia was eventually vanquished by Aurelian and brought to Rome in chains, Hawthorne's queen in The Blithedale Romance utterly conquered the territory of Coverdale's dreams. He spent his first night at Blithedale in that fevered state "when a fixed idea remains in the mind, like the nail in Sisera's brain" (III, 38). The analogy to Jael was particularly effective for this point in The Blithedale Romance, where Zenobia brought a bowl of execrable gruel to Coverdale's sickbed. In the Song of Deborah, Sisera, commander of the Canaanites, was slain in his sleep by Jael ("of tent-dwelling women most blessed") in the following manner:

> He asked water and she gave him milk,
> she brought him curds in a lordly bowl.
> She put her hand to the tent peg and her right hand to the workmen's mallet;
> She struck Sisera a blow,
> she crushed his head,
> she shattered and pierced his temple. (Judges 5:25–26)

Finally, in *The Marble Faun* Miriam bears the name of the Old Testament prophetess who was the sister of Moses and Aaron. An equivocal figure, she led the women with timbrel and dance in celebrating the deliverance of the Children of Israel from their Egyptian captivity but was cursed with leprosy as long as she challenged the authority of Moses and believed to have her own voice from God.

Against the murderously seductive images associated with Miriam in *The Marble Faun*, fair Hilda offers no significant artistic or sensual counterweight. Like Sophia Hawthorne, Hilda "had produced sketches that were seized upon by men of taste" in America. But while she is recognized as "incomparably the best copyist in Rome," Hilda lacks originality and creativity and, especially compared to a seminal force like Miriam, seems just an "exquisitely effective piece of mechanism" (IV, 55, 59). Like Guido's Beatrice Cenci, the subject of her finest work, Hilda needs a sin to soften her, but Hawthorne allows her to sin only vicariously through observing the murder of Miriam's model. One wonders whether the author's wife felt more ennobled or demeaned by the essentially sterile characterization of Hilda.

In both his art and his affections the sculptor Kenyon is caught between the creative force of Miriam and the white light of Hilda. The busts he carves, as Miriam remarks, "turn feverish men into cool, quiet marble" (IV, 119), and he treats his particular "treasure of Hilda's marble hand" with such reverence for her "remote and shy divinity" that he dares not kiss the image he himself has made (IV, 122). The frozen classical image that signifies Kenyon's relation with Hilda demonstrates his talent but not genius. Far more expressive of the latent passions and energies in the soul of the artist is Kenyon's inspired statue of Cleopatra, to which the author turns immediately after the presentation of Hilda's marble hand: " 'MY NEW STATUE!' said Kenyon, who had positively forgotten it, in the thought of Hilda.—'Here it is, under this veil' " (IV, 123). Alone with Miriam in his studio, Kenyon removes the veil from his still moist clay model and discloses an idea of woman that is strikingly like Miriam's self-portrait—the one Egyptian, the other Jewish. Opposite to the snow image inspired by Hilda, Kenyon's statue of Cleopatra is aflame with tropical heat: "Cleopatra sat attired in a garb proper to her historic and queenly state, as a daughter of the Ptolemies, and yet such as the beautiful woman would have put on, as best adapted to heighten the magnificence of her charms, and kindle a tropic fire in the cold eyes of Octavius." There was "a great, smouldering furnace" deep in the woman's heart and, despite her total repose, a "latent energy and fierceness," as if "she might spring upon you like a tigress, and stop the very breath that you were now drawing, midway in your throat."

> The face was a miraculous success. The sculptor had not shunned to give the full Nubian lips, and other characteristics of the Egyptian physiognomy. His courage and integrity had been abundantly rewarded; for Cleopatra's beauty shone out richer, warmer, more triumphantly, beyond comparison, than if, shrinking timidly from the truth, he had chosen the tame Grecian type. (IV, 126)

Earlier in the novel Miriam remarked to Hilda that the sweet air she breathed drifted far above "our moral dust and mud" (IV, 53). Kenyon's original woman, to the contrary, rises from the depths of the earth under his creative hand with the primordial mud and fire still clinging to her.

> In a word, all Cleopatra—fierce, voluptuous, passionate, tender, wicked, terrible, and full of poisonous and rapturous enchantment—was kneaded into what, only a week or two before, had been a lump of wet clay from the Tiber. Soon, apotheosized in an indestructible material, she would be one of the images that men keep forever, finding a heat in them which does not cool down, throughout the centuries.
>
> "What a woman is this!" exclaimed Miriam, after a long pause.—"Tell me, did she never try—even while you were creating her—to overcome you with her fury, or her love? Were you not afraid to touch her, as she grew more and more towards hot life, beneath your hand?" (IV, 127)[51]

Kenyon cannot answer Miriam's challenge satisfactorily, even to himself. Like the woodcarver Drowne in Hawthorne's earlier tale, he regards the fruit of his artistic passion with wonder: "But I know not how it came about, at last. I kindled a great fire within my mind, and threw in the material—as Aaron threw the gold of the Israelites into the furnace—and, in the midmost heat, uprose Cleopatra, as you see her" (IV, 127). Kenyon's Cleopatra traces Hawthorne's dark lady to her source. In the 1844 tale, Drowne liberated a hamadryad locked in New England oak; in *The Romance of Monte Beni* in 1860, Hawthorne's Pygmalion removes the veil and reads the hieroglyphics of woman. "She was draped from head to foot in a costume, minutely and scrupulously studied from that of ancient Egypt, as revealed by the strange sculpture of that country, its coins, drawings, painted mummy-cases, and whatever other tokens have been dug out of its pyramids, graves, and catacombs" (IV, 125–126).

Miriam marvels at the depth of understanding represented in Kenyon's Cleopatra. "Where did you get that secret?" she asks; "You never found it in your. gentle Hilda." "No, surely, it was not in Hilda," Kenyon answers; "Her womanhood is of the ethereal type, and incompatible with any shadow of darkness or evil" (IV, 127–128). In the presence of the fierce, voluptuous figure of Cleopatra, Miriam and Kenyon come closer to knowing one another than they ever will again. Crying out to him "with sudden passion, 'will you be my friend, indeed?' "—Miriam pleads: "Perhaps—perhaps—but Heaven only knows—you might understand me! Oh, let me speak!' " (IV, 128). Had Kenyon responded with an equal warmth of spirit, possibly they would have become more than friends. But his characteristic timidity and reserve dispel the possibilities of the moment, and the sensual communication they were able to achieve through their expressive art ends with neither a poisonous nor a rapturous embrace.[52] After this, the relationship of Kenyon and Miriam is resolutely sublimated to one approximating that of friend, or brother and sister.

At the end of the novel Miriam and Kenyon have said their last farewell, she withdrawing into an unknown seclusion, he finally securing the living hand of Hilda, who, through the agency of vicarious sin, has come down "from her old tower, to be herself enshrined and worshipped as a household Saint, in the light of her husband's fireside" (IV, 461). Throughout *The Marble Faun*, except for those chapters in which Miriam and Kenyon display their respective art, Hawthorne kept a tighter grip on his characters than in *The Blithedale Romance*. There is no artificial, stammering revelation of love for the fair maiden at the end of the novel. Kenyon is overtly committed to winning Hilda from the outset. But the fair and formal life that lies ahead of them in the "broad and simple daylight" of their native land, it goes without saying, will never again rise to the level of passion and knowledge that Kenyon experienced at the crossroads of the world, where East and West meet.

It is common to regard *The Marble Faun* as the least artistically successful of Hawthorne's four major romances and a preview of his abortive struggles in the early 1860s. Roy Harvey Pearce has attributed the inadequacy of *The Marble Faun* to Hawthorne's loss of "the special cultural richness of his New England" that he had appropriated in the first novels and his failure to discover its equivalent in Italy, where "he was entirely out of contact with such richly formalized and institutionalized elements in the culture of which he wrote."[53] The results of the present study would suggest a somewhat different explanation: that what we experience as the genius of *The Scarlet Letter* is not the rich domestic life of seventeenth-century New England alone but the counterweight which that grave and orthodox culture provided to Hawthorne's "Oriental" flights of imagination; and that what we find unsatisfactory in *The Marble Faun* is the loss not only of native footing but also of tension between the foreign and the domestic as he moved the locus of his fiction ever closer to the geographical and historical source of the romance in the East. Imaginative distance, not proximity, was imperative to Hawthorne's work. He might have declined to visit nearby Roxbury when writing *The Blithedale Romance* in West Newton, Massachusetts, for fear that the realities of the decade before would press too closely upon him again.[54] When the difficulty of finding romantic inspiration in America, or adapting foreign atmosphere to the native landscape, became too great, Hawthorne turned to the easier exoticism of the Mediterranean and the East as George William Curtis and a host of popular writers had done before him.

By the time Hawthorne turned his English notes into *Our Old Home*, his consular experiences had taken on a "sense of illusion" and seemed the experience of another man (V, 38). So too his Italian holiday left him with a spirit of disenfranchisement. The author spoke for himself as much as for Kenyon and Hilda when he wrote of the "kind of emptiness" felt by those who spend too many of their years on a foreign shore.

We defer the reality of life, in such cases, until a future moment, when we shall again breathe our native air; but by-and-by, there are no future moments;

or, if we do return, we find that the native air has lost its invigorating quality, and that life has shifted its reality to the spot where we have deemed ourselves only temporary residents. Thus, between two countries, we have none at all, or only that little space of either, in which we finally lay down our discontented bones. It is wise, therefore, to come back betimes—or never. (IV, 461)

The author's lament on behalf of Kenyon implied the same two great and often irreconcilable adventures of life—travel and domestic love—that Hawthorne's Story Teller had failed to realize a quarter century earlier. "The mind wanders wild and wide," Kenyon said to Hilda, "and, so lonely as I live and work, I have neither pole-star above, nor light of cottage-windows here below, to bring me home. . . . Oh, Hilda, guide me home!" (IV, 460–461).

After reading through Hawthorne's career one finds in *The Marble Faun* a resolution of long-standing dialectics. That the syntheses achieved there failed to generate new and effective antitheses is all too apparent from the mannerism and machinery of *The American Claimant* and *The Elixir of Life* manuscripts, which Hawthorne struggled in vain to shape during the four years of life remaining to him after his return to America in 1860. The random Oriental imagery in those last works, like their plot, characterization, and symbolism in general, is devoid of psychological or cultural necessity.[55]

When Hilda and Kenyon visited St. Peter's Cathedral, the daughter of New England Puritans approved the untinted white light that poured into the temple of faith. The artist, on the other hand, would have preferred painted windows. "Yonder square apertures," Kenyon told Hilda, "filled with ordinary panes of glass are quite out of keeping with the superabundant splendor of everything about them. They remind me of that portion of Aladdin's palace which he left unfinished, in order that his royal father-in-law might put the finishing touch" (IV, 366). Henry Wadsworth Longfellow had this image in mind, as well as the unfinished *Dolliver Romance*, when he commemorated the burial of Hawthorne in a poem for the *Atlantic Monthly* entitled "Concord. May 23, 1864." Longfellow's elegy concluded:

> There in seclusion and remote from men
> The wizard hand lies cold,
> Which at its topmost speed let fall the pen,
> And left the tale half told.
> Ah, who shall lift the wand of magic power,
> And the lost clue regain?
> The unfinished window in Aladdin's tower
> Unfinished must remain![56]

There is no great distance between the Sleepy Hollow cemetery in Concord, Massachusetts, and Hawthorne's birthplace in Salem. During his mortal pilgrimage of sixty years Hawthorne's world travels were relatively modest, whether in comparison with peripatetic contemporaries like Irving, Longfellow, and Melville or his own seafaring forefathers. Yet in his imagination and in his art Hawthorne was very much a citizen of the world. His writing chambers in Salem and elsewhere were as large as the deserts of Arabia and the jungles of Hindostan. The Orient played a prominent role in the development of Hawthorne's romance as in America's international culture.

APPENDIX A

Eastern Materials Borrowed from the Salem Athenaeum
1826–1839, 1848–1850

The following titles and dates of use are based on Marion L. Kesselring, *Hawthorne's Reading 1828–1850: A Transcription and Identification of Titles Recorded in the Charge-Books of the Salem Athenaeum* (New York: The New York Public Library, 1949). Several of the citations have been expanded in order to clarify the subject matter of the books.

Works listed below that are not concerned solely with the East (e.g., Coryat's *Crudities*, Picart's *Religious Ceremonies and Customs*, Pliny's *Historie of the World*) figured prominently, nonetheless, in the Occidental effort to comprehend the geography, beliefs, and practices of the Orient. Kesselring identifies still other encyclopedias and general histories not mentioned here that chronicled the changing state of knowledge on the Near East and Asia down to the nineteenth century. While I have included Byron's *Works* because of his Turkish tales, I have not cited the 49 volumes of Voltaire borrowed by Hawthorne from October 1829 to September 1831, the three-volume *Plays of Philip Massinger* taken in 1833, or other collections where Eastern tales and commentary were parts of much larger wholes. Reviews, essays, travel sketches, and scholarly dissertations on the East permeated the 130 sets of the *Gentleman's Magazine*, the 19 sets of the London *Monthly Magazine*, and other serials taken from the Salem Athenaeum. Winnowing such materials from the 487 titles (books and serials) identified by Kesselring would extend this checklist but not alter significantly the contours of Hawthorne's reading interests.

Titles	Dates on Loan
Antar, A Bedoueen Romance. Trans. from the Arabic, by Terrick Hamilton. London, 1819–1820. 4 vols.	
Vol. 1	June 25–July 5, 1836
Asiatic Society of Bengal. *Asiatic Researches.* London, 1801–1811. 11 vols.	
Vol. 1?	Oct. 2–Oct. 6, 1831
Bruce, James. *Travels to Discover the Source of the Nile.* London, 1790. 5 vols.	
Vol. 1	Feb. 20–Mar. 16, 1833
Vol. 3	Mar. 16–Mar. 26, 1833
Vol. 4	Apr. 3–Apr. 10, 1833
Vol. 5	Apr. 10–Apr. 20, 1833
Bünting, Heinrich. *Itinerarium totius Sacrae Scripturae; or, The Travels of the Holy Patriarchs, Prophets, Judges, Kings, our Saviour Christ, and His Apostles.* London, 1629.	Mar. 19–Mar. 24, 1828
Busbecq, Ogier Ghislain de. *Travels into Turkey.* London, 1744.	Feb. 27–Feb. 28, 1827
Bush, George. *The Life of Mohammed.* New York, 1830.	May 6–May 10, 1836

Titles	Dates on Loan
Byron, George Gordon Byron, 6th baron. *Works*. Philadelphia, 1829.	Aug. 4–Oct. 31, 1834 Aug. 20–Oct. 9, 1838
Camoes, Luiz de. *The Lusiad: or, The Discovery of India*. Trans. by William Julius Mickle. London, 1798.	July 23–July 26, 1830
Chandler, Richard. *Travels in Asia Minor*. London, 1776. Or *Travels in Greece*. Oxford, 1776.	June 2–June 4, 1828
Chardin, Sir John. *The Travels of Sir John Chardin into Persia and the East Indies*. London, 1686.	Nov. 1–Nov. 6, 1831
Chishull, Edmund. *Travels in Turkey and back to England*. London, 1747.	July 16–Aug. 4, 1832
Cochrane, John Dundas. *Narrative of a Pedestrian Journey through Russia and Siberian Tartary, from the Frontiers of China to the Frozen Sea and Kamchatka; Performed during the Years 1820, 1821, 1822, and 1823*. Philadelphia, 1824.	Oct. 7–Oct. 14, 1831.
Coryate, Thomas. *Coryat's Crudities . . . Being a More Particular Account of His Travels (Mostly on Foot) in Different Parts of the Globe, than any Hitherto Published*. London, 1776. 3 vols. [This edition includes Coryat's account of India.]	
Vol. 1	Dec. 22–Dec. 25, 1826
Vol. 2	Dec. 24–Dec. 26, 1827
Vol. 3	Dec. 27–Dec. 29, 1827
Hanway, Jonas. *An Historical Account of the British Trade over the Caspian Sea: with the Author's Journal of Travels from England through Russia into Persia*. London, 1754. 2 vols.	
Vol. 1	Dec. 3–Dec. 17, 1831
Harris, John. *Navigantium atque Itinerantium Bibliotheca. Or, A Complete Collection of Voyages and Travels. Consisting of above six hundred of the most Authentic Writers*. London, 1744–1748. 2 vols.	Mar. 1–Mar. 5, 1830
Vol. 1	Mar. 8–Mar. 15, 1831
Heber, Reginald. *Narrative of a Journey through the Upper Provinces of India, from Calcutta to Bombay, 1824–1825. (With Notes upon Ceylon,) an Account of a Journey to Madras and the Southern Provinces, 1826, and Letters Written in India*. Philadelphia, 1828. 2 vols.	
Vol. 1	June 25–Aug. 4, 1834
Vol. 2	Aug. 4–Oct. 31, 1834
The Koran, Commonly Called the Alcoran of Mohammed. Trans into English with an "Historical Discourse" by George Sale. London, 1734.	Oct. 2–Oct. 4, 1827
Le Blanc, Vincent. *The World Surveyed; or, The Famous Voyages & Travailes of Vincent Le Blanc . . . through Most Parts of the World. Viz. The East and West Indies, Persia, Pegu, the kingdoms of Fez and Morocco, Guinny, and through all Africa*. London, 1660.	Mar. 21–Mar. 23, 1827

Titles	Dates on Loan
Lockman, John. *Travels of the Jesuits into Various Parts of the World: Compiled from their Letters* [Particularly China and the East Indies]. London, 1743. 2 vols.	
Vol. 1	Feb. 5–Feb. 9, 1827
Vol. 2	Apr. 24–Apr. 30, 1829
Ludolf, Hiob. *A New History of Ethiopia.* London, 1682.	Aug. 13–Aug. 22, 1836
Madden, Richard Robert. *Travels in Turkey, Egypt, Nubia and Palestine, in 1824, 1825, 1826, and 1827.* London, 1829. 2 vols.	
Vol. 1	Sept. 30–Oct. 7, 1834
Vol. 2	Nov. 19–Nov. 29, 1834
Maundrell, Henry. *A Journey from Aleppo to Jerusalem at Easter,* A.D. *1697.* London, 1810.	Mar. 19–Mar. 28, 1831
Morier, James Justinian. *The Adventures of Hajji Baba, of Ispahan.* Philadelphia, 1824. 2 vols.	
Vol. 1	July 12–July 14, 1827
Vol. 2	July 14–July 17, 1827
Olearius, Adam. *The Voyages and Travels of the Ambassadors Sent by Fredrick, Duke of Holstein, to the Great Duke of Muscovy and the King of Persia.* London, 1662.	June 30–July 4, 1827
Picart, Bernard. *Religious Ceremonies and Customs.* London, 1731. 6 vols.	
Vol. 1	Apr. 18–Apr. 24, 1829
Vol. 2	May 5–May 8, 1829
	June 5–June 12, 1829
Vol. 3	Apr. 24–Apr. 27, 1829
Vol. 4	Apr. 27–May 5, 1829
Vol. 6	May 30–June 5, 1829
Plinius Secundus, C. *The Historie of the World. Commonly Called, the Naturall Historie of C. Plinius Secundus.* Trans. by Philemon Holland. London, 1601. 2 vols.	
Vol. 1?	May 21–Aug. 25, 1836
Pococke, Richard. *A Description of the East, and some other Countries.* London, 1743–1745. 2 vols. in 3.	
Vol. 1	Dec. 17–Dec. 31, 1831
[Porter, David.] *Constantinople and Its Environs. In a Series of Letters . . . By an American, Long Resident at Constantinople.* New York, 1835. 2 vols.	
Vol. 1	May 28–June 1, 1836
Vol. 2	May 28–June 1, 1836
Reynolds, J[eremiah] N. *Voyage of the United States Frigate Potomac . . . During the Circumnavigation of the Globe, in the Years 1831, 1832, 1833, and 1834; Including a Particular Account of the Engagement at Quallah-Battoo, on the Coast of Sumatra; With All the Official Documents Relating to the Same.* New York, 1835.	June 1–June 18, 1836

Titles	Dates on Loan
Russell, Alexander. *The Natural History of Aleppo.* London, 1794. 2 vols.	
Vol. 1	Nov. 17–Nov. 24, 1831
Rycaut, Sir Paul. *The History of the Turkish Empire from the Year 1623 to the Year 1677.* London, 1679–1680.	Apr. 18–Apr. 24, 1829
[Sandys, George.] *A Relation of a Journey Begun An:Dom: 1610. Foure Bookes. Containing a Description of the Turkish Empire, of Egypt, of the Holy Land.* London, 1627.	Dec. 10–Dec. 12, 1827
Shaw, Samuel. *The Journals of Major Samuel Shaw, the First American Consul at Canton.* Boston, 1847.	Sept. 25–Nov. 14, 1848
Tott, François, baron de. *Memoires of the Baron de Tott, on the Turks and the Tartars.* London, 1785. 2 vols.	
Vol. 1	Sept. 24–Sept. 27, 1827
Tournefort, Joseph Pitton de. *A Voyage into the Levant.* London, 1741. 3 vols.	
Vol. 1	Aug. 16–Aug. 25, 1830.
Wilkinson, Sir John Gardner. *Modern Egypt and Thebes.* London, 1843. 2 vols.	
Vol. 1	Oct. 10–Nov. 14, 1848

Two precautions should be observed when crediting Nathaniel Hawthorne with the choice and reading of the materials identified by Kesselring. First, until May 21, 1828, when the membership was transferred to him, borrowings were recorded under the name of his aunt Mary Manning, who had purchased a share in the Athenaeum in October 1826, the year after Hawthorne's graduation from Bowdoin and return to Salem. Kesselring conjectured, however, that "Aunt Mary went to this expense more for her nephew than for herself," and that Hawthorne bought the share in his own right as soon as he was able. There is no difference of taste or subject matter between the items charged before and after May 1828, and the use of multi-volume works continued without interruption across the change of ownership. Furthermore, although her brother William Manning held a share in the Athenaeum from 1820 to 1827, there is no record that Aunt Mary or anyone else in the family had used the borrowing rights it provided.[1]

The second consideration, and a more significant one, concerns the use Hawthorne's sister Elizabeth made of his Athenaeum privileges. She wrote after his death: "It was one of my brother's peculiarities that he would never visit [the Athenaeum] himself, nor look over the Catalogue to select a book, nor indeed do anything but find fault with it; so that it was left entirely to me to provide him with reading, and I am sure nobody else would have got half so much out of such a dreary old library as I did."[2] In light of Hawthorne's own references to mornings and afternoons spent at the Salem Athenaeum in the early 1840s, when he was between memberships in the Athenaeum but living under the same roof with his sister, Elizabeth's claim seems rather too absolute.[3] Yet her role in obtaining books and magazines for him was considerable, and most likely she chose material for her reading as well as her brother's.

Works charged to Hawthorne's membership while he was away from Salem presumably were for Elizabeth's own use. He was "rambling about," for instance, when Byron's *Works* were taken the second time in 1838,[4] and he was in Boston editing the *American Magazine of Useful and Entertaining Knowledge* when several of the titles listed above were borrowed in 1836. It is possible in the latter case, however, that Hawthorne directed his sister, who was supplying material for the *American Magazine*, to specific works at the Athenaeum or had them posted on the Mannings' stagecoaches, which traveled daily between Salem and Boston, so that he could search out material himself. The valise that passed back and forth between Hawthorne in Boston and his sisters in Salem carried books as well as laundry and mail. On March 3, he wrote urgently to his sister Louisa: "Why dont Uncle Robert send those books?" (XV, 239).

It is not necessary completely to disentangle what Nathaniel or Elizabeth Hawthorne read from the Salem Athenaeum. Elizabeth was the closest confidante of Hawthorne's apprentice years, a collaborator and incisive critic, intimately acquainted with his interests and themes, ambitious for his career, and resentful when the softer presence of Sophia Peabody entered his life. Immediately after their connection with the *American Magazine* ended, Nathaniel and Elizabeth co-authored *Peter Parley's Universal History*, and a few years later he invited her to join in writing his other books for children. She was, Hawthorne said, "the most sensible woman I ever knew in my life, much superior to me in general talent, and of fine cultivation."[5] Her use of the Salem Athenaeum, whatever it was, became part of his own environment of information and ideas.

There is no reason, in any case, to attribute the Eastern materials cited above to Elizabeth Hawthorne's preferences rather than to her brother's. Although in later life she turned increasingly to history and read "some travel books," she did not share his taste for Robert Southey's Oriental verse narratives and seems to have been unaffected by the Oriental romances that were fashionable into the 1870s.[6] Circumstantial evidence as well as the direct use Hawthorne made of names and figures from his Athenaeum borrowings enable us to regard Kesselring's bibliography as an accurate index to his tastes and mental peregrinations in these years.

APPENDIX B

Eastern Materials in *The American Magazine of Useful and
Entertaining Knowledge* March–August, 1836

The following 69 notes, articles, and extracts from other works appeared in the six
monthly issues of the *American Magazine of Useful and Entertaining Knowledge* (March
through August, 1836) that Nathaniel Hawthorne edited with the assistance of his
sister Elizabeth. Ranging in length from two lines on the building of the pyramids in
the March issue to Hawthorne's fully worked essays on "Jerusalem" (March) and "The
Culture of Rice" (April) and lengthy extracts describing "The Valley of the Sweet
Waters" at Constantinople (May) and "Peking, in China" (July), each of the items
listed below is chiefly when not exclusively concerned with the cultures extending
eastward from the Muslim states and the Holy Land to the East Indies, China, and
Japan. Items referring only incidentally to the East are not included. The sources and
references identified parenthetically next to the essay titles correspond to the bibliography in the second part of this appendix. Items marked *from* were extracted verbatim from the sources indicated.

EASTERN SUBJECT MATTER BY ISSUE AND PAGE

March 1836 (Vol. 2, no. 7)
"Jerusalem," pp. 269–270
Two untitled lines on the pyramids, p. 288
"Death of Hindoos on the Ganges," p. 297
April 1836 (Vol. 2, no. 8)
"The Egyptian Papyrus," p. 315 (refers to Pliny, *Naturall History*)
"Chinese Magnets," p. 315
"A Man-Mountain," p. 315
"Armed Chariots," p. 315
"An Ourang Outang," pp. 321–322
"The Culture of Rice," pp. 323–325 (refers to Belzoni, *Egypt and Nubia*)
Untitled note on the "grand scale" of nature in India, p. 335
"Rubies," p. 336
May 1836 (Vol. 2, no. 9)
"Lawsuits in Pegu," p. 356
"The Valley of the Sweet Waters," pp. 361–362 (from Porter, *Constantinople*)
"Tonquinese Soldiers," p. 362
"An Annual Fair, in India," pp. 363–364 (from Roberts, *Hindostan*)
"Tower of Babel," p. 366
"Moorish Peculiarities, Taken at Random," pp. 368–369
"Turtle," p. 369 (refers to Kempthorne, "Survey Along the . . . Persian Gulf")
"The Camel's Thorn," p. 369
"Polygamy," p. 371
"The Gardens of Etawah, in India," pp. 375–376 (from Roberts, *Hindostan*)
"Leathern Rafts," p. 384
"Ancient Bricks," p. 389
"Female Protection," p. 389
"Suicides in Canton," p. 394
June 1836 (Vol. 2, no. 10)

The pioneer exposition of Hawthorne's work on the *American Magazine* is Arlin Turner, *Hawthorne as Editor: Selections from His Writings in The American Magazine of Useful and Entertaining Knowledge* (University, La.: Louisiana State University Press, 1941). Turner reproduced and annotated the items he believed particularly bear Hawthorne's authorial stamp and offered a ten-page list of "authors and works drawn on or mentioned in Hawthorne's six issues of *The American Magazine.*" The 20 items listed below were first identified by Turner, but the citations have been amplified and brought into conformity with *National Union Catalog* entries.

Sources and References

Titles	Issues and Pages
Belzoni, Giovanni Battista. *Narrative of the Operations and Recent Discoveries within the Pyramids, Temples, Tombs, and Excavations in Egypt and Nubia.* London, 1820.	April, p. 323
Cochrane, John Dundas. *Narrative of a Pedestrian Journey through Russia and Siberian Tartary.* Philadelphia, 1824.	May, p. 384
Conolly, Arthur. *Journey to the North of India Overland from England, through Russia, Persia, and Afghaunistaun.* London, 1830. 2 vols.	June, p. 427
Gützlaff, Charles [Karl Friedrich August]. *A Sketch of Chinese History, Ancient and Modern; Comprising a Retrospect of the Foreign Intercourse and Trade with China.* New York, 1834. 2 vols. Or: *Journal of Three Voyages along the Coast of China; in 1831, 1832, & 1833, with Notices of Siam, Corea, and the Loo-Choo Islands.* London, 1834.	June, pp. 423–424
Holman, James. *A Voyage Round the World, Including Travels in Africa, Asia, Australasia, America.* London, 1834–1835. 4 vols.	August, p. 515
Johnson, Samuel. *The Prince of Abissinia: A Tale* [*Rasselas*]. London, 1759. 2 vols.	July, p. 442
Kempthorne, G. B. "Notes Made on a Survey Along the Eastern Shores of the Persian Gulf in 1828," *Journal of the Royal Geographical Society of London*, 5 (1835), 263–285.	May, p. 369
Lord, Perceval Barton. *Algiers, with Notices of the Neighbouring States of Barbary.* London, 1835. 2 vols.	August, p. 520
Macartney, George Macartney, earl. *An Historical Account of the Embassy to the Emperor of China, Undertaken by Order of the King of Great Britain.* London, 1797.	June, p. 423
Niebuhr, [Carsten]. *Travels through Arabia, and Other Countries in the East.* Trans. by Robert Heron. Edinburgh, 1792. 2 vols.	August, p. 494

Titles	Issues and Pages
The Oriental Annual; or, Scenes in India. 7 vols. London, 1834–1840.	June, p. 422
[Pliny the Elder.] The Historie of the World. Commonly Called, the Naturall Historie of C. Plinius Secundus. Trans. by Philemon Holland. London, 1601. 2 vols. in 1.	April, p. 315 August, pp. 489–490, 510, 518
[Porter, David.] Constantinople and Its Environs. New York, 1835. 2 vols.	May, pp. 361–362 July, p. 467 August, pp. 491, 492, 500
Purchas, Samuel. Purchas His Pilgrimage. Or, Relations of the World and the Religions. London, 1613.	July, p. 476
Reynolds, J[eremiah] N. Voyage of the United States Frigate Potomac. New York, 1835.	August, p. 486
Roberts, Emma. Scenes and Characteristics of Hindostan. London, 1835. 3 vols. Or: Philadelphia, 1836. 2 vols.	May, pp. 363–364 June, p. 425
Anon. Three Weeks in Palestine and Lebanon. London, 1833. Or: Boston, 1836.	June, pp. 406, 412, 426
Timkovskii, Egor Fedorovich. Travels of the Russian Mission Through Mongolia to China, and Residence in Pekin, in the Years 1820–1821. Trans. by H. E. Lloyd. London, 1827. 2 vols.	July, pp. 477–478
[Trelawny, Edward John.] Adventures of a Younger Son. London, 1831. 3 vols.	June, pp. 417–418 July, pp. 459–460
White, John. A Voyage to Cochin China. London, 1824. First published as History of a Voyage to the China Sea. Boston, 1823.	June, p. 418

Hawthorne did not attribute all of his material in the *American Magazine*, and it was outside Turner's purview in *Hawthorne as Editor* either to inspect at first hand the sources he was able to identify through Hawthorne's references or to look for additional sources. Many of Hawthorne's anecdotes and some of the longer essays were synthesized from a decade's continuous reading. Other materials were pulled from the shelves of the Boston Athenaeum, where the editor of the *American Magazine* had reading but not borrowing privileges.

If Hawthorne's sources and editorial process for the *American Magazine* ever are explicated in more detail, the charge records of the Salem Athenaeum should be of special importance. Turner used an early checklist of Hawthorne's borrowings published in the *Essex Institute Historical Collections* in 1932 (Vol. 68, pp. 65–87) but did not have the benefit of Marion Kesselring's carefully arranged and thoroughly detailed account that appeared in 1949. Based on the earlier list Turner noted, "Two dozen or more books and periodicals from which material was taken for use in the magazine during Hawthorne's editorship were drawn against his card at the Salem Athenaeum Library." Turner thought, "They were doubtless borrowed and used by Elizabeth. A check on the references in the magazine to these books shows that almost without exception they were used to supply only direct quotations. These quotations are rather numerous, many of them long, and it is quite possible that they represent the bulk of Elizabeth's assistance in the editorial venture."[2] In fact, the evidence is not so definitive, at least as it concerns the works by Cochrane, Pliny, Porter, and Reynolds that appear here in both Appendixes A and B.

Hawthorne had Cochrane's *Narrative of a Pedestrian Journey through Russia and Siberian Tartary* out of the Salem Athenaeum in 1831 and probably wrote his note on the "Great Gun" at Moscow (May) from memory. Pliny's *Historie of the World* was on loan from the Athenaeum for three months, from May 21 to August 25, 1836, and might well have been on Hawthorne's desk in Boston during this time. Since the first reference to Pliny appeared in the April issue of the *American Magazine*, a month before the *Historie* was taken from the Athenaeum, Hawthorne had been previously acquainted with the work. The response to Pliny's "fantastical illusions" in the essay "Natural History Among the Ancients" (August) obviously was of his authorship.

The articles based on David Porter's and Jeremiah Reynolds's works are more likely to have been extracted by Elizabeth and forwarded to Boston. Porter's *Constantinople and Its Environs* appears five times in the *American Magazine*, first as two lengthy extracts in the May and July numbers, and then, in the final August issue, through three shorter notes that Hawthorne seems to have digested from material on hand. In the course of his editing Hawthorne accumulated copy that he would insert as space required. He advised Elizabeth in March, "You may continue to make extracts; for they will all come into play, sometime or other."[3] The article "Transplantation of Foreign Products," also in the August issue, was taken intact from Reynolds's *Voyage of the United States Frigate Potomac*, which was out of the Salem Athenaeum from June 1 to June 18. Even in these cases, however, the choice of what he would publish was Hawthorne's, and the three responses to *Constantinople and Its Environs* in August are in his own voice.

Introduction

1. D. H. Lawrence, *Studies in Classic American Literature* (New York: Thomas Seltzer, 1923), pp. 139–140, 121. In *S.* (1988), his third novel based on characters from *The Scarlet Letter*, John Updike has reorientalized Hester Prynne by turning her modern avatar (Sarah Worth) into a *Kundalini* and sending her to an ashram in Arizona.

2. David Levin, "Introduction" to *The Blithedale Romance* (New York: Dell, 1960), p. 11.

3. Buford Jones, "The *Fairy Land* of Hawthorne's Romances," *Emerson Society Quarterly,* 48 (III Quarter 1967), 118.

4. Neal Frank Doubleday, *Hawthorne's Early Tales: A Critical Study* (Durham, N.C.: Duke University Press, 1972), p. 67.

5. Charles H. Foster, "Hawthorne's Literary Theory," *PMLA* 57 (March 1942), 242.

6. Nina Baym, "Hawthorne," in *American Literary Scholarship 1973,* ed. James Woodress (Durham, N.C.: Duke University Press, 1975), p. 22.

7. William H. Goetzmann, *New Lands, New Men: America and the Second Great Age of Discovery* (New York: Viking, 1986), p. ix.

8. Raymond Schwab, *The Oriental Renaissance: Europe's Rediscovery of India and the East, 1680–1880,* trans. Gene Patterson-Black and Victor Reinking (New York: Columbia University Press, 1984), p. 7. Schwab's work first appeared in French in 1950.

9. Schwab, pp. 4, 6. Italics added.

10. Edward W. Said, *Orientalism* (New York: Random House, 1979), pp. 14–15, 1–2. Italics added. As A. L. Rowse pointed out in his foreword to John Steadman's *The Myth of Asia* (New York: Simon and Schuster, 1969), p. 11: "There are at least three Asias—the cultural complex of China and Japan, that of India and its related cultures, and Islam." "The notion of Asian unity" and the geographical and cultural "dichotomy of East and West" are both illusory, Steadman noted, but they strongly influenced the "universal histories" of the eighteenth and nineteenth centuries and have left their mark on comparative criticism down to the present day (pp. 39, 43).

11. Said, *Orientalism,* pp. 3–4.

12. Edward W. Said, "Foreword" to Schwab, *The Oriental Renaissance,* p. xix.

13. *Peter Parley's Universal History, on the Basis of Geography* (Boston: American Stationers' Company, 1837), I, 21–23, 28, vii. The four panels on the frontispiece of *Parley's Universal History* depict "The Savage," "The Barbarous," and "The Civilized State" of mankind and then the "Highest State of Civilization." "The Civilized State" is represented by a city scene in India, with temple worshippers and howdah-decked elephants; the "Highest State" by a pastoral American landscape, complete with church, farmers, train, and steamboat.

14. Hugh Henry Brackenridge and Philip Freneau, *Father Bombo's Pilgrimage to Mecca, 1770,* ed. and intro. Michael Davitt Bell (Princeton, N.J.: Princeton University Library, 1975), p. ix; and Frank Luther Mott, *Golden Multitudes: The Story of Best Sellers in the United States* (New York: Macmillan, 1947), p. 305.

15. See, for example, Arthur Christy, *The Orient in American Transcendentalism* (New York: Columbia University Press, 1932); James Baird, *Ishmael* (Baltimore: The Johns Hopkins Press, 1956); John T. Irwin, *American Hieroglyphics: The Symbol of the Egyptian Hieroglyphics in the American Renaissance* (New Haven: Yale University Press,

1980); Mukhtar Ali Isani, "The Oriental Tale in America through 1865: A Study in American Fiction" (Ph.D. dissertation, Princeton University, 1962); Patricia Clark Smith, "Novel Conceptions, Unusual Combinations: The Arabesque in Poe" (Ph.D. dissertation, Yale University, 1970); Franklin Walker, *Irreverent Pilgrims: Melville, Browne, and Mark Twain in the Holy Land* (Seattle: University of Washington Press, 1974); Dorothee Melitsky Finkelstein, *Melville's Orienda* (New Haven: Yale University Press, 1961); Beongcheon Yu, *The Great Circle: American Writers and the Orient* (Detroit: Wayne State University Press, 1983); and R. K. Gupta, *The Great Encounter: A Study of Indo-American Literary and Cultural Relations* (New Delhi: Abhinav, 1986).

16. Journal entry for October 30, 1841; *The Journals and Miscellaneous Notebooks of Ralph Waldo Emerson*, ed. William H. Gilman and J. E. Parsons, Vol. 8 (Cambridge, Mass.: Harvard University Press, 1970), p. 60.

17. Irwin, *American Hieroglyphics*, p. 277.

18. Harry Levin, *The Power of Blackness: Hawthorne, Poe, Melville* (New York: Alfred A. Knopf, 1958), p. 37.

1. A Hawthorne and a Salemite

1. Nathaniel Hathorne's log for the *Herald* is owned by The Huntington Library. Unless otherwise indicated his entries provide the quotations that follow.

2. Samuel Eliot Morison describes the *Herald's* cargo to and from Madeira and India in *The Maritime History of Massachusetts 1783–1860* (Boston: Houghton Mifflin, 1921), pp. 87–88. Arlin Turner, who also used Hathorne's logbook, misdates the *Herald's* departure as February 3, 1800, and its return to America as January 23, 1801. Turner, *Nathaniel Hawthorne* (New York: Oxford University Press, 1980), p. 6. The extant log lacks its first two pages (one sheet), which apparently recorded four days' sailing. Page 3, for January 3 and 4, is marked "out 5 days" and "out 6 days." The January 29, 1800, departure is corroborated by Nathaniel Silsbee, "Biographical Notes," *Essex Institute Historical Collections*, 35 (January 1899), 21. Silsbee's account of the *Herald's* voyage, written before his death in 1850, varies only in minor details from Hathorne's contemporary record. Silsbee mentions taking his younger brother Zachariah with him as clerk but says nothing of Hathorne or other officers. Nor is Hathorne mentioned by Morison. The nature of his log, however, and of his previous and subsequent voyages to the East Indies suggests that Hathorne served the *Herald* as first mate.

3. Morison, pp. 87–88. Silsbee, p. 22, put the total value of his stock of specie, merchandise, and bank credits at over one hundred thousand dollars.

4. Silsbee, p. 22.

5. Silsbee, p. 22.

6. I have added end punctuation and capitals as indicated but transcribed Hathorne's spelling without change.

7. Brantz's painting, now in the Peabody Museum at Salem, is reproduced in Edgar Stanton Maclay, *A History of American Privateers* (New York: D. Appleton, 1899), facing p. 220.

8. The *Salem Gazette* reported on February 27, 1801: "Capt. Silsbee, of this port has arrived at New-York from Calcutta. Capt. Gibeau, of this town, came passenger with him, in good health." And on March 3, 1801: "Port of Boston. Friday, Feb. 27. Ship Herald, Capt. Silsbee, 115 days from Calcutta."

9. See James Duncan Phillips, *Salem and the Indies* (Boston: Houghton Mifflin, 1947), Chap. 4, "First Voyages to India and China," pp. 44–60. Phillips notes, p. 48, that when the *Grand Turk* anchored at Whampoa alongside the *Empress of China* and the *Hope*, both of New York, she was "the third American ship to reach China and the first from New England." The first ship to take the American flag to India was the *United States* out of Philadelphia, which arrived at Pondicherry December 26,

1784. G. Bhagat, *Americans in India 1784–1860* (New York: New York University Press, 1970), p. 4.

10. For further dates and details about Hathorne's voyages from 1795 to 1808 see Turner, *Nathaniel Hawthorne*, pp. 6–11; Vernon Loggins, *The Hawthornes* (New York: Columbia University Press, 1951), pp. 197–206; and Hubert H. Hoeltje, "Captain Nathaniel Hathorne: Father of the Famous Salem Novelist," *Essex Institute Historical Collections*, 89 (October 1953), 329–356. Neither Loggins nor Hoeltje was aware, however, of Hathorne's voyage on the *Herald*.

11. Julian Hawthorne, *Nathaniel Hawthorne and His Wife: A Biography* (Boston: James R. Osgood/Printed at the University Press, 1884), I, 99.

12. Elizabeth Manning, "The Boyhood of Hawthorne," *Wide Awake*, November 1891, p. 501; Hoeltje, p. 330.

13. Julian Hawthorne probably authenticated the logbook for sale to the St. Louis collector William K. Bixby, who in turn sold it to Henry E. Huntington at the Anderson Galleries on March 29–31, 1916. Julian concludes his inscription: "This is the only log-book of Capt. Hawthorne in existence," which is obviously untrue. When the three logbooks now at the Essex Institute left the Hawthorne family, however, is unknown.

14. Hawthorne also copied entries for November 16, 1800, and February 15 and 23, 1801. I have compared annotations in the four logbooks considered here with holograph letters at the Essex Institute written by Nathaniel Hawthorne in 1820 and with examples of his later script published in *Hawthorne's Hand: An Exhibition from the Collection of C. E. Frazer Clark, Jr.* (New York: Grolier Club, 1973). The May 28, 1800, entry for the *Herald* also bears the signature "Mr George G. Sawyer."

15. Randall Stewart, "Recollections of Hawthorne by His Sister Elizabeth," *American Literature*, 16 (January 1945), 331. Elizabeth Hawthorne's "Recollections" comprise five letters to James T. Fields in December 1870 and January 1871. Fields used her accounts in his series of essays on Hawthorne for "Our Whispering Gallery," *Atlantic Monthly*, 27 (February–May 1871), which later were drawn together in his *Yesterdays with Authors* (1900).

16. Julian Hawthorne, *Nathaniel Hawthorne and His Wife*, I, 96.

17. Captain Hathorne's logbooks for the *America*, *Perseverance*, and *Mary and Eliza* are owned by the Essex Institute.

18. Phillips, *Salem and the Indies*, p. 185.

19. The last pages of the *America* log were noted as missing in 1952. According to Hoeltje, p. 338, however, Hathorne made his final entry after the ship approached Long Island on April 10, 1796. The *America* continued on to Salem in late April or early May.

20. The ownership and command of the *Perseverance*, not mentioned by Hathorne, are established in the directories to shiplogs at the Essex Institute and elsewhere.

21. Loggins, pp. 189, 197, believed that Hathorne was chief mate on both the *America* and the *Perseverance* but offers no documentation. Based on Hathorne's references to other officers, Hoeltje, p. 339, concluded that he was neither first nor second mate on the *Perseverance*.

22. Hoeltje, pp. 346–347; Loggins, p. 201. Hathorne assumed command of the ship at some point during the voyage; the *Mary and Eliza* had left Salem in December 1803 under the captaincy of Henry White.

23. The departure of the *Morning Star* for Malaga under Captain Daniel Hathorne was announced in "Ship News," *Salem Gazette*, August 24, 1804.

24. Hoeltje, pp. 347–348.

25. Quoted by Walter Muir Whitehill, *The East India Marine Society and the Peabody Museum of Salem: A Sesquicentennial History* (Salem, Mass.: Peabody Museum, 1949), pp. 6, 8. Whitehill, p. 162, lists Captain Nathaniel Hathorne as the 97th member of the Society.

26. Loggins claims, pp. 200–201, that Hathorne "took over command" of the *Astrea* for a voyage to Sumatra and Java but gives no source for his information. Hoeltje, pp.

344–345, offers circumstantial evidence that Hathorne was on a voyage to Russia at the time. Turner, however, has found additional reason to believe that Hathorne "probably sailed for the Orient again late in 1801, or early the next year, possibly in command of the *Astrea*." Turner, *Nathaniel Hawthorne*, pp. 7, 397, note 14. If Hathorne commanded the *Astrea* in 1801–1803, would he not have been admitted to membership in the East India Marine Society at this earlier time?

27. Turner, *Nathaniel Hawthorne*, p. 397, note 15.

28. See note 10, above, especially Hoeltje.

29. Five weeks passed between the gift of the logbook to Hathorne by his "esteamed" but unidentified friend "Mr. Robert Robinnet" and his first entry on December 3, 1795.

30. Reprinted under "Domestic Affairs," *Salem Gazette*, May 3, 1796. The *Gazette* welcomed the *America's* return home in its May 10, 1796, issue offering Buffon's description of elephants and a compliment to Crowninshield: "We are pleased with the ardent wishes of one of our young, and enterprising Citizens, Captain Jacob Crowninshield, to gratify his Country with one of the noblest animals in Creation. And we are happy to learn that success has crowned his ambition, and that he has attained a reward, which will be finally paid by a grateful and inquisitive public."

31. "The Modern Job; or, The Philosopher's Stone," *The Token and Atlantic Souvenir*, ed. S.G. Goodrich (Boston: Charles Bowen, 1834), p. 300.

32. Hoeltje, pp. 341–342, reads the obscure script here as "Romanticist."

33. Letter to Louisa Hawthorne, February 17, 1836; XV, 238.

34. *American Magazine of Useful and Entertaining Knowledge*, 2 (March 1836), 302. Even closer to home was Hawthorne's poem "The Ocean," which appeared in the *Salem Gazette* for August 26, 1825. The lines "Calmly the wearied seamen rest/ Beneath their own blue sea" state its melancholy theme. "The Ocean" was soon reprinted in *The Mariner's Library or Voyager's Companion* (Boston: Lilly, Wait, Colman and Holden, 1833), p. 34.

35. That the author studied the *America* and *Perseverance* logs after graduating from Bowdoin as well as before is known by his inscription on the entry for January 28, 1796: "Nathaniel Hathorne, Salem, Massachusetts, 1825."

36. Hoeltje, p. 355.

37. Hoeltje, p. 342. Arlin Turner summed up "such an attitude as the marks in the journals seem to reflect: a curiosity to know his father, to imitate and to experience vicariously his career, and yet to add an ironic, critical touch of his own." Turner, *Nathaniel Hawthorne*, p. 9.

38. Van Wyck Brooks, *The World of Washington Irving* (New York: E. P. Dutton, 1944), pp. 370–371.

39. Letter to Horatio Bridge, May 3, 1843; XV, 686–687.

40. Letter to Horatio Bridge, March 25, 1843; XV, 683. Italics added.

41. B. Bernard Cohen, "Hawthorne's Library: An Approach to the Man and His Mind," *The Nathaniel Hawthorne Journal 1971*, ed. C. E. Frazer Clark, Jr. (Washington, D.C.: NCR Microcard Editions, 1971), pp. 126–127.

42. Julian Hawthorne, *Hawthorne Reading: An Essay* (Cleveland: The Rowfant Club, 1902), pp. 16–17.

43. James T. Fields, *Yesterdays with Authors* (Boston: Houghton Mifflin, 1900), p. 43.

44. Manning Hawthorne, "Parental and Family Influences on Hawthorne," *Essex Institute Historical Collections*, 76 (January 1940), 8.

45. Norman Holmes Pearson, "Elizabeth Peabody on Hawthorne," *Essex Institute Historical Collections*, 94 (July 1958), 268.

46. Hawthorne to Richard Henry Stoddard; quoted by Julian Hawthorne, *Nathaniel Hawthorne and His Wife*, I, 96.

47. Letter to James T. Fields, March 6, 1851; XVI, 400.

48. Fields, *Yesterdays with Authors*, p. 43.

49. Turner, *Nathaniel Hawthorne*, p. 11.

50. See, most notably, Frederick C. Crews, *The Sins of the Fathers: Hawthorne's Psychological Themes* (New York: Oxford University Press, 1966).

51. Nina Baym, "Nathaniel Hawthorne and His Mother: A Biographical Speculation," *American Literature*, 54 (March 1982), 11–12.

52. Gloria C. Erlich, *Family Themes and Hawthorne's Fiction: The Tenacious Web* (New Brunswick, N.J.: Rutgers University Press, 1984).

53. Manning Hawthorne, "Parental and Family Influences on Hawthorne," pp. 9, 12.

54. George Parsons Lathrop, *A Study of Hawthorne* (Boston: James R. Osgood, 1876), pp. 61–62.

55. Stewart, "Recollections of Hawthorne by His Sister Elizabeth," p. 321.

56. Lathrop, p. 64.

57. Young Hawthorne grew up in a colony of grieving widows. From her marriage in 1801 until the death of her husband at Surinam in 1808, Elizabeth Manning Hawthorne and her children lived with her husband's mother, Rachel Phelps Hathorne, who not only lost both her sons at sea (Daniel and Nathaniel) but also her son-in-law Captain George Archer (on a return passage from Hamburg, 1799) and another son-in-law, John Crowninshield (at age 25), from a disease likely contracted in a foreign port. The author's maternal grandmother, with whom the family lived thereafter, also mourned a son, John Manning, who unlike his landbound brothers had heard the call of the sea and disappeared at age fourteen or fifteen. The first Hawthorne to be claimed by the sea was the novelist's great-great uncle Captain Benjamin Hathorne, drowned with a crew of four in a great wind in 1732. Another Nathaniel Hathorne died on the schooner *Eliza* in the Havana harbor in 1801. There were other fortuitous escapes. See Loggins, *passim*.

58. Lathrop, p. 134.

59. Letter to Horatio Bridge, July 22, 1851; XVI, 462.

60. Fields, *Yesterdays with Authors*, p. 92. Among the fanciful concoctions Hawthorne recommended as a cure for Fields's seasickness were ingredients from *The Arabian Nights*: "a few roc's eggs beaten up by a mermaid on a dolphin's back" and "love-lorn nightingales cooked briskly over Aladdin's lamp." The *roc*, a legendary bird of great strength and size believed to inhabit the Indian Ocean area, plays an important part in "Sindbad the Sailor" as well as other Arabian and Persian legends.

61. Lathrop, p. 80; Elizabeth Manning, p. 504.

62. Horatio Bridge, *Personal Recollections of Nathaniel Hawthorne* (New York: Harper & Brothers, 1893), p. 41.

63. Letter to Henry W. Longfellow, January 12, 1839; XV, 287.

64. Letter to George P. Morris, January 11, 1839; XV, 285.

65. Letter to Sophia Peabody, March 26, 1840; XV, 428. Horatio Bridge claimed of Hawthorne's customs and consular posts, p. 159: "In all these places he for the time subordinated his finer and higher qualities to his matter-of-fact duties, and applied his common-sense to the prosaic tasks that those commercial offices imposed. In all of them he performed his obligations faithfully, and to the entire satisfaction of the Government." Looking back at his three years in the Salem Custom House, Hawthorne himself allowed, "There was no occasion to make much moan about this state of affairs. I had ceased to be a writer of tolerably poor tales and essays, and had become a tolerably good Surveyor of the Customs" (I, 38). He was succeeded in his maritime post by Captain Allen Putnam, an ex-shipmaster and president of the Salem East India Marine Society.

66. William H. Goetzmann, *New Lands, New Men: America and the Second Great Age of Discovery* (New York: Viking, 1986), pp. 274, 288.

67. Stewart, "Recollections of Hawthorne by His Sister Elizabeth," p. 326.

68. Bridge, p. 83.

69. Letter to Henry W. Longfellow, June 4, 1837; XV, 253.

70. See Hawthorne's entry for December 28, 1854, *The English Notebooks*, p. 98.

71. Stewart, "Recollections of Hawthorne by His Sister Elizabeth," p. 326.

72. Hawthorne to Richard Henry Stoddard; quoted by Julian Hawthorne, *Nathaniel Hawthorne and His Wife*, I, 97.

73. Robert Heron, "Preface by the Translator" in *Travels through Arabia, and Other Countries in the East, Performed by* M. *Niebuhr* (Edinburgh, 1792), I, vi–vii.

74. *The Memoirs of Julian Hawthorne*, ed. Edith Garrigues Hawthorne (New York: Macmillan, 1938), p. 6.

75. Robert Cantwell, *Nathaniel Hawthorne: The American Years* (New York: Rinehart, 1948), p. 139. James Duncan Phillips, *Pepper and Pirates: Adventures in the Sumatra Pepper Trade to Salem* (Boston: Houghton Mifflin, 1949), p. 43.

76. Turner, *Nathaniel Hawthorne*, p. 5.

77. Loggins, pp. 23, 54, 101, 109.

78. Loggins, pp. 153, 157–160.

79. Loggins, pp. 161, 182.

80. Hawthorne wrote: "This grandfather (about whom there is a ballad in Griswold's 'Curiosities of American Literature') died long before I was born." Julian Hawthorne, *Nathaniel Hawthorne and His Wife*, I, 95.

81. The complete ballad is printed in Loggins, pp. 176–179.

82. Hoeltje, p. 329.

83. Julian Hawthorne, *Nathaniel Hawthorne and His Wife*, I, 95.

84. The series ran in *Cosmopolitan* for July-November 1897.

85. *The Nathaniel Hawthorne Society Newsletter*, 11 (Fall 1985), 6; *The Biographic Register*, U.S. Department of State (July 1971), p. 175.

86. Hoeltje, p. 332.

87. Quoted in Julian Hawthorne, *Nathaniel Hawthorne and His Wife*, I, 95.

88. Cantwell, p. 139.

89. Manning Hawthorne, "Hawthorne's Early Years," *Essex Institute Historical Collections*, 74 (January 1938), 6–7. In refuting the pallid picture of Salem drawn in Henry James's *Hawthorne* (1879), the Rev. Dr. George Batchelor observed in 1887: "It seems incredible that [Hawthorne] should not have been drawn to the wharf, a few rods from his home, where came the richest cargoes, spices, gums, tea, coffee, ivory, silks, the fragrant spoils of the western islands and many foreign lands." See "The Salem of Hawthorne's Time," *Essex Institute Historical Collections*, 84 (January 1948), 68.

90. Loggins, p. 219.

91. *The Memoirs of Julian Hawthorne*, p. 6.

92. Phillips, *Pepper and Pirates*, pp. 2, 43, 111.

93. Batchelor, in "The Salem of Hawthorne's Time," p. 68.

94. "Yankee Traders and Indian Merchants, 1785-1865," an exhibition presented at the Peabody Museum, Salem, Massachusetts, in conjunction with the 1985 Festival of India in the United States. Unfortunately, no exhibition catalog was published.

95. Morison, pp. 84, 82.

96. Van Wyck Brooks, *The Dream of Arcadia: American Writers and Artists in Italy 1760-1915* (New York: E.P. Dutton, 1958), p. 30, note 2.

97. Morison, pp. 8–9, 292; James A. Field, Jr., *America and the Mediterranean World, 1776-1882* (Princeton, N.J.: Princeton University Press, 1969), pp. 114–115.

98. Morison, p. 92.

99. David H. Finnie, *Pioneers East: The Early American Experience in the Middle East* (Cambridge, Mass.: Harvard University Press, 1967), pp. 243–245. See also: Edward H. Berman, "Salem and Zanzibar: 1825-1850; Twenty-five Years of Commercial Relations," *Essex Institute Historical Collections*, 105 (October 1969), 338–362; and for the period 1875-1880, Norman R. Bennett, "William H. Hathorne: Merchant and Consul in Zanzibar," *Essex Institute Historical Collections*, 99 (April 1963), 117–146.

100. Morison, p. 84; Loggins, p. 211; Berman, p. 340.

101. Morison, p. 215.

102. Logbooks at the Essex Institute record the voyages of these and such like-named vessels as the *Calcutta, Canton, Ceylon, Indus, Koran, Levant, Loo Choo, Madagascar, Magi, Nabob, Rajah, Rasselus, Rupee, Saracen,* and *Siam.*

103. Manning Hawthorne, "Hawthorne's Early Years," pp. 1–2.

104. Batchelor, in "The Salem of Hawthorne's Time," p. 68.

105. *The Diary of William Bentley, D.E.* (Salem, Mass.: The Essex Institute, 1905), I, 228; Morison, p. 92.

106. Hermann Frederick Eilts, "Ahmad bin Na'aman's Mission to the United States in 1840, the Voyage of *Al-Sultanah* to New York City," *Essex Institute Historical Collections,* 98 (October 1962), 222.

107. Charles E. Goodspeed, *Nathaniel Hawthorne and the Marine Museum of the Salem East India Marine Society or the Gathering of a Virtuoso's Collection* (Boston: The Club of Odd Volumes, 1946).

108. Nina Fletcher Little, "Carved Figures by Samuel McIntire and His Contemporaries," *Essex Institute Historical Collections,* 93 (April-July 1957), 196.

109. The artifacts mentioned in this paragraph were displayed at the "Yankee Traders and Indian Merchants, 1785–1865" exhibition, Peabody Museum, 1985–1986.

110. James Duncan Phillips, "Salem in the Nineties," *Essex Institute Historical Collections,* 90 (January 1954), 37.

111. Quoted in the exhibition "Yankee Traders and Indian Merchants, 1785–1865."

112. Van Wyck Brooks, *New England: Indian Summer, 1865–1915* (New York: E.P. Dutton, 1940), p. 310.

113. Pearson, "Elizabeth Peabody on Hawthorne," p. 267. Julian Hawthorne, *Nathaniel Hawthorne and His Wife,* I, 4–5.

114. John T. Irwin, "The Symbol of the Hieroglyphics in the American Renaissance," *American Quarterly,* 26 (May 1974), 104.

115. See Hermann Frederick Eilts, "Sayyid Muhammed bin Aquil of Dhufar: Malevolent or Maligned?" *Essex Institute Historical Collections,* 109 (July 1973), 177–230. Hawthorne's interest in the Red Sea is suggested by an encounter in Boston he recorded late in the 1830s: "An old seaman, seventy years of age . . . has voyaged all over the world—for instance, I asked him if he had ever been in the Red Sea, and he had, in the American sloop of war that carried General Eaton, in 1803" (VIII, 194).

116. Field, p. 124.

117. Hubert J. Hoeltje, *Inward Sky: The Mind and Heart of Nathaniel Hawthorne* (Durham, N.C.: Duke University Press, 1962), pp. 57–59. All other citations of Hoeltje refer to his article "Captain Nathaniel Hathorne."

118. Review of *Constantinople and Its Environs,* in *Knickerbocker,* 6 (July 1835), 73.

119. Finnie, p. 94.

120. Field, p. 181.

121. *The English Notebooks,* pp. 107–108. On December 7, 1857, p. 610, Hawthorne commented on the relics brought to England by Layard, which were placed in the Assyrian Room of the British Museum. His joy upon beholding "the brilliancy of [several] oriental fragments of glass" after coming from the classical sculpture of the Townley Gallery typified an attitude that will be discussed in a later chapter. The iridescent fragments were, for his taste, "indescribably beautiful, and unimaginably, unless one can conceive of the colors of the rainbow, and a thousand glorious sunsets, and the autumnal forest-leaves of America, all condensed upon a little fragment of a glass cup." He concluded, "I think this chaste splendour will glow in my memory for years to come."

122. Dorothee Melitsky Finkelstein, *Melville's Orienda* (New Haven: Yale University Press, 1961), pp. 22–23. Finkelstein's chapter "The Near East on the American Scene, 1810–1850" is a fine introduction to the subject.

123. Irwin, p. 104.

124. Clay Lancaster, "Oriental Forms in American Architecture, 1800–1870," *The Art Bulletin*, 29 (September 1947), 183–193. Lancaster describes and illustrates three styles within the eclectic Orientalism: the Egyptian, the Mohammedan, and the Far Eastern.

125. George W. Curtis et al., *Homes of American Authors* (New York: G. P. Putnam, 1853), pp. 305–306.

126. *Hawthorne's Lost Notebook 1835–1841*, p. 26.

127. Field, p. 87. See Field's third and eighth chapters, "The Missionary Impulse" and "Leavening the Levant."

128. "Bowdoin College," *American Magazine of Useful and Entertaining Knowledge*, 3 (March 1837), 217.

129. Finnie, p. 3.

130. Fred Lewis Pattee, *The Development of the American Short Story* (New York: Harper & Brothers, 1923), p. 97.

131. Edwin Fussell, *Frontier: American Literature and the American West* (Princeton, N.J.: Princeton University Press, 1965), pp. 69–70.

132. "A Brief Summary of Japan-U.S. Cultural Relations (1837–1982)," a checklist distributed at "The 13th U.S.-Japan Conference on Cultural and Educational Interchange," Tokyo, July 1986.

2. Hawthorne's Reading

1. James R. Mellow, "Literary Archaeology: Attempting to Reconstruct Certain Days and Nights in the Lives of the Hawthornes and Their Concord Friends and Neighbors," *Essex Institute Historical Collections*, 118 (January 1982), 9. See also Mellow's *Nathaniel Hawthorne in His Times* (Boston: Houghton Mifflin, 1980).

2. Julian Hawthorne, *Nathaniel Hawthorne and His Wife* (Boston: James R. Osgood, 1884) I, 100. Julian Hawthorne, *Hawthorne Reading* (Cleveland: The Rowfant Club, 1902), p. 63.

3. Letter to Louisa Hawthorne, September 28, 1819; XV, 114. Letter to Elizabeth M. Hawthorne, October 31, 1820; XV, 132. Fragment to Elizabeth M. Hawthorne [?], ca. 1820–1821; XV, 134.

4. Julian Hawthorne, *Nathaniel Hawthorne and His Wife*, I, 96.

5. Letter to Henry W. Longfellow, June 4, 1837; XV, 251.

6. Letter to Sophia Peabody, October 4, 1840; XV, 494.

7. Julian Hawthorne, *Nathaniel Hawthorne and His Wife*, I, 97.

8. Arlin Turner, "Needs in Hawthorne Biography," *The Nathaniel Hawthorne Journal 1972*, ed. C. E. Frazer Clark, Jr. (Washington, D.C.: NCR/Microcard Editions, 1973), p. 43.

9. Letter to Henry W. Longfellow, June 4, 1837; XV, 252.

10. Randall Stewart, "Recollections of Hawthorne by His Sister Elizabeth," *American Literature*, 16 (January 1945), 324.

11. Marion L. Kesselring, *Hawthorne's Reading 1828–1850: A Transcription and Identification of Titles Recorded in the Charge-Books of the Salem Athenaeum* (New York: The New York Public Library, 1949).

12. Letter to Sophia Peabody, September 3, 1841; XV, 566. Letter to Sophia Hawthorne, December 2, 1844; XVI, 69.

13. R. Mead, "Preface" to Edmund Chishull, *Travels in Turkey and back to England* (London, 1747), p. iii.

14. Kesselring, pp. 12, 9.

15. Alfred Weber, *Die Entwicklung der Rahmenerzählungen Nathaniel Hawthornes "The Story Teller" und andere frühe Werke (1825–1835)* (Berlin: Erich Schmidt, 1973), p. 291, note 4. I have counted *Coryat's Crudities* as both a European and an Eastern

travel. The identification numbers cited by Weber include James Morier's fictional *Adventures of Hajji Baba, of Ispahan* and Camoes's *The Lusiad* but omit two other works cited in Appendix A of this study: Rycaut's *The History of the Turkish Empire* (Kesselring, #379) and Russell's *A Natural History of Aleppo* (Kesselring, #377).

16. Arlin Turner, *Hawthorne as Editor: Selections from His Writings in The American Magazine of Useful and Entertaining Knowledge* (University, La.: Louisiana State University Press, 1941), p. 9.

17. *American Magazine of Useful and Entertaining Knowledge*, 2 (August 1836), 520. Other references to the March-August 1836 issues of the magazine, which were paginated consecutively, will be located with page numbers in the text of this and the following chapters. The Boston Bewick Company was first organized as the American Engraving and Printing Company.

18. Letter to Elizabeth M. Hawthorne, January 25, 1836; XV, 230. Letter to Louisa Hawthorne, March 13, 1836; XV, 240. Letter to Elizabeth M. Hawthorne, March 15, 1836; XV, 241.

19. Stewart, "Recollections of Hawthorne by His Sister Elizabeth," p. 328.

20. Turner, *Hawthorne as Editor*, pp. 10, 12.

21. *Portico*, 1 (June 1816), 538; *American Quarterly Review*, 5 (June 1829), 343.

22. *Monthly Review*, n.s. 3 (October 1835), 239.

23. *American Magazine of Useful and Entertaining Knowledge* 2 (September 1835), 1.

24. Letter to Louisa Hawthorne, March 13, 1836; XV, 240.

25. Manning Hawthorne, "*Nathaniel & Elizabeth HAWTHORNE, Editors*," *The Colophon*, n.s. 3 (September 1939), [no page no.]; Turner, *Hawthorne as Editor*, p. 8.

26. Reynolds's entire account of the *Potomac* would have held Hawthorne's attention, for he wrote extensively on the role of Salem in opening the pepper trade with Sumatra, the hazards of commerce in the China Sea, and the trade routes followed by Massachusetts sea captains. A friend of Edgar Allan Poe as well as President Andrew Jackson, Reynolds was almost single-handedly responsible for generating the Great Exploring Expedition.

27. John Livingston Lowes, *The Road to Xanadu: A Study in the Ways of the Imagination* (Boston: Houghton Mifflin, 1927), p. 115.

28. Turner, *Hawthorne as Editor*, p. 10.

29. John Aldrich Christie, *Thoreau as World Traveler* (New York: Columbia University Press [with the American Geographical Society], 1965), pp. 4, 130–131.

30. Norman Holmes Pearson, introduction to *The French and Italian Notebooks. By Nathaniel Hawthorne* (Ph.D. dissertation, Yale University, 1941), I, ii–iii.

31. In characterizing and adding context for the works mentioned in this section, I have drawn on Edward Godfrey Cox's *A Reference Guide to the Literature of Travel*, "University of Washington Publications in Language and Literature," 2 vols. (Seattle: University of Washington, 1935–1938).

32. Percy G. Adams, *Travel Literature and the Evolution of the Novel* (Lexington: University Press of Kentucky, 1983), pp. 72–73.

33. Letters to Henry W. Longfellow, March 7 and June 4, 1837; XV, 249, 252–253.

34. In footnoting Hawthorne's reference to "sandal-shoon" in his letter to Longfellow, the editors of the Centenary Edition cite "*Hamlet*, IV, v, 26" (XV, 254, note 12). Although Hawthorne knew his Shakespeare through and through, he was obviously responding here, and later in *The Blithedale Romance*, not to Shakespeare but to Byron. Neither Ophelia's song nor the verses from *Childe Harold*, however, allude to the pilgrim's staff. Hawthorne also might have had in mind the pilgrimages of Thomas Coryat, who doted on the staff and the restless shoes that constantly ran ahead of his hands and head.

35. Edward Seymour Forster, "Introduction" to *The Turkish Letters of Ogier Ghiselin de Busbecq* (Oxford: At the Clarendon Press, 1927), pp. ix–x.

36. Cox, I, 204.

37. Sarah Searight, *The British in the Middle East*, 2d ed. (London: East-West Publications, 1970), pp. 68–69.

38. Cox, I, 227; Searight, p. 77.

39. *The Complete Letters of Mary Wortley Montagu*, ed. Robert Halsband (Oxford: At the Clarendon Press, 1965–1967), I, 363. For a handsome text and illustrations of an exhibition presented at the Metropolitan Museum of Art in 1973–1974, celebrating the fiftieth anniversary of the founding of the Republic of Turkey, see Alexandrine N. St. Clair, *The Image of the Turk in Europe* (New York: The Metropolitan Museum of Art, 1973); on Lady Montagu, pp. 18–19.

40. In the *English Notebooks* for July 4, 1855, p. 150, Hawthorne mentioned that the monument to Lady Montagu at the Lichfield cathedral was "erected by a lady in gratitude for having been benefitted by inoculation." Arlin Turner has suggested that Hawthorne might have found the name "Dr. Heidegger" (for his story "Dr. Heidegger's Experiment") "in Lady Mary Wortley Montagu's *Letters and Works* ... which he is known to have read." See Turner, "Hawthorne's Literary Borrowings," *PMLA*, 51 (June 1936), 560, note 131. It is also possible that one or more of four entries in the Salem Athenaeum's charge books for Hawthorne from 1827 to 1831 reading "Montague's Lett^{rs}" and "Mrs. Montagu's Letters" referred not to Elizabeth (Robinson) Montagu, as Kesselring assumed (p. 57), but to the *Letters* of Mary Wortley Montagu (or "Montague," as her name occasionally was spelled). According to its 1842 and 1858 catalogs the Athenaeum owned the letters of both women. The first of these four borrowings, for three weeks in February 1827, was simultaneous with Hawthorne's reading of Lockman's *Travels of the Jesuits* and immediately followed by Busbecq's *Travels into Turkey*.

41. Cox, I, 250; Searight, p. 79.

42. Cox, I, 255.

43. "James Justinian Morier," *Dictionary of National Biography*, Vol. 39 (London: Smith, Elder, 1894), p. 51.

44. Searight, p. 72.

45. Review of Richard Hole's *Remarks on the Arabian Nights' Entertainments* (London, 1797), in *Gentleman's Magazine*, 67 (December 1797), 1047.

46. According to Julian Hawthorne, *Hawthorne Reading*, p. 64, *The Arabian Nights* was among the early readings that "had survived" his father's frequent changes of residence to appear in the library of their Wayside home at Concord.

47. "Antar," *Encyclopedia American*, 1 (1829), 270.

48. Harriet Martineau, *Eastern Life, Present and Past* (Philadelphia: Lea and Blanchard, 1848), p. iv.

49. William Julius Mickle, "Introduction" to *The Lusiad: or, The Discovery of India* (London, 1798), p. cxlvii.

50. Sir William Jones, "A Discourse on the Institution of a Society for Inquiring into the History, Civil and Natural, the Antiquities, Arts, Sciences, and Literature, of ASIA," *Asiatic Researches*, Vol. 1 (London, 1801 [reprinted from the Calcutta Edition]), ix–x.

51. Hawthorne drew passages from *Adventures of a Younger Son* twice for the *American Magazine* and also referred to the work in *The French and Italian Notebooks* for August 12, 1858, when visiting the villa of Seymour Kirkup, who had two pictures of the adventurer, "one a slight sketch on the wall, the other a half-length portrait in a Turkish dress" (XIV, 395).

52. Quoted in "Koran," *Encyclopedia Americana*, 7 (1831), 348.

53. Ernest Bernardt-Kabisch, *Robert Southey* (Boston: Twayne, 1977), p. 19.

54. "Arabian Literature and Language," *Encyclopedia Americana*, 1 (1829), 317.

55. Samuel Terrien, "Job," *The Interpreter's Bible*, ed. George A. Buttrick, *et al.* (New York: Abingdon, 1951–1957), III, 886 *et passim*. It was a special pleasure, James T. Fields later remembered, "to hear [Hawthorne] talk about the Book of Job." Fields, *Yesterdays with Authors* (Boston: Houghton Mifflin, 1900), p. 94.

56. In *The French and Italian Notebooks* for June 2, 1858, Hawthorne mentioned "a well which Boccaccio has introduced into one of his stories, I forget which" (XIV, 269). See also Werner Peterich, "Hawthorne and the 'Gesta Romanorum': The Genesis of 'Rappaccini's Daughter' and 'Ethan Brand,' " in *Kleine Beiträge zur amerikanischen Literaturgeschichte*, ed. Hans Galinsky and Hans-Joachim Lang (Heidelberg: Carl Winter, 1961), pp. 11–18.

57. See especially Donald F. Lach's chapter "The Westward Migration of Story," in his *Asia in the Making of Europe*; Vol. 2, *A Century of Wonder*; Book 2, *The Literary Arts* (Chicago: University of Chicago Press, 1977), pp. 99–109; and H. A. R. Gibb's essay "Literature," in *The Legacy of Islam*, ed. Thomas Arnold and Alfred Guillaume (Oxford: At the Clarendon Press, 1931), pp. 180–209. Gibb wrote, p. 192: "The vogue of Arabic philosophical and scientific works [in the Middle Ages] brought with it an interest in other sides of Arabic literature, more especially in the apologues, fables, and tales, which constitute the bulk of Arabic belles-lettres. Already before this, however, oral transmission had broadcast elements of Arabic and other oriental story over a wide area."

58. Louis Wann, "The Oriental in Elizabethan Drama," *Modern Philology*, 12 (January 1915), 426, 447.

59. Gibb, pp. 180, 200.

60. Martha Pike Conant, *The Oriental Tale in England in the Eighteenth Century* (New York: Columbia University Press, 1908), pp. viii, xxvi, 84–85.

61. Donald Greene, *Samuel Johnson* (New York: Twayne, 1970), p. 28.

62. Julian Hawthorne, *Hawthorne Reading*, 65, 118; B. Bernard Cohen, "Hawthorne's Library," *The Nathaniel Hawthorne Journal 1971*, ed. C. E. Frazer Clark, Jr. (Washington, D.C.: NCR Microcard Editions, 1971), p. 126. In "Books of Memory," *The Bookman*, 61 (March 1925), 567, Julian remembered seeing "all the works of Voltaire, poor of paper and print and bound in paper" on the top shelves of the Wayside library.

63. See *The Letters of Henry Wadsworth Longfellow*, ed. Andrew Hilen (Cambridge, Mass.: Harvard University Press, 1966–1972), V, 417. Hawthorne counted on Sophia Peabody's familiarity with Goldsmith when he described for her "a little Mediterranean boy, from Malaga" who was "already a citizen of the world" (Letter of May 30, 1840; XV, 466).

64. Gibb, p. 201.

65. Searight, p. 253.

66. Notes to *The Giaour*, in *Lord Byron: The Complete Poetical Works*, ed. Jerome J. McGann (Oxford: At the Clarendon Press, 1980–1986), III, 423.

67. William Bysshe Stein believed *Vathek* to be the source for Chillingworth's burning heart and Dimmesdale's gesture of covering this enflamed organ with his right hand. See *Hawthorne's Faust: A Study of the Devil Archetype* (Gainesville: University of Florida Press, 1953), p. 37. Arlin Turner, "Hawthorne's Literary Borrowings," p. 556, associated Fanshawe's power to force Butler to retire "solely by the strength of his stare" with the like powers of Caliph Vathek and Melmoth the Wanderer.

68. Richard Harter Fogle claimed to have found "some hundreds of parallels" in Hawthorne's tales to Coleridge, Shelley, Keats, Byron, and Wordsworth. See "Nathaniel Hawthorne and the Great English Romantic Poets," *Keats-Shelley Journal*, 21–22 (1972–1973), 220; and also the first chapter, "Hawthorne, Literary History, and Criticism," in Fogle's *The Permanent Pleasure* (Athens: University of Georgia Press, 1974). Fogle did not enlarge his scope, however, to include Southey and Moore or the Romantics' Orientalism.

69. Besides the works of Richard Harter Fogle, see Janet Harris, "Reflections of the Byronic Hero in Hawthorne's Fiction," *Nathaniel Hawthorne Journal 1977*, ed. C. E. Frazer Clark, Jr. (Detroit: Gale Research, 1980), pp. 305–317; and Michael G. Cooke, "Hawthorne and Byron," *The Byron Journal*, No. 13 (1985), 22ff.

70. Quoted by Stuart Curran, *Poetic Form and British Romanticism* (New York: Oxford University Press, 1986), p. 135.

71. Letter to Sophia Peabody, June 20, 1842; XV, 631. Randall Stewart, *Nathaniel Hawthorne: A Biography* (New Haven: Yale University Press, 1948), p. 105. Hawthorne's signed copy of *The Poetical Works of Robert Southey, Collected by Himself* (New York: D. Appleton, 1839) is in the Bowdoin College Library.

72. "Preface" to *The Curse of Kehama*, Vol. 8 of *The Poetical Works of Robert Southey, Collected by Himself* (London: Longman, 1838), xiii–xiv. "Preface to the Fourth Edition," *Thalaba the Destroyer*, Vol. 4 of *The Poetical Works of Robert Southey, Collected by Himself* (London: Longman, 1838), xv.

73. Southey, "Preface" to *The Curse of Kehama*, p. xv.

74. Southey, "Preface to the Fourth Edition," *Thalaba the Destroyer*, p. xv.

75. "Robert Southey," *Dictionary of National Biography*, Vol. 53 (London: Smith, Elder, 1898), p. 286.

76. Curran, p. 135.

77. See, for example, references to *Childe Harold* in "Passages from a Relinquished Work" (X, 410) and in Hawthorne's letter to Sophia Peabody on April 6, 1840 (XV, 437–438). According to a Manning relative who visited the Herbert Street house around 1812–1813, Hawthorne was reading *Childe Harold* when he was only eight or nine years old. Manning Hawthorne, "A Glimpse of Hawthorne's Boyhood," *Essex Institute Historical Collections*, 83 (April 1947), 180.

78. "Advertisement" to *The Giaour*, p. 39.

79. *Lalla Rookh* sold at least 75,000 copies in the United States in its first decade. Frank Luther Mott, *Golden Multitudes* (New York: Macmillan, 1947), p. 305.

80. Jay B. Hubbell, *The South in American Literature, 1607–1900* (Durham, N.C.: Duke University Press, 1954), p. 627.

81. Stephen Gwynn, *Thomas Moore*, "English Men of Letters" (New York: Macmillan, 1905), p. 58.

82. *The Corsair*, in *Lord Byron: The Complete Poetical Works*, III, 148–149. Marie E. de Meester, *Oriental Influences in the English Literature of the Nineteenth Century*, Heft 46 of *Anglistische Forschungen* (Heidelberg: Carl Winter, 1915), p. 31.

83. *Lalla Rookh*, in *The Poetical Works of Thomas Moore*, ed. A. D. Godley (London: Henry Frowde, 1910), p. 342.

84. Julian Hawthorne, *Hawthorne Reading*, p. 118; Stewart, *Nathaniel Hawthorne*, p. 105; Julian Hawthorne, "Books of Memory," p. 567.

85. Letter to James T. Fields, August 18, 1851; XVI, 475.

86. Thomas De Quincey, *Confessions of an English Opium-Eater*, in *The Collected Writings of Thomas De Quincey*, ed. David Masson (Edinburgh: Adam and Charles Black, 1890), III, 441–442.

87. For example, Shelley's *Prometheus Unbound*, "Ozymandias," and "From the Arabic, an Imitation" (an adaptation from *Antar*); Tennyson's "The Expedition of Nadir Shah into Hindostan," "Persia," "Egypt," and "Written by an Exile of Bassorah, while sailing down the Euphrates." Although Hawthorne read little German, he probably had some acquaintance also with the Orientalism of Schlegel, Rueckert, Goethe, Lessing, and the other German Romantics, as well as with Victor Hugo's *Les Orientales* (1829). See Gibb, pp. 204–205.

88. *The Leader*, 7 (January 5, 1856), 15.

89. Mukhtar Ali Isani, "The Oriental Tale in America through 1865" (Ph.D. dissertation, Princeton University, 1962), pp. 2–4.

90. Hugh Henry Brackenridge and Philip Freneau, *Father Bombo's Pilgrimage to Mecca, 1770*, ed. and intro. Michael Davitt Bell (Princeton University Library, 1975), p. 51.

91. Isani, pp. 23–25.

92. B. Bernard Cohen, "Hawthorne's Library," p. 135, note 8.

93. William L. Hedges, *Washington Irving: An American Study, 1802–1832* (Baltimore: The Johns Hopkins Press, 1965), p. 26; Isani, p. 139.

94. *Letters of Jonathan Oldstyle, Gent.* [and] *Salmagundi; or The Whim-Whams and Opinions of Launcelot Langstaff, Esq. & Others*, ed. Bruce I. Granger and Martha

Hartzog, Vol. 6 of *The Complete Works of Washington Irving* (Boston: Twayne, 1977), pp. 91–92.

95. Mott, p. 305.

96. L. Moffitt Cecil, "Poe's 'Arabesque'," *Comparative Literature*, 18 (Winter 1966), 58. See also Patricia Clark Smith, "Novel Conceptions, Unusual Combinations: The Arabesque in Poe" (Ph.D. dissertation, Yale University, 1970).

97. See Barton L. St. Armand, "The 'Mysteries' of Edgar Poe: The Quest for a Monomyth in Gothic Literature," in *The Gothic Imagination: Essays in Dark Romanticism*, ed. G. R. Thompson (Pullman: Washington State University Press, 1974), p. 69.

98. Dorothee Melitsky Finkelstein, *Melville's Orienda* (New Haven: Yale University Press, 1961), pp. 26–27.

99. Isani, p. 57.

100. Van Wyck Brooks, *The World of Washington Irving* (New York: E. P. Dutton, 1944), p. 474. For an account of Melville's own travels to Turkey and beyond, see his *Journal of a Visit to Europe and the Levant, October 11, 1856–May 6, 1857*, ed. Howard C. Horsford (Princeton, N.J.: Princeton University Press, 1955).

101. Gordon Milne, *George William Curtis & the Genteel Tradition* (Bloomington: Indiana University Press, 1956), pp. 51, 57.

102. Stewart, *Nathaniel Hawthorne*, p. 105.

103. William Dean Howells, quoted by Milne, p. 51.

104. George William Curtis, *Nile Notes of a Howadji* (New York: Harper & Brothers, 1851), pp. 129–130, 137.

105. Bayard Taylor, *The Lands of the Saracen; or Pictures of Palestine, Asia Minor, Sicily, and Spain* (New York: G. P. Putnam, 1855), [no page no.].

106. Carl Bode, *The Anatomy of American Popular Culture, 1840–1861* (Berkeley: University of California Press, 1959), pp. 230–231, 235.

107. George W. Curtis, quoted by John Tomsich, *A Genteel Endeavor: American Culture and Politics in the Gilded Age* (Stanford, Calif.: Stanford University Press, 1971), p. 39.

108. See Randall Stewart, "Hawthorne's Contributions to *The Salem Advertiser*," *American Literature*, 5 (January 1934), 327–333; and Stewart, "Two Uncollected Reviews by Hawthorne," *New England Quarterly*, 9 (September 1936), 504–506.

109. John M. Steadman, *The Myth of Asia* (New York: Simon and Schuster, 1969), p. 183.

110. Samuel C. Chew, *The Crescent and the Rose: Islam and England during the Renaissance* (New York: Oxford University Press, 1937), p. 3.

111. Ogier Ghislain de Busbecq, *The Four Epistles of A. G. Busbequius, Containing his Embassy into Turkey* (London, 1694), p. 10.

112. *Three Weeks in Palestine and Lebanon* (New York: Protestant Episcopal Sunday School Union, [1833]), pp. 19–20.

113. Quoted in Robert A. Colby, *Thackeray's Canvass of Humanity: An Author and His Public* (Columbus: Ohio State University Press, 1979), pp. 43–44. Hawthorne makes numerous references to Thackeray and his works in the *English Notebooks*.

114. See Franklin Walker, *Irreverent Pilgrims: Melville, Browne, and Mark Twain in the Holy Land* (Seattle: University of Washington Press, 1974).

115. *Three Weeks in Palestine and Lebanon*, p. 142.

116. Joseph Pitton de Tournefort, *A Voyage into the Levant* (London, 1741), I, 19. Carsten Niebuhr, *Travels through Arabia, and Other Countries in the East* (Edinburgh, 1792), II, 194. *Memoirs of the Baron de Tott, on the Turks and the Tartars* (London, 1785), I, vii. Montagu, I, 415.

117. Alexander Russell, *The Natural History of Aleppo, Containing a Description of the City* (London, 1794), I, 145.

118. Niebuhr, II, 264–265.

119. Richard Madden, *Travels in Turkey, Egypt, Nubia and Palestine* (London: Henry Colburn, 1829), I, 345, 350–351.

120. Tournefort, III, 235. *The Travels of Sir John Chardin into Persia and the East Indies* (London, 1686), p. 85. *The World Surveyed; or, The Famous Voyages & Travailes of Vincent Le Blanc* (London, 1660), p. 139.

121. Russell, I, 245.

122. Tournefort, II, 247, 321–322.

123. Madden, I, 43–44.

124. *Three Weeks in Palestine and Lebanon*, p. 13.

125. Madden, I, 2, 6.

126. Tournefort, II, 199.

127. Chardin, p. 115.

128. Montagu, I, 385.

129. Niebuhr, II, 1–2, 396–397; italics added.

3. Providence, Destiny, and Choice of Life in the Early Tales

1. A clear facsimile of the poem, which is dated Salem, February 13, 1817, is found in Elizabeth Manning, "The Boyhood of Hawthorne," *Wide Awake*, November, 1891, p. 505. The texts of this and similar meditations—e.g. "Earthly Pomp" (1819) and "The Darken'd Veil" (1820)—appear in *Nathaniel Hawthorne: Poems*, ed. Richard E. Peck (The Bibliographical Society of the University of Virginia, 1967).

2. Manning Hawthorne, "Hawthorne's Early Years," *Essex Institute Historical Collections*, 74 (January 1938), 15–16.

3. *Hawthorne's Lost Notebook*, p. 40 (1837).

4. Randall Stewart, "Recollections of Hawthorne by His Sister Elizabeth," *American Literature*, 16 (January 1945), 327.

5. Thomas Woodson, "A New Installment of Hawthorne's *Spectator*," *Nathaniel Hawthorne Review*, 12 (Fall 1986), 1–2.

6. Arlin Turner stated the still prevailing view in "Hawthorne's Literary Borrowings," *PMLA*, 51 (June 1936), 553: "Hawthorne's literary indebtednesses are . . . chiefly to English writers. It was to Spenser, Shakespeare, Milton, Bunyan, Scott, and the Gothic romancers that he owed most of all, though he took definite hints from certain lesser writers."

7. Martha Pike Conant, *The Oriental Tale in England in the Eighteenth Century* (New York: Columbia University Press, 1908), p. xxv.

8. Edward Wagenknecht, *Nathaniel Hawthorne: Man and Writer* (New York: Oxford University Press, 1961), p. 33.

9. Conant, p. xv.

10. Robert Southey, *Thalaba the Destroyer*, Vol. 4 of *The Poetical Works of Robert Southey* (London: Longman, 1838), p. 407.

11. *The Complete Writings of Nathaniel Hawthorne*, Autograph Edition (Boston: Houghton Mifflin, 1900), XVI, ix.

12. Turner, "Hawthorne's Literary Borrowings," p. 556; Conant, p. 68.

13. Compare Ellen and Fanshawe's exchange on the dumb felicity of animal existence, and the anxiety of human consciousness, with Chapter Two of *Rasselas*, "The Discontent of Rasselas in the Happy Valley": "What," asked Rasselas, "makes the difference between man and all the rest of the animal creation?" "Ye," he said to the animals around him, "are happy, and need not envy me that walk thus among you, burthened with myself; nor do I, ye gentle beings, envy your felicity; for it is not the felicity of man." Samuel Johnson, *The History of Rasselas, Prince of Abissinia*, ed. Geoffrey Tillotson and Brian Jenkins (London: Oxford University Press, 1971), p. 6. Hereafter noted simply as *Rasselas*.

14. Hyatt H. Waggoner, *Hawthorne: A Critical Study* (Cambridge, Mass.: Harvard University Press, 1963), p. 189; B. Bernard Cohen, "Hawthorne's Library," *The Na-*

thaniel Hawthorne Journal 1971, ed. C. E. Frazer Clark, Jr. (Washington, D.C.: NCR Microcard Editions, 1971), p. 132. The moral and artistic kinship of Johnson and Hawthorne has received some limited attention. See, for example, Marvin Fisher, "The Pattern of Conservatism in Johnson's *Rasselas* and Hawthorne's *Tales*," *Journal of the History of Ideas*, 19 (April 1958), 173–196; and Robert Eugene Gross, "Hawthorne's First Novel: The Future of a Style," *PMLA*, 78 (March 1963), 60–68. Gross establishes *Fanshawe*'s stylistic indebtedness to *Rasselas* and links the abrupt chapter transitions of the novel, which usually are attributed to the influence of Scott, to "arbitrary plotting in *Rasselas*, with its tenuously connected occasions for wisdom" (p. 63). He does not however, move beyond style to the important matters of setting, characterization, and theme that also join the two works.

15. Arlin Turner, *Nathaniel Hawthorne* (New York: Oxford University Press, 1980), p. 42.

16. *Rasselas*, p. 3.

17. Hiob Ludolf, *A New History of Ethiopia* (London, 1682), pp. 7–8. Ludolf gave the accepted judgment that "the *Abassenes* formerly inhabited *Arabia*" and noted that *Ethiopian* continued to refer to peoples on both sides of the Red Sea.

18. Sometime in 1836, Hawthorne recorded this note: "The Abyssinians, after dressing their hair, sleep with their heads in a forked stick, in order not to discompose it." *Hawthorne's Lost Notebook*, p. 25.

19. *The Famous Voyages & Travailes of Vincent Le Blanc*, pp. 214, 238. Compare John Milton, *Paradise Lost*, IV, 280–284:

> Nor, where Abassin kings their issue guard,
> Mount Amara (though this by some supposed
> True Paradise) under the Ethiop line
> By Nilus' head, enclosed with shining rock,
> A whole day's journey high. . . .

Amara also appears as *Mount Abora* in Coleridge's "Kubla Khan."

20. Roy Harvey Pearce, "Introduction to *Fanshawe*" (III, 305).

21. Manning Hawthorne, "Nathaniel Hawthorne at Bowdoin," *New England Quarterly*, 13 (June 1940), 275.

22. Manning Hawthorne, "Nathaniel Hawthorne at Bowdoin," p. 246.

23. John R. Byers, Jr., and James J. Owen, *A Concordance to the Five Novels of Nathaniel Hawthorne* (New York: Garland, 1979), II, 823.

24. Horatio Bridge, *Personal Recollections of Nathaniel Hawthorne* (New York: Harper & Brothers, 1893), p. 10; *Rasselas*, p. 55.

25. The setting and topography of Hawthorne's earlier tale "The Hollow of the Three Hills" particularly reminded Ely Stock of the depiction of grottos in Henry Maundrell's *A Journey from Aleppo to Jerusalem*. Stock, "Witchcraft in 'The Hollow of the Three Hills,' " *American Transcendental Quarterly*, No. 14, Part 1 (Spring 1972), 31–33.

26. *Rasselas*, p. 2.

27. *Rasselas*, p. 4.

28. Italics added. Hawthorne might have encountered the name *Fanshawe* in his Oriental readings. *The Arabian Nights' Entertainments*, published in four volumes by David Huntington in New York in 1815, carried the imprint "Fanshaw & Clayton, Printers," and Voltaire based his harsh criticism of Camoes' *Lusiad* on "the unfaithful and unpoetical version of Sir Richard Fanshawe," which was published in 1655.

29. *Rasselas*, p. 10.

30. *Rasselas*, p. 37.

31. *Rasselas*, p. 20, 33. Hawthorne named his absent-minded college president after the protagonist of Robert Charles Maturin's Gothic novel *Melmoth the Wanderer*

(1820). Although no rival to *Vathek* in the genre, *Melmoth* is also laced with Orientalism. The four-volume work draws frequent references and quotations from *Thalaba the Destroyer*, besides Coryat's *Crudities*, Pliny's *Natural History*, and Bruce's *Travels to Discover the Source of the Nile*. Much of the third volume is set in India.

32. *Rasselas*, p. 79.

33. Robert H. Hopkins, *The True Genius of Oliver Goldsmith* (Baltimore: The Johns Hopkins Press, 1969), p. 94.

34. Compare also the landscape of Goldsmith's *valley of ignorance* to the setting of *Fanshawe*. Goldsmith's tutor offered to conduct his young adventurer "to that land of happiness thro' those intervening regions you see hung over with fogs and darkness, and horrid with forest, cataracts, caverns, and various other shapes of danger." As they proceeded, "the skies became more gloomy and the way more intricate and they often inadvertently approached the brow of some frightful precipice, or the brink of a torrent." "Letter 37" of *The Citizen of the World*, in *Collected Works of Oliver Goldsmith*, ed. Arthur Friedman (Oxford: Clarendon Press, 1966), II, 156–159.

35. *Rasselas*, p. 79.

36. *Rasselas*, p. 7.

37. Bridge, p. 23.

38. *Rasselas*, p. 115. Imlac's discourse on "The Dangerous Prevalence of Imagination" is especially apropos to Hawthorne's "haunted chamber" in Salem during the latter 1820s and early 1830s when he "only seemed to live." Nina Baym noticed that Hawthorne's writings after 1830 "show one attempt after another to write more rational and conservative fiction" and suggested that his wariness of "the dangerous power of the imagination" might be traced to Charles W. Upham's lectures on Salem witchcraft. Baym, *The Shape of Hawthorne's Career* (Ithaca, N.Y.: Cornell University Press, 1976), pp. 38–40. Whatever the effect of Upham's lectures, Hawthorne had learned the lessons of Dr. Johnson, "the great conservative," at least a decade earlier.

39. John M. Aden, " 'Rasselas' and 'The Vanity of Human Wishes,' " *Criticism*, 3 (Fall 1961), 299, 302; William Kenney, "*Rasselas* and the Theme of Diversification," *Philological Quarterly*, 38 (January 1959), 84–85.

40. *Rasselas*, pp. 122–123.

41. *Rasselas*, p. 69.

42. Barbara Snow Hartman, "*Fanshawe* and Hawthorne's Strategy to 'Open an Intercourse with the World,' " *Nathaniel Hawthorne Review*, 12 (Fall 1986), 19.

43. Michael J. Colacurcio, *The Province of Piety: Moral History in Hawthorne's Tales* (Cambridge, Mass.: Harvard University Press, 1984), p. 106.

44. Colacurcio, p. 100.

45. Marion L. Kesselring, *Hawthorne's Reading 1828–1850* (New York: The New York Public Library, 1949), p. 63.

46. A. Owen Aldridge, *Voltaire and the Century of Light* (Princeton, N.J.: Princeton University Press, 1975), p. 88.

47. Lea B. V. Newman, *A Reader's Guide to the Short Stories of Nathaniel Hawthorne* (Boston: G. K. Hall, 1979), p. 328. Colacurcio, pp. 100–101, found it "not unthinkabable" that "The Wives of the Dead" was written for *Seven Tales of My Native Land*.

48. Baym, p. 30.

49. Julian Hawthorne, *Nathaniel Hawthorne and His Wife* (Boston: James R. Osgood, 1884), I, 131–132. The biographical origins of "The Wives of the Dead" are apparent from its outset, "a hundred years ago, in a principal seaport of the Bay Province" (XI, 192). A century before Nathaniel Hawthorne's generation the family had turned decisively from the land to the sea and begun to suffer the chances and casualties of ocean life. The deaths of Daniel and Nathaniel Hathorne in 1804 and 1808, and the forms of widowhood the writer saw in the Hawthorne household, surely had some role in inspiring this paradigmatic tale.

50. Aldridge, pp. 155–156.

51. *Zadig, and Other Tales by Voltaire* trans. Robert B. Boswell (London: George Bell and Sons, 1901), pp. 49–50. Hawthorne read Voltaire in the original French, but all quotations here are from the Robert Boswell translation.

52. *Zadig*, pp. 53–57.

53. *Zadig*, p. 131.

54. *Zadig*, p. 138.

55. *Zadig*, p. 143.

56. Aldridge, p. 159. According to Norman L. Torrey, "Voltaire's belief that design and purpose are manifest in nature was the basis of his religion. A consistent and finally a militant theist (he himself used that term in preference to 'deist,' as he has often been called), he can readily be shown to have accepted at least three of the Thomistic proofs of the existence of God as First Cause, Prime Mover, and the Supreme Intelligence." Furthermore, Voltaire believed God had "endow[ed] man with reason and feelings of benevolence, which, if properly directed, were all that was needed for man to gain happiness in life. Voltaire's 'general providence' would be described today as a benevolent universe." See Torrey's essay "François-Maret Arouet de Voltaire," *The Encyclopedia of Philosophy*, Vol. 8 (New York: Macmillan, 1967), pp. 264–265.

57. *Zadig*, p. 138. According to Ronald M. Green, theodicies are "specific explanations or justifications of suffering in a world believed to be ruled by a morally good God." Green, "Theodicy," *The Encylopedia of Religion*, ed. Mircea Eliade (New York: Macmillan, 1987), XIV, 431. Given Voltaire's extensive engagement with the Theodicy Problem, and the impact of his thought on the American Renaissance, it is remarkable that Voltaire is mentioned not at all in Richard Forrer's *Theodicies in Conflict: A Dilemma in Puritan Ethics and Nineteenth-Century American Literature* (New York: Greenwood Press, 1986).

58. Aldridge, p. 156.

59. *Zadig*, p. 93.

60. Compare Job 2:10: "But he said unto her, Thou speakest as one of the foolish women speaketh. What? shall we receive good at the hand of God, and shall we not receive evil? In all this did not Job sin with his lips." Despite her immoderate perturbations, however, Margaret is treated much more sympathetically than Voltaire's silly Semina. The narrator of "The Wives of the Dead" continues: "Yet she trembled at these rebellious expressions, almost as soon as they were uttered, and, by degrees, Mary succeeded in bringing her sister's mind nearer to the situation of her own" (XI, 193).

61. When word of the safety of her husband came to Margaret, the reporter's lantern brought into view "indistinct shapes of things, and the fragments of a world, like order glimmering through chaos" (XI, 196). In projecting this recoalescence of Margaret's spirit, Hawthorne might have had in mind Zadig's confrontation with followers of the world religions in a chapter called "The Supper," and in particular the protest of a Greek merchant: "Is it possible that you do not know that Chaos is the father of all things, and that form and matter have brought the world into the state in which it is?" (*Zadig*, p. 97) Zadig leads the Greek to admit that form and matter depend on the existence of a Supreme Being.

62. Southey, *Thalaba the Destroyer*, pp. 4–5

63. Southey, *Thalaba the Destroyer*, p. 28; italics added.

64. George Sale, "The Preliminary Discourse," *The Koran, Commonly called The Alcoran of Mohammed* (London, 1734), p. 63. Compare the following remark on the Muslims in Bernard Picart's *The Ceremonies and Religious Customs of the Various Nations* (one-volume abridged edition; London, 1741), p. 525: "When they make their Addresses to the Throne of Grace for any particular mercies, their Prayers must be offered up with an entire Resignation to the Divine Will, and they are directed to say, *My God, I beseech thee not to grant those Blessings which I ask, if they are not for my real Advantage.*" See also Edward Lane's disquisition "On Fate and Destiny" in *The Thousand and One Nights* (London: Charles Knight, 1839), I, 58, note 5.

65. Newman, p. 330.

66. Park Benjamin; quoted by Lillian B. Gilkes, "Hawthorne, Park Benjamin, and S. G. Goodrich: A Three-Cornered Imbroglio," *Nathaniel Hawthorne Journal 1971*, ed. C. E. Frazer Clark, Jr. (Washington, D.C.: Microcard Editions, 1971), p. 108.

67. Thomas J. Assad, "Sir Richard Francis Burton," *Encyclopedia Americana* (1983), V, 30.

68. Newman, p. 132; Henry Wadsworth Longfellow, Review of *Twice-told Tales* in *North American Review*, 54 (April 1842), 498.

69. Julian Hawthorne, *Nathaniel Hawthorne and His Wife*, I, 132–133.

70. Nathaniel Hawthorne, "Preface" to *The Gentle Boy: A Thrice Told Tale* (Boston: Weeks, Jordan, 1839), [p. 4].

71. Seymour L. Gross, "Hawthorne's Revisions of 'The Gentle Boy,' " *American Literature*, 26 (May 1954), 208.

72. Colacurcio, pp. 194, 170–172, 177.

73. Colacurcio, p. 166.

74. George Edward Woodberry, *Nathaniel Hawthorne* (Boston: Houghton Mifflin, 1902) p. 134.

75. Colacurcio, p. 515, note 15.

76. Kesselring, pp. 25, 58. The *National Union Catalog* lists the English language translation as: *The Religious Ceremonies and Customs of the Several Nations of the Known World. Represented in Above an Hundred Copperplates Designed by the Famous Picart. Together with historical explanations, and several curious Dissertations,* 7 Vols. in 6 (London, 1731–1739). Volume 5, which Hawthorne did not borrow from the Salem Athenaeum, concerns "Ceremonies of the Greeks and Protestants."

77. Colacurcio, p. 575, note 13.

78. Willem Sewel, *The History of the Rise, Increase, and Progress, of the Christian People Called Quakers*, 3rd ed. (Burlington, N.J.: Isaac Collins, 1774), p. 294. Kesselring, p. 61. See also G. Harrison Orians, "The Sources and Themes of Hawthorne's 'The Gentle Boy,' " *New England Quarterly*, 14 (December 1941), 672.

79. Kesselring, p. 60. Kesselring provided only the short title of Rycaut's history; later scholars have looked no farther.

80. Paul Rycaut, *The History of the Turkish Empire from the Year 1623 to the Year 1677* (London, 1679–1680), p. 36.

81. Kesselring, p. 61.

82. Rycaut, p. 14.

83. Ogier Ghislain de Busbecq, *The Four Epistles of A. G. Busbequius, Containing his Embassy into Turkey* (London, 1694), p. 288.

84. For a fine presentation of analogies that were made between Eastern religions, particularly Islam, and liberal Christianity in the United States prior to 1830, and the use of visionary and Oriental tales by American writers to subvert Calvinist orthodoxy, see Chapter 1, "The Oriental Connection," of David S. Reynolds, *Faith in Fiction: The Emergence of Religious Literature in America* (Cambridge, Mass.: Harvard University Press, 1981), pp. 13–37.

85. Sale, p. 33.

86. Rycaut, p. 8.

87. Kesselring, p. 56; Clarence D. Rouillard, *The Turk in French History, Thought, and Literature (1520–1660)* (Paris: Boivin & Cie, [1941]), pp. 369–376. Hawthorne's library at the Wayside also contained "Montaigne, in a large quarto." See Julian Hawthorne, "Books of Memory," *The Bookman*, 61 (March 1925) p. 567.

88. Lane, I, 27, note 13.

89. Sale, p. 29.

90. Busbecq, p. 28.

91. Voltaire, *A Treatise Upon Religious Toleration*, trans. T. Smollett (Dublin, 1764), pp. 49–50, 268.

92. In *Le Fanatisme, ou Mahomet le prophète* Voltaire borrowed from Catholic tradition to depict the founder of Islam as a manipulative fanatic, but even there he

added his personal touch in crediting Mohammed with a grandeur of spirit. Voltaire's *Les Guèbres, ou La Tolérance* (1768) was another allegory with contemporary applications about the "innocent victims of religious persecution." Aldridge, pp. 125–126, 348.

93. Sale, p. 39.

94. Picart, p. 523.

95. Aldridge, p. 126. See also Djavâd Hadidi, *Voltaire et l'Islam* (Paris: Association Langues et Civilisations, 1974), pp. 180, 194.

96. Torrey, p. 266.

97. Torrey, p. 266.

98. Roy R. Male, *Hawthorne's Tragic Vision* (New York: W. W. Norton, 1957), p. 45.

99. Busbecq, p. 94.

100. *The Token*, ed. S. G. Goodrich (Boston: Gray and Bowen, 1832 [1831]), p. 240.

101. Torrey, p. 267. As a further indication of Hawthorne's ameliorative view, see his brief essay in the *American Magazine of Useful and Entertaining Knowledge* for April 1836, p. 338, on Archbishop Laud, who is mentioned in "The Gentle Boy" as a model of religious tyranny. Albeit in a defensive and bantering tone, Hawthorne dared to suggest that Laud was "perhaps the greatest benefactor that ever New England had."

102. Edwin Fussell, *Frontier: American Literature and the American West* (Princeton, N.J.: Princeton University Press, 1965), p. 122.

103. For another description of the *Khanes*, "or as they are sometimes called, caravansaries," see Alexander Russell, *The Natural History of Aleppo* (London, 1794), I, 18. Russell's discussion of Turkish toleration, hospitality, and "resignation under misfortune" further substantiated the cultural bases of the Eastern ethics Hawthorne espoused in "The Wives of the Dead" and "The Gentle Boy."

4. The Story Teller

1. Randall Stewart, "Recollections of Hawthorne by His Sister Elizabeth," *American Literature*, 16 (January 1945), 323; Nelson F.Adkins, "The Early Projected Works of Hawthorne," *Papers of the Bibliographical Society of America*, 39 (II Quarter 1945), 121–122, 127.

2. George Parsons Lathrop, *A Study of Hawthorne* (Boston: James R. Osgood, 1876), pp. 173–174.

3. Michael J. Colacurcio, *The Province of Piety* (Cambridge, Mass.: Harvard University Press, 1984), p. 496.

4. The snarled publication history of *The Story Teller* is still being untangled. What is known can be traced best through Adkins, pp. 132–133; the "Historical Commentary" of the Centenary Edition of *Twice-told Tales*, IX, 492–496; Lillian B. Gilkes, "Hawthorne, Park Benjamin, and S. G. Goodrich: A Three-Cornered Imbroglio," *The Nathaniel Hawthorne Journal 1971*, ed. C. E. Frazer Clark, Jr. (Washington, D.C.: NCR Microcards Editions, 1971), p. 83–112; and David W. Pancost, "Evidence of Editorial Additions to Hawthorne's 'Fragments from the Journal of a Solitary Man,'" *The Nathaniel Hawthorne Journal 1975*, ed. C. E. Frazer Clark, Jr. (Englewood, Colo.: Microcard Editions, 1975), pp. 210–226.

5. Letter to Elizabeth Peabody, August 13, 1857; XVIII, 89. Moncure D. Conway, *Life of Nathaniel Hawthorne* (London: Walter Scott, 1890), p. 32.

6. Letter to William D. Ticknor, June 7, 1854; XVII, 225, 227.

7. Alfred Weber, who has made the most thoroughgoing reconstruction of *The Story Teller* to date (based largely on itinerary), identifies thirty-six items as certain, probable, or possible components. Weber, *Die Entwicklung der Rahmenerzählungen*

Nathaniel Hawthornes "The Story Teller" und andere frühe Werke (Berlin: Erich Schmidt, 1973), 360–362. The editors of the Centenary Edition are equally embracive, offering a half dozen titles not admitted by Weber but withholding a like number (IX, 494–496). Nina Baym, who conceives the narrative primarily in relation to the narrator-protagonist's psychological evolution, most conservatively does "not accept in *The Story Teller* any material published in other magazines than the *New England/American Monthly Magazine*, or even published there after 1836." Baym, *The Shape of Hawthorne's Career* (Ithaca, N.Y.: Cornell University Press, 1976), p. 40.

8. See the historical collation in the Centenary Edition, IX, 631.

9. Julian Hawthorne, *Nathaniel Hawthorne and His Wife* (Boston: James R. Osgood, 1884), I, 97.

10. Letter to Louisa Hawthorne, August 17, 1831; XV, 211–215. Letter to J. S. Dike, September 9, 1831; XV, 216–219. Weber, p. 132.

11. Letter to Franklin Pierce, June 28, 1832; XV, 224. Hawthorne's eagerness to visit Canada in June 1832 and its consequence for the book he planned have perplexed some readers. Exploring the actual historic and scenic landscape of Canada might have been less important to him than the symbolic act of crossing the national boundaries of the United States and laying claim, in however limited a degree, to the title of international traveler.

12. Letter to Elizabeth C. Hawthorne, September 16, 1832; XV, 226.

13. "Mr. Higginbotham's Catastrophe" was later republished separately in *Twice-told Tales* (1837); the other elements, as "Passages from a Relinquished Work" in *Mosses from an Old Manse* (1854).

14. Letter to Elizabeth C. Hawthorne, March 13, 1821; XV, 138–139.

15. Horace Lorenzo Conolly, recalling many years later a conversation at Yale University in October 1828; quoted in Manning Hawthorne, "Hawthorne and 'The Man of God,' " *The Colophon*, n.s. 2 (Winter 1937), 265.

16. Barbara Hardy, *Tellers and Listeners: The Narrative Imagination* (London: Athlone Press, 1975), pp. [165], xii, 172.

17. Alexander Russell, *The Natural History of Aleppo* (London, 1794), I, 148–150.

18. Particularly striking is the use of the term *catastrophe* both by Russell and by Hawthorne, in three consecutive settings. Here and elsewhere Hawthorne gives the term the technical meaning assigned by Samuel Johnson: "The change or revolution which produces the conclusion or final event of a dramatic piece"—the denouement.

19. Adkins, p. 145; "Historical Commentary," Centenary Edition of *Twice-told Tales*, IX, 492.

20. "Introductory Note" to Henry Wadsworth Longfellow, *Outre-Mer and Drift-Wood* (Boston: Houghton Mifflin, 1904), p. 5. After returning to his native village, Longfellow's School Master, like Hawthorne's Story Teller, continues to travel by memory.

21. Washington Irving, *The Sketch Book of Geoffrey Crayon, Gent.*, ed. Haskell Springer, Vol. 8 of *The Complete Works of Washington Irving* (Boston: Twayne, 1978), p. 8.

22. See also the ironic reminiscences of "P.'s Correspondence" (1845): "I remember, too, a lad just from college, Longfellow by name, who scattered some delicate verses to the winds, and went to Germany and perished, I think, of intense application, at the University of Gottingen. Willis—what a pity!—was lost, if I recollect rightly, in 1833, on his voyage to Europe, whither he was going, to give us sketches of the world's sunny face" (X, 379).

23. Stanley T. Williams, *The Life of Washington Irving* (New York: Oxford University Press, 1935), II, 221.

24. Washington Irving, *Oliver Goldsmith: A Biography*, ed. Elsie Lee West, Vol. 17 of *The Complete Works of Washington Irving* (Boston: Twayne, 1978), p. 47.

25. "Tales," *Encyclopedia Americana*, 12 (1832), 124.

26. "The Arts of the Islamic People," *Encyclopedia Britannica*, 15th ed. (1974), IX, 958.

27. "Short Story," *Encyclopedia Britannica*, 15th ed. (1974), XVI, 712–713.

28. "Benevolence; Or, the Good Samaritan," *Massachusetts Magazine*, 1 (February 1789), 76–77.

29. Julian Hawthorne, *Nathaniel Hawthorne and His Wife*, I, 145.

30. John Neal, "Story-Telling," *New-England Magazine*, 8 (January 1835), 2. Three years later in his "Divinity School Address" Emerson said of the moral sentiment among the Eastern writers: "This thought dwelled always deepest in the minds of men in the devout and contemplative East; not alone in Palestine, where it reached its purest expression, but in Egypt, in Persia, in India, in China. Europe has always owed to oriental genius, its divine impulses." *Nature, Addresses and Lectures*, Vol. 1 of *The Complete Works of Ralph Waldo Emerson* (Cambridge, Mass.: Riverside Press, 1903), p. 126.

31. Elizabeth Peabody, whose retrospective account of *The Story Teller* was decidedly biographical, identified Eliakim with a reclusive neighbor of Hawthorne, "who felt an internal call to convert the whole world." Quoted by Conway, p. 31. When Hawthorne became acquainted with Jones Very, he found a living embodiment of the conception he had tried to portray in the Story Teller's Fellow-traveler (XV, 482).

32. Edward Lane, *The Thousand and One Nights* (London: Charles Knight, 1839–1841), I, 24, note 3.

33. See, for example, Hawthorne's reference to his wife and himself as "wandering Arabs" whom Providence took by the hand, in "Mosses from an Old Manse" (X, 33). Around this same time, Hawthorne also referred to the story of the "wandering Arab girl" (the original for "Evangeline") that he had agreed to turn over to Longfellow. Manning Hawthorne, "Hawthorne and 'The Man of God,' " p. 278.

34. *Memoirs of the Baron De Tott, on the Turks and the Tartars* (London, 1785), I, 215. An article "The Turcomans" in the July 1836 *American Magazine of Useful and Entertaining Knowledge*, p. 427, drawn from Arthur Conolly's *Journey to the North of India* (1834), juxtaposes Eastern hospitality and mendacity: "Perhaps at the very moment you are eating his salt, your host is thinking, how, at a future occasion, he can best transfer part of your wealth to himself." Hawthorne's own essay "Salt; Its Origin and Manufacture" in the May 1836 *American Magazine*, pp. 393–394, begins with a section on the phenomenal abundance of salt in the Near Eastern countries.

35. Letter to Horace L. Conolly, June 17, 1850; XVI, 345.

36. Adkins, pp. 139–142. While acknowledging that "it is now virtually impossible to trace the itinerary of the story teller," Adkins based this particular sequence on Hawthorne's letter to Franklin Pierce in June 1832. Weber, p. 363, on the other hand, suggests that Hawthorne's travelers toured the White Mountains, the setting for "The Ambitious Guest" and "The Great Carbuncle," before coming to the Erie Canal.

37. On September 28, 1832, Hawthorne received a printed certificate attesting that he had "passed behind the Great Falling Sheet of Water to Termination Rock." James R. Mellow, *Nathaniel Hawthorne in His Times* (Boston: Houghton Mifflin, 1980), p. 51. Elizabeth McKinsey might assume too much in calling *The Story Teller* "a collection of disconnected sketches unified by the story narrator's wanderings and the growth of his sensibility and art." But, no doubt, within that framework Hawthorne's sketch "My Visit to Niagara" did mark "a climactic turning point." McKinsey, *Niagara Falls: Icon of the American Sublime* (Cambridge: Cambridge University Press, 1985), p. 197.

38. From "The Canal-Boat" (X, 429–430).

39. The "Fragments" are well-named, for they bring together three disparate types of material: random sketches that apparently were interspersed with the interior tales; reflections by the melancholy Story Teller after his return home; and comments by a second voice, an executor for the Story Teller (who is here called "Oberon"), on the passages he has assembled from the journals of his now-deceased friend. The shifts in narrator and introduction of a second voice have perplexed critics. They are, at least, "internally inconsistent." Baym, *The Shape of Hawthorne's Career*, p. 41. While "Oberon" was Hawthorne's popular nickname at Bowdoin and later, the narrators of

"The Seven Vagabonds" and "The Story Teller No. I and No. II" are unnamed. Furthermore, some of the executor's testamentary information—e.g., the age of the Story Teller when orphaned, the duration of his travels—disagrees with earlier revelations. David Pancost (see note 4) probably has solved this riddle by surmising that the executor's passages, which introduce and bind the "Fragments" together, were supplied not by Hawthorne but by Park Benjamin, who combed enough leftover material from Hawthorne's manuscript for *The Story Teller*, including his conclusion, to make an article for the July 1837 *American Monthly Magazine*. Benjamin was sufficiently familiar with "Oberon" to write of familiar visits to his office in the metropolis, and too rushed, or too distant from the introduction to *The Story Teller* in the 1834 *New-England Magazine*, to be wholly consistent with what went before. Hawthorne left his Story Teller at age twenty-four preoccupied with thoughts of death; Benjamin, it seems, killed him off.

40. "Pilgrimage to Mecca," *American Magazine of Useful and Entertaining Knowledge*, 3 (December 1836), 125.

41. References to such other great travel writers as Cervantes, Swift, Scott, Chaucer, Lesage, and Goldsmith crop up in "The Seven Vagabonds" and "The Story Teller No. I," but only the Eastern storytellers, the "prototypes" of them all, seem to have run throughout the frame of *The Story Teller*, from "The Seven Vagabonds" to "Fragments from the Journal of a Solitary Man."

42. "The Storyteller," in Walter Benjamin, *Illuminations*, ed. and intro. Hannah Arendt; trans. Harry Zohn (New York: Schocken Books, 1969), pp. 84–85.

43. C. S. B. Swann, "The Practice and Theory of Storytelling: Nathaniel Hawthorne and Walter Benjamin," *American Studies*, 12 (August 1978), 188. I am grateful to Swann for calling my attention to Benjamin's essay.

44. Benjamin, pp. 86–87.

45. See, however, the tales told by Holgrave, Zenobia, and Donatello: Coleman W. Tharp, "The Oral Storyteller in Hawthorne's Novels," *Studies in Short Fiction*, 16 (Summer 1979), 205–214.

46. In Northrop Frye's scheme of archetypes these forms are related, respectively, to "the 'idyllic' fictional world 'associated with happiness, security and peace' [and] to the 'demonic or night world' of exciting adventures." Percy G. Adams, *Travel Literature and the Evolution of the Novel* (Lexington: University Press of Kentucky, 1983), pp. 148–149. The tension in Hawthorne's works between the "poetics of adventure" and the "poetics of domesticity" has been addressed more theoretically by William C. Spengemann in *The Adventurous Muse: The Poetics of American Fiction, 1789–1900* (New Haven: Yale University Press, 1977).

47. Dan Vogel, "A Lexicon Rhetoricae for 'Journey' Literature," *College English*, 36 (October 1974), 189.

48. Hawthorne also showed his appreciation for the merry journeys and beguiling tales of the "Ancient Pilgrims" in an essay of that name for the April 1836 *American Magazine of Useful and Entertaining Knowledge*, p. 332. "Generally," he wrote, "a pilgrimage, though imposed or undertaken as a religious penance, must have been a very pleasant interlude in a man's life . . . and when completed, the pilgrim was a travelled man, and had a stock of fireside stories for the remainder of his days."

49. Adams, p. 153.

50. Sargent Bush, "Hawthorne's Domestic Narratives of the 1830s: 'The Threefold Destiny' and Other Quests for Home," *Nathaniel Hawthorne Review*, 12 (Fall 1986), 21.

51. Adams p. 160.

52. "Jerusalem" and "An Ontario Steamboat" appeared respectively on pp. 269–270 and 270–272 of the *American Magazine of Useful and Entertaining Knowledge* for March 1836 and are reprinted together in Arlin Turner, ed., *Hawthorne as Editor* (University, La.: Louisiana State University Press, 1941), pp. 55–64. The following quotations from "An Ontario Steamboat" are taken from the *American Magazine*

without further pagination. The vivid detail and fresh reactions of the narrator suggest that Hawthorne wrote the sketch shortly after the fact of his own travels to the Great Lakes in the fall of 1832. Hard-pressed to compose his monthly issues of the *American Magazine* early in 1836, Hawthorne probably inserted the sketch on hand, giving it added meaning by its juxtaposition to the article "Jerusalem." Weber, p. 362, lists the piece as a "possible" element of *The Story Teller*; Adkins, p. 140, felt "reasonably certain that this sketch belonged originally to *The Story Teller*."

53. *The Travels of Sir John Chardin into Persia and the East Indies* (London, 1686), p. 115.

54. The essay "Wives of Emigrants" appeared in the *American Magazine of Useful and Entertaining Knowledge* for July 1836.

55. Seymour L. Gross, "Four Possible Additions to Hawthorne's 'Story Teller,'" *Papers of the Bibliographical Society of America*, 51 (I Quarter 1957), 95, finds "The May-Pole of Merry Mount," which appeared in *The Token* for 1836, "very probably" a part of *The Story Teller*. "The Canterbury Pilgrims" was published in *The Token* for 1833 alongside "The Seven Vagabonds" and like that prefatory tale may have been involved in the genesis of *The Story Teller*. An outgrowth of the trip Hawthorne took to New Hampshire in the summer of 1831, "The Canterbury Pilgrims" could have been incorporated comfortably in the two volumes Hawthorne rounded off in 1834, whether composed for that purpose or not.

56. Patrick Morrow, "A Writer's Workshop: Hawthorne's 'The Great Carbuncle,'" *Studies in Short Fiction*, 6 (Winter 1969), 157–164.

57. Following the Cynic's initial address to his "fellow-pilgrims" delivered with his characteristic sneer, the term is used in a satirical fashion that emphasizes the lack of commonality among the adventurers. In a more straightforward fashion the narrator speaks of the particular "quest" of Master Ichabod Pigsnort. (IX, 159, 164)

58. On Hawthorne's transformation of *Cacafogo* into *Cacaphodel*, see Luther S. Luedtke, "Hawthorne's Doctor Cacaphodel: The Significance of a Name," *The Nathaniel Hawthorne Journal 1977*, ed. C. E. Frazer Clark, Jr. (Detroit: Gale Research, 1980), pp. 167–172.

59. The tale had been published by the fall of 1834, several months before *The Story Teller* began to appear in the *New-England Magazine*, but Goodrich may well have siphoned it from the two-volume manuscript Hawthorne presented to him.

60. Weber, pp. 363–364. For the place of "Little Annie's Ramble" in *The Story Teller*, see Gross, p. 91.

61. Vathek told Nouronihar: "But at all events we will not stay long at his [the Giaour's] fiery palace. I esteem your beautiful body more highly than all the treasures of the pre-Adamite sultans; and it is my wish to possess it at my ease and in the good air of heaven for many moons, before burying myself in the earth." William Beckford, *Vathek*, trans. Herbert B. Grimsditch (London: The Bodley Head, 1929), p. 90.

62. Beckford, p. 122.

63. Robert Southey, *Thalaba the Destroyer*, Vol. 4 of *The Poetical Works of Robert Southey* (London: Longman, 1838), pp. 425, 197–198.

64. Southey, *Thalaba the Destroyer*, p. 232.

65. Weber, p. 288.

66. *Hawthorne's Lost Notebook*, p. 40.

67. Elizabeth Peabody to Horace Mann, March 3, 1838; quoted in Wayne Allen Jones, "Sometimes Things Just Don't Work Out," *The Nathaniel Hawthorne Journal 1975*, ed. C. E. Frazer Clark, Jr. (Englewood, Colo.: Microcard Editions, 1975), p. 19. The composition of "The Threefold Destiny" around the turn of the year 1837–1838 prevents us from associating the figure of Faith Egerton exclusively with Sophia Peabody since she was only one of three young women Hawthorne was someways romantically interested in during these months, the other two being Elizabeth Peabody and Mary Silsbee, the daughter of Nathaniel Silsbee, who was captain of the *Herald* when Hawthorne's father sailed to the Orient in 1800–1801.

68. Buford Jones, "The *Faery Land* of Hawthorne's Romances," *Emerson Society Quarterly*, No. 48 (III Quarter 1967), 108.

69. "The Threefold Destiny" splendidly illustrates Walter Benjamin's two archetypes of the storyteller. When the village selectmen come to call, Ralph Cranfield's mother proudly encourages him: "Now do tell them a good long story about what you have seen in foreign parts" (IX, 477). Henceforth he would combine this lore of the traveler with the homelier instruction befitting his role as a schoolmaster.

70. Southey, *Thalaba the Destroyer*, pp. 27, 263.

71. Jones, pp. 108–109. Aside from the stories and sketches discussed in this chapter, the influence of the Eastern tales of the eighteenth century is apparent in "David Swan: A Fantasy," "The Man of Adamant: An Apologue," "Fancy's Show Box: A Morality," and "The Prophetic Pictures," which all appeared in *The Token* for 1837 alongside "The Great Carbuncle"—as well as in "The Lily's Quest: An Apologue," which was first published in 1839. Except for "The Great Carbuncle" Weber does not connect these works with *The Story Teller*, but the editors of the Centenary Edition (IX, 495–496) suggest that the tales published in *The Token* for 1837 may well have come into Samuel Goodrich's hands by way of Hawthorne's manuscript for the comprehensive work. Neal Frank Doubleday, *Hawthorne's Early Tales* (Durham, N.C.: Duke University Press, 1972), pp. 66–67, dissociated Hawthorne's allegorical method from both Bunyan and Spenser. The morality of these tales is not, like Christian allegory, concentrated on a salvation drama but rather is more concerned with matters of fate and circumstance, destiny and chance, resignation and supplication that are typical of Islamic thought.

72. Agnes Rush Burr, *Russell H. Conwell and His Work* (Philadelphia: John C. Winston, 1917), p. 409. Conwell claimed to have been told the fable of Al Hafed by an Iraqi guide while making a trip down the Tigris River in 1870.

73. Quotations respectively are from James F. Folsom, *Man's Accidents and God's Purposes: Multiplicity in Hawthorne's Fiction* (New Haven: College and University Press, 1963), p. 75; and Henry James, *Hawthorne* (New York: Harper & Brothers, 1879), p. 55. James continued: "When I think of it, I almost envy Hawthorne's earliest readers; the sensation of opening upon *The Great Carbuncle*, *The Seven Vagabonds*, or *The Threefold Destiny* in an American annual of forty years ago, must have been highly agreeable."

74. *Hawthorne's Lost Notebook*, p. 74.

5. The Fairy-Land of Hawthorne's Romance

1. Letter to Louisa Hawthorne, July 10, 1842; XV, 639.

2. J. Donald Crowley, "Historical Commentary" to *Mosses from an Old Manse* (X, 508, 535).

3. Letter to E. A. Duyckinck, July 1, 1845; XVI, 105.

4. *Nature, Addresses and Lectures*, Vol. 1 of *The Complete Works of Ralph Waldo Emerson* (Cambridge, Mass.: Riverside Press, 1903), p. 17.

5. As further evidence of his interest in the manuscripts of the East see Hawthorne's item "Mahometan Libraries" in the August 1836 issue of the *American Magazine of Useful and Entertaining Knowledge*.

6. See the *American Notebooks* (VIII, 182); and Manning Hawthorne, "Hawthorne and 'The Man of God'," *The Colophon*, n.s. 2 (Winter 1937), 278.

7. Letter to Sophia Hawthorne, December 2, 1844; XVI, 67.

8. Horatio Bridge, *Personal Recollections of Nathaniel Hawthorne* (New York: Harper & Brothers, 1893), pp. 188–189. Hawthorne probably was responsible around this time also for the comparison in Bridge's *Journal of an African Cruiser* (1845) between the crusty sailors' fondness for yarns and the story addiction of "the Sultan in the Arabian Nights."

9. Sophia Hawthorne to Horatio Bridge, July 4, 1845; XVI, 109.

10. Sarah Searight, *The British in the Middle East*, 2d ed. (London: East-West Publications, 1979), p. 184.

11. Searight, p. 271.

12. Bayard Taylor, *The Lands of the Saracen* (New York: G. P. Putnam, 1855), p. 140.

13. Michael Davitt Bell's *The Development of American Romance: The Sacrifice of Relation* (Chicago: University of Chicago Press, 1980) is representative in operating entirely within an Anglo–American scheme. Robert D. Richardson, Jr.'s *Myth and Literature in the American Renaissance* (Bloomington: Indiana University Press, 1978) restores a large part of the historical and perceptual context in which Hawthorne and his contemporaries worked by incorporating two major events of the late eighteenth century: "The first was the Nordic Renaissance, the rediscovery and subsequent popularization of old North European myth and epic; the second was the Oriental Renaissance, the European discovery of the ancient sacred writings of the East, and of India in particular" (pp. 28–29). While Richardson traces the effect of Anquetil-Duperron's translation of the Zoroastrian *Zend-Avesta* on an expanded, comparativist point of view in religion and mythological research, his scope does not include the other great event of the eighteenth century, that is, the *Mille et une Nuits*, nor does it leave room for the more fanciful productions of Longfellow, Irving, and Hawthorne. Some qualification must be made in John C. Stubbs' remark: "Certainly history more than anything else in the nineteenth century gave the romancer his simplest solution to the problem of artistic distance." Stubbs, "Hawthorne's *The Scarlet Letter*: The Theory of the Romance and the Use of the New England Situation," *PMLA*, 93 (October 1968), 1443. As "Rappaccini's Daughter" and *The Marble Faun* would make clear, geographical and cultural remoteness was a very potent romantic device, and one often used in combination with distance in time.

14. *Peter Parley's Universal History* (Boston: American Stationers' Company, 1837), I, vii.

15. *The Corsair; A Tale*, in *Lord Byron: The Complete Poetical Works*, ed. Jerome J. McGann (Oxford: At the Clarendon Press, 1980–1986), III, 148–149.

16. Thomas Warton, *The History of English Poetry, from the Close of the Eleventh Century to the Commencement of the Eighteenth Century*, from the 1824 edition by Richard Price (London: Thomas Tegg, 1840), I, i–ii.

17. Warton, I, xliv, lvi.

18. H. A. R. Gibb, "Literature," in *The Legacy of Islam*, ed. Thomas Arnold and Alfred Guillaume (Oxford: At the Clarendon Press, 1931), p. 202.

19. "An Essay on Romance," in *Chivalry, Romance, and the Drama*, Vol. 6 of *The Miscellaneous Prose Works of Sir Walter Scott* (Edinburgh: Adam and Charles Black, 1852), pp. 147, 174–176.

20. Hawthorne had the two-volume 1818 Philadelphia edition of Schlegel's *Lectures* from July 12 to August 11, 1828. Marion L. Kesselring, *Hawthorne's Reading 1828–1850* (New York: The New York Public Library, 1949), p. 60.

21. Henry Wadsworth Longfellow, *Origin and Growth of the Languages of Southern Europe and of Their Literature* (Brunswick, Me.: Bowdoin College Library, 1907), pp. 36, 79, 99. Longfellow also balanced the claims for the Scandinavian and the Arabian sources of the modern romance in his essay "The Trouveres" in *Outre-Mer*.

22. Quoted by Fred Lewis Pattee, *The Development of the American Short Story* (New York: Harper & Brothers, 1923), p. 17.

23. Hawthorne withdrew nine volumes of the *Americana* from the Salem Athenaeum between September 1833 and February 1838 (Kesselring, p. 49), reprinted its articles in the *American Magazine of Useful and Entertaining Knowledge*, and reworked other *Americana* materials for *Peter Parley's Universal History*.

24. "Arabian Literature and Thought," *Encyclopedia Americana*, 1 (1829), 318, 320.

25. "Troubadours," *Encyclopedia Americana*, 12 (1832), 355; "Fairies, Fairy Tales," *Encyclopedia Americana*, 5 (1831), 39.

26. "Arabian Nights," *Encyclopedia Americana*, 1 (1829), 321.

27. "Tales," *Encyclopedia Americana*, 12 (1832), 124.

28. "Grotesques," *Encyclopedia Americana*, 6 (1831), 73.

29. "Oriental Literature," *Encyclopedia Americana*, 9 (1832), 425–428.

30. "Arabia," *Encyclopedia Americana*, 1 (1823), 316.

31. *The Sketch Book of Geoffrey Crayon, Gent.*, ed. Haskell Springer, Vol. 8 of *The Complete Works of Washington Irving* (Boston: G. K. Hall, 1978), p. 225.

32. Carsten Niebuhr, *Travels through Arabia* (Edinburgh, 1792), II, 1–2.

33. Longfellow's mother, for instance, entertained the boy with stories from *The Arabian Nights* in 1815 while he was confined with a foot injury, and among the affinities of Longfellow and his second wife, Fanny Appleton Longfellow, was reportedly this, that "In her youth she passionately loved *The Arabian Nights*." Lawrence Thompson, *Young Longfellow (1807–1843)* (New York: Macmillan, 1938), pp. 16–17; Edward Wagenknecht, *Longfellow: A Full-Length Portrait* (New York: Longmans, Green, 1955), p. 239.

34. Clay Lancaster, "Oriental Forms in American Architecture, 1800–1870," *The Art Bulletin*, 29 (September 1947), 183, 187.

35. *Hawthorne's Lost Notebook*, p. 22.

36. Hawthorne's next entry continues the Eastern strain of thought with regard to the symbol of the *talisman*, which is discussed below: "To consider a piece of gold as a sort of talisman—or as containing within itself all the forms of enjoyment that it can purchase—so that they might appear, by some fantastical chemical process, as visions" (VIII, 242).

37. *Peter Parley's Universal History*, II, 347–348.

38. Luther S. Luedtke, "Hawthorne on Architecture: Sources for *Parley's Universal History* and *The American Notebooks*," *Papers of the Bibliographical Society of America*, 71 (I Quarter 1977), 88–98.

39. *Gentleman's Magazine*, n.s. 3 (June 1835), 619–620.

40. *English Notebooks*, June 7, 1857, p. 493.

41. See, for example, Hawthorne's note on April 11, 1843, in anticipation of Sophia's homecoming: "To-night—to-night—yes, within an hour—this Eden, which is no Eden to a solitary Adam, will regain its Eve" (VIII, 379).

42. The Oriental structures in Mount Auburn include the pyramid-shaped tomb of Col. John Mountfort and his parents, the ornate sarcophagus of Johannes T. Kirkland, and the emblematic designs of the Masonic order on the J. Foss monument. Wilson Flagg, *Mount Auburn: Its Scenes, Its Beauties, and Its Lessons* (Boston: James Monroe, 1861), p. 27 *et passim*.

43. In lieu of the *momento mori* of Egypt, Hawthorne apparently based his image of immortality on the classical Binney Monument, which depicted a child "lying on her pallet, after death. The hands are crossed upon the breast and the feet bare, and likewise crossed." According to Flagg, p. 53, this was "the first marble statue executed in Boston."

44. *Thalaba the Destroyer*, Vol. 4 of *The Poetical Works of Robert Southey* (London: Longman, 1838), p. 189.

45. *Gentleman's Magazine*, 101 (November 1831), 454–455.

46. John Neal, "Story-Telling," *New England Magazine*, 8 (January 1835), 2.

47. Hawthorne noted in "The Egyptian Papyrus" (AM, p. 315) that manuscripts found with the Egyptian mummies contained both alphabetic characters and "hieroglyphics, in which the meaning is expressed by pictures and symbols." See also John T. Irwin, *American Hieroglyphics* (New Haven: Yale University Press, 1980).

48. Richard D. Rust, " 'I Seek for Truth': Hawthorne's Use of the Talisman," *Nathaniel Hawthorne Review*, 12 (Spring, 1986), 5.

49. "Talisman," *Encyclopedia Americana*, 12 (1832), 125.

50. *The Poetical Works of Thomas Moore*, ed. A. D. Godley (London: Oxford University Press, 1910), p. 402.

51. "The Talisman of Truth," *Massachusetts Magazine*, 3 (October 1791), 614–617.

52. Henry A. Beers, *Nathaniel Parker Willis* (Boston: Houghton Mifflin, 1885), p. 99.

53. For a further depiction of the kinds, origin, and legendary associations of these gems, see Pliny's *Historie of the World*, Book 37, Chapter 7: "Of Carbuncles or Rubies."

54. James Sullivan, *The History of the District of Maine* (Boston: I. Thomas and E. T. Andrews, 1795), pp. 74–75. By contrasting the early explorers' illusory expectations of mountains of precious metals in New England with the true natural resources of the land, Sullivan foreshadowed one of Hawthorne's primary situations, where jewels of great price, sought in far off places, turn to dross when compared to the earthly riches at home. Hawthorne also mentions the Great Carbuncle in his French and Italian notebooks (XIV, 96) and in his American Claimant manuscripts (XII, 198). There he also recalls the naked sword that lay "between the Arabian prince in the tale and the princess whom he wedded" (XII, 171). Hawthorne apparently knew that in the Middle Ages, and later, the carbuncle was thought to emit a light in the dark, for such is the use to which Matthew and Hannah wish to put it in "The Great Carbuncle." In Sir Walter Raleigh's *The Historie of the World* (London, 1652), I, 96—which he had from the Salem Athenaeum in April 1828 (Kesselring, p. 22)—Hawthorne could have read a terse remark on "the foolery of the *Hebrews*," who supposed that Noah's Ark was lighted by a carbuncle. For other connections of precious stones with Hindostan see "Earth's Holocaust" (X, 385).

55. Southey, *Thalaba the Destroyer*, p. 17.

56. *The Curse of Kehama*, Vol. 8 of *The Poetical Works of Robert Southey* (London: Longman, 1838), p. 137.

57. Southey, *Thalaba the Destroyer*, pp. 425–426.

58. Southey, *The Curse of Kehama*, pp. 188–192.

59. Seymour Gross, "Hawthorne's 'Vision of the Fountain' as a Parody," *American Literature*, 27 (March 1955), 101–105.

60. "Dr. Bullivant," *The Complete Writings of Nathaniel Hawthorne*, Autograph Edition (Boston: Houghton Mifflin, 1900), XVII, 269–273; italics added.

61. Max Meyerhof, "Science and Medicine," in *The Legacy of Islam*, ed. Thomas Arnold and Alfred Guillaume (Oxford: At the Clarendon Press, 1931), pp. 353, 326–327.

62. Richard Pococke, *A Description of the East* (London, 1743–1745), I, 181.

63. Niebuhr, II, 41, 285.

64. Richard Madden, *Travels in Turkey, Egypt, Nubia and Palestine* (London: H. Colburn, 1829), II, 274, 288–289.

65. Compare Ramona E. Hull, "Hawthorne and the Magic Elixir of Life: The Failure of a Gothic Theme," *Emerson Society Quarterly*, 18 (II Quarter 1972), 97–107.

66. Southey, *The Curse of Kehama*, pp. 202–209. In "Hawthorne's Literary Borrowings," *PMLA*, 51 (June 1936), 554, Arlin Turner suggested that Kehama's "eternal burning and suffering probably contributed to Hawthorne's conception of the undesirability of an immortal life on earth."

67. Other Eastern artifacts in the Virtuoso's collection include Mohammed's favorite cat, Aladdin's lamp, the crown of Semiramis, the "sacred ibis of Egypt," "the crooked blade of Saladin's scimetar," "some Egyptian darkness in a blacking jug," "the original manuscript of the Koran," and a jewelled casket of Darius fragrant with Persian perfumes.

68. Letter to Evert Duyckinck, April 15, 1846; XVI, 153.

69. Roy Harvey Pearce, "Historical Introduction" to *True Stories, A Wonder-Book and Tanglewood Tales* (VI, 305).

70. Julian Hawthorne, *Nathaniel Hawthorne and His Wife* (Boston: James R. Osgood, 1884), I, 368.

71. Julian Hawthorne, *Nathaniel Hawthorne and His Wife*, I, 372.

72. Patricia C. Smith, "Novel Conceptions, Unusual Combinations: The Arabesque in Poe" (Ph.D. dissertation, Yale University, 1970), pp. 116-117.

73. Julian Hawthorne, *Nathaniel Hawthorne and His Wife*, I, 386.

74. Julian Hawthorne, *Nathaniel Hawthorne and His Wife*, I, 471-473.

75. Pearce (VI, 310).

76. George W. Curtis et al., *Homes of American Authors* (New York: G. P. Putnam, 1853), pp. 305-306.

77. In " 'Proper Evidences of Madness': American Gothic and the Interpretation of 'Ligeia,' " *Emerson Society Quarterly*, 18 (I Quarter 1972), 30-49, G. R. Thompson has suggested that *Gothic, Arabesque,* and *Grotesque* were nearly equivalent terms from the third quarter of the eighteenth century well into the nineteenth—although the Gothic retained its sense of the "ponderous, sombre, and depressing," and an atmosphere of weird and terrifying events, while the Arabesque was given a lighter, more soaring, fanciful, and decorative air.

78. When eulogizing Hawthorne contemporary poets like Longfellow, E. C. Stedman, Oliver Wendell Holmes, and Bronson Alcott all wrote of the Magi's rod and his wizard touch. Edwin H. Cady, " 'The Wizard Hand': Hawthorne, 1864-1900," in *Hawthorne Centenary Essays*, ed. Roy Harvey Pearce (Columbus: Ohio State University Press, 1964), pp. 317-334. His daughter Rose compared his passion to "flashes of a scimitar, as rapidly sheathed as it was sprung." *The Complete Writings of Nathaniel Hawthorne*, Autograph Edition, I, xxvii. Julian Hawthorne remembered his father at the time of *The Scarlet Letter* in similar imagery: " . . . the forehead was hollowed at the temple and rounded out above, after the Moorish style of architecture." And he said of his unfulfilled intention to rework *Doctor Grimshawe's Secret*: "But these last transfiguring touches to Aladdin's Tower were never to be given; and he has departed, taking with him his Wonderful Lamp." Maurice Bassan, *Hawthorne's Son* (Columbus: Ohio State University Press, 1970), p. 6; *The Complete Writings of Nathaniel Hawthorne*, Autograph Edition, XV, xii.

79. *The English Notebooks*, September 27, 1855, pp. 238-239.

80. Gibb, p. 182.

81. See, for example, Richard Price's preface to Warton, I, 34-35.

82. *Webster's Third New International Dictionary* (1964), p. 1679. The *Encyclopedia Americana*, 10 (1832), 16, defined *peri* in essentially the same terms: "The Peris, in Persian mythology, are the descendants of fallen spirits, excluded from paradise until their penance is accomplished."

6. Hawthorne's Oriental Women: The First Dark Ladies

1. Gloria Erlich, "Deadly Innocence: Hawthorne's Dark Women," *New England Quarterly*, 41 (June 1968), 164. Nina Baym, "Thwarted Nature: Nathaniel Hawthorne as Feminist," in *American Novelists Revisited: Essays in Feminist Criticism*, ed. Fritz Fleischman (Boston: G. K. Hall, 1982), p. 62.

2. Philip Rahv, "The Dark Lady of Salem," *Partisan Review*, 8 (September-October 1941), 367, 369.

3. *Lilith* (meaning "night monster") derives from the Babylonian-Assyrian demon *Lilit* and appears in both Jewish and Muslim folklore. In Rabbinical literature Lilith was the first wife of Adam. She claimed equality with Adam but refused to serve him and was expelled from Eden before God created Eve.

4. Ralph P. Boas, "The Romantic Lady," in *Romanticism in America*, ed. George Boas (Baltimore: The Johns Hopkins Press, 1940), pp. 66-67, 79, 81.

5. See especially Frederick C. Crews, *The Sins of the Fathers* (New York: Oxford University Press, 1966); Gloria C. Erlich, *Family Themes and Hawthorne's Fiction* (New Brunswick, N.J.: Rutgers University Press, 1984); and Philip Young, *Hawthorne's Secret* (Boston: David R. Godine, 1984).

6. Peter Gay, *The Bourgeois Experience: Victoria to Freud*, Vol. 1 of *The Education of the Senses* (New York: Oxford University Press, 1984), p. 456.

7. Letter to Sophia Peabody, July 15, 1839; XV, 326.

8. Letter to Sophia Peabody, January 20, 1842; XV, 606.

9. Gay, p. 118.

10. Ca. April 11, 1843; quoted by Gay, p. 457, from the notebook Nathaniel and Sophia shared in 1843 (Pierpont Morgan Library, New York). Only his part is published in the Centenary Edition of *The American Notebooks*.

11. Rahv, p. 381.

12. Sophia Hawthorne to Louisa Hawthorne, February 6, 1844; XVI, 12–14.

13. Arlin Turner, *Nathaniel Hawthorne* (New York: Oxford University Press, 1980), pp. 168–169.

14. Letter to G. W. Hillard, March 24, 1844; XVI, 22–23.

15. Letter to Sophia Hawthorne, March 16, 1843; XV, 679.

16. William Dean Howells, *Literary Friends and Acquaintances*, ed. David F. Hiatt and Edwin H. Cady, Vol. 32, *A Selected Edition of William Dean Howells* (Bloomington: Indiana University Press, 1968), p. 49.

17. Letter to Louisa Hawthorne, March 3, 1844; XVI, 15. Letter to John Frost, March 11, 1844; XVI, 17.

18. Lea Bertani Vozar Newman, *A Reader's Guide to the Short Stories of Nathaniel Hawthorne* (Boston: G. K. Hall, 1979), p. 74.

19. Neal Frank Doubleday, *Hawthorne's Early Tales* (Durham, N.C.: Duke University Press, 1972), p. 187.

20. Millicent Bell, *Hawthorne's View of the Artist* (New York: State University of New York, 1962), p. 127.

21. For an illustration of the practical conditions of life at the Old Manse following the birth of Una, see Hawthorne's letter to his sister Louisa, March 15, 1844; XVI, 19.

22. Erlich, "Deadly Innocence: Hawthorne's Dark Women," p. 175.

23. Hawthorne continued, interestingly, with the same double metaphor he applied to Sophia: "Had [Warland] become convinced of his mistake through the medium of successful love; had he won Annie to his bosom, and there beheld her fade from *angel* into *ordinary woman*, the disappointment might have driven him back, with concentrated energy, upon his sole remaining object" (X, 464). Italics added.

24. Doubleday, p. 191.

25. Bell, p. 133.

26. Turner, p. 162.

27. Quoted by Turner, p. 162.

28. *Hawthorne's Lost Notebook*, p. 85. Several years later, sometime before July 27, 1844, Hawthorne also referred in his notes to Madame Calderón de la Barca's account in *Life in Mexico* (Boston, 1843) of the inoculation with rattlesnake venom of persons who thus became themselves poisonous (VIII, 238).

29. Henry G. Fairbanks, *The Lasting Loneliness of Nathaniel Hawthorne* (Albany, N.Y.: Magi Books, 1965), p. 138.

30. David Cody believes that Hawthorne had begun to read Browne's works at least as early as 1836 and cites effects on Hawthorne's tales in the early 1840s, including parallels between Browne's *Fragment on Mummies* and the grinning Egyptian skeleton in "The Christmas Banquet." Cody, "Invited Guests at Hawthorne's 'Christmas Banquet': Sir Thomas Browne and Jeremy Taylor," *Modern Language Studies*, 11 (Winter 1980–1981), 17–26.

31. See, for example, *Sir Thomas Browne's Works: Including His Life and Correspondence*, ed. Simon Wilkin (London: William Pickering, 1835), p. 358. Quoted from the copy in the James T. Fields Collection, The Huntington Library.

32. Julian Hawthorne, *Nathaniel Hawthorne and His Wife* (Boston: James R. Osgood, 1884), I, 128.

33. Carol Marie Bensick has argued for the dense historical foundations of "Rappaccini's Daughter" in Padua in the years 1527–1533 in *La Nouvelle Beatrice: Renaissance and Romance in "Rappaccini's Daughter"* (New Brunswick, N.J.: Rutgers University Press, 1985). While referring several times to Penzer's *Poison-Damsels* (see note 46, below), however, she shows no particular concern for the Indian associations of the legend or the Oriental presence in the culture and the scientific studies pursued at Padua from the twelfth century forward. That major themes and images of Renaissance literature derived from Eastern origins is well demonstrated in Samuel Chew's *The Crescent and the Rose* (New York: Oxford University Press, 1937), and the authority of "Arabism" in the study of botany, zoology, physics, alchemy, and medicine at the University of Padua throughout the period Bensick covers is well presented in Max Meyerhof's essay, "Science and Medicine," in *The Legacy of Islam*, ed. Thomas Arnold and Alfred Guillaume (Oxford: At the Clarendon Press, 1931), pp. 311–355. Averroës's *Colliget* was translated into Latin in Padua in 1255, and the process of translating the works of Avicenna, Averroës, and other Arab philosophers and scientists went on well into the sixteenth century. The effect of "translations from the Graeco-Arabic literature . . . on the barren scientific soil of Europe," according to Meyerhof, "was that of a fertilizing rain." Not until 1543, when Copernicus published his *De Revolutionibus Orbium caelestium* and Andreas Vesalius edited his anatomy— that is, a decade *after* the period of Bensick's concern—did the direct influence of Scholasticism and Arabian science begin to wane. In pharmacology the Arabic influence "survived into the nineteenth century."

34. George Sales drew special attention to *al Jannat* and the Islamic images of Paradise in his "Preliminary Discourse" to the Koran (London, 1734), pp. 96–97:

> But all these glories will be eclipsed by the resplendent and ravishing girls of paradise, called, from their large black eyes, *Hûr al oyûn*, the enjoyment of whose company will be a principal felicity of the faithful. These, they say, are created not of clay, as mortal women are, but of pure musk; being, as their prophet often affirms in his *Korân*, free from all natural impurities, defects, and inconveniences incident to the sex, of the strictest modesty, and secluded from public view in pavilions of hollow pearls.

35. *The Complete Letters of Lady Mary Wortley Montagu*, ed. Robert Halsband (Oxford: At the Clarendon Press, 1965–1967), I, 343. For a like description of the garden, "pleasure house," kiosk, and fountain in the home of an *effendi* at Smyrna at the end of the seventeenth century, see Edmund Chishull, *Travels in Turkey and back to England* (London, 1747), p. 6.

36. Alexander Russell *The Natural History of Aleppo* (London, 1794), I, 29.

37. Montagu, I, 326.

38. Joseph Pitton de Tournefort, *A Voyage into the Levant* (London, 1741), II, 322.

39. [James J. Morier], *The Adventures of Hajji Baba, of Ispahan* (London: John Murray, 1824), I, 245.

40. See Chapter 2 for a further discussion of Hawthorne's essay "Natural History Among the Ancients" in the August 1836 *American Magazine*. Pliny's original depiction associates the Astomes with their flowers no less intimately than Beatrice Rappaccini is wed to hers: "[T]hey live onely by the aire, and smelling to sweet odours, which they draw in at their nosethrils: No meat nor drinke they take, onely pleasant savours from divers and sundrie roots, floures, and wild fruits growing in the woods they entertaine." *The Historie of the World, Commonly called the Naturall Historie of C. Plinius Secundus*, trans. Philemon Holland (London, 1601), I, 156.

41. Jac Tharpe has pointed out parallels between *Shakuntala* and "Rappaccini's Daughter," and between the *Ramayana* and "Roger Malvin's Burial," in "Hawthorne and Hindu Literature," *Southern Quarterly*, 10 (1973), 107–115. Most striking are

Shakuntala's identification with a flowering plant ("O most radiant of twining plants, receive my embraces, and return them with thy flexible arms") and the wish of her adoptive father, Canna, to gain her "a husband equal to thyself." Canna: "I will marry thy favourite plant to the bridegroom Amra, who sheds fragrance near her." *Shakuntala*, Act IV; quoted by Tharpe, p. 110.

42. Montagu, I, 326.

43. *The Adventures of Hajji Baba*, III, 237.

44. Julian Hawthorne, *Nathaniel Hawthorne and His Wife*, I, 360–361. In *Hawthorne Reading* (Cleveland: The Rowfant Club, 1902), pp. 122–123, Julian Hawthorne mentioned his father's reluctance to read his tales even to his wife before they were completed, but noted exceptions in the cases of "Rappaccini's Daughter" and *The Scarlet Letter*. Hawthorne's discomposure both times suggests not only the dramatic similarity in the two works but also a strong personal struggle to bring his male and female characters into alignment with his own ideals.

45. A brief account of Alexander's rule and campaigns can be found in *Peter Parley's Universal History* (Boston: American Stationers' Company, 1837), I, 232–238.

46. N. M. Penzer, *Poison-Damsels and Other Essays in Folklore and Anthropology* (London: Chas. J. Sawyer, 1952), p. 18.

47. Penzer, pp. 18–19.

48. Penzer, p. 22.

49. Werner Peterich, "Hawthorne and the 'Gesta Romanorum.' The Genesis of 'Rappaccini's Daughter' and 'Ethan Brand,' " *Kleine Beiträge zur amerikanischen Literaturgeschichte*, ed. Hans Galinsky and Hans-Joachim Lang (Heidelberg: Winter, 1961), pp. 11–18. In the *Gesta Romanorum* account of the poison-maiden (tale No. 11 in the Charles Swan translation) it is the Queen of the North (Regina Aquilonis) who nourishes her daughter on poison and sends her to Alexander.

50. Penzer, pp. 12–18, 70–71. Penzer, mentions, p. 28, "The most recent adaptation of the story is probably that of the American poet [sic] Nathaniel Hawthorne. It appeared under the title of "Rappacini's [sic] Daughter.' " He does not offer any specific connections, however.

51. Penzer, p. 36.

52. Penzer, p. 16 *et passim*. Penzer also mentions, p. 63, stories in Middle India of poisonous snakes hiding in the vagina or belly, another analogue, perhaps, to Hawthorne's "Egotism; or, The Bosom-Serpent" (1843). His descriptions of diseased clothing and poisoned shirts among the Rajputs and in the court of the Emperor Aurangzeb, pp. 3, 8–9, might hold clues for further exploration of "Lady Eleanor's Mantle" (1838).

53. S. D. Trevidi, *Secret Services in Ancient India: Techniques and Operations* (New Delhi: Allied Publishers, 1984); Appendix 2, "Visakanya (Poison-damsel): An Intelligence Operation," pp. 171–177.

54. *Gesta Romanorum: or, Entertaining Moral Stories*, trans. Charles Swan (London: George Bell & Sons, 1877), pp. 21–22.

55. An exploration of Pliny's commentaries on "counterpoisons" could lend more precision to our understanding of the drugs used to remove the mortal stains in "Rappaccini's Daughter" and "The Birth-mark." In his chapter on "Aconite" (the chief poison mentioned in Sir Thomas Browne's story of the poison-damsel) Pliny noted that this and other counterpoisons are effective only when a body is *partially* poisoned. It is "a wonderfull thing to observe," he wrote, "that two poisons, both of them deadly of themselves and their own nature, should die one upon another within the bodie, and the man by that mean only escape with life." If the body is *wholly* poisonous, it will be completely destroyed. Similarly, if the body is pure of contamination, and if the counterpoison "meet not with some poison or other in mens bodies for to kill, it presently setteth upon them and soone brings them to their end." Pliny's *The Historie of the World*, II, 270. Applying Pliny's pharmacology to "Rappaccini's Daughter" presents two possibilities concerning the antidote prepared by Baglioni: either that there was no poison in Beatrice's system for it to attack and so it killed

the pure tissues; or that her physical being was *wholly* poisonous. Hawthorne's entire account of "*La Belle Empoisonneuse*" contradicts the former possibility, but either approach would exonerate Baglioni. He prescribes the means to remove a partial poison and is as horrified as Giovanni with the result.

56. Letter to Louisa Hawthorne, June 22, 1845; XVI, 173.

57. *English Notebooks*, September 14, 1855, p. 225.

58. Mark Van Doren, *Nathaniel Hawthorne* ([New York]: William Sloan, 1949), p. 154. D. H. Lawrence, *Studies in Classic American Literature* (New York: Thomas Seltzer, 1923), p. 139.

59. "Mrs. Hutchinson," *The Complete Writings of Nathaniel Hawthorne*, Autograph Edition (Boston: Houghton Mifflin, 1900), XVII, 3.

60. *Three Weeks in Palestine and Lebanon* (New York: Protestant Episcopal Sunday School Union, [1833]), pp. 13–14.

61. Letter to Horatio Bridge, February 4, 1850; XVI, 311–312.

62. Letter to Horatio Bridge, July 22, 1851; XVI, 461. Italics added.

63. Holgrave's legend of Alice Pyncheon draws one's attention, again, to "The Threefold Destiny." Holgrave's tale also concerns the search for a treasure hidden behind a cryptic sign (in this instance, the deed to the Pyncheon properties) and for the maiden and the three sages through whom it will be made known. Putting Alice Pyncheon into a trance, Matthew Maule evoked through "her spiritualized perception . . . three visionary characters" who "possessed a mutual knowledge of the missing document" (II, 206–207). Like the wise men Ralph Cranfield glimpsed at the Great Geyser, the Alhambra, and the Pyramid of Cheops, the spectres from the Pyncheon and Maule families failed to divulge their secret. Only generations later is the sign rightly interpreted through Phoebe and Holgrave. The village maid, the downward pointing hand, and the command "Effode-Dig!" that instructed Ralph Cranfield in home economics in 1837 also hold the key to Holgrave's self-discovery a decade and a half later.

64. Compare Hawthorne's *English Notebooks* for June 30, 1854, p. 64: "I had an Uncle John, who went a voyage to sea about the beginning of the war of 1812, and has never returned to this hour. But, as long as his mother lived (as many as twenty years afterwards) she never gave up the hope of his return, and was constantly hearing stories of persons whose descriptions answered to his." It is possible that memories of his Grandmother Manning or other grieving widows in the family affected Hawthorne's characterization of Hepzibah. Besides references noted in the text above, Hepzibah's "turban" also appears on pp. 135, 136 and 246 of the Centenary Edition.

65. For a lavishly illustrated account of Soleiman's empire, see Merle Severy, "The World of SÜLEYMAN the Magnificent," *National Geographic*, 172 (November 1987), 552–601.

66. I am grateful to Arlin Turner for this information, based on Sophia Hawthorne's journal in the Berg Collection.

7. Hawthorne's Oriental Women: The Female Sovereigns

1. See the frontispiece to John W. McCoubrey, *American Art 1700–1960* (Englewood Cliffs, N.J.: Prentice-Hall, 1965).

2. Carl Bode, *The Anatomy of American Popular Culture 1840–1861* (Berkeley: University of California Press, 1959), p. 99.

3. McCoubrey, frontispiece.

4. Quoted in William H. Gerdts, *The Great American Nude: A History in Art* (New York: Praeger, 1974), p. 87.

5. *French and Italian Notebooks*, June 13, 1858; XIV, 311. Letter to Franklin Pierce, October 27, 1858; XVIII, 157.

6. *English Notebooks*, August 7, 1856, p. 393.

7. Lesley Blanch, *The Wilder Shores of Love* (New York: Simon and Schuster, 1954), pp. 208, xiv.

8. Marion L. Kesselring, *Hawthorne's Reading 1828–1850* (New York: The New York Public Library, 1949), p. 54.

9. Gerdts, p. 97. "In those pre-Freudian days, the mixture of sex and sadism was fully displayed," Gerdts remarks, "if never discussed."

10. Letter to George W. Curtis, April 29, 1851; XVI, 424–425.

11. Georgiana Bruce Kirby, *Years of Experience: An Autobiographical Narrative* (New York: G. P. Putnam's Sons, 1887), pp. 151–152.

12. Hyatt H. Waggoner, *Hawthorne: A Critical Study* (Cambridge, Mass.: Harvard University Press, 1963), p. 189.

13. Letter to Sophia Peabody, January 3, 1840; XV, 398.

14. "Progress of Literature in Different Ages of Society," *Gentleman's Magazine*, 91 (May 1821), 415–416.

15. Ogier Ghislain de Busbecq, *The Four Epistles of A. G. Busbequius* (London, 1694), p. 144.

16. *Memoirs of the Baron De Tott* (London, 1785), I, 25.

17. George William Curtis, *Nile Notes of a Howadji* (New York: Harper & Brothers, 1851), pp. 129–130.

18. *Don Juan*, in *Lord Byron: The Complete Poetical Works*, ed. Jerome J. McGann (Oxford: At the Clarendon Press, 1980–1986), V, 71.

19. *The Complete Letters of Lady Mary Wortley Montagu*, ed. Robert Halsband (Oxford: At the Clarendon Press, 1965–1967), I, 363.

20. For a "Persian" disquisition on the natural superiority of the male sex, and subjection of women, see "RICA to IBBEN," *Gentleman's Magazine*, 4 (February 1734), 76–77, which Hawthorne might have read in 1829 (Kesselring, p. 51). For a modern discussion of "Zenobia's half-hearted feminism" and sexual bondage in the novel, see Thomas F. Strychacz, "Coverdale and Women: Feverish Fantasies in *The Blithedale Romance*," *American Transcendental Quarterly*, No. 62 (December 1986), 29–45.

21. Tott, I, 199. In *The Adventures of Hajji Baba* (London: John Murray, 1824), II, 300, another Zeenab is thrown, "a mangled and mutilated corpse," at the feet of her lover, the blood still flowing from her mouth. Drowning concubines in weighted sacks was a standard means of ridding the seraglios of disobedient or tiresome females. See Merle Severy, "The World of SÜLEYMAN the Magnificent," *National Geographic*, 172 (November 1987), 576.

22. On the increasing spirituality and decreasing credibility of Hawthorne's brown-haired maidens, see Virginia Ogden Birdsall, "Hawthorne's Fair-Haired Maidens: The Fading Light," *PMLA*, 73 (June 1960), 250–256.

23. John W. Hirsch names some of the major dramatizations and depictions of Zenobia in his article "Zenobia as Queen: The Background Sources to Hawthorne's *The Blithedale Romance*," *The Nathaniel Hawthorne Journal 1971*, ed. C. E. Frazer Clark, Jr. (Washington, D.C.: Microcard Editions, 1971), pp. 182–190.

24. Robert Southey, *Thalaba the Destroyer*, Vol. 4 of *The Poetical Works of Robert Southey* (London: Longman, 1838), p. 28.

25. The Essex Institute has two logbooks from the *Zenobia's* voyage to the East Indies and China in June 1839–February 1840.

26. The nine "Lucius M. Piso" letters that appeared in volumes 7–9 of the *Knickerbocker* were republished as the first volume of the two-volume *Letters of Lucius M. Piso, from Palmyra, to his Friend Marcus Curtius at Rome* (New York: C. S. Francis, 1837).

27. *Knickerbocker*, 10 (July 1837), 68.

28. Letter to E. P. Whipple, May 2, 1852; XVI, 536–537.

29. "Palmyra, or Tadmor," *American Magazine of Useful and Entertaining Knowledge*, 2 (February 1836), 263–264.

30. Edward Gibbon, *The History of the Decline and Fall of the Roman Empire* (New York: Harper & Brothers, 1851), I, 350.

31. "Zenobia," *Encyclopedia Americana*, 13 (1833), 325.

32. Ralph P. Boas calls attention to these traits in "The Romantic Lady," *Romanticism in America*, ed. George Boas (Baltimore: The Johns Hopkins Press, 1940), p. 86.

33. [William Ware], *Zenobia; or, The Fall of Palmyra: An Historical Romance* (New York: C. S. Francis, 1838), I, 113, 106. Beginning with the second, 1838 edition, Ware's novel was published under the title *Zenobia* rather than *Letters of Lucius M. Piso*. The following quotations are from the 1838 edition.

34. *Zenobia*, I, 5, 94.

35. *Zenobia*, I, 258.

36. *Zenobia*, II, 35–36; I, 90, 141

37. *Zenobia*, I, 104.

38. John Harris, *Navigantium atque Itinerantium Bibliotheca* (London, 1744), I, 439.

39. *Zenobia*, II, 281.

40. Van Wyck Brooks, *The Flowering of New England* (New York: E. P. Dutton, 1936), p. 473.

41. Harris, I, 439.

42. *Zenobia*, II, 144. Ware's development of Queen Zenobia's pride and the enervating effect of personal love is perhaps his greatest contribution to Hawthorne's conception of the figure. In Ware's romance Queen Zenobia's ambition "is boundless, almost insane" (I, 89). She confesses, "I am charged with pride and ambition. The charge is true, and I glory in its truth. Who ever achieved any thing great in letters, arts, or arms, who was not ambitious?" (II, 31). Her militant force focuses both on the cause of her country and on the vindication of "her sex against the tyranny of her ancient oppressors and traducers" (I, 90).

43. *Zenobia*, I, 105.

44. See the lengthy account of Captain Gibson's Gulliverian adventures in the *English Notebooks*, October 19, 1854, pp. 93–95.

45. See *The Consular Letters, 1853–1855*; XIX, 165–226.

46. *English Notebooks*, August 13, 1856, p. 321.

47. *English Notebooks*, August 13, 1856, pp. 320–321. See also Patrick Brancaccio, "Emma Abigail Salomons: Hawthorne's Miriam Identified," *The Nathaniel Hawthorne Journal 1978*, ed. C. E. Frazer Clark, Jr. (Detroit: Gale Research, 1984), pp. 95–103.

48. On February 10, 1858, Hawthorne recorded in his notebooks the discovery of another such obelisk in the Piazza di Monte Cavallo. "The obelisk was, as the inscription said, a relic of Egypt; the basin of the fountain was an immense bowl of oriental granite, into which poured a copious flood of water discolored by the rain" (XIV, 66–67).

49. For another appreciative description of Hosmer's "high, heroic" sculpture of Zenobia, see Hawthorne's *French and Italian Notebooks*, March 15, 1859; XIV, 508–510.

50. Lynne Thornton's *The Orientalists: Painter-Travellers 1829–1908* (Paris: ACR Edition, 1983) offers a lavishly illustrated introduction to this culture of taste.

51. Even schoolchildren of Hawthorne's time were treated to arousing depictions of Cleopatra. *Peter Parley's Tales about Ancient Rome, with Some Account of Modern Italy* (Boston: Carter, Hendee, 1833), pp. 130–131, offered adolescent readers an illustration of Cleopatra's Barge arrayed with nude sylphs, their hair tied back and breasts displayed. "Captivated by her beauty," Peter Parley warned, Antony sacrificed everything to possess Cleopatra. "He followed the queen into Egypt, and remained there buried in luxury and dissipation." Neglecting all affairs of state, "he was servant and slave to the pleasures of Cleopatra." Peter Parley's rationale for offering such salacious history to ten- and twelve-year-olds was the moral to be learned, the same

caution against sloth and luxury that the *Gesta Romanorum* drew from the tale of Alexander and the poison-damsel of India.

52. At the end of the novel Miriam acknowledges that she had often thought of revealing her secret to Kenyon: "On one occasion, especially, (it was after you had shown me your Cleopatra,) it seemed to leap out of my heart, and got as far as my very lips. But, finding you cold to accept my confidence, I thrust it back again. Had I obeyed my first impulse, all would have turned out differently" (IV, 432–433).

53. Roy Harvey Pearce, "Hawthorne and the Twilight of Romance," in *Historicism Once More* (Princeton, N.J.: Princeton University Press, 1969), p. 181.

54. Julian Hawthorne, *Nathaniel Hawthorne and His Wife* (Boston: James R. Osgood, 1884), I, 431.

55. For instance, casting around in his *Etherege* manuscript for some picturesque characteristic of the Lord of Brathwaite Hall that would breathe life into his plot, Hawthorne wrote in exasperation: "Something monstrous he must be, yet within nature and Romantic probability—hard conditions. A murderer—'twon't do at all. A Mahometan?—pish" (XII, 265).

56. *Atlantic Monthly*, 14 (August 1864), 170.

Appendix A

1. Marion L. Kesselring, *Hawthorne's Reading 1828–1850* (New York: The New York Public Library, 1949), p. 6.

2. Randall Stewart, "Recollections of Hawthorne by His Sister Elizabeth," *American Literature*, 16 (January 1945), 324.

3. See Chapter 2.

4. Letter to Henry Wadsworth Longfellow, October 12, 1838; XV, 276.

5. Letter to William D. Ticknor, May 17, 1862; XVIII, 456.

6. Raymona E. Hull, " 'Aunt Ebe,' Critic of Books and Their Writers," *The Nathaniel Hawthorne Journal 1978*, ed. C. E. Frazer Clark, Jr. (Detroit: Gale Research, 1984), p. 27. See also Hawthorne's letter to Sophia Peabody, June 20, 1842; XV, 631.

Appendix B

1. Turner incorrectly attributed this report on the Parsee "Fire Worshippers" of Bombay to Barthold George Niebuhr (1776–1831), a renowned historical scholar, rather than to his father Carsten Niebuhr (1733–1815). See Millicent Bell, "Hawthorne's 'Fire Worship': Interpretation and Source," *American Literature*, 24 (March 1952), 31–39.

2. Arlin Turner, *Hawthorne as Editor* (University, La.: Louisiana State University Press, 1941), p. 7.

3. Letter to Elizabeth M. Hawthorne, March 15, 1836; XV, 241.

INDEX